World City Syndrome

Routledge Studies in Human Geography

World City Syndrome

Neoliberalism and Inequality in Cape Town

David A. McDonald

Routledge
Taylor & Francis Group
New York London

Front cover photo credit: Under the rail bridge in Kalk Bay (David McDonald)

Back cover photo credits:

top left: City Bowl (City of Cape Town)
top right: Security company sign (David McDonald)
middle left: Road sign in Muizenburg (David McDonald)
middle right: Pit latrines in informal settlement (City of Cape Town)
bottom left: Strike rally (David McDonald)
bottom right: Old City Hall (David McDonald)

Routledge
Taylor & Francis Group
270 Madison Ave,
New York NY 10016

Routledge
Taylor & Francis Group
2 Park Square,
Milton Park, Abingdon,
Oxon, OX14 4RN

© 2008 by Taylor & Francis Group, LLC
Routledge is an imprint of Taylor & Francis Group, an Informa business

Transferred to Digital Printing 2009

International Standard Book Number-13: 978-0-415-95857-8 (Hardcover)

Library of Congress Cataloging-in-Publication Data

McDonald, David A. (David Alexander)
    World city syndrome : neoliberalism and inequality in Cape Town / David A. McDonald.
        p. cm. -- (Routledge studies in human geography)
    Includes bibliographical references and index.
    ISBN 978-0-415-95857-8 (hardback : alk. paper)
    1. Cape Town (South Africa)--Geography. 2. Human geography--South Africa--Cape
Town. 3. Cape Town (South Africa)--Politics and government. 4. Neoliberalism--South
Africa--Cape Town. 5. Cape Town (South Africa)--Economic conditions. 6. Cape
Town (South Africa)--Social conditions. 7. Urbanization--South Africa--Cape Town. 8.
Equality--South Africa--Cape Town. 9. Racism--South Africa--Cape Town. 10. Sociology,
Urban--South Africa--Cape Town. I. Title.

DT2405.C364M38 2007
968.73'55066--dc22   2007007173

ISBN10: 0-415-95857-1 (hbk)
ISBN10: 0-415-87500-5 (pbk)

ISBN13: 978-0-415-95857-8 (hbk)
ISBN13: 978-0-415-87500-4 (pbk)

Visit the Taylor & Francis Web site at
http://www.taylorandfrancis.com

and the Routledge Web site at
http://www.routledge.com

For Barrett and Joan

Contents

PART III

Tables

Figures

Acronyms

ACSA   Airports Company of South Africa
AEC   Anti-Eviction Campaign
AIDC   Alternative Information and Development Centre
ANC   African National Congress
BEE   black economic empowerment
BIG   Basic Income Grant
BLA   Black Local Authority
BOTT   Build, Operate, Train and Transfer
CBD   central business district
CBO   community-based organization
CCC   Cape Town City Council
CCT   City of Cape Town
CDS   Centre for Development Studies
CID   City Improvement District
CMA   Cape Metropolitan Authority
CMC   Cape Metropolitan Council
CMNF   Cape Metropolitan Negotiating Forum
Cosatu   Congress of South African Trade Unions
CPA   Cape Provincial Administration
CSIR   Council for Scientific and Industrial Research
CTRCCI   Cape Town Regional Chamber of Commerce and Industry
DA   Democratic Alliance
DBSA   Development Bank of South Africa
DFID   Department for International Development
DME   Department of Minerals and Energy
DWAF   Department of Water Affairs and Forestry
EDI   Electricity Distribution Industry
FFC   Financial and Fiscal Commission
FIRE   finance, insurance and real estate
GATT   General Agreement on Tariffs and Trade
GaWC   Globalization and World Cities
GDP   gross domestic product

GEAR   Growth, Employment and Redistribution
GGP   gross geographic product
GVA   geographic value added
HSL   Household Subsistence Level
HSRC   Human Sciences Research Council
ICT   information and communication technology
ID   Independent Democrats
IDP   Integrated Development Plan
IHRG   Industrial Health Research Group
Ilrig   International Labour Research and Information Group
Imatu   Independent Municipal and Allied Trade Union
IRIN   Integrated Regional Information Networks
ISP   Internet service provider
LDO   Land Development Objective
LGDB   Local Government Demarcation Board
LGTA   Local Government Transition Act
LGWSETA   Local Government Water and Related Services Sector Educa-
              tion Training Authority
MIG   Municipal Infrastructure Grant
MIIU   Municipal Infrastructure Investment Unit
MSDF   Metropolitan Spatial Development Framework
MSP   municipal service partnership
NCOP   National Council of Provinces
Nedlac   National Economic Development and Labour Council
NEF   National Empowerment Fund
Nepad   New Partnership for Africa's Development
NGO   nongovernmental organization
NLGNF   National Local Government Negotiating Forum
NNP   New National Party
NPA   National Ports Authority
O&M   operating and maintenance
OECD   Organization for Economic Cooperation and Development
PAC   Pan African Congress
PGWC   Provincial Government of the Western Cape
PPP   public-private partnership
PPPUE   Public-Private Partnerships for the Urban Environment
PSP   private sector partnership
PuP   public-public partnership
RDP   Reconstruction and Development Programme
RED   Regional Electricity Distributor
RSA   Republic of South Africa
RSC   Regional Service Council
SACN   South African Cities Network
Sacob   South African Chamber of Business
SACP   South African Communist Party

SADC	Southern African Development Community
SAHRC	South African Human Rights Commission
Salga	South African Local Government Association
Samwu	South African Municipal Workers' Union
Sanco	South African National Civic Organization
Satawu	South African Transport and Allied Workers Union
Seta	Sector Education and Training Authority
SMME	small, medium and micro enterprises
SSA	Statistics South Africa
SUPPS	Support Unit for Public Provision of Services
TCTA	Trans Caledon Tunnel Authority
UCLGA	United Cities and Local Governments of Africa
UNDP	United Nations Development Programme
UNEP	United Nations Environment Programme
UNHCR	United Nations High Commission on Refugees
Unicom	Unicity Commission
USAID	United States Agency for International Development
V&A	Victoria and Albert
WCEDF	Western Cape Economic Development Forum
WLA	White Local Authority
WRC	Water Research Commission
WRC	Water Resources Council
WSSD	World Summit on Sustainable Development

Preface and Acknowledgments

I must admit to a love/hate relationship with Cape Town. On the positive side, there is much to love about the city. It is a fascinating mix of African, Malay and European cultural heritages, with a strong Muslim influence and an increasingly cosmopolitan flavour. From Xhosa initiation rights in Langa to mosques in Mitchell's Plain to outdoor concerts in Kirstenbosch Gardens and fish *braais* on the Cape Flats, Cape Town offers a rich tapestry of traditions, sanded by centuries of grit, determination and resistance.

The built environment is equally wonderful. From the decaying but vibrant Victorian working-class housing of Salt River to the art deco factories in Observatory to the Dutch colonial estates of Constantia and the bright colours of the Bo-Kaap, the city has a wide range of fascinating architectural streetscapes.

And, of course, there is the city's stunning physical beauty—possibly the most beautiful natural urban environment in the world. Table Mountain is the most obvious (and most photographed) physical feature. With its 1000-metre cliffs framing and cradling the city centre, visible from up to 80 kilometres away, it is the focal point of the city.

But it is not just this northern face of the mountain that is spectacular. The Table Mountain chain runs for some 70 kilometres south to Cape Point, along which there are seemingly endless nooks and crannies for exploration, and an equally remarkable coastline. It is these smaller, less well-known spots which I enjoy the most, and into which one can disappear from the city in a matter of minutes. The sight and sound of urbanness vanishes, with a sense of wilderness that is achieved more quickly than in any other large city I know. From the hiking trails in Silvermine to the hidden mountain forests of Newlands to the sandy beaches of Cape Point, one could spend a lifetime exploring new and interesting corners of this city's amazing natural setting.

But it is exactly this physical beauty that makes it such a painful place to be. I find it impossible to see the natural splendour through the city's social ugliness. Much of this stems from centuries of colonialism and apartheid, but contemporary neoliberalism is leaving its own unsightly imprint. One third of the city's population lives below the poverty line in makeshift or overcrowded housing, and another third are just getting by. HIV and AIDS are ravaging many of the city's townships, and Cape Town has one of the highest rates of tuberculosis in the world—due in part to poor quality housing in cold, damp winters. A quarter of the city's population is unemployed, thousands do not have access to basic services such as water and electricity (or cannot afford to pay for these services) and public transport in the townships is underfunded and dangerous. Life for township-based women is that much more difficult, struggling to work and take care of their families while also being targets of crime and rape.

As a result of these inequalities, the natural amenities of the city (its beaches, parks and hiking trails) are populated largely by wealthier, white Capetonians and tourists. There are black faces in some of the more accessible attractions—e.g. Muizenburg beach—but for the most part Cape Town's natural splendour is for those who can afford to enjoy it, with Table Mountain little more than an imposing outline in the sky from 30–40 kilometres out in the townships.

Ironically, it is largely black Capetonians who have built Cape Town's beauty. From the colonial facades of Long Street to the stone steps up Platterkloof Gorge, the city is haunted by centuries of invisible black labour. And this is still the case. Black workers clean the streets, remove dead seals from the beach, water the plants in the parks and clean the dishes in the restaurants—most of it unacknowledged by the people who benefit from it.

Cape Town is not alone in this regard, of course, but it is arguably the most uneven and spatially segregated city in the country, especially with its unique white, coloured and African demographics. It may be the most ghettoized and spatially uneven city in the world.

Underlying this inequity is a smug, white liberalism that permeates all manner of activity in Cape Town—from the pedantic treatment of black store clerks, to a suburban sense of entitlement, to policies that keep the poor 'in their place'. Cape Town smacks of a privileged elite that feels it has little to apologize for, while at the same time suggesting it has all the answers for future development. Cape Town may have been the most 'liberal' city in South Africa under apartheid, but it is exactly this liberalism that has made it such a *neo*liberal place today.

It is for both these reasons then—love and hate—that I have written this book. I hate what the city has done (and not done) since the end of apartheid, but it is because Cape Town is such an interesting and dynamic place, and one that has been a second home to me, that I want to contribute in some small way toward positive change.

CAPE TOWN AS 'MOVING TARGET'

One of the most difficult things about conducting research in South Africa is that the country is like a moving target. Most countries are undergoing rapid change with the ever-quickening pace of neoliberalism but South Africa's emergence out of apartheid, its rapid adjustment to neoliberal policies and its highly politicized environment have made it even more volatile than most. Cape Town has gone through more political, institutional and economic changes in the past ten years than many cities have been through in a century.

All of this means that research can quickly become outdated. By the time one collects data, analyzes it, writes about it and publishes it, the situation on the ground may be very different. Budgets adjust, political parties morph, new legislation is introduced, and more homes and water taps are built. No doubt the same will apply to this book. I have done my best to get the most up-to-date material possible, but the target keeps moving.

Nonetheless, I have also come to realize that the more things change in Cape Town, the more they stay the same. After more than a dozen years of research what stands out most is the city's single-minded pursuit of neoliberalism. There may be more low-income houses and toilets than there were 15 years ago, but the policies underlying these shifts have changed little since the mid-1990s. Behind the façade of party political debates lies a much deeper convergence toward the development and implementation of outward-looking, market-oriented urban reforms. This applies equally to the two dominant political parties in the city: the African National Congress (ANC) and the Democratic Alliance (DA). Though not without their differences, these two parties have had essentially the same governance records and mandates in Cape Town, and continue to push for neoliberal reform.

What this means analytically is that the target may be moving but it is moving in a relatively predictable (if volatile) direction. As a result, one can acknowledge the dramatic changes taking place in Cape Town, and recognize the significant gains that have been made in some areas, but also point to the record of neoliberal reform and predict its impact into the future.

It is essential, in other words, not to become analytically paralyzed by the rapid pace of change in the city, or to succumb to the brow-beating of mainstream policymakers and academics who insist that the change is bringing deep-seated improvements (or will in the near future).

In attempting to illustrate these larger ideological trends I will necessarily miss out on some of the more subtle nuances of policymaking and implementation in Cape Town, those behind-the-scenes debates about policy direction or investment priorities that can seem incredibly important to those involved in it at the time but often make little difference to the overall picture. This is not due to a lack of appreciation of the multifaceted and contested ways in which neoliberal change takes place in the city, but rather because I want to sweep away the often distracting discourse of this neoliberal policymaking and expose the more naked capital accumulation strategies that are the real driving force behind post-apartheid change in the city.

A NOTE ON RACIAL TERMINOLOGY

Although apartheid-era racial classifications are a social construct with no objective significance, the legacies of apartheid and the heavy correlation between race and class in South Africa are such that racial classifications remain an integral part of political analysis in the country. There are, however, many different versions of racial terminology, and a brief explanation of the use of terms in this book is in order. Following the tradition of the anti-apartheid movement, "African", "coloured", "Asian" and "white" will be used to describe the four major racial categories of apartheid South Africa, with the most common use of upper and lower case letters being adopted. The term "black" is employed to refer to Africans, coloureds and Asians as a whole, in recognition of their common oppression under apartheid.

ACKNOWLEDGMENTS

The research for this book stems back to my doctoral research in the mid-1990s. From the University of Toronto I would like to thank Jonathan Barker, Richard Stren and Gerry Helleiner. From York University a special thanks to John Saul, from whom I learned the meaning of scholar activism.

Zunade Dharsey first convinced me to conduct research in Cape Town and it was his parents—Amen and Zora—who met us at the airport and gave us such a warm first welcome. *Hamba kahle* Zunade.

Salie Manie was instrumental in getting me involved in municipal issues in Cape Town and in connecting me with the South African Municipal Workers' Union (Samwu). Samwu has been an invaluable connection ever since, assisting with logistical and political matters related to research and opening my eyes to a world of physical work that I had largely taken for granted myself. At the national office, Roger Ronnie has been a strong intellectual and political colleague and an inspiration for what it takes to effect change in difficult and shifting terrains. Jeff Rudin, John Mawbey, Lance Veotte, Petrus Mashishi, Xolile "Boss" Nxu, Sandra van Niekerk, Anna Weekes and many others at the head office have been invaluable sources of information and assistance over the years.

At the Cape Town and Western Cape offices of Samwu, Andre Adams has been enormously supportive and resourceful. Much of the city-specific data and insights that I have collected would not have been possible without him. There are also dozens of Samwu shop stewards and workers in Cape Town that I have met with and interviewed over the years who have given generously of their time and thoughts. It never ceases to amaze me how knowledgeable these workers are of the goings-on in the city (and yet how little management listens to them!).

This connection with Samwu eventually led to the formation of the Municipal Services Project (MSP)—the single most important influence on my work over the past seven years. Founded in partnership with Samwu, the MSP has come to include a wide range of academic institutions, unions, NGOs and social movements. The most important individuals have been Greg Ruiters and Patrick Bond who have served as co-directors of the MSP with me over the years and whose work and thinking on cities and service delivery have impacted fundamentally on my own. They have been the best kind of academic colleagues one could ask for—collegial yet challenging, academic yet activist, serious yet fun. I regard them as two of the leading scholarly lights in the country and am privileged to have been able to work so closely with them.

Another major partnership in the MSP has been with the International Labour Research and Information Group (Ilrig), from whom I have learned not only about research but about research dissemination and the art of making academic work accessible to a wider audience. John Pape, Lenny Gentle, Moses Cloete, Mthetho Xali, Mskoli Qotole and Hameda Deedat have all played an important role in this.

Other key players in the MSP have been David Hemson, Melanie Samson, Laïla Smith (with whom I worked closely on some of the data collection and analysis included in this book), Rene Loewenson, and Godfrey Musaka. We have also been lucky to have excellent project administrators over the years: Debbie Bruinders, Rebecca Pointer and Emma Harvey.

There are many other researchers who have worked on MSP projects whose insights have influenced my thinking. Though not an exhaustive list, these include: Nick Henwood, Franco Barchiesi, Maj Fiil-Flynn, Ben Cashdan, Alex Loftus, Leslie Swartz, Danwood Mzikenge Chirwa, Sean Flynn, Ebrahim Harvey, Peter McInnis, Stephen Greenberg, Rekopanstwe Mate, Karen Cocq, Horacio Zandamela, Grace Khunou, Eddie Cottle, David Sanders, Mickey Chopra, Farhaad Haffajee, Mandisa Mbali, Rob Reese, Dinga Sikwebu, Peter van Huesden, Anne-Marie Debanne and Jackie Dugard.

International colleagues associated with the MSP include a strong group at the Canadian Union of Public Employees (Morna Ballentyne, Jane Stinson, Anthony Pizzino, Stan Marshall and Graham Deline), people at the Public Services International Research Unit (notably David Hall and Kate Bayliss) and others who have taken part in the project in some way and from whom this book has benefited (Maude Barlow, Tony Clarke, Karl Flecker, Daniel Chavez, Oscar Olivera, Patrick Apoya).

In terms of funding, the International Development Research Centre of Canada (IDRC) has been the largest and most supportive backer. Jean-Michel Labatut has been there from the beginning and Christina Zarowsky has lent regular support. Additional funding from the Social

Sciences and Humanities Research Council of Canada (SSHRCC) is also acknowledged.

There are two other clusters of people I want to mention. The first involves those in the environmental justice movement in South Africa with whom I have had sustained contact and who have a keen interest in cities and municipal services: Farieda Khan, Lianne Greef, Bobby Peek, Thabo Madihlaba, Jacklyn Cock, David Fig, Peter Lukey, Greg Knill, Jan Glazewski, Thabang Ngcozela, David Hallowes and Mark Butler.

The second (and much more loosely-defined) includes those associated with social movements. This is a large and diverse group and I will mention only those that I have had the most contact with over the years and who have provided me with regular assistance and inspiration: Trevor Ngwane, Virginia Setshedi, Dale McKinley, Ashraf Cassiem, Faizel Brown, George Dor, and Ismael Peterson.

Friendships have also been an important part of my Cape Town experience, but I will restrict myself to our two longest-standing friends—Alastair Rendall and Gita Govan—who have been housemates, hosts and political sounding boards over the years. If all of the planners and architects in the city had the same commitment as they do to sustainable and equitable development Cape Town could be a very different place.

No acknowledgment would be complete, of course, without reference to my family. In this, it has been a truly joint road of discovery. My partner, Lea Westlake, has been a co-traveller and -inquisitor from the start, providing insightful (and level-headed) analyses of her own and critical feedback on my work. My young kids, Hannah and Eli, have also helped me to see Cape Town through more innocent eyes. Though sometimes remarkably penetrating in their naivety, there is a hopefulness in their perceptions that sometimes eludes my more jaded existence.

On a final, technical note, I would like to thank Meg Freer for her peerless editorial assistance, Ben Holtzman at Routledge for his efficient and positive support, Jennifer Grek-Martin for her assistance with the maps, Derek Brine for assistance with some of the diagrammatic figures, and the anonymous reviewers for their useful comments on the original manuscript.

Maps of Cape Town and Its Regional Setting

Figure P.1 Map of Municipal Boundaries and Major Suburbs/Townships of the City of Cape Town (effective January 2001)

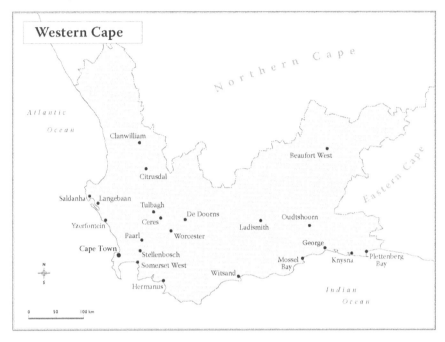

Figure P.2 Map of Province of the Western Cape, South Africa

Figure P.3 Map of South Africa

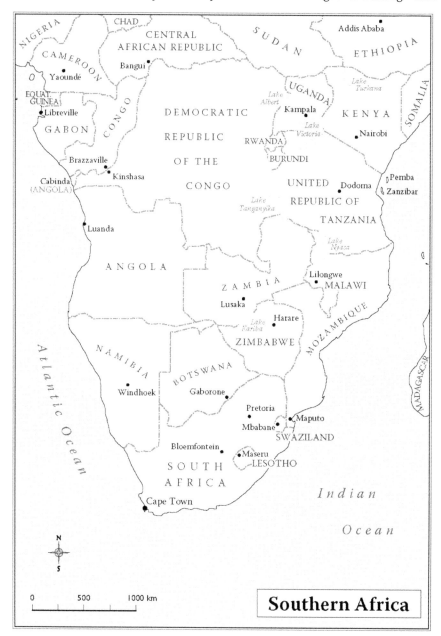

Figure P.4 Map of Southern Africa

Introduction
World City Syndrome

> As a well connected global city set in an environment of great natural beauty,
> Cape Town offers more than just an investment opportunity. Perhaps more
> than any other city in the world, Cape Town offers unbeatable quality of life.
>
> *From "Welcome to Cape Town: One of the World's Great Cities",*
> *2004 brochure from the City of Cape Town*

Is Cape Town a world city? In many respects, yes. It fits the description
of world cities laid out in the academic literature on the subject (albeit as
a peripheral player) and has an increasingly complex global network of
connections.

But the academic description of a world city does not adequately capture
or explore the dynamics of urbanization in Cape Town. As useful as this
theoretical paradigm may be in describing the service-oriented, globally
linked and polarized nature of the city, it fails to assess and address the key
features of urban capitalist crisis that shape Cape Town and the neoliberal
policies and institutions that have emerged as a result.

Despite this, politicians and policymakers in Cape Town, as well as business leaders and the media, have become fixated with the idea of being a
'world city'. From Cape Town's claim to offering world-class amenities, to
its promotion of itself as a lucrative investment centre, one can barely read
a policy statement or promotional brochure that does not make some kind
of reference to Cape Town's world city ambitions.

And yet there has never been a systematic study of where and how Cape
Town—or other South African cities for that matter—fit into this world
city system. Cape Town and Johannesburg have been categorized as world
cities in a number of global surveys (e.g. Friedman 1986, Taylor 2004,
van der Merve 2004), and there is growing use of the concept in urban
academic writing in the country (e.g. Watson 2002, Rogerson 2004, van
der Merve 2004, Sihlongonyane 2004, Beavon 2006), but there has been
no close theoretical analysis of this paradigm in the South African context
and little empirical data to back up positivistic claims. Despite hundreds of
academic books, articles, chapters, theses and research reports having been
written about Cape Town over the past two decades (Pirie 2005) there has

not been a single detailed examination of whether it should be classified as a world city or what the implications of this analysis may be.

My first task, therefore, is to demonstrate that Cape Town does fit the world city model. Chapter 1 will argue that Cape Town should, in fact, be seen as paradigmatic of the genre: an 'ideal' world city, of sorts, exemplifying the socioeconomic and urban characteristics portrayed in the literature, including an outward-focused service economy, the creation of tightly networked business hubs connected to other world cities via high-tech transportation and telecommunication systems, and the development of world-class facilities to cater to a transnational elite.

Things fall apart conceptually, however, when we look at the deeper, structural processes of uneven capitalist development in the city. Relying, as much of the 'mainstream' world city literature does, on an ill-defined and under-problematized concept of 'globalization', the world city hypothesis does not provide us with the analytical tools necessary for properly investigating the source and outcomes of capital accumulation and inequality in Cape Town.

For this we must turn to a more radical literature on urban development, one that situates Cape Town's (re)emergence as a global urban player in the 1990s within a larger, historical context of capitalist crisis and as part of a new neoliberal hegemony of urban development policy. It is here that I hope to contribute conceptually to the broader world city debate while at the same time shedding light on the unequal and unsustainable development path of the city of Cape Town.

Surprisingly, these radical criticisms have not been raised explicitly in the urban literature on world cities to date (though the substance of the arguments I will make in this book feature prominently in radical urban writing more generally, and some scholars have pointed to such theoretical tensions in the world city literature (e.g. Amen, Archer and Bosman 2006a, Brenner and Kiel 2006). This lack of direct criticism may be due in part to the conceptual affinity between the world city hypothesis and urban Marxist thought—a point I will return to in Chapter 2. It may also be a result of the fact that the two literatures come to the same general descriptive conclusions about contemporary world cities in terms of their socioeconomic and spatial profiles and their highly unequal characteristics. Whatever the reasons, a critical review of the world city hypothesis from a Marxist perspective is overdue and, I hope, will contribute to a more layered debate on the strengths and weaknesses of the world city literature in general.

This is not to suggest that there have been no criticisms of the world city literature at all. There has been a substantial, and sometimes quite heated, debate within the world city literature itself. None of this internal debate fundamentally challenges the conceptual frameworks of the world city hypothesis, however, and none of it makes the kind of structural critiques I will make here.

There have also been criticisms of the world city literature for being too Euro- and North American-centric, with insufficient attention being paid to cities in the South. Some of this criticism has come from within the world city literature itself, with no less an authority than Saskia Sassen (2002b, 2006) lamenting the lack of studies on urban centres in the 'third world'. The response, however, has been to apply a largely unreconstructed world city hypothesis to cities in Asia, Africa and Latin America, uncritically investigating world cityness in major centres such as Shanghai, Buenos Aires and Johannesburg (see, for example, Sassen 2002b, Gugler 2004). There has been no fundamental questioning of the analytical integrity of the world city hypothesis within this literature.

Deeper, epistemological challenges have, however, come from outside the world city tradition. Robinson (2002, 535–38), for example, has argued in a widely cited article that the world city hypothesis sets up "*a priori* analytical hierarchies", dividing cities into predefined categories of world city status based on "narrow economistic" criteria. Those toward the top of the world city ladder receive enormous academic attention while hundreds of millions of other people—predominantly those living in less important cities in the South—are left "off the world city map", relegated to "irrelevance" and rendered invisible to world city researchers (see also Smith 1998, McCann 2004, Short 2004a, Davis 2005).

Worse yet, argues Robinson (2002, 545), the normative tone of the world city literature has convinced many policymakers that world city status is a positive—even inevitable—goal to strive for and that planners and politicians should do what they can to get their city on the world city map or move it up the world city ladder.

Academics have contributed to this normative discourse by uncritically employing these hierarchical frameworks, thereby "severely limit[ing] the imaginations of possible futures for cities" (Robinson 2002, 534). Friedman's (1995, 36) experiences in this regard are instructive:

> A few years ago I was invited by the government of Singapore to speak on world cities. In private conversations with senior government officials it became clear to me what the government really wanted. Singapore was embarking on 'the next lap' and officials hoped to hear from me how their city state might rise to the rank of 'world city'. The golden phrase had become a badge of status.

Some of this normativeness would appear to be intentional, even boosterish in tone. Gu and Tang (2002, 274), for example, argue that in Shanghai "infrastructure *has to* keep pace with functional change in the city". Clark, Green and Grenell (2001, 58–59) argue that "globalization ... *requires* cities to become much more entrepreneurial". Chernotsky (2001, 30) states that "changes in trade, immigration and the movement of capital ... [make it] *necessary* [for American cities] to promote economic growth", noting that "only a few have *advanced* to the elite core of world cities" (all emphases added).

While some of this language should perhaps be seen as detached observation by 'objective' academics—i.e. a description of the trends affecting world cities and not necessarily an endorsement of the processes or their outcomes—there is a strong and persistent air of aspiration in the world city literature, an intellectual surrender of sorts to the "almost inevitable continuity" of world city formation (Felbinger and Robey 2001, 64).

I would argue that most of this normativeness is the product of default rather than design. With no intrinsic theoretical opposition to the conceptual assumptions around what constitutes "economic globalization", many world city researchers and practitioners simply choose between what they see as the lesser of two evils: playing the world city game and being good at it (while doing the best to mitigate negative side-effects) or risking a slide into oblivion on the periphery of the world city system. Though not necessarily happy with these two options, it may be that many researchers and urban policymakers see little choice.

Illustrative of the latter is the UN-Habitat's (2001, chapter 5) portrayal of world cities. As the UN's foremost urban policy agency, and one that is enormously influential in policymaking in cities in the South (along with its partners in the World Bank), the UN-Habitat's normative take on world cities is emblematic of a broader intellectual submission to the concept and benefits of world city formation. Drawing on Sassen's work on the subject, the UN-Habitat raises concerns about growing urban inequalities, deunionization and other negative characteristics associated with globalization, but shares Sassen's optimistic perspective that the world city process will bring with it a respect for multiculturalism, a culture of human rights and a "greater empowerment of women" via the informalization of the workforce and the growing "business opportunities" offered to a "new professional stratum".

At best, then, the mainstream world city literature raises important concerns about globalization and the growing sociospatial and economic inequalities of world cities, indicating ways in which these can perhaps be compensated for and/or mitigated against. At worst, it contributes to a policy discourse that sees world cityness as a process that is unavoidable but manageable, marginalizing critically minded policymakers, academics, unionists and activists and failing to encourage alternative urban visions.

This is all part of a world city 'syndrome' that permeates the discursive terrain of academic and government debates on urban development around the world and has come to dominate the discourse on urban policymaking and planning in Cape Town and other South African cities.

A purging of this normative discourse will depend, in part, on new analytical models. What, then, is on offer in this regard?

ALTERNATIVES TO THE WORLD CITY HYPOTHESIS

Critics of the world city hypothesis—scarce though they are—have offered some thoughts on alternative analytical frameworks. Robinson (2002, 2006) argues for a more "cosmopolitan" approach to the study of cities; one that overcomes the "strident economism" of the world city literature, opening researchers and practitioners to the full "diversity and complexity" of cities (particularly those in the South). Such a move would open up new urban "imaginaries", helping academics and urban policymakers "break free of the categorizing imperative" of the world city thesis. Her solution, following Amin and Graham (1997), is to think of all cities as "ordinary cities", a "broader and less ambitious approach" to urban studies.

What constitutes this "cosmopolitan", "postcolonial" approach to urban studies, and what, if anything, might objectively differentiate one "ordinary" city from another or help inform policy and action? The answer, unfortunately, takes us to the other analytical extreme. Unlike world cities, ordinary cities have no universally distinguishing social, political, economic or spatial patterns. They are, instead, to be seen as open-ended, "diverse, creative [and] modern", with the "possibility to imagine ... their own futures and distinctive forms of cityness" (Robinson 2006, 110). There are "constraints of contestations and uneven power relations" that may limit these "possible urban futures", but the conceptual imaginary is thrown wide open as we are asked not to limit our investigative focus or our policy prescriptions lest we miss some important analytical features of an individual city or ride roughshod over different ideological perspectives (see also Sihlongonyane 2004 and Simone 2004).

Short (2004a, 301) takes a different approach, arguing for an expanded, but tightly conceptualized, set of city definitions: "the poor city, the collapsed city, the excluded city, and the resisting city". Although only "exploratory" in nature, these categories are intended to analytically capture cities that are "ignored, abandoned, or excluded by global capital or [that are] sites of resistance against capitalist incorporation". Short calls for "theorized case studies" of these conceptual "black holes" in the world city research, arguing that they would "present an intriguing opportunity to understand and explore the underside of globalization" and expand our understanding of cities in the South beyond the constraints of the world city literature.

The problem with these alternative analytical approaches is that they throw out the proverbial baby with the bath water. As problematic as the world city hypothesis is, it nevertheless offers enormously useful insights into contemporary urbanization. More importantly, these insights apply—to varying degrees—to virtually every city in the world today. Some cities—such as Pyongyang, Havana and Tehran—clearly fall outside the 'normal' international urban flow, for various reasons, but none can escape the homogenizing and hegemonic influences of capitalist globalization entirely (Marcuse and van Kempen 2000).

In this respect, *all* cities are world cities—a point made by King (1990, 82) some years ago and one that Robinson (2002, 534), interestingly enough, notes in her critique of the world city literature as well. It is not, therefore, a question of whether a particular city is on or off the world city map, but rather the extent to which it is affected by the same socioeconomic trends that create world cities everywhere. Understanding the world city hypothesis can help us comprehend cities on the global periphery as much as it can help us understand those in the metropolitan core (as well as the linkages between them).

The real question is whether the world city hypothesis tells us the right things about globalization and urbanization. Herein lie the most fundamental conceptual problems with the world city literature: its vague and overly optimistic conceptualization of globalization, and its virtual silence on the nature and impacts of (urban) neoliberalism.

But rather than abandoning the world city hypothesis, I want to extract from it its most useful analytical and empirical lessons and use these as a base for rebuilding a conceptual framework for Cape Town's place in a global economy.

My argument, in a nutshell, is that Cape Town is a world city, but not for the reasons outlined in the world city hypothesis. It is a world city because it is a capitalist city. More importantly, it is a world city because it is a neoliberal city.

It is impossible to understand Cape Town's emerging position in the global economy, its shifting socioeconomic and spatial makeup, and its massive and growing inequalities without first understanding the nature of uneven capitalist development and neoliberal policymaking, and how it is that these developments have created the characteristics described in the world city hypothesis.

For this we need a radically different interpretation of globalization than that offered up by the mainstream world city literature. Unlike the world city writing, radical urban theory tells us that global capitalist forces are fundamentally negative, pulling cities into a downward spiral of instability (though seemingly stable at times), perpetuating and deepening sociospatial and economic inequalities and serving the interests of a transnational elite. It is here, to quote Harvey (2000, 68), that a "shift of language from 'globalization' to 'uneven geographical development' has most to offer". This discussion is taken up at length in Chapter 2.

Chapter 3 tackles the question of neoliberalism. Although the world city literature does make repeated references to neoliberal reforms (such as the deregulation of the finance industry) there is virtually no theorization of the concept and very little in the way of assessing its impacts on inequality. My argument—drawing once again on an existing radical literature on the subject—is that neoliberalism is part and parcel of the world city formation process and outcome, shaping the particular forms of uneven urban capitalist development we see in world cities today.

In making these arguments the book is unapologetically structural in its approach, focusing on the economic, physical and institutional organization of Cape Town, evaluating the ways in which these structures have (or have not) changed since the end of apartheid, and assessing the impact of these structural reforms on inequality and the scope for socioeconomic justice in the future. Investments in transportation, telecommunications, electricity and other core services are not the only important things going on in Cape Town but they tell us a lot about the priorities of urban policy-makers and of foreign and domestic capital.

These structural features take precedence over cultural indicators of change in my analysis not because the latter are unimportant, but because the former are the most critical determinants of the daily, material lives of Capetonians. Housing, refuse collection, Internet access and municipal governance systems have a direct and profound impact on peoples' ability to lead a healthy and fulfilling life, and it is here that we see the biggest barriers to positive change for the poor majority of the city. Racism, religious beliefs, xenophobia and other sociocultural factors play into these dynamics in important ways—as we shall see in different parts of the book, particularly Chapter 9—but they are not the primary focus of my discussion.

Nevertheless, the theoretical framework I adopt is explicitly dialectical in nature, hopefully highlighting the complex links between economy and culture—structure and agency, if you will—stressing the elliptical character of socioeconomic change. In this sense we can recognize the diversities and complexities of a city such as Cape Town while at the same time foregrounding the more universal structural constraints to socioeconomic justice and the homogenizing tendencies of global urban reforms. Cultural practices, institutional legacies and social norms all serve to complicate this universalizing tendency but we can bridge some of this epistemological gap with the best of Marxist theory.

I should also note that although the focus of the book is on the impact of neoliberalism on the urban poor, world city developments must also be seen to limit the life choices of the well-to-do (though without the same life-and-death consequences). The homogenization and commodification of lifeworlds through brand-name shopping, blockbuster entertainment and the creation of gated communities exemplifies the narrowing of sociocultural landscapes in general, even for those who benefit most from world city formation: the transnational capitalist class.

I begin my empirical review of this transition in Chapter 4 with a look at the political remapping of Cape Town since 1996 and the reorganization and restructuring of local government institutions designed to bring the city in line with international political norms. The redrawing of boundaries and the reconfiguration of intergovernmental relations and powers have had profound effects on the city. From more than 60 fragmented local government authorities under apartheid to a single metropolitan government in the 1990s, the City of Cape Town now has the financial clout, the managerial know-how and the political centralization required to compete effectively as a world city.

Chapter 5 explores the physical restructuring of the city, with a focus on spatial and infrastructural changes. Here we see the most concrete and explicit expression of Cape Town's repositioning as a world city and the capitalist pressures behind it. The perceived need to make Cape Town more responsive to the demands of outward-looking, service-oriented transnational capital has resulted in a pattern of investment that has seen the intensification of gated communities and office complexes, specialized transportation and communication corridors, and leisure amenities and conference facilities for the elite, largely at the expense of low-income households. Efforts to improve and expand housing and basic services in low-income areas have made some important differences to the lives of the poor, but these pale in comparison to the massive private and public sector investments in the business nodes and upper-income residential areas of the city.

Chapter 6 looks at the scale and character of privatization in Cape Town, including the corporatization and commercialization of services ranging from sanitation to tourism. Little has been left off the marketization agenda in the city, as intensive pressures have been applied by capital to open up new spaces for investment, to reduce the costs of doing business and to create a multi-tiered service delivery system. We look in this chapter at the extent to which privatization pressures have impacted on service delivery and how they have exacerbated inequality in the city.

A closely related development is the neoliberal push for cost recovery on services and this is the focus of Chapter 7. More accurately, it is the uneven pressures for cost recovery that are the focus of my discussion, with low-income households being squeezed for payments they can barely afford (while being threatened with cutoffs and service restrictions if they do not pay) while businesses and middle-class suburbanites continue to benefit from massive municipal subsidies, all in the name of international competitiveness.

Not surprisingly, there has been intense opposition to these uneven reforms, particularly from public sector unions and township-based community organizations. But the post-apartheid state (local and national) has been extremely effective at containing this resistance and Chapter 8 looks at the ways in which opposition voices have been 'disciplined' and marginalized through the manipulation of public participation in decision making, the harassment and jailing of vocal opposition and even the use of physical violence (with numerous deaths having occurred at the hands of the police since 1996).

None of this was supposed to happen in post-apartheid South Africa, of course. The African National Congress (ANC) had long been committed to a model of democratic development and governance that promised a fairer distribution of wealth (if not an equalization) and broad-based participation in decision making by people from all walks of life. There has certainly been progress in this regard when compared to the apartheid era, but for the most part the city of Cape Town remains remarkably unreformed and undemocratic when it comes to participation in decision making on the part of low-income residents.

Chapter 9 is the final critical chapter in the book and looks at the (de)Africanization of the city. By (de)Africanization I mean the contradictory but simultaneous effects of Cape Town becoming more African than it has ever been—a result of internal migration and cross-border migration from other parts of Africa—while at the same time entrenching and expanding the racially-segregated nature of the city. From its (always overstated) reputation as a racially tolerant and relatively mixed city under apartheid, Cape Town has arguably become the most racially segregated and racist city in the country. Vast swaths of low-income coloured and African townships continue to grow and spread out across the Cape Flats—though with sharp physical barriers still dividing them, by and large—while the lily-white suburbs and business nodes increasingly become a refuge for whites fleeing 'darker' parts of the country and for (white) Europeans and North Americans seeking a relatively cheap piece of paradise near the ocean. How this plays into the larger, socioeconomic changes taking place in the city, and its links to a global urban network, are discussed in that chapter.

ALTERNATIVE DEVELOPMENT STRATEGIES

What remains is an investigation of alternatives to Cape Town's world city neoliberalism. Chapter 10 offers two seemingly opposite but potentially synergistic approaches. The first is an exploration of short-term, ameliorative ways of addressing the inequities thrown up by the current system, both at a national and local level. These include: keeping services in public hands and putting resources into revitalizing and strengthening the public sector; introducing more progressive forms of municipal taxation and tariffs; transferring more resources from national to local government; allowing for more effective and broad-based participation in local decision making; spending more money on public transport; improved densification and diversification of urban planning; and an end to all service cutoffs and restrictions on low-income households. These and many other Keynesian-style reforms could go a long way in a short period of time to addressing some of the worst inequities and injustices of the city and are implicit in all of the critical chapters leading up to this discussion.

But do these reforms tackle the underlying pressures and inherent inequities of capital accumulation? Is capitalism—even its more welfarist variants—ultimately sustainable? My answer, in short, is no, and the second half of Chapter 10 outlines a more radical perspective on change.

The arguments made here are intentionally indicative in nature. My own hope is for an explicitly anti-capitalist future: some kind of nationally-driven but locally vibrant form of socialism that allows for considerable participation and local autonomy in decision making, with limited market exchange in a decommodified environment. The actual ideological and institutional character of this system cannot and should not be predetermined, however, and it is not my intent to suggest a blueprint for change. What I hope to provide is an indication of the range of possibilities for a noncapitalist Cape Town, drawing on a wealth of theoretical and 'actually existing' radical alternatives, couched in a clear framework of structural constraints.

How likely is a radically different development path for Cape Town (or for South Africa more generally)? Not very, to be honest, at least not in the near future, given the current configurations of power locally and internationally. But radically different politico-economic models are being discussed in the country once again and there are encouraging lessons from cities elsewhere in the world (e.g. Brazil, Venezuela, Kerala). Cuba and Havana also remain beacons of hope for many, having produced impressive gains for their citizens over the past five decades despite intense external pressures.

Cape Town and Havana may, in fact, be polar opposites in the world city stakes. At one end is Cape Town, arguably the most unequal and spatially segregated city in the world. At the other is Havana, arguably the most equitable city in the world, offering housing for all, some of the highest levels of health, literacy and education in Latin America and a sense of security that capitalist world cities can only dream of. It is unclear how long this revolutionary agenda can last in Cuba given the American trade embargo and the creeping commodification associated with a dualized economy that has emerged since the collapse of the Soviet Union (Dilla 1999, Carmona Báez 2004), but the contrast with Cape Town could not be more stark and serves as a reminder that 'another (urban) world is possible'.

Convincing a critical mass of South African policymakers of these radical alternatives may never take place, but we can continue to chip away at the smug, self-confidence of neoliberal boosterism in the country. More importantly, there are thousands of activists working on the ground toward more radical change in South Africa, and though this trend is still weak and fragmented in Cape Town the city is pregnant with the potentiality for radicalized politics, inherent as this tendency is in the very inequalities of neoliberal reforms. Far from suggesting paralysis in the face of homogenizing global capital, therefore, the concluding chapter points to the existence and scope for resistance to neoliberalism as intrinsic to the contradictions of capitalist development.

If nothing else, the analysis provided here should make it clear that 'going global' in a capitalist world is not the only option for Cape Town and is anything but a panacea for positive change. Despite the claim by the neoliberal

South African Cities Network (SACN 2004, 12) that "South African cities are doing what the economic consensus of the moment says they should do—go global ... [and that] there is no evidence that this will not work", the reality of externally oriented neoliberal reform in Cape Town and other South African cities has been one of increasing and entrenched inequality, with growing international evidence to reinforce these findings.

This is not a particularly cheerful or optimistic take on Cape Town's future, but it is an attempt to critically and realistically understand the underlying dynamics of reform in this complex and fascinating city.

Part I

1 Cape Town as World City

The term "world city" is widely and increasingly used in popular and academic writing, making it one of the most familiar and influential ways of describing and understanding large cities in a globalized world. Countless books, articles, conferences and policy papers use the phrase to describe the links between globalization, cities and the growth of the service economy.

This chapter provides an overview of the world city hypothesis and tests it against the city of Cape Town. I begin with an assessment of the primary tenets of the world city hypothesis. The purpose of this review is to clarify my own interpretation of the conceptual and methodological characteristics of the literature, while at the same time ensuring that readers are familiar with the basic theory. There is no single interpretation of what constitutes a world city, though it is possible to identify central lines of analyses.

In doing so, I hope to demonstrate the complexity and sophistication of the world city hypothesis. Despite my criticisms of the concept in later chapters, the world city hypothesis is an enormously useful descriptive and analytical tool, offering important insights into urbanization in a global economy.

I start with a discussion of the different terminology employed in the world city literature, followed by an overview of the core concepts. I conclude by asking whether Cape Town fits the analytical bill, arguing that it is in fact a paradigmatic example of the world city hypothesis.

DEFINING THE TERMS

Originally attributed to Goethe, the term "world city" (*Weltstad*) found its way into contemporary academic literature through the work of Peter Hall (1966) (who, in turn, drew inspiration from Patrick Geddes' work on proposals to establish a "world league of cities" in the 1920s (Taylor 2004, 21)). Hall's book did not, however, draw systematic links *between* individual cities. Couched as it was in the 'national urban systems' thinking of the day, and the Fordist world economy of the time, the book presented

world cities as relative islands of cultural, political, economic and technological development.

It was not until the 1980s—most notably with the reworking of the
term by Friedman (1982, 1986)—that the concept of a world city came to
be associated with a broader "world economy". This reconceptualization
made the *links* between cities as important to their study as their individual, internal dynamics. World city research as we know it today began
"when the economic restructuring of the world-economy made the idea of
a mosaic of separate urban systems appear anachronistic and irrelevant....
New thinking about cities was required and a world cities literature emerged
in the 1980s and flowered in the 1990s as a central theme of globalization"
(Taylor 2004, 21).

This is not to say that contemporary cities are the only urban conglom-
erations that could be considered 'worldly'. Hall's cities of the mid-twentieth century and many cities of medieval Europe and precolonial Asia and
Africa were also world cities in their own right, trading and engaging in
international ways (Braudel 1984, Abu-Lughod 1989, King 1990). It is the
post-Keynesian, post-Fordist capitalism of the last three decades, and the
massive geographical expansion of production via new forms of technology
and telecommunication, that sets contemporary world cities apart from
these formerly global urban centres. Today's world cities are quantitatively
and qualitatively different from their predecessors and require a different
set of analytical tools.

Given this larger historical perspective it could be said that Cape Town
has always been a world city, having played a significant political and economic role in the European colonial system since its founding as a Dutch
supply station in the seventeenth century. But it is Cape Town's role and
place in the contemporary global network of cities that we are interested
in here and it is in this more limited, temporal sense that the term "world
city" will be used in this book.

World city is not the only term used in the literature, however. Saskia
Sassen (1991), in her seminal work on the subject, consciously chose to use
the phrase "global city". In the Preface to the second edition to the book,
Sassen (2001, xix) argues that she chose not to use the phrase 'world city'
exactly because of its historical significance, because it "referred to a type
of city which we have seen over the centuries, and most probably in much
earlier periods in Asia than in the West". But as we shall see in our analysis
of her global city model below there is no fundamental difference between
what she calls a global city and what other analysts call a world city, and
the terms are used interchangeably in the larger literature on the subject.
My own terminological preference is world city, though I will use global
city at times to minimize repetition of one phrase and when quoting other
authors.

One other small terminological point of note is the use of the phrase
'world-class city'. Although not an integral feature of the academic litera-

ture on world cities the phrase has come to be something of a proxy for world cityness in popular writing and in government publications. So pervasive has the expression become in South Africa that it is now used to describe virtually anything a major city has to offer. As such, Table Mountain becomes a 'world-class urban park', Cape Town's new conference centre becomes a 'world-class' conference centre, and Cape Town itself a 'world-class' tourist destination. The term has also come to represent a strong ideological commitment to 'going global' and is an important discursive example of the normative desire of policymakers in Cape Town to see it become a 'world city' in the more academic sense of the term.

DEFINING A WORLD CITY

The following overview of the world city hypothesis is by no means a comprehensive review of what is a very large and sometimes divergent literature on the subject (readers are referred to the growing number of texts that have been compiled for just that purpose: King 1990, Kawano 1992, Knox and Taylor 1995, Marcuse and van Kempen 2000, Clark 2003, Amen, Archer and Bosman 2006b, Brenner and Kiel 2006, to name but a few). My objective here is simply to outline the central conceptual and empirical arguments of the writings.

In doing so I have adopted what Taylor (2004, 21–22), in his own summary of the literature, calls the "nugget approach": an attempt to identify the most important "signposts" of the genre. But unlike Taylor, who reviews three of the "seminal contributions" to the writing (Friedman 1986, Sassen 1991, and Castells 1996), I will focus primarily on Sassen's work, and in particular her 1991 contribution, *The Global City* (though I will largely cite the second edition of the book published in 2001 because of its updated empirical data, its partially revised conceptualization, and its useful Preface and Epilogue).

I use Sassen's work for several reasons. First, and most importantly, I consider it to be the single most representative and comprehensive body of work in the genre. Although she does not deal with every facet of the world city debate in detail—or in sufficient detail—her writing nonetheless encompasses the central facets of the writing. Sassen is also one of the most prolific authors in the field. Some of her writing is only indirectly related to world cities but all of it helps to fill out the gaps in her *Global City* contribution (Sassen 1988, 1991, 1994, 1995, 1996, 1998, 1999, 2000, 2003). She has also edited and contributed to a collection of essays that look specifically at world cities in the South, helping to fill another important gap in the world city literature (Sassen 2002a, 2004, 2006).

Sassen's writing is also the most influential, and certainly the most widely cited, work in the field. Friedman's (1995, 29) reference to Sassen's 1991 book as a "masterful summation" of the world city hypothesis is one indication of this acclaim, as are Castells' (1996, 378) adoption of her thesis, the use of her work in various 'readers' on cities (LeGates and Stout 1996, Brenner and Kiel 2006), and the use of her work by influential organizations such as the UN-Habitat (2001, chapter five).

I frame my summary of the literature around Sassen's "seven global city hypotheses", in the order that she presents them. I have rephrased some of the language (for stylistic consistency), and have inserted some references to other scholarship to fill out her ideas, but the conceptual framework remains hers.

Globalization Creates the Need for Spatial Concentration

The first, and perhaps most critical, world city hypothesis is that the global spread of manufacturing since the 1970s has necessitated the centralization of corporate control functions. With operations in many countries multinational firms need to centralize their command and control structures in order to coordinate their activities. Not all functions are done at head office, but there are important centralized activities such as corporate planning that require a corporate headquarters. This geographic dispersal of corporate production—what Sassen refers to as "economic globalization"—is facilitated by advances in telecommunications and transportation, effectively compressing the space-time limitations of earlier forms of international trade and production.

There is, then, a spatial irony to this new "organizational architecture": it contains "not only the capabilities for enormous geographic dispersal and mobility but also pronounced territorial concentrations of resources necessary for the management and servicing of that dispersal and mobility" (Sassen 2002b, 2). In other words, the globalization of economic activity has made place both less and more important. In this regard, the predicted death of the city in the mid-twentieth century, with some analysts assuming that advances in transportation and telecommunication would create ever-spreading suburbanization and de-urbanization as people did not need to be in cities, was fundamentally wrong (Williamson 1990).

There has been some deconcentration of urban corporate headquarter activities due to these technological developments, and not all corporate headquarters need to be in major urban centres, but the increasing dispersal of corporate activities has necessitated a spatial concentration of core activities, not their diffusion. This need for command and control centres is true of all sectors, from manufacturing and services to nongovernmental organizations.

The Rise of a Producer Service Economy

The second hypothesis is that centralized command and control corporate functions have become so complex that they have been increasingly outsourced. This outsourcing has, in turn, created a secondary site of control functions outside of the producing firm, leading to the rapid and massive expansion of a 'producer services' sector—i.e. firms that service the centralization requirements of globalized manufacturing companies.

Most notable amongst these producer service firms are accounting, law, advertising, corporate travel, security, public relations, management consulting, information technology, real estate, storage, data processing and insurance companies. Although not entirely separate in corporate ownership terms from 'consumer services' (i.e. services intended for consumption by individuals, such as leisure travel or home insurance) producer services overwhelm even the large and growing consumer services sector.

Driven initially by the manufacturing sector, the producer services sector has now taken on a life of its own. As specialized service companies have grown and internationalized so too have their own requirements for specialized outsourcing of the same command and control functions as their manufacturing counterparts. A multinational advertising firm, for example, may require the services of a legal firm, a financial services company, IT specialists, and so on. In what has become a self-perpetuating cycle of producer services growth and service company expansion we have witnessed a fundamental transformation of the global economy from manufacturing at its centre to one with producer services at the core.

Producer services now dominate international trade, foreign direct investments, and job creation, with the fastest growth in producer service employment being in cities. This is especially true in the North as urban manufacturing jobs continue to move offshore, but it is generally true in the South as well where growth in urban manufacturing jobs has been slight (Sassen 2002a, Gugler 2004).

Of special significance is the immense growth in financial services, which has grown faster than all other producer services and now dominates the producer services sector. This growth is primarily the result of deregulation, starting in the US and spreading rapidly in the 1990s to virtually every country in the world. Securities markets have seen the most dramatic change and growth but similar expansion has occurred in international financial flows, currency markets and so on.

The complex requirements of the finance sector have also meant the development of sophisticated and wide-ranging service support inputs (e.g. changing legislative environments, new international regulatory mechanisms) while the potential for super-profits has proven highly attractive to service support firms. Moreover, this potential for massive profits—and the (perceived) potential for job growth—has led to the relative devalorization of the manufacturing sector in terms of support from the state.

This de(re)valorization dynamic has also heightened the influence of service sector firms in public policymaking. Witness, for example, the increasing influence of financial firms in city budgeting processes and real estate developers in urban planning. Even if the services sector "accounts for only a fraction of the economy of a city, it imposes itself on that larger economy" through policymaking pressure, creating a "new valorization dynamic ... [that] has had devastating effects on large sectors of the urban economy" (Sassen 2002b, 16–17).

This is not to say that manufacturing is irrelevant to service-dominated cities. Even in New York, London and Tokyo, three of the most service-intensive urban economies in the world, approximately 10% of formal employment is still in the manufacturing sector (Sassen 2001, 208, 213, 221). Moreover, jobs that were once in the manufacturing sector (e.g. assembly) have, with the introduction of new technologies, been moved from the shop floor to the office floor (e.g. data entry). The increasingly intensive automation of production—much of which is now outsourced to the producer services sector—has created a whole new assembly line workforce. This may not be the manufacturing sector of old, but "modern technology has not ended nineteenth-century forms of work", it has simply shifted them around (Sassen 2001, 10).

Agglomeration Economies

The third hypothesis is that the outsourcing of centralized control functions by multinational firms in the manufacturing sector has meant that the head offices of these firms are relatively free to locate where they want. This is demonstrated empirically by the exodus of the headquarters of manufacturing multinationals from cities like London and New York over the past two decades to smaller cities (or edge cities) where office space is cheaper and where there may be other locational factors that come into play (such as quality of life considerations).

The specialized service firms that have taken over core corporate functions are, on the other hand, increasingly subject to agglomeration economies and have little choice but to locate in major world cities (and certain parts of these cities at that) where related service firms are located. Because no single service company is capable of managing all the affairs of a large multinational corporation, law firms must meet with advertising firms who must meet with finance firms, and so on. A dense and intense information loop is required to manage the complex, uncertain, and (ever-quickening) pace of corporate decisions that need to be made in a global economy.

This spatial concentration of service firms in a central business district—or in networked business nodes within a city—allows members of different service firms to meet face-to-face to share ideas and information and broker deals. To be outside of this spatial loop is to create inherent inefficiencies in productivity, to risk missing out on crucial information, or to be shut out altogether from lucrative business opportunities with correlated firms. Mergers and acquisitions within the producer services sector have made this agglomeration all the more important, allowing firms to provide seamless, one-stop shopping (Sassen 2002b, 23–24).

Proximity also matters because firms and individuals need to share information (both formal and informal) that simply cannot be digested and analyzed adequately electronically. This is information that requires "interpretation/evaluation/judgement" (Sassen 2001, 120) and is crucial to decision making in a climate of rapidly changing legislation and trade agreements, technological innovations and political upheavals. The sheer mass of information in today's electronic world is itself reason enough for continued face-to-face contact as service firms try to make sense of what Thrift (1999, 272–74) has called a "blizzard of transactions", creating a decision-making world of "unimaginable complexity".

Sassen (2002, 23) calls this personal networking "specialized social connectivity", while others speak of it as a form of "social capital" (see, for example, García 2002, 47; Meyer 2002, 268). Here we see another seeming contradiction in world city formation: in the most electronically dependent and technologically advanced economic sectors in the world it is the need for personal contact that shapes a world city's spatial configuration.

Critical to the success of this agglomeration economy is the infrastructure required to make it all work: 'smart buildings', conference centres, transportation networks (airports, roads, transit), telecommunications systems, as well as the less formal 'soft' infrastructure required for networking and the daily living requirements of the individuals that run these firms such as restaurants, entertainment venues, education facilities and accommodation. Political infrastructure is also critical, with access to political decision makers (local, national and international) critical to many firms' operations. All are part of an agglomeration package that determines how well a city works for the service firms that inhabit it (or whether these firms choose to locate elsewhere). The most important world cities are those best provisioned with this infrastructure, hard and soft.

Manufacturing Headquarters No Longer Critical

The fourth hypothesis is a corollary of the previous one, emphasizing that multinational manufacturing firms have been moving their headquarters away from large cities because they are no longer subject to agglomeration economies (at least not to the same extent as their producer service suppliers). From an empirical point of view, this hypothesis is important because it challenges the simplistic argument that the number of headquarters is what specifies a global city. While this may still be the case in some countries where urban primacy is such that alternative urban locations are not available to a corporation, a simplistic counting of multinational headquarters is no longer a useful indication of a city's world cityness.

World City Networks

The fifth hypothesis argues that agglomeration economies operate on different scales. As important as it is for specialized service firms to be able to interact with each other in a single city, so too must they be able to communicate effectively with their counterparts in other world cities. Infrastructure is once again critical here, especially that which facilitates intercity linkages such as airports, fibre-optic telecommunication and convention centres.

The result is a "transnational urban system" (Sassen 2001, xxi) where cities—or relevant sections thereof—are economically and technologically linked, and socially and politically connected. Not all cities are as deeply integrated as others, but virtually all cities in the world today are linked in some way into this international urban "space of flows" (Taylor 2000).

Interestingly, as important as this concept is to Sassen's work at a conceptual level, she fails to provide much in the way of detailed empirical evidence—a point that Taylor (2004, 39) takes up in his extended critique of the "evidential crisis" of the world city literature. Taylor and his colleagues have addressed this empirical gap by mapping out intercity connectivity for several hundred cities around the world, providing a comprehensive connectivity map.[1]

From this connectivity argument flow three conceptual corollaries. The first is that cities and regions compete with each other for positioning on this transnational loop in an attempt to place themselves as close as possible to the inner circle of world city connections (Harvey 1989c, Begg 1999, Gordon 1999, Lever and Turok 1999, Campagni 2002). We see this competition in the form of subsidized infrastructure and tax incentives to attract and retain firms that play a part in this urban networking.

Less prominent in the world city literature is the second corollary: that world cities *cooperate* with each other. Sassen makes two poignant observations here. The first is that the connectivity of world cities requires a certain degree of mutuality, driven in large part by the interest of international firms. Companies with offices in more than one city (some have offices in dozens of cities around the world) do not want to see an intercity bloodbath of competition that might jeopardize their own operations. As Sassen (2001, 357) notes:

> [G]lobal firms and global markets do not necessarily operate as if these cities were competing with each other, but rather as forming a cross-border network for their operations. Such firms and markets need to ensure state of the art infrastructure and resources in a network of cities, not in a single city.

In other words, producer service firms depend not only on business nodes within individual cities but in the vitality of the linkages between these nodes. Even peripheral cities are important here. It could even be argued that the vitality of peripheral cities (especially those in the South) is all the more important to maintain because there are so few viable alternatives in which to locate large offices. If Buenos Aires or Bangkok were wiped out by intercity competitive pressures it would create serious problems for national and international capital wanting to operate in those countries or regions. Keeping these cities fiscally and infrastructurally healthy (or, more specifically, healthy in those sections of the city that are required for networking and accumulation purposes) is just as important as ensuring that they are offering competitive tax rates.

Sassen (2001, 357–58) also notes that intercity cooperation has increasingly led to a complex division of labour amongst service firms in these cities, adding an additional layer of urban interdependence. The finance sector in Frankfurt, for example, once thought to be challenging London for supremacy in the European finance market, actually operates in a more collaborative than competitive manner with its counterpart (Taylor 2004, 211). Frankfurt-based firms tend to manage European portfolios while London-based firms manage the more global contracts, ultimately complementing each other rather than competing (Poon et al. 2004).

A third corollary is that intercity connectivity (be it cooperative or competitive) is contributing to the homogenization of cities around the world: socially, economically, politically and spatially. Yet another irony of the world city phenomenon is that as cities strive to become more remarkable than other cities it is their very unremarkability that defines them. Glass office towers, chain stores, entertainment spectacles, hotels, restaurants and related business infrastructures are more noteworthy today for their bland homogeneity and increasing levels of oligopolistic control than for their uniqueness. One can operate between Singapore, London and Johannesburg in a business-class bubble that barely differs from one place to the next (save for the ubiquitous 'local flavour' served up as 'exoticism', itself a message that is as bland and unconvincing from one location to the next as the office towers from which these messages are transmitted). In a world of increasing homogeneity, world cities are at the cutting edge of 'sameness'.

There are, of course, still significant differences between world cities. Paris remains different in many ways from Tokyo, Manila and Cape Town, "nested" as these cities are in their own national or regional systems with different historical "pathways" (to use the parlance of the world city literature). Political, economic, cultural and spatial distinctiveness has not disappeared and probably (hopefully!) never will, given that cities continue to respond to the pressures of capitalism in different ways. 'Economic globalization' is homogenizing cities on a scale and at a pace that are historically unprecedented, but these processes are also uneven and not entirely predictable.

Local Disconnections

A sub-hypothesis of this networking argument is that cities have become correspondingly *dis*connected from their immediate "hinterlands" (to use Johnson's (1967) now antiquated term). Rural and smaller urban areas that were once a significant part of a city's economy have typically become less important to the social, economic and political life of world cities. No city can ever delink completely from its adjacent areas—biophysical constraints for water and energy are reason alone for this—and socioeconomic and political links remain, particularly for cities in the South with strong circular migration patterns and a heavier dependence on foodstuffs from immediate rural areas.

Nevertheless, there is ample evidence that these local connections are weakening. This is particularly true of important business nodes of world cities where access to amenities and infrastructure is increasingly designed for a transnational elite (not for the country bumpkins of the surrounding areas), and where the sociocultural relevance of these urban cores is increasingly detached from local realities.

This disconnect is also playing itself out on a wider scale, with the most important world cities becoming disconnected from even their larger regional and national contexts. It can be easier, for example, to fly from New York to Paris than from New York to Dallas (at least a direct flight), a pattern that is amplified in cities in the South where transport hubs cater primarily to world city networking. The emergence of national and international airport hubs to service this urban interconnectivity is itself both a product and a producer of these global networking trends.

Socioeconomic and Spatial Polarization

The last two hypotheses address the socioeconomic effects of world city development. "Different types of economic growth promote different types of social forms" argues Sassen (2001, 255, xxi), in asking what the new social geography of the global city looks like, noting that a "growing number of high level professionals and high-profit making specialized service firms have the effect of raising the degree of spatial and socioeconomic inequality evident in these cities".

From an economic point of view world cities have seen heightened levels of income inequalities and job insecurity. The hyper-valorization of upper-level service sector jobs (especially in finance) and the related devalorization of manufacturing have created sharp and growing income disparities (Elliot 1999; Sassen 2001, 244–49).

These patterns of growing inequity are true for world cities in the South as well. In one of the few books that looks specifically at world cities in "developing" countries, Sassen (2002, 15) comments that urban inequalities have not been improved in any of the places examined: "Even in the face of massive upgradings and state-of-the-art infrastructure", socioeconomic inequalities have not been reduced—a point that is echoed in virtually every article written about world cities in the South (e.g. Sassen 2002a, Clammer 2003, Marcotullio 2003, Gugler 2004, Douglass and Boonchuen 2006, Tyner 2006).

The high-growth, producer service industry has contributed to this income polarization directly via the creation of low-wage, casualized and insecure production-line jobs such as data processing. But it is not only working-class positions that are affected by this growing insecurity. High-paid jobs in the producer services sector (particularly in newer, more 'innovative' sectors such as financial securities) are also vulnerable to this flexibility, as was witnessed with massive layoffs in the dot.com industry in the late 1990s, albeit with greater opportunities for reemployment and healthy severance packages after massive profit taking.

The rise of the services economy has contributed to wage polarization and job insecurity *indirectly* as well. A new class of highly paid service economy professionals drives a large sphere of personal services consumption (e.g. restaurants, tourism), which has in turn created a large and growing low-wage, casualized, insecure and labour-intensive workforce (e.g. dishwashers, dry cleaning services, nannies). This stratum of high-income earners is not a new urban phenomenon but has expanded dramatically with the rise of producer services in world cities (e.g. from less than 5% of New York City in the early 1900s to over 30% by the end of the century (Sassen 2001, 286)) and has become a structural feature of world city formation.

Spatially, world cities have seen two major polarizing developments. The first relates to work space: that hyper-concentration of buildings, transport nodes and related infrastructure required to connect city-bound firms to other firms and other cities in the network. Although much of it is technically 'public space'—most notably the leisure facilities associated with the new urban elite such as shopping centres, entertainment complexes, restaurants and the ubiquitous 'waterfront' developments—in reality much of it is effectively closed to large parts of the general public through disciplinary mechanisms such as zero-tolerance policing, entrance fees or just plain cultural alienation as these homogenized spaces become increasingly detached from the social milieu in which they are located. These new spatial developments may be *in* the city but they are not necessarily *of* or *for* the city.

Personal space has also been radically altered in world cities. The transnational elites that run the producer services economy increasingly want to live closer to where they work, network and play. This has created a heightened level of gentrified urban living space in central business districts (and within closely networked residential nodes within a city). Without the pretence of having to be 'public', these personal living spaces have increasingly become security compounds, serving to further alienate and polarize the non-elite of the city. Rapidly rising rental rates in city centres have driven working-class and unemployed families to more peripheral areas, making for longer commutes and contributing to a new form of geographically peripheralized ghettoization (Smith et al. 2001). These living spaces have also become increasingly homogenized by a new transnational architectural aesthetic, epitomized by the 'downtown loft'. This segregation is not unique to contemporary world cities, of course, "but the extent of spatial segmentation and spatial unevenness has reached dimensions not typical of earlier decades" (Sassen 2001, 260).

Finally, the privatization of consumer services such as water, refuse collection, health care and education has further exacerbated these socio-economic and spatial inequities. Private service providers have served to undermine the quality and quantity of public service delivery systems, creating multi-tiered service structures whereby transnational elites receive better services than others in a city, serving to differentiate the quality of place and space in the internationally connected business and residential nodes of the city as compared to lower-income areas.

The Informalization of World Cities

Yet another seemingly ironic characteristic of world cities—and Sassen's final hypothesis—is that urban economies are becoming increasingly informalized. As outsourcing of the formal economy works it way down the chain of production, particularly in less specialized aspects of the service industry, we see the rise of small, unregistered firms providing services ranging from photocopying to the watering of office plants. There has also been a massive increase in in formalization in the spin-off services economy driven by the personal services sector: dry cleaning, catering, household renovations, child care, and so on.

A rise in informalization in the light manufacturing sector has taken place as well, with increases, for example, in 'sweatshops' for clothing. Rising unemployment and the demand for inexpensive goods (many big-city sweatshops in the North are able to compete with cheap imports from the South) have been driving these developments, quite literally under the nose of the most formalized and technologically driven economies the world has ever seen. Sassen points out that much of this informal work is being done by women and immigrants (Sassen 2001, 305–23; see also Sassen 1988, 1995, 1999), adding yet another dimension of inequality to the social geography of world cities.

IS CAPE TOWN A WORLD CITY?

Given this set of definitions, is Cape Town a world city? In short, yes. But measuring these characteristics is not a simple task. As Sassen (2001, 354) notes in her own attempts at quantifying world cityness, "When it comes to identification and measurement … we enter a somewhat fuzzy domain".

In what follows I present empirical data that corresponds as closely as possible to the seven hypotheses outlined above in an effort to illustrate Cape Town's world city status. Not every aspect of Cape Town's world cityness is discussed in detail here—much of the empirical data around infrastructure development, for example, is provided in subsequent chapters—but the data offered below serves to at least establish Cape Town's world city standing.

Cape Town's Producer Service Economy

The first empirical point is that Cape Town is a service-oriented economy, with finance (32%), transport (11%) and other services (19%) dominating geographic value added (GVA) for the metropolitan area in 2004 (SACN 2006, 3–14). Manufacturing is still a major player in the city's economy (at 16% of GVA) but it has never dominated Cape Town's economy as it has in Durban and Johannesburg. Moreover, most of the city's manufacturing is light industry such as textiles and clothing. The latter has been a major employer in the city for decades but has seen dramatic changes since the mid-1990s, losing some 12,000 jobs in 2004 alone (personal interview, Shoemaker). The Finance Minister, Trevor Manuel, has also given notice to this sector, saying that it must face up to the "tough realities" of a global economy rather than expect handouts from the state or a tariff increase for imports (*Business Report*, November 26, 2004). Overall, performance in the manufacturing sector in Cape Town has been considered "very disappointing, at an average annual growth of just 0.5%, lower than the national performance of 1.8%" (PGWC 2005, 2).

Nevertheless, provincial and municipal governments have been targeting investments in manufacturing to adjust to these "tough realities" and there are new manufacturing areas targeted for growth, such as the building of luxury yachts (for which the city hopes to become the number two supplier in the world (CCT 2002b, 19)) and automotive parts (Cape Town produces 10% of the world's catalytic converters). There has also been growth in the fishing and agriculture sectors within the greater Cape Town area—most notably with the export of fruit and wine—which has had some impact on the growth of these sectors within the city boundaries and with spin-off effects in the service sector.

Overall, though, the strongest economic growth has been in personal and producer services. In direct contrast to manufacturing, the provincial Western Cape economy (of which Cape Town makes up some 85%) has seen "higher growth than the national average in catering and accommodation, transport and storage, business services and other producer services" (PGWC 2005, 2). According to Thomas (2003, 12), "the dominance of the service sectors [has] increased steadily ... with export-orientated, high value-adding niches rapidly gaining significance".

Job growth has not kept pace in the service sectors, however, with employment rates in key services having stayed level or dropped off between 2001 and 2005 (SACN 2006, 3–28). Nor is there much optimism from policymakers in this regard, with the provincial government lamenting in a 2005 review of the Western Cape economy that there has not been "net employment creation in finance and business services, transport and communication, nor in wholesale and retail trade, hotels and restaurants ... [and] there is little indication of increased employment resulting from tourism and other services such as telecommunications (PGWC 2005, 2).

Figure 1.1 provides a sectoral breakdown of GVA for the city in 2004 while Table 1.1 illustrates the percentage growth (or decline) of these sectors. Of particular note is the growth in the FIRE sector (finance, insurance and real estate), which dominates the service sector scene, although growth has tapered off somewhat in recent years, in line with trends in the rest of the country (SACN 2004, 50).

The service sector that has seen the most growth is communications and transportation, with call centres expected to be a large part of this growth in the future (one of the "fastest growing industries" in the country with growth rates of 20–30% per annum (Wiser 2001a, 5)). It is expected that the call centre industry will double by 2008 with as many as 100,000 new jobs (*Business Report*, November 9, 2004; *The Economist*, August 25, 2005).

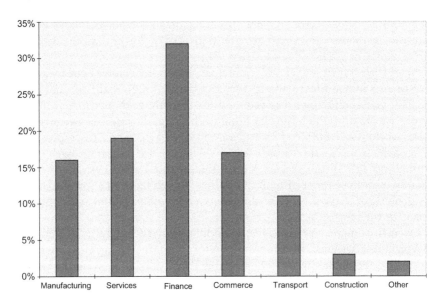

Figure 1.1 Geographic Value Added by Sector in Cape Town—2004. Source: SACN 2006, 3–14.

Table 1.1 Growth in Gross Value Added per Sector for Cape Town

Sector	1996–2001 annual growth (%)	2001–2002 annual growth (%)
Agriculture, forestry, fishing	0.76	4.00
Mining and quarrying	0.35	–8.49
Manufacturing	0.07	1.59
Electricity, gas, water	–0.52	3.37
Construction	5.55	–1.00
Wholesale and retail trade	2.22	–0.03
Transportation, storage, communications	5.84	4.58
Finance, insurance, real estate and business services	3.47	2.03
Community, social and personal services	0.28	1.11
TOTAL	2.24	1.65

Source: SACN 2004, 50.

The city and province also hope to grow the film and television sector in Cape Town, flagging it as one of the "top five growth industries" (Wiser 2001b, 2). There are plans to build a "Film City" near Cape Town where a DreamWorks studio would be based, and the national Department of Trade and Industry has launched a Film and Television Incentive Scheme for the country as a whole.

Film and television generate approximately R2bn a year in revenues in South Africa and this has been growing at about 20% per annum. Cape Town has seen most of this growth, with feature film productions increasing by 140% between 2002 and 2003 and with the city considered one of the top five production destinations in the world for television commercials (CTRCCI 2004a, 38). The film industry does not provide many jobs, however, and only contributes about R3m a year in direct municipal revenues through filming fees (CCT 2004a, 70) (though the spin-off effects are obviously larger).

Oil and gas is another growth area for services. The city hopes to become a servicing hub for the massive new gas production industry recently developed off the coasts of Namibia and the Western Cape of South Africa, as well as for the oil industry in West Africa (most of which is currently done in the United States). It is expected that a 1% share of the West African oil servicing market (financing, accounting, repairs, etc.) would provide a 1% increase in the GGP of Cape Town. To this end, the city hopes to sign a twinning agreement with the Nigerian state of Bails where 30% of Nigeria's oil is produced (personal interview, Albert Shoemaker; *Cape Argus*, October 20, 2004).

Tourism is another service area the city hopes to develop. It is already a large part of the city's economy, generating over R11 billion per annum (about 10% of GGP), employing over 50,000 people and with an asset base of at least R70 billion in land, buildings and equipment in 2002 (CCT 2002b, 17). It is also one of the fastest growing sectors of the city's economy. Conventions are a big part of this growth, with the completion of the Cape Town International Convention Centre in 2003 being a major component of this development strategy.

The same trends are reflected in South Africa's other major cities as well, illustrated by the fact that the service economy represented 55.4% of value added in the national GDP in 1990, rising to 65.6% in 2001, and still growing (DBSA 2003, 243).

Agglomeration Economies

Service firms in Cape Town are also subject to agglomeration economies and therefore benefit from a spatial concentration of firms in specialized business nodes. Chapters 4 and 5 discuss these spatial (re)developments in detail, but it is useful to highlight here that Cape Town has always had, and continues to have, a relatively strong and robust central business district (CBD).

Unlike Johannesburg, which effectively lost its CBD as a meaningful operational node in global business terms when it was abandoned by service economy firms in the 1980s and 1990s (Beal et al. 2002, Gaga 2003), and which has seen large parts of its urban residential core abandoned by the middle class and resettled by lower-income (and increasingly immigrant) populations, Cape Town's CBD has largely maintained its demographic and socioeconomic profile and remains at the centre of the city's economy (Miraftab 2006). Most of the city's service firms have their offices in the central CBD and there are a growing number of national and international firms with their headquarters here. Considerable efforts have gone into averting capital flight from the central CBD and a powerful public-private initiative has been launched to strengthen the CBD's appeal as both an office and residential location (see Chapter 6).

There are other business nodes in the city as well and these are connected by strong transportation and communication infrastructure. Even the Afrikaner-dominated business node in the edge city of Stellenbosch, half an hour's drive from Cape Town's CBD, and home to some of the largest finance and insurance firms in the country, is strongly linked to Cape Town's central CBD by highways, and has easy access to the city's international airport.

The city's dense business nodes therefore facilitate the kind of face-to-face networking required of a world city. Cape Town may not be as well-equipped with 'smart buildings' and other cutting-edge technologies as some of its northern world city counterparts, but it is remarkably well-positioned from a spatial point of view to facilitate the interpersonal net-working required of a competitive global city.

The new convention centre, ever-expanding shopping and entertainment facilities (catering as much to international tourists as to the city's residen-tial transnational elites) and upmarket housing developments with 24-hour security in the CBD have further served to entrench the city centre as an effective place to live and do business. The presence of the South African parliament, the head offices of the provincial government and those of the city council serve to reinforce the attractiveness of the city core for service firms.

In many respects Cape Town is an 'ideal' world city. The urban core is a mix of new office towers and old colonial buildings (the latter being ripe for yuppie renovation) and there is still considerable room for office expan-sion in the Foreshore and in the eastern section of the core. Nestled into the 'city bowl', framed by Table Mountain and the harbour, and with white sand beaches and spectacular cliff-side housing within an easy 5–10 minute drive, there are few city centres that can rival the efficiency and beauty of Cape Town.

The spatial legacy of apartheid has also meant that the city core, and vir-tually all of the upper-income housing in the city (situated in the city centre and along the mountain spine and coastline that run southward from the city centre), are separated from the vast, sprawling low-income townships on the Cape Flats by rail and road corridors, commercial and industrial space and/or parkland.

Figure 1.2 illustrates this socio-spatial economic reality, with the poor-est areas of the city being the African townships in the southeast quadrant of the map (in dark red). Low-income coloured townships are the next poorest (in pink) while middle-income coloured townships are represented by the yellow and light green. White/wealthier suburbs are largely repre-sented by the dark green, largely clustered around Table Mountain and along the ocean.

Figure 1.3 adds another layer to this spatial inequity, illustrating the correlation of poverty and population density, while Figures 1.4–1.8 offer photographic representation of these disparities.

Although mushrooming informal settlements along the main highways out of the city mean that there is some visual exposure to the grinding poverty and homelessness that grip the majority of the city's population, the city's business elite can—and do—operate in a spatial bubble that has more in common with San Francisco or Sydney than with the townships of the Cape Flats.

No other city in South Africa—and arguably no other city in the world—has been able to create such an insulated and insular central busi-ness district. Ironically, then, it is Cape Town's long, but still relatively recent, history of race and class segregation, which has given it a competi-tive edge as a contemporary world city.

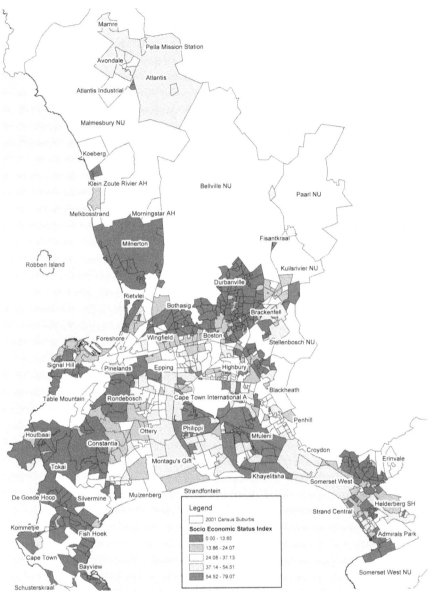

Figure 1.2 Socio-Economic Status in Cape Town by Township and Suburb. Source: CCT 2006e, Figure 3.

Headquarter Locations

Johannesburg has traditionally been the centre of manufacturing activity in South Africa but manufacturing headquarters are less and less a feature of the urban politico-economic landscape. South Africa has seen an increasing

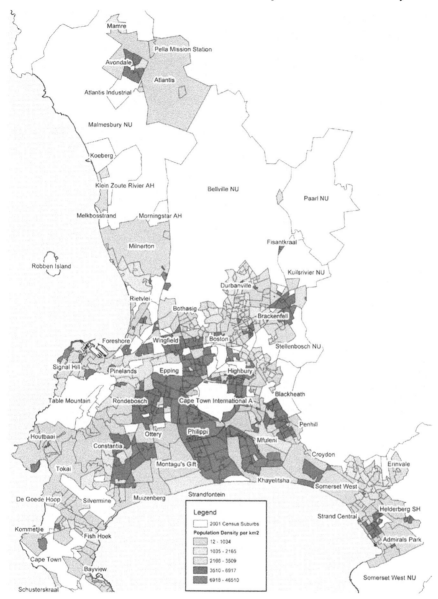

Figure 1.3 Population Density in Cape Town by Township and Suburb. Source: CCT 2006e, Figure 7.

dispersal of production to smaller urban centres, to industrial development zones and to export processing centres (Jauch 2002). There has also been a significant movement of manufacturing offshore, with some of the largest South African manufacturing firms locating all or part of their administrative, financial and manufacturing activities outside of the country.

Figure 1.4 Central Business District, Cape Town. Photo: Courtesy of City of Cape Town.

Cape Town has never been home to a large number of manufacturing headquarters (oil refining being an important exception, with the South African headquarters of Shell, BP and Caltex located in the city). Cape Town has, however, been successful at attracting and retaining head offices in the service and retail sectors. The head offices of Pick 'n Pay, Shopright/Checkers and Woolworths (retail), Protea Hotels (tourism), and Sanlam and Investec (financial and insurance services) are all located in various business hubs in the city (with Rembrandt Group, another financial services powerhouse, having its headquarters in nearby Stellenbosch). In total the city is home to the head offices of approximately 50 medium- to large-size firms.

Cape Town is also the 'second city' for service firms that have their headquarters in Johannesburg, particularly in the finance sector (with Durban a distant third in this regard (Padayachee 2002)) and there are important

Figure 1.5 Seaside Housing in Clifton, Cape Town. Photo: Courtesy of City of Cape Town.

Figure 1.6 Middle-Income Housing in Mitchell's Plain, Cape Town. Photo: Courtesy of City of Cape Town.

Figure 1.7 Low-Income Council Housing in Grassy Park, Cape Town. Photo: Courtesy of the City of Cape Town.

Figure 1.8 Low-Income Informal Housing in Khayelitsha, Cape Town. Photo: David McDonald.

regional offices for many global producer service players such as PricewaterhouseCoopers and KPMG.

It is worth noting as well that some of South Africa's largest service firms have moved their global headquarters offshore, most notably Old Mutual—the largest financial and insurance services business in the country, which used to be headquartered in Cape Town. Nevertheless, Cape Town appears to be gaining the upper hand on Johannesburg in terms of attracting and retaining service sector head offices, with the physical infrastructure of the city's business nodes and 'quality of life' for executives playing a key part in the decision-making process of managers—a point which the Cape Town Regional Chamber of Commerce and Industry trumpeted in its 200th Anniversary publication, pointing in particular to the decision of Pick 'n Pay CEO, Raymond Ackerman, to keep his head office in the city for these reasons (CTRCCI 2004b).

It is unlikely that Cape Town will supersede Johannesburg as the dominant headquarters location in South Africa in the near future, but the city's world-class business amenities, and a quality of life that appeals to active urban professionals, is helping the city to hold its own in this regard—especially for producer services—and these factors may eventually contribute to a tipping of the balance in headquarter locations in this sector (particularly if Johannesburg's (perceived) crime situation worsens).

One notable countertrend is that Cape Town is increasingly seen to be a 'white' city by black professionals, most of whom would appear to prefer the Johannesburg-Pretoria hub for social and political reasons. It could be argued at the same time, however, that it is exactly this renewed racialization of Cape Town that makes it all the more attractive to (white) transnational elites, a matter that will be taken up in more detail in Chapter 9.

International Connectivity

We turn now to the most important aspect of Cape Town's status as a world city: its degree of connectivity to other centres in the world city network. We have seen that Cape Town has a strong producer service economy with the necessary infrastructure and spatial configuration to make it a prototypical world city, but is it actually connected into the world city network? I will use Taylor's (2004) data to argue that Cape Town is in fact well-connected, if only as a tertiary player.

Cape Town is one of only six African cities that make it to the "operational roster of world cities" in Taylor's (2004, 71–100) research, and it is only the second time that the city has been identified in this way (the other being Petrella 1995, 21). Johannesburg is also on the list and has been identified as a world city in at least six other studies (Durban, by contrast, has not been listed on any world city roster that I am aware of).

The fact that Cape Town makes it to this list after having only recently re-emerged as an international centre makes its ranking all the more significant. A relatively sleepy, inward-looking city in the 1970s and 1980s, Cape Town has quickly joined the international business elite, highlighting not only the quantitative importance of its connections but also the qualitative robustness of this growth.

What makes Taylor's empirical work particularly important is that previous world city research has not adequately investigated the interfirm ("subnodal") linkages that are so critical to a city's connectivity. Earlier research relied on unsubstantiated hypotheses about connectivity—e.g. assuming that large service firms *must* be well-connected with other cities (Sassen comes in for particular criticism from Taylor (2004, 39) in this regard, but it is a common assumption in the literature)—or it depended on analyses of telecommunication linkages (e.g. Graham and Marvin 1996, 2001) or airline linkages (Friedman 1986, Keeling 1995, Rimmer 1998) where data is either too narrow to capture the full scope of interfirm/intercity connectivity or is even misleading (with popular holiday destinations being over-represented using the airlinks analysis, for example).

Taylor and his colleagues define connectivity by the degree to which producer service firms are connected to one another across different cities; through common ownership (e.g. the same firm with locations in many different cities) and/or through transactions between firms. This methodology is applied to 100 large international producer service firms (those with offices in at least 15 cities). Additional connectivity is defined via important multilateral institutions and international NGOs (such as Red Cross and United Nations organizations) (see Taylor 2004, chapter three).

Figure 1.9 illustrates Cape Town's placement in this world city network (the higher the connectivity ratio number the greater the international connectivity of a city). Notable is the fact that Cape Town is located in the bottom sixth of world cities in terms of its degree of connectivity, putting it on par with Portland, Stuttgart, Rio de Janeiro, Bangalore, Casablanca, Kiev, Wellington and Guangzhou. But this bottom tier standing does not mean it is unimportant. Both Cape Town and Johannesburg fall into what Taylor (2004 169–70) calls "major regional world cities", playing a critical role on the continent.

Nonetheless, Johannesburg is a more important city in terms of connectedness. With a connectivity ratio of 0.239, Cape Town is only about two-thirds as connected as Johannesburg (with a ratio of 0.414), prompting Taylor (2004, 74) to refer to the latter as the "clear leading regional city".

And yet, the connectivity ratio between the two cities (Cape Town and Johannesburg) is relatively low, indicating that much of their connectivity is with cities outside of South Africa and not just with each other. The opposite is true in many other 'emerging country' economies, where one city dominates the national scene and the 'second' city is more like a local satellite (e.g. in Korea, Mexico, Turkey, Russia). Many OECD countries also face this kind of urban primacy (Austria, Denmark, Britain, Japan) with considerably higher "top two city" connectivity ratios than Johannesburg and Cape Town. The implication here is that there is a considerable degree of international parity between Cape Town and Johannesburg, despite Johannesburg's stronger overall position, suggesting that Cape Town is in a position to maintain, and even expand, its role as an independent city of choice for international organizations.

Cape Town is certainly well-positioned relative to other sub-Saharan African cities in this regard. Of the other four African cities on Taylor's world city roster only two are from sub-Saharan Africa (Lagos and Nairobi), with Nairobi's appearance being due almost entirely to the presence

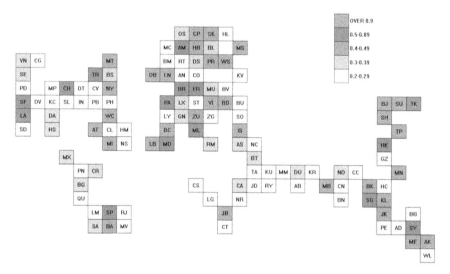

Figure 1.9 Global Connectivity of Major Nodes in the World City Network. Source: Taylor 2004, 73, Figure 4.2. (Note: This cartogram places cities in their approximate relative geographical positions. The codes for cities are: AB Abu Dubai; AD Adelaide; AK Auckland; AM Amsterdam; AS Athens; AT Atlanta; AN Antwerp; BA Buenos Aires; BB Brisbane; BC Barcelona; BD Budapest; BG Bogota; BJ Beijing; BK Bangkok; BL Berlin; BM Birmingham; BN Bangalore; BR Brussels; BS Boston; BT Beirut; BU Bucharest; BV Bratislava; CA Cairo; CC Calcutta; CG Calgary; CH Chicago; CL Charlotte; CN Chennai; CO Cologne; CP Copenhagen; CR Caracas; CS Casablanca; CT Cape Town; CV Cleveland; DA Dallas; DB Dublin; DS Dusseldorf; DT Detroit; DV Denver; FR Frankfurt; GN Geneva; GZ Guangzhou; HB Hamburg; HC Ho Chi Minh City; HK Hong Kong; HL Helsinki; HM Hamilton(Bermuda); HS Houston; IN Indianapolis; IS Istanbul; JB Johannesburg; JD Jeddah; JK Jakarta; KC Kansas City; KL Kuala Lumpur; KR Karachi; KU Kuwait; KV Kiev; LA Los Angeles; LB Lisbon; LG Lagos; LM Lima; LN London; LX Luxembourg; LY Lyons; MB Mumbai; MC Manchester; MD Madrid; ME Melbourne; MI Miami; ML Milan; MM Manama; MN Manila; MP Minneapolis; MS Moscow; MT Montreal; MU Munich; MV Montevideo; MX Mexico City; NC Nicosia; ND New Delhi; NR Nairobi; NS Nassau; NY New York; OS Oslo; PA Paris; PB Pittsburgh; PD Portland; PE Perth; PH Philadelphia; PN Panama City; PR Prague; QU Quito; RJ Rio de Janeiro; RM Rome; RT Rotterdam; RY Riyadh; SA Santiago; SD San Diego; SE Seattle; SF San Francisco; SG Singapore; SH Shanghai; SK Stockholm; SL St Louis; SO Sofia; SP São Paulo; ST Stuttgart; SU Seoul; SY Sydney; TA Tel Aviv; TP Taipei; TR Toronto; VI Vienna; VN Vancouver; WC Washington DC; WL Wellington; WS Warsaw; ZG Zagreb; ZU Zurich.)

of important UN headquarters such as UNEP and UN-Habitat. The other 25 sub-Saharan cities studied for the ranking (including Durban) scored well below that of Cape Town.

Together with Johannesburg, then, Cape Town plays a commanding role in the region and on the continent as a whole in terms of facilitating and generating investment pathways for international capital.

Taylor (2004, 83–86) and his colleagues have also shown that there are service sectors in which Cape Town's international connectivity ratios are stronger than those of Johannesburg. Accountancy is particularly pronounced, with additional relative strengths in law, management consulting and advertising. Cape Town is relatively weaker than Johannesburg, however, in the areas of banking/finance and insurance.

Competition/Cooperation

The world city hypothesis argues that connectivity leads to both competition and cooperation between urban centres and Cape Town is no different in this regard. On the competitive front the city finds itself in hard-pitched battles for foreign investment with cities throughout the world, selling itself as a relatively low-cost emerging economy while at the same time offering OECD-quality business and leisure facilities. The low-cost angle is used to attract such entities as call centres (pitting Cape Town against Delhi and Bombay, for example) while the 'first world' angle is used to attract filmmakers, biotech companies and finance firms (pitting Cape Town against cities such as Los Angeles, Toronto and Sydney).

Attracting and retaining these firms—and the transnational elites that run them—require significant investments in infrastructure and Cape Town has been doing its share on this front. The scale and character of these investments will be explored in detail in Chapter 5. Suffice it to say at this point that the city has invested enormous sums of money in the hard and soft infrastructures it deems relevant to international (and national) urban competitiveness, using public and private funds.

On the cooperation front, Cape Town is equally in synch with international trends. Municipal politicians and bureaucrats in the city are regular and active participants in multilateral organizations related to urban networking such as the World Bank and the UN-Habitat. City officials also play a key role in organized local government in South(ern) Africa and beyond (e.g. the South African Local Government Association, the United Cities and Local Governments of Africa, and the International Association of Local Governments (with Cape Town having hosted the first world congress of the latter in February 2006)). Cape Town also has twinning arrangements with numerous cities around the world, with strong social and cultural ties and with funding to assist with the city's development initiatives (e.g. the Federation of Canadian Municipalities' support for urban programming in South Africa).

As the world city literature makes clear, there is a simultaneous—if schizophrenic—relationship between competitiveness on the one hand and cooperation on the other, perhaps best exemplified by the World Bank's annual "Competitive Cities" conference which brings together senior city officials from around the world to learn how to out-compete each other, in a collegial way. Cape Town appears a willing participant in this urban paradox and has sent representatives to these World Bank meetings.

Homogenization

To what extent is Cape Town also affected by the increasing homogenization of world cities? There are, to be sure, many remarkable physical, political and cultural features to the city. Its built environment (most notably the Dutch colonial architecture), the strong presence of Cape Malay religious and cultural traditions, its unique demographic makeup (home to the largest coloured population in South Africa) and, of course, the looming presence of Table Mountain, all serve to distinguish Cape Town from other world cities.

And yet one cannot but be struck by the growing similarity of the city—particularly its business and related leisure facilities—to other world cities. The office towers are clones of other business hubs. The new airport terminals, casinos, shopping malls, 'loft' developments, conference centre and the ever-expanding waterfront (with its seemingly endless capacity for new shops, restaurants, entertainment facilities and up-market residences) are similarly devoid of any organic sense of place or personality.

This is not to say that planners and architects have not attempted to attach a unique sense of identity to these developments. Enormous efforts have gone into making shops, hotels, restaurants and business facilities (such as lounges at the airport) feel different by wrapping them in African flavours. But as South African architectural scholar Lindsay Bremner (2004, 11) notes: "[I]f we are honest, architecture's most widespread contribution to the first 10 years of democracy [in South Africa] is its use of fake, of artifice, of 'theme-ing', as the primary instruments of its interpretation of new socio-economic realities". As with other world cities, Cape Town's attempts to be different are more noteworthy for their indistinguishableness than for any real social or cultural variation.

Significantly, it is exactly this strength in creating artifice that "has made South African architecture extremely exportable to other centres seeking similar global positioning". With Cape Town firms amongst them, South African architects are "busy remaking Beijing, Bujumbura, Dubai, Kigali, Lagos, Luanda, Maputo [and] Shanghai" (Bremner 2004, 11).

Local Disconnections

Another feature of world cities that applies to Cape Town is its increasing disconnect from its immediate geographic surroundings. As Cape Town becomes increasingly networked into a global system, its immediate hinterland is of less and less importance to its economic and political viability. A rapidly growing international tourist market (now earning 50% more foreign exchange for the country than gold (*Business Report*, October 13, 2004)), producer service firms that cater largely to a regional and global network of manufacturers, and a municipal government with increasing ties to other world cities are all indications of a city detaching itself from its surrounds.

Elsewhere in the country, Cape Town's connections are primarily with other large cities, and it plays a key role in the recently established South African Cities Network (SACN)—an association of South Africa's nine largest cities that "encourages the exchange of information, experience and best practices on urban development and city management" (SACN 2004, 2). The links between these cities—and in particular between the 'golden triangle' of Cape Town, Durban and Johannesburg-Pretoria—play a much larger role in the networking consciousness of local government and corporations than do links with the smaller towns and districts of Cape Town's contiguous surrounds.

Size dictates much of this dynamic. With an overall budget of close to R18bn in 2005–06 (CCT 2005a), Cape Town's budget is larger (and more flexible) than that of the province within which it is situated (the latter's budget being approximately R14b in 2006–07 (PGWC 2005, 5) and is even larger than that of several neighbouring Southern African states.

Cape Town has quite simply outgrown its hinterland, requiring what Taylor (2004) has coined a much larger "hinterworld". Figure 1.10 is an illustration of Cape Town's hinterworld, indicating areas of strong and weak linkages with other world cities.

SOCIOECONOMIC AND SPATIAL INEQUALITIES

Finally, to what extent does Cape Town exhibit the spatial and socioeconomic inequalities characteristic of other world cities? Once again, the fit is strong, with Cape Town being one of the most—if not *the* most—unequal cities in the world.

Cape Town's Gini coefficient is certainly indicative of this inequality, with a score of 0.67 (SACN 2006, 3–45). This is not surprising given that South Africa's national coefficiency figure makes it one of the most unequal countries in the world (a dubious honour it shares from year to year with countries such as Brazil and Namibia). Cape Town's coefficiency figure is slightly lower than the national average, and also lower than that of

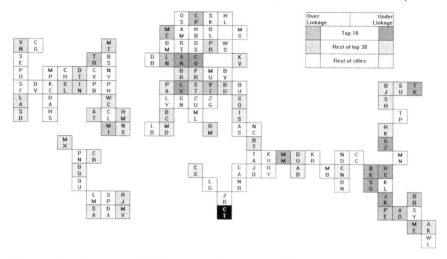

Figure 1.10 Cape Town's "Hinterworld." Source: Globalization and World Cities (GaWC) Study Group and Network website (www.lboro.ac.uk/gawc/visual/hw_ct.html). See Figure 1.3 for an index of city names.

Johannesburg (0.75) and Durban (0.72), but this is due in large part to the sizeable lower-middle income demographic in Cape Town's coloured community, which skews the city's figures. A more triangulated perspective shows enormous gaps between white, coloured and African residents of Cape Town, with the latter being as poor on average as Africans living in other South African cities. As the South African City Network (SACN 2004, 86) notes in its gloomy review of urban income distribution in the country, all South African cities are characterized by "deepening wealth divisions"—a point borne out by the fact that 36% of Cape Town households (about 1.2 million people) are estimated to be earning incomes below the government-determined household subsistence level of R1600 per month (CCT 2006e, 32).

But it is not just income that marks Cape Town's extreme inequities. As Table 1.2 outlines, the city is unequal across a wide range of fronts, from wealth to health to crime to employment, with unemployment rates having increased from 13.3% in 1997 to about 26% in 2005 (CCT 2006d, 21).

There are also signs of increasing dependency rates in single-parent, low-income households, rising service costs relative to incomes, huge distances between residential location and workplaces, and decreasing job security and benefits (to name but a few of the quantitative differences between the haves and have-nots of Cape Town (see SACN 2004, chapter five).

There are qualitative features to this inequality as well: the inferiority of service delivery in the townships; bleak, treeless streets on the Cape Flats; the angst and humiliation of water cutoffs for nonpayment of services; and the fear of gang violence.

Once again, Cape Town is not alone is this regard but what makes the city's inequalities so exceptional are the highly spatially segregated ways in which they operate. More than any other city in South Africa, well-to-do residents can live a life that is largely separated from their socioeconomic 'other'. The grinding poverty of the Cape Flats is far removed from the suburbs and hidden behind concrete fences, transport corridors and industrial zones.

There is relatively little indication of this poverty in the urban core. There is some informal economic activity, and there are some 'street children' in the CBD, but even this has been aggressively beaten back and pushed out to the margins by the private sector-dominated City Improvement District (CID) (Miraftab 2006). Cape Town has not experienced the massive capital flight or inner-city decay witnessed in Johannesburg and Durban over the past 15–20 years and has become even more corporate than ever.

These inequalities cannot simply be blamed on Cape Town's world city status of course. Three centuries of colonialism and four decades of apartheid put in place one of the deepest and most structured forms of inequality in the world.

What we do need to ask, though, is the extent to which these inequalities have been alleviated by, or exacerbated by, Cape Town's world city status since the end of apartheid. This is the question that we focus on in the rest of the book and which lies at the heart of the debates over globalization and cities. Are Cape Town's attempts at 'going global' worsening its inequalities or improving them? Will the service sector create the kinds of jobs and wealth required for poverty alleviation? Does the privatization of amenities and decision making create a more efficient or more unequal city?

Similar questions must be asked with respect to the informalization of Cape Town's economy (estimated to produce about 12% of economic output and employ 18% of the economically active population of the city, growing by 6% a year from 2001–04 (CCT 2002b, 23; SACN 2006, 3–18)), as well as the impact of (im)migration on Cape Town. Foreign and internal migration have altered the demographics of the city significantly over the past ten years and would appear to have contributed to the informalization of the economy as well. To what extent should these dynamics be attributed to Cape Town's world city status and to what extent are they the result of other dynamics?

Does the world city hypothesis provide us with the conceptual tools needed for answering these questions? My position, as outlined in the introduction to this book, is that we can use the world city hypothesis as a guide for describing and partially understanding contemporary urbanization in major cities—Cape Town included—but it fails to provide us with the necessary insights into understanding the contradictions of capital accumulation and the neoliberal policies now shaping it. The world city literature correctly points to the shift toward agglomerated service-based urban economies and the hyper-connectivity and specialized built environments

Table 1.2 Indicators of Inequality in Cape Town

Indicator	Informal Settlements	Low-income public housing	Low-income private housing	Lower-middle income	Higher-middle income
Average household income per annum	< R10,000	R10-R20,000	R20-R30,000	R30-R60,000	> R60,000
Median age	22	24	21	25	31
% household earnings less than Household Subsistence Level (HSL)	60%	31%	21%	13%	10%
% households with potable water on-site or in-dwelling	52%	97%	98%	99%	100%
% households with flush toilet	52%	97%	98%	99%	100%
% households using electricity for lighting	45%	91%	98%	99%	100%
Infant mortality rate (per 1000 live births)	Brown Farms - 62 KTC - 51	Mannenberg - 19 Hanover Park -12	Tafelsig - 11 Eastridge - 19	Strandfontein - 5	Claremont - 7 Tableview - 8
Low birth weight as % of all births	Brown Farms - 10% KTC - 12%	Mannenberg - 14% Hanover Park - 16%	Tafelsig - 13% Eastridge - 18%	Strandfontein - 12%	Claremont - 9% Tableview - 7%
New TB cases per 10,000 of population	Brown Farms - 114 KTC - 141	Mannenberg - 49 Hanover Park - 87	Tafelsig - 33 Eastridge - 45	Strandfontein - 6	
AIDS deaths as % of all deaths	Brown Farms - 12% KTC - 15%	Mannenberg - 2% Hanover Park - 2%	Tafelsig - 2% Eastridge - 2%	Strandfontein - 0%	Claremont - 1%

(Continued)

Table 1.2 Continued

Indicator	Informal Settlements	Low-income public housing	Low-income private housing	Lower-middle income	Higher-middle income
Reported violent crime cases per 10,000 of population	Khayelitsha - 154	Mannenberg - 218 Bishop Lavis - 185	Mitchell's Plain - 193	Lansdowne - 106	Rondebosch - 76 Kirstenhof - 117
Reported cases of murder per 10,000 of population	Khayelitsha - 12	Mannenberg - 6 Bishop Lavis - 7	Mitchell's Plain - 7	Lansdowne - 2	Rondebosch - 0.5 Kirstenhof - 1
Reported property crime cases per 10,000 of population	Khayelitsha - 99	Mannenberg - 326 Bishop Lavis - 425	Mitchell's Plain - 415	Lansdowne - 594	Rondebosch - 1612 Kirstenhof - 697
Reported cases of residential burglary per 10,000 of population	Khayelitsha - 32	Mannenberg - 64 Bishop Lavis - 63	Mitchell's Plain - 93	Lansdowne - 180	Rondebosch - 262 Kirstenhof - 185
% Economically active (< Matric education)	90%	83%	82%	59%	26%
% Unemployed males	32%	25%	19%	11%	4%
% Unemployed females	53%	29%	25%	12%	4%
Number of formal businesses as % of all businesses	4.7%	2.6%	0.3%	42%	49%
Existing formal jobs as % of all jobs	1.4%	0.6%	0%	75.7%	21.7%

Note: 'Service provision and basic infrastructure in lower-income areas have improved since these statistics were gathered but the scale of the disparities remains enormous both quantitatively and qualitatively.'

that allow for this kind of global networking but it tells us very little about why this is happening, how it leads to the kinds of sociospatial polarization that seem endemic to world cities or what kinds of alternative development strategies might be developed to address these concerns.

As an essentially normative framework, it could be argued that the world city literature does the exact opposite, naturalizing neoliberal ideological trends and perpetuating policies that are constitutive of world city inequalities.

The next two chapters are an attempt to provide better analytical purchase on these world city dynamics. Building on the conceptual and empirical insights of the world city hypothesis my objective is to highlight the deeper, structural reasons for the geographic dispersal of production, the valorization of service sectors (particularly finance) and the spatial reconfiguration and infrastructural investments in Cape Town. Drawing on a radical urban literature it will be argued that the changes so aptly described in the world city hypothesis are but an expression of the inherent cycles of the overaccumulation of capital and the tendency toward inequality within capitalist systems of production.

World cities, in other words, are world cities because they are capitalist cities, and it is an understanding of capitalist urbanization that we must have for our review of Cape Town. But rather than throwing out the world city 'baby' with its bath water, we can retain many of the descriptive insights that it has to offer. We just need to wrap them in new conceptual clothing.

2 Cape Town as Capitalist City

The previous chapter made a case for defining Cape Town as a world city, albeit a peripheral one. But as useful as the world city literature is as a descriptor of contemporary urbanization in South Africa, it does not provide us with the analytical tools necessary for understanding the extent of urban inequalities or the role that capital accumulation plays in sustaining and redefining unstable patterns of urban development.

The current chapter discusses this critique of the world city hypothesis, looking in particular at the world city literature's vague conceptualization of 'globalization'. In its place, I argue, we need to insert a much more critical interpretation of the internationalization of economic production and how this has manifested itself in urban South Africa; a perspective that sees major urban centres such as Cape Town as *necessarily* global in their orientation, *inherently* unequal in their make-up, and *intrinsically* unstable in their social, political and infrastructural constitution.

The Marxist analytical tradition I draw on here does not explain everything we might want to know about post-apartheid Cape Town, but it does help us better orient the city in relation to contemporary capitalism than the world city literature does, and helps to determine the extent to which 'going global' is a positive or negative development strategy for the city.

It is only when we see Cape Town as a capitalist city, and not just as a world city, that we understand more fully the nature of its inequalities and the limits and contradictions of market-based post-apartheid reforms. Rather than providing opportunities for poverty alleviation and just, sustainable growth, Cape Town's reinsertion into the global market economy has trapped it in an unequal pattern of crisis-ridden urban development, entrenching rather than mitigating the enormous inequalities and instabilities of the past.

The chapter begins with a review of the conceptual weakness of the world city literature's interpretation of globalization. I then invoke a more radical thesis on uneven urban development and discuss how this both parallels and differs from the world city hypothesis. The chapter concludes with a review of how this alternative analytical framework applies to urbanization in South Africa in general and Cape Town in particular, preparing the ground for a discussion in Chapter 3 of why Cape Town must, ultimately, be seen as a neoliberal city.

WEAKNESSES IN THE WORLD CITY HYPOTHESIS

Sometimes referred to as "economic globalization", sometimes "internationalization", and sometimes "global processes" (Sassen 2001, 4), the concept of "globalization" lies at the heart of the mainstream analysis of world cities. Once again I will use Saskia Sassen as my reference point, starting with her argument that, "with globalization come [the] conditions for the ascendance of ... cities and regions.... I locate the emergence of global cities in this context" (Sassen 2001, xviii–xix). Her global city thesis is fundamentally grounded in the argument that globalization "is a key factor feeding the growth and importance of central corporate functions.... In order to understand why major cities with different histories and cultures have undergone parallel economic and social changes we need to examine transformations in the world economy" (Sassen 2001, xix, 4).

But despite the centrality of the concept, we are never offered a detailed explanation of what these "transformations" are. Sassen (2001, 4) argues that "global processes" are "important to my theoretical framework" but also states that they are "not examined at length in my study". What we are offered instead is an interesting, but undertheorized, list of "geographical areas, industries and institutional arrangements that are central to the current process of globalization" (Sassen 2001, 23). The two chapters in her *Global City* book describing "The Geography and Composition of Globalization" provide a useful discussion of the "global dispersal of manufacturing" as it has been facilitated by technological developments in transport and telecommunications, but there is no overarching theoretical framework, nothing to pull together an otherwise disparate set of useful descriptive factors offered up as conceptual model.

This is not a problem unique to Sassen. Much of the world city literature falls into the same nontheoretical trap, assuming, it would appear, that globalization is such a well-known concept that there is no need to explain it. Indexes of books on world cities and keyword references in journal articles invariably contain the term "globalization" but seldom explicitly define it (e.g. Felbinger and Robey 2001, Chernotsky 2001, Clark et al. 2001, Boshken 2003, Clammer 2003, Marcotullio 2003; notable exceptions include Marcuse and van Kempen 2000, Short 2004b, Taylor 2004).

Nor is this a problem restricted to the world cities literature. As a number of 'globaloney' critics have pointed out, the term is uncritically used in a wide range of popular and academic discourses—on both the left and the right—with insufficient attempt to define or problematize its conceptual foundations. As Hay and Marsh (2000, 100) note: "The concept of globalization may give the impression of explanation, but it cannot in itself explain anything. It is in fact merely to redescribe, and to redescribe in the most imprecise and obscurantist terms at that, the object of our attentions. It is, in short, a redescription masquerading as an explanation. As such, our critical hackles should rise whenever globalization is appealed to as a causal factor". Strange (1995, 293) is equally scathing, arguing that it is "a term used by a lot of woolly thinkers who lump together all sorts of superficially converging trends ... and call it globalization without trying to distinguish what is important from what is trivial, either in causes or in consequences (see also Harvey 2000, 53–73; Petras and Veltmeyer 2001).

This lack of critical perspective is understandable in some respects. Despite differences of opinion on the pros and cons of globalization there is at least a general (if under-articulated) consensus as to what it constitutes: the global spread of capitalist production and market ideology; the deregulation of the economy (particularly the finance sector); a heightened international movement of capital and labour (and culture); and rapid technological changes in production, transport and communications that have facilitated and speeded up these changes (see, for example, Held and McGrew 2000).

But all too often conceptualizations of globalization stop here. We are told what globalization is in descriptive terms—and sometimes told that it is a 'good' or 'bad' thing—but are often left in the dark as to how this descriptive/normative assessment fits into a broader world view.

In Sassen's case this conceptual fuzziness leaves her in a sort of theoretical limbo, with ambiguous conclusions as to the role and impact of globalization on urbanization. For example, she argues on the one hand that globalization clearly has "its own specific impacts in producing [inequalities in world cities]", but then immediately qualifies this by saying: "I would agree with my critics that it is not the sole cause and that it is very difficult to establish for how much it accounts" (Sassen 2001, 362).

Might there, then, be more to be gleaned from Sassen's focused discussion of "the basic traits of contemporary capitalism"? Here there would appear to be more promise, with a commitment at the start of *The Global City* to providing "a theoretical elaboration of the concept of capital mobility" and "capital-labor relations" and how these fit within the "broader organization and control of the economy in the current phase of the world economy" (Sassen 2001, 23–24).

Unfortunately, we are once again provided with a list of facts and variables but no overarching theoretical framework. Classic locational theory forms part of the analysis (i.e. the argument that firms tend to (re)locate where the cost of production is lowest: "the movement of manufacturing jobs from highly developed areas to less developed, low-wage areas"). Sassen also insists that there are "other components of importance", including: efforts to "maximize the use of low-wage labor and to minimize the effectiveness of mechanisms that empower labor vis-à-vis capital"; increases in the "transnationalization of ownership and control of major corporations";

shifting patterns in the organization of office work; "the entry of large corporations into the retailing of consumer services"; the "development of export processing zones"; "several changes in the financial industry"; the "onset of the so-called Third World debt crisis"; and the "formation of international labor markets" (Sassen 2001, 23–34).

But how these concepts of capital mobility and capital/labour relations fit into a larger theoretical whole is again unclear. Sassen moves (albeit eloquently) from one conceptual point to another without pulling them into a discernable theoretical interpretation of globalization. Even her references to the "dismantling of Fordism" fail to draw any theoretical links to the vast literature on post-Fordist economies and what this dismantling means for globalization.

Three additional points in Sassen's work further illustrate my point. The first has to do with the concept of "crisis" in the global capitalist economy. Sassen plays with the idea but does not develop it beyond a series of questions. She asks about the "durability of an economic system dominated by management, servicing and financing activities" but fails to tell us if this system is sustainable, preferring instead to say that there is "considerable debate" on the matter (Sassen 2001, 334, 336). Similarly, when talking about the sustainability of socioeconomic inequalities in cities, Sassen (2001, 335) can only ask questions: "At what point do these tensions become unbearable? At what point is the fact of homelessness a cost for the leading growth sectors? How many times do high-income executives have to step over the bodies of homeless people till this becomes an unacceptable fact or discomfort?" We are not told whether these inequalities are inherent to globalization (and therefore intrinsically unstable), or whether they have the potential for resolution within the current system.

A similar, and related, theoretical ambiguity arises in Sassen's discussion of the built environment. Arguing that "[t]he place-ness of the global city is a crucial theoretical and methodological issue in my work", Sassen (2001, 350) agrees with "Harvey's notion of capital fixity as necessary for hypermobility"—i.e. the Marxist argument about a "spatio-temporal fix" that we will develop in more detail below.[1] But rather than adopting the Marxist position that spatial fixes play a "vital role in crisis formation and resolution [inherent to] the internal contradictions of capitalism", as Harvey (1982, 350) has argued in his seminal work on the subject, Sassen makes no reference to crisis. She speaks rather of "instances where the leading growth trends have ... made possible totally new land uses or sociospatial forms" (Sassen 2001, 257). Spatial fixes are not "rendered necessary" by capitalism, as they are in the Marxist literature, but rather "made possible" by amorphous "growth trends". Are these "trends" merely accidental? Are there underlying characteristics or dynamics that help us understand their formation and/or outcomes? Sassen does not provide us with the conceptual tools to pursue these questions.

And finally, what of the class tensions implicit in Sassen's discussion of "capital-labor relations"? Here too we find no discernable theoretical reference point. There is the "upper class" (those who own sufficient capital to "make them into important investors"), the "high income workforce" (that well-paid stratum of "professionals and managers" who make decisions about capital investments but are not significant owners of capital themselves) and a diverse group belonging to the "working class" (composed of a shrinking "labour aristocracy", a growing "offshore proletariat" of women and migrants, and a vast pool of "low-wage" labourers), but we are given no indication as to the ontological status of these class categories or the nature of (potential) class conflicts (Sassen 2001, 286, 322).

Are these objective economic actors operating independently of the capitalist "traits" around them, or are they subjected somehow to the demands of a market system (or some combination thereof)? Are highly paid professionals inclined in some way to ally with the working class because of their own vulnerability in an ever-quickening boom-and-bust economy, or do their allegiances lie with the "upper class"? And who are the "upper class" exactly; what role do they play in contemporary capitalism and how does one define 'ownership' in today's world of publicly traded multinational corporations? Sassen (2001, 323) asks some important questions (e.g. Do growing class inequalities in world cities "represent changes in magnitude along an upward or downward gradient, or are they ruptures and discontinuities in the social fabric of these cities?") but once again there are no theoretical reference points to orient us in this regard.

The world city literature grounded in "world-systems" analysis comes closer to theorizing these questions (e.g. Knox and Friedman 1995, Taylor 2004) but this writing also leaves us with an indeterminate conceptualization of a global market economy. To illustrate, Taylor (2004, 199–200), one of the leading proponents of the "world cities in a world-systems" theorem, points to the cyclical nature of "over-production and under-demand" in the global economy and comments on how these trends "favour capital over labour", but there is no sense that the system may be inherently unstable or unequal. Just the opposite in fact: "I will assume", he argues, "that the world city network as part of globalization processes is not inherently regressive in nature. The world city network can do more than service global capital". Taylor also argues that there are many different types of globalization—a useful acknowledgement of the diversity of global forces at play and their different social, geographic and economic manifestations—but does not tell us what might tie these different globalizations together and what (if any) core characteristics they may share.

Short (2004b) makes a more concerted effort to date to draw links between globalization and world cities but the analysis falls short of the book's promising subtitle ("Globalizing Cities in a Capitalist World"), plagued as it is by vague and underconceptualized concepts of capitalism and often conflating descriptive features (e.g. "global urban networks") with explanatory theory.

In the end, we are left with a useful but analytically limited conceptualization of globalization in the world city literature. We can agree with its main descriptive parameters—the global dispersal of manufacturing, the rise of an outsourced producer services economy subject to agglomeration economies, the concentration of these command and control centres in key world cities and the related growth in the networking of these world cities as a result—but the hypothesis does not adequately tell us how capitalism shapes and determines these dynamics or whether it is possible to mitigate or reverse their negative impacts in a market system. For this we must turn to Marxist literature on cities.

UNEVEN DEVELOPMENT AND URBAN THEORY

It is useful to note at the outset of this discussion that the Marxist urban literature is in general agreement with the basic descriptive features of the world city literature and with the "global processes" that it says shape cities today. Likewise, few Marxist writers would deny the broad quantitative changes to the global economy that Sassen highlights in her world city hypothesis or the centrality of these dynamics in understanding cities.

Where the analytical divergence occurs is in the *qualitative* interpretation of these changes—i.e. whether they represent a 'new' set of political, social and economic processes (as the world city literature explicitly or implicitly argues) or whether they are a continuation of older dynamics. Here is where radical theory is critical to our understanding of world cities, and where, to quote Harvey (2000, 68), a "shift of language from 'globalization' to 'uneven geographical development' has most to offer".

The Marxist argument, in essence, is that world cities are but the most recent manifestation of a long-term capitalist trend toward the valorization of finance capital and an increasing concentration of wealth (and poverty) in urban centres. As firms are continually forced to scour the earth in search of cheaper ways to produce their goods, sell their stock and invest their capital, urban networks of command and control have emerged as a 'natural' progression of this accumulation dynamic. The spatial configuration and infrastructural fixity of cities are a manifestation of these global market processes, concretely expressed in the form of transportation networks, residential layouts and other infrastructural, institutional and ideological formations. This accumulation and investment process is inherently unequal and unstable, however, making it prone to crisis and bound to change. The same capitalist dynamics that lead to world city formation, in other words, invariably lead to their change or demise.

It is worth looking at these dynamics in some detail, in part because there has not been a systematic review of this literature as it relates to the world city hypothesis, despite the apparent similarities between the world city literature and the more radical writing on uneven development, and in part because it helps us better situate Cape Town's emergence as a global urban centre.

What follows is by no means a comprehensive review of theories of uneven development. I have simply identified key conceptual points as they relate to world city formation and to my own interpretation of urban developments in South Africa. I have also attempted to highlight elements of this radical thesis that capture what I deem to be the universal, constituent elements of capitalist cities, while at the same time highlighting the need (and the theoretical possibility) for conceptual flexibility—i.e. a theoretical framework that reflects the variations of the global urban experience while at the same time capturing what Marx referred to as the "absolute general laws of capital accumulation".

Crises of Overaccumulation

The first of these "absolute general laws" is that capitalist firms must make a profit if they are to survive. One strategy for this is to invest in labour-saving technologies, but since competition compels all firms to invest in the same way, labour-saving technology negates individual profit increases in the longer run, driving down the overall rate of profits and leading to what Marx called the "tendency" or "law" of a "falling rate of profit". The irony—or, more appropriately, the inherent contradiction—of this process is that in trying to maximize their profits through the introduction of technology, capitalists end up doing the exact opposite: "[T]he capacity to produce surplus value ... is diminished over time by the very technological revolutions that individual capitalists institute in their pursuit of surplus value" (Harvey 1982, 180).

This tendency toward decreasing profits can be countered in various ways: through a higher intensity of exploitation of workers (e.g. sweat-shops), by a lowering of the social wage (e.g. reducing benefits), by accessing cheaper sources of constant capital (e.g. environmental exploitation), by slowing down the pace of technological change (e.g. patent laws) and by an increase in the 'industrial reserve army' of unemployed labour (e.g. by tapping into new pools of wage labour such as China). All of these counter-trends have been employed at various times over the years—in South Africa as well, some of which we will have cause to return to in this book—but none can stave off the general tendency toward falling rates of profit for-ever. Heightened competition and new technological innovations inevitably bring firms back to the same profit pressures to invest in cost-saving plants and equipment.

Capitalist firms are also compelled to continuously search for cheaper ways of producing and of finding new consumers if they are to remain prof-itable. One of the most common strategies has been to relocate to another country (or outsource production) where social wages are lower and/or environmental laws more lax.

Here we see the first, and most fundamental, point of departure from the world city hypothesis. Rather than a mysterious and unexplained dynamic driving the "global dispersal of manufacturing", we see a clear, structural set of forces that impel capitalist firms to internationalize their operations. The intensity and timing of this imperative differ from sector to sector, and region to region, but the underlying structural necessity of profit seeking compels all capitalist firms to globalize in some way or other.

Equally important is the fact that this incessant and excessive investment in profit-seeking strategies inevitably results in a crisis of 'overaccumulation' (in the form of commodity, money or productive capital) which, when combined with a growing pool of displaced labour, creates a situation where it is no longer possible to bring all goods produced to the market profitably. This overaccumulation typically takes place in subsectors of the economy, creating bottlenecks and disruptions here and there, but slowly spreads to the broader national/international economy, creating a more general accumulation crisis (with the Depression of the 1930s being the most significant and expansive thus far).

This is not a problem of "underconsumption", notably, but one where underconsumption is a consequence of overaccumulation. As a result, efforts to increase consumption through Keynesian welfare mechanisms can only have ameliorative effects. Though these welfare reforms can have important—even lifesaving—impacts in the short run, they are inherently limited and transitory. The real crisis lies with the creation of idle productive capacity and pools of unemployed labour.

How does capital overcome these general crisis tendencies (as it regularly has in the past)? The answer is complex and involves a series of potential strategies and developments. The most spectacular—and often catastrophic—response has been massive devaluations of assets in what Marx called the "primary circuit of capital". In this case, large swaths of hitherto productive assets can become worthless (in monetary terms) due to overcapacity in the system. In some cases, firms are able to move or reconfigure their assets to become profitable again (refitting a textile plant to become a high-end clothing manufacturer, for example) but these shifts can be difficult if not impossible in practical terms and often take place in periods of general recession where the incentive for reinvestment, and the potential for profitable returns, are diminished. The long, painful process of deindustrialization in cities in the United States over the past three decades exemplifies this devaluation dynamic.

A second, and related, response to overaccumulation crisis has been for the state to invest in secondary (e.g. roads, communications infrastructure) and tertiary (e.g. education, health care) circuits of capital, with the aim of rebuilding and/or reformulating the base upon which new primary circuits of capital accumulation can be built. In other words, investing in the medium- to long-term reconfiguration of a place—or network of places—to prepare the ground for a renewed period of profit making. The reinvention of cities such as Baltimore into postindustrial centres of services investment are illustrative of the kinds of efforts that have gone into reestablishing the conditions for capitalist growth in urban areas (Fee et al. 1991, Wallace 2004), as is Cape Town's reconstitution of itself as a service-oriented, internationally connected city.

Spatiotemporal Fix

This investment in different circuits of capital is what Marx originally coined the "spatial fix", a concept that Marxist analysts have fruitfully expanded on more recently (Harvey 1982, 1989b, 2003; Smith 1984). Here we see investments in the built environment that are, quite literally, fixed into the ground, without which new rounds of capital accumulation would be impossible. Airports, conference centres, universities and water and electricity systems are crucial to the redevelopment of cities, which would be unable otherwise to host competitive, profit-seeking capitalist firms.

But as permanent as these fixed investments may seem, they are also perpetually unstable. Overinvestments in secondary and tertiary circuits of capital can exacerbate periods of devaluation (as happened with overcapacity in electricity generation in South Africa in the 1980s and with education in the United States in the 1970s), putting investments in the primary circuit at additional risk of becoming obsolete or devalued.

As a result, spatial fixes are necessarily temporary, unpredictable and unstable, potentially resetting the equilibrium required for another cycle of capital accumulation but then exposing capitalist firms to the same general tendencies of a falling rate of profit in the longer run. The spatial fix is therefore a transitory and partial solution to accumulation crises, staving off one disaster and laying the ground for the next (though it may take years or even decades for the cycle to run its course). The aggregate effect, argue Brenner and Theodore (2002, 354), is that capitalism "continually renders obsolete the very geographical landscapes it creates and upon which its own reproduction and expansion hinges".

The analytical differences with the world city hypothesis could not be more stark. Although Sassen notes the importance of fixing *in* space the infrastructure required to work *across* space, her world city hypothesis has none of the structural features described here: profit-seeking crises incessantly leading to new forms of built environments, creating a situation of perpetual change and instability.

Nor does Sassen discuss the ways in which this cycle of boom and bust leads to infighting amongst ruling elites keen to minimize their own losses and maximize their potential future gains. Theories of uneven development, on the other hand, tell us that different factions of capital are forced to fight it out over the downward, devaluation stage of crisis as well as over strategies for renewed capital accumulation. Manufacturing, agrarian, rentier and finance capital can have very different investment interests and time horizons, creating major conflicts over investment priorities and policies.

The outcomes of these struggles, and the resultant shapes of the urban built environment, depend in part on the relevant strengths and historical positionality of the different players as well as the mediating role of the state. What was once an "operating fraternity of the capitalist class" during boom times can become a "fight amongst hostile brothers" during a bust, as capitalists within the same sector, and across sectors, slug it out for survival (Marx, as quoted in Harvey 1982, 202).

This leads to another key point of difference with the world city literature: How is it that finance capital increasingly plays the role of kingmaker in managing periods of accumulation crisis? For Marxists, the answer is built into the very nature of the crisis itself. As overaccumulation begins to set in, as structural bottlenecks emerge, and as "profit rates fall in the productive sectors of the economy, capitalists begin to shift their investable funds out of reinvestment in plant, equipment and labour power and instead seek refuge in financial assets" (Bond 1999b, 11). In other words, finance capital enriches itself at the expense of other forms of capital during periods of devaluation crisis, setting in train a long-term (and accelerating) cycle of strengthening its position vis-à-vis other factions of capital *because of* the boom-and-bust process.

Here, then, is the real source of ongoing valorization and strengthening of finance capital. Sassen, for her part, can only point to this phenomenon in empirical terms, missing out on a crucial conceptual point about the inevitable shift toward finance-dominated decision-making structures and criteria in cities. Without this understanding we cannot fully appreciate the shifting trends in urban investment and policy priorities.

So too must we understand the mediating role of the state as part of the structural makeup of accumulation crises. Accumulation can happen without a state or with a weak state, and so too can recovery from an overaccumulation crisis, but "the preferred condition for capitalist activity is a bourgeois state in which market institutions and rules of contract (including those of labour) are legally guaranteed, and where frameworks of regulation are constructed to contain class conflicts and to arbitrate between the claims of different factions of capital" (Harvey 2003, 91).

We will return to the role of the state—and its shifting ideological and scalar composition—in greater detail in Chapter 3. What I want to emphasize here is that the state continues to play a strong role in dealing with capitalist crises (this is not a state that is 'withering away'), and it is essential to see this role as inextricably bound up with the larger structural changes of capitalism—yet another point missing from the world city hypothesis.

Inherently Unequal

A final, critical difference between theories of uneven development and the world city hypothesis relates to interpretations of inequality. As noted above, the world city literature is quick to point to a pattern of extreme sociospatial inequalities in world cities but fails to provide a consistent or structured explanation of it. Sassen tells us about homelessness in the streets and sweatshops in the back alleys of New York but she cannot tell us if this is an intractable problem of capitalist cities or just another anomaly of 'globalization', ready for resolution.

Marxism tells us that this kind of inequality is inherent to the capitalist system, that profit seeking and surplus extraction inevitably lead to uneven development and that any efforts to ameliorate the situation through Keynesian welfarist mechanisms will only push the problem elsewhere and/or be temporary in its resolution (though 'temporary' can last for several decades, as the postwar welfare states of Europe and North America have shown).

In this respect, there is little to be optimistic about when it comes to 'globalization'. We can, along with Harvey (2000, chapter twelve), be hopeful about the potential of a more rational harnessing of technologies and a universalization of certain human rights, but we can reject the possibility of sustainable, equalized development under capitalism. While recognizing that market systems are different throughout the world (American capitalism differs in important ways from Swedish and South African capitalism, for example) we can nonetheless point to a core set of profit dynamics that will always be unequal and unstable.

From this perspective, the world cities of today are but a new manifestation of a much older capitalist dynamic. They are not, as Sassen (2001, 34–36) asserts, a response to the "new economic logic" of globalization. In making this mistake Sassen conflates the outcomes of world city formation with the practices that drive it, assuming that new *forms* of space economy represent new *logics* of a space economy. The Marxist position is fundamentally different, arguing that the logic of capitalism remains essentially the same but the spatial form and sociopolitical shape that it takes on are always changing.

Harvey (2000, 54, 68) makes the point as follows: "If the word 'globalization' signifies anything about our recent historical geography, it is most likely to a new phase of exactly this same underlying process of the capitalist production of space.... [T]here has not been any fundamental revolution in the mode of production and its associated social relations and if there is any real qualitative trend it is toward the reassertion of early nineteenth-century capitalist values coupled with a twenty-first century penchant for pulling everyone (and everything that can be exchanged) into the orbit of capital while rendering large segments of the world's population permanently redundant in relation to the basic dynamics of capital accumulation".

CAPITALIST CRISES IN SA

What can be gleaned from this analysis in the South African context? The following sections use this analytical framework to outline key developments in the crisis of capital accumulation during apartheid and illustrate how this led to a major reconfiguration of urban development policymaking and investments, and to the eventual dismantling of the apartheid system in favour of a liberal democracy.

This brief historical review is followed by an outline of the major institutional, ideological and infrastructural trends in South African cities since the fall of apartheid in the early 1990s. The analysis here is also brief, in preparation for the more detailed empirical discussion of these developments in later chapters. My objective at this point is to highlight the extent to which Cape Town and other South African cities have been, and continue to be, fundamentally shaped by the same capitalist dynamics that affect other world cities.

Racial Capitalism's Collapse

Since the 1880s when gold and diamonds were first discovered in South Africa, capital accumulation in the country has been based on access to cheap black labour (made artificially available through colonial and then apartheid labour and land policies) and on the availability of heavily subsidized, state-run energy and water supplies. As the economy expanded beyond mineral extraction and agriculture to manufacturing—particularly with the onset of the Second World War—the accumulation strategies and systems to support this growth necessarily became more complex, but the fundamental features of access to cheap pools of black labour and subsidized infrastructures remained key to the economy's expansion (Saul and Gelb 1981, Fine and Rustomjee 1996, Bond 2000, Marais 2001).

The industrialization of South Africa did, however, threaten the viability of Afrikaner-dominated farming and English-dominated mining in the first half of the twentieth century and it is here that we see the earliest signs of crisis arise. Mine and farm owners petitioned for legislation to stem the flow of African labour to better-paying factory jobs in towns and cities, and pre-apartheid governments acceded to these requests by enacting a series of labour influx control measures—most notably the Natives (Urban Areas) Act of 1923 (Bonner et al. 1993).

It was not until the late 1940s, though, that social, economic and administrative conditions were ripe for full-blown racial segregation. The rapid economic expansion of the war years had heightened the tensions around African labour migration and further threatened the livelihoods of under-capitalized Afrikaner farmers and the white, urban working class (who were experiencing an erosion of real wages due to the influx of cheap black labour). Campaigning on a ticket of Afrikaner nationalism and racist ideology the National Party was able to attract sufficient votes from the most economically threatened elements of white South Africa (white workers, white farmers and petty bourgeois Afrikaners) to win the national election of 1948 and implement its grand vision of "separate development".

These racial policies had their desired economic effects. Pools of cheap labour were maintained in the rural areas and the jobs and wages of white workers were protected in the cities. But serious tensions remained in the system. Urban capitalists wanted unfettered access to cheap black labour and the apartheid state could not turn its back on the labour needs of the most economically vibrant sectors of the nation's economy simply to enforce the racial principles of 'pure' apartheid.

The state was therefore faced with the difficult task of balancing the flow of labour between rural and urban areas. This balancing act proved relatively easy in the 1950s and 1960s: the South African economy was booming; black resistance movements had been all but silenced; and the central and local states had the managerial, financial, and military capabilities to adequately control the movement of people. Although urban-based capital did complain that migrant labour costs were still artificially inflated by influx laws, protest was muted. There were, after all, enormous profits still to be made from relatively cheap black labour. Significant also was the fact that the costs of maintaining the township/homeland system were still manageable.

The real economic contradictions of what Saul and Gelb (1981) referred to as "racial capitalism" were to surface in the 1970s with the development of numerous structural barriers to continued capital accumulation. The first, and arguably most important, of these was the heavy, capital-intensive growth path of the previous decades (due in part to the subsidy and incentive policies of the apartheid state), which made it impossible to absorb adequate numbers of the growing ranks of unemployed black South Africans. This overcapacity was particularly acute in manufacturing, creating large pools of underutilized stock and capital. This rising organic composition of capital—central, we should recall, to all overaccumulation crises—led to growing unemployment, falling rates of productivity throughout the economy (GDP growth fell from an annual average of 6% in the 1960s to about 1.7% from 1973 to 1990 (Marais 2001, 30)), falling rates of profit (from 40% during the 1950s to less than 15% during the 1980s) and a virtual collapse in net fixed capital investment by the early 1990s (Bond 1999b, 21).

This particular overaccumulation crisis was exacerbated by the peculiarities of the apartheid economy. Import-substitution strategies had provided a base for much of the growth in manufacturing during the 1950s and 1960s but by the 1970s the white consumer market had been effectively saturated. Moreover, there were not enough black consumers to buy the goods being produced due to insufficient (or nonexistent) disposable incomes, high rates of un(der)employment and weak or nonexistent infrastructure, particularly in the heavily populated rural areas (i.e. the 'consumption fund' necessary for mass consumption did not exist).

International sanctions—though having little effect on the export of key commodities such as gold—played a role here as well, making it difficult for South African manufacturing firms to sell their goods internationally. Sanctions also made it difficult to access international capital for additional growth and/or to export capital for growth options outside of the country. South Africa's reliance on a few export commodities (especially gold) made the economy particularly vulnerable to currency fluctuations, contributing to a chronic balance of payments deficit from the late 1970s.

Making matters worse for capital was a growing anti-apartheid protest movement—renewed from the mid-1970s. The management and maintenance of the apartheid system became increasing expensive to maintain. Strategies of 'ungovernability' and boycotts against the payment of rates and housing bonds, coupled with an increase in military resistance by the armed wing of the ANC, saw a dramatic increase in the cost of the security apparatus required to sustain apartheid's institutions (including the by-now bankrupt Black Local Authorities, the puppet administrations set up by the neo-apartheid state to give a semblance of self-governance in the townships).

A revived (black) labour movement intensified the crisis, with dramatic increases in industrial action from the early 1980s (Fine and Davis 1991, Kraak 1993). The impact of this unionization was also felt in the civic arena, as highly organized 'political unionism' had knock-on effects on activist discipline and organizational capacity amongst community-based groups, with organizations such as the United Democratic Front benefiting from the solidarity and assistance of union-based cadre (Seekings 2000).

By the mid-1980s the South African economy was mired in crisis, with massive overcapacity and very few ways of relieving these accumulation pressures.

Calls for a New Accumulation Strategy

The looming crisis did not go unnoticed by capitalists. As early as the mid-1970s big capital in South Africa began to realize that the accumulation strategy of apartheid was bumping up against barriers. There had been some half-hearted reforms introduced by the state to try and address these problems in the early 1970s but capital's frustration with the lack of more substantive government reform, particularly after the Soweto uprisings of 1976, led to the formation of a pro-business think tank to address the problem—the Urban Foundation. Founded in 1977 and funded by Anglo American (English capital) and the Rembrant Group (Afrikaner capital), the Urban Foundation operated with the expressed intent of trying to resuscitate the South African urban economy by improving the material living conditions of urban blacks and influencing urban policymaking (McCarthy 1991).

The Urban Foundation was openly critical of attempts by the apartheid state to create ever more bureaucratic versions of apartheid, arguing that more serious reform in the townships was necessary to "spearhead economic growth and demonstrate the opportunities of an expanding domestic market" (Bernstein 1991, 329), articulating corporate South Africa's newfound interest in upgrading urban areas to create more black consumers and healthy, skilled workers for better workplace productivity. In the words of Mr Justice Steyn (Executive Director of the Urban Foundation in the early 1980s): "If people want the free-enterprise system to continue [in this country], they are going to have to get off their butts and make contributions towards housing" (as quoted in Soni 1992, 45).

Equally important was the corresponding "transformation of both the ideology and the class basis of Afrikaner Nationalism" by the end of the 1970's, leading to a definitive split within the National Party on whether more substantial reform should be adopted (O'Meara 1983, 254). A new "class of Afrikaner financial, industrial and commercial capitalists" had emerged from decades of state assistance for Afrikaner business and had become the "dominant faction" within the National Party. Under this new leadership the National Party began gradually to "cut itself away from its old constituency ... leav[ing] the cause of defending fully institutionalized racism to strata more immediately vulnerable to black advance—the marginalized white farmers of the plattenland and the remnants of the white working-class" (Saul 1993, 94–95). No longer the poor cousins of English enterprise, the elites of Afrikanerdom had transcended their dependence on a racist election ticket and allied themselves with corporate South Africa in an "attempt to secure the political and economic conditions for renewed capitalist prosperity and stability" in the country (O'Meara 1983, 254–55).

By the mid-1980s, "thinking within the National Party and senior civil service circles to a large extent reflected the liberal paradigm" of English capital (Hendler 1991, 201), and with its 1986 White Paper on Urbanization the apartheid state had officially acknowledged that black urbanization was not only inevitable but economically desirable. Rather than spending billions of rand to try and keep blacks out of cities, "the urbanization of the African population was to be turned from problem to solution, with the processes of industrialization and cultural change expected to transform a discontented and threatening people into more compliant members of a mass-consumption society" (Smith 1992, 2).

Realizing that renewed economic growth and profitability in a market economy depended on a dramatic change in the racial policies of the day, large-scale capital and its allies were anxious to establish a new political order, a "new national consent" involving the adjustment and eventual overturn of "the political and ideological bases of apartheid rule" (Marais 2001, 41). To this end, executives from Anglo American and other large firms began talking openly with ANC officials in exile in Lusaka, Zambia, from the mid-1980s, and the National Party began secret negotiations with Nelson Mandela (while he was still in prison in South Africa) in 1986. The election, in 1989, of F.W. De Klerk to head the National Party signalled the end of an era in the party and a triumph of (neo)liberal reformers within the apartheid state, leading to the unbanning of anti-apartheid organizations and calls for multiparty negotiations for a new constitution in early 1990 (Murray 1994, O'Meara 1996).

The nature of these negotiations, and the neoliberal dispensation that emerged from them, are the subject of later chapters. The point to emphasize here is that the transition out of apartheid was driven in large part by a crisis in capitalist accumulation and by efforts on the part of a ruling elite to preserve the market and rekindle economic growth.

This interpretation stands in stark contrast to the liberal assessment of apartheid's demise as a failure of a morally corrupt system of racial oppression and an awakening on the part of the ruling National Party to these wrongs (e.g. Sparks 1995). Although there are undeniably moral aspects to the post-apartheid transition—the heart-wrenching testimonials and apologies of the Truth and Reconciliation Commission being sufficient evidence of the complexity of the situation—the demise of apartheid was largely the result of a concerted effort on the part of a new, liberal ruling elite to reconstitute a revised capital accumulation strategy.

A New (Urban) Accumulation Regime

Of particular interest is the extent to which cities factor into this new accumulation strategy. In short, South African cities are essential to capital growth: opening the doors to new investment opportunities in producer services domestically; creating a platform for outward-oriented growth and for foreign direct investment in South Africa; creating new and expanded patterns of elite consumption and the facilities necessary for the attraction and retention of a transnational capitalist class; and unleashing the potential for mass black consumption.

To accomplish these goals a new spatial fix was required (though many of the spatial legacies of apartheid would offer a good start), with massive investments in secondary and tertiary circuits of capital. Most important has been the hard infrastructure of the city—airports, seaports, telecommunication systems, etc.—to better link South African cities with the rest of the world. Also necessary has been expanding and strengthening the business nodes of cities to allow them to host sophisticated agglomerated service economies (smart buildings, conferences centres, etc.).

Elite spaces of consumption have been a major investment focus as well, with massive growth in high-end shopping malls, leisure areas and residential developments, often overlapping into one, integrated gated community (such as the Waterfront and Century City developments in Cape Town).

Expanding and improving basic infrastructure in urban townships has been important too. Billions of rand have been spent since the mid-1990s on the provision of water, roads, electricity, schools and health clinics (amongst other things) and many millions of low-income South Africans have received new or improved service delivery (though these investments pale in comparison to those in upper-income areas and are tempered by policies of cost recovery, as we shall see in later chapters).

Part of the rationale for these township investments has been the moral and humanitarian commitment to addressing the wrongs of apartheid. But the state and big business have also made it clear from the outset that improving township services is required to boost economic growth (McDonald 1998). This interest is confirmed in part by the enthusiastic support of the Reconstruction and Development Programme (RDP) by big business, as illustrated by the full-page newspaper advertisements taken out by organizations such as Anglo American and Old Mutual when the RDP was first introduced and by the financing of government publications on the RDP (such as the glossy 20-page review published by the Office of the President on the first anniversary of the new government, financed by BMW, Iscor, Land Rover, SA Finance, Liberty Life, Siemens and Standard Bank (RSA 1995b, 21)).

The RDP White Paper (RSA 1994b, 23–24) puts this accumulation rationale front and centre in the government's justification of the program:

> Investments that follow the logic of the RDP offer tremendous opportunities for the South African industry. In particular, major investments will be made in electricity, health, housing, education, telecommunications and the information infrastructure, transport, and public works such as roads, water and sanitation.... In this respect ... [t]he RDP creates a large local market for industry which allows it to design and develop products with a stable home base. This also provides the predictability to allow the extensive restructuring that is needed to make the country's industries more efficient and effective. For instance, the domestic appliance industry expects its local market to increase by millions of new consumers, and is thus restructuring itself and designing new products.

With more than 80% of South Africa's GDP produced in urban areas, the need to create competitive investment and production environments is critical, as highlighted in an early post-apartheid Discussion Document on Urban Development Strategy (RSA 1997b, 13): "Better working towns and cities are crucial ... to restoring and speeding up economic growth, and to enhancing the global competitiveness of the national economy.... South

Africa's cities are more than ever strategic sites in a transnationalised production system".

This transition to a new accumulation regime did not happen overnight. It was a contested and uncertain struggle, with competing visions of what a post-apartheid urban economy could look like and what kind of spatial fix would be required. There have also been major struggles over the ideological and institutional character of urban reform.

There was no guarantee of the direction that these reforms would take, either, but the resulting 'rationalization' of local government has had a decidedly neoliberal tone, creating municipal authorities that are more responsive to the demands of domestic and international capital than to the needs of the urban poor. In this respect the ANC is no different than any other bourgeois government in actively intervening to manage the accumulation process.

CONCLUSION

The specifics of how these respatializing initiatives have played themselves out in Cape Town are the subject of Chapters 4 and 5. What I hope to have established here are the general conceptual principles around capitalist crisis, how it manifests itself in cities and the kinds of strategies employed to establish new patterns of accumulation.

With this theoretical lens we can see beyond the mere descriptive features of world cities to understand Cape Town as a capitalist city, prone to the same patterns of instability and sociospatial reconstitution as other capitalist urban centres. While retaining the descriptive insights of the world city hypotheses we can leave behind its optimistic—even boosterish—position on the positive impacts of 'globalization', adopting a much more critical perspective on both the motivations and the outcomes of contemporary urban reform.

But this is not the end of the analytical story. Just as important to understanding Cape Town as a capitalist city is understanding it as a 'neoliberal city', and it is to this subject that we turn next to investigate the role, scale, ideology and institutional makeup of state involvement in the new urban accumulation strategies of South Africa.

3   Cape Town as Neoliberal City

Having established that world cities are a new manifestation of a much older capitalist dynamic, the challenge in this chapter is to determine the specific ideological and institutional character of this urban capitalism. What are the reforms that capitalist cities have adopted to make themselves into world cities and how do these patterns apply in Cape Town?

I will argue here that policies being adopted in world cities are largely *neoliberal* in character—intended to attract and retain service-oriented transnational capital and to induce the kinds of sociospatial restructuring required to (re)establish new regimes of capital accumulation—and that Cape Town is no different in this respect. The specific forms of neoliberalism that have been adopted in Cape Town since 1996 are, of course, specific to its social, political and economic past, but the city's overall approach to urban development is remarkably similar to that of urban neoliberalism elsewhere in the world.

More importantly, it is the *process* of neoliberalization that makes Cape Town's experience so universal—i.e. the dynamic by which neoliberal policies and institutions emerge and then adjust to their own internal contradictions. Mapping out this process and its outcomes is an important conceptual task.

The purpose of this chapter is to define neoliberalism (what it is and what it is not) and the process of neoliberalization. I start with a review of national-level neoliberalism and then look at how it manifests itself locally. In both cases I compare the international experience of "actually existing neoliberalisms" with that of South Africa and argue that the national government and Cape Town's local government are neoliberal regimes (though much more robust and dynamic than is often argued in writings on the subject).

This conceptual discussion prepares the ground for an empirical review of neoliberalism in Cape Town in later chapters, looking at decentralization, privatization, cost recovery, and other neoliberal policy developments, as well as the impacts of these institutional and policy reforms on equity in the city. This theoretical discussion helps to explain the shifting nature of neoliberalism and how it is that apparently progressive policy reforms (e.g. 'free water') can actually be just the opposite, serving the interests of transnational capital rather than the urban poor.

Remarkably, none of these issues is being discussed in the mainstream world city literature. Neoliberal policies such as deregulation, privatization and liberalization certainly feature in world city writing—and are often identified as central to the formation and reconfiguration of world cities— but there is little in the way of critical engagement with these policies or the processes that shape them. The world city literature tells us very little about the historical emergence of neoliberalism (beyond the fact that it has superseded Keynesianism), how it has changed over time (and continues to change), how these ideas have come to dominate national and urban policymaking worldwide or what they mean for urban inequality. In fact, the term "neoliberalism" seldom even appears in the 'keywords' of journal articles or in the indexes of books on world cities (Sassen's *The Global City* (2001), Taylor's *World City Network* (2004) and Short's *Global Metropolitan* (2004) being prominent examples of the latter). Most telling of all, perhaps, is that the recent *Global Cities Reader*—a comprehensive collection of the most representative and important writings in the genre over the past two decades—has only one single reference to "neoliberalization" in its index (and even that is in an Introduction written by the editors) (Brenner and Kiel 2006).

Nor is it clear from most of the world city literature where an author stands on the matter: should cities stop or reverse neoliberal policies or should they simply be modified to try and make them work better for the poor? There is also little in the way of nuanced discussion about subtle variations of neoliberalism or what their different outcomes might be (e.g. comparisons of divesting state assets versus public-private partnerships). This quietude, I would argue, has served to strengthen—if inadvertently— the very neoliberal agenda that much of the world city literature laments.

So too is the world city literature silent on the links between neoliberalism (as an ideological and institutional construct) and capitalism (as a mode of production). The literature tells us virtually nothing about the connections between different policies of neoliberalism and the (changing) dynamics of capital accumulation. Are privatization, deregulation and liberalization just random policy developments or are they linked to particular phases (and crises) of capital accumulation?

These missing links are not surprising given the fuzzy conceptualization of capitalism in the world city literature, but they do serve to further highlight the analytical gaps in the world city hypothesis.

This is not a simple matter to take up, however. As we shall see below there are shades of uncertainty as to what constitutes neoliberalism, and its constantly changing character makes it difficult to identify and universalize.

Nor is the labelling of South Africa as neoliberal a simple or straightforward position to adopt. While few would deny that the post-apartheid government (at all levels) is pro-market in its orientation, there are many who insist that it is more Keynesian than neoliberal in its orientation. Seekings (2002, 3, 14), for example, argues that "observers of South Africa in the late 1990s might be forgiven for seeing the South African case as yet another example of the triumph of 'neoliberalism'", insisting that the ideas of the ANC—at least in the area of welfare reform, to which his comments refer—should be associated with "new liberalism" or "social democracy".

At one level Seekings is right. South African welfare programs do not necessarily follow crude neoliberal policy prescriptions. As he notes, the "South African pension system serves to redistribute from the rich to the poor to an extent unmatched almost anywhere else in the south" (Seekings 2002, 11). In comparative terms the country's noncontributory welfare system is indeed quite progressive.

We must be careful, therefore, not to generalize neoliberalism across all arenas of social and economic policy in South Africa or to assume a particular, universalized character. Neoliberal policies can be implemented in one arena and not another, or by one level of government and not another. As we shall see, this is inherent to the neoliberal process itself, depending as it does on the historical trajectories and concrete realities of the persons and institutions through which it has evolved (and been resisted). It would be wrong to suggest that *all* policymaking in South Africa is neoliberal or that there is a monolithic or static form of neoliberalism that has descended on the country.

Nevertheless, I will argue that the *general* character of post-apartheid policymaking is neoliberal—some of which is orthodox in nature—and nowhere is this more evident than in the country's cities. There are policy variations across cities and regions, and in the way policies are implemented and articulated, but the general tone of post-apartheid ANC urban policymaking is solidly neoliberal in its orientation.

This urban neoliberalism also casts a long shadow over the country, in some cases reversing what might otherwise be considered progressive gains in other sectors. In this respect, Seekings' (2002, 6) depiction of post-apartheid welfare reform as "generous" must be seen in light of what has happened in other policy arenas, such as cost recovery on municipal services. Households may receive old-age pensions but millions are still without adequate access to basic services such as water and electricity because they cannot afford to pay the high cost of connection fees or because they cannot afford to pay the tariffs (or at least not for as much as they would like to consume) (McDonald and Pape 2002). These are the types of knock-on effects that can serve to hollow out gains made in other—less neoliberal—policy arenas.

But it is not enough to simply weigh the costs of one policy against the benefits of another. We must develop a more dialectical understanding of the dynamism of neoliberalism to see how it moves and responds to the contradictions of capitalism as well as its own internal inconsistencies.

Neoliberalism, like its market progenitor, is inherently unstable and constantly in need of adjustment.

The rest of this chapter looks at these neoliberal dialectics and draws connections to the larger structural contradictions of capitalism outlined in Chapter 2—keeping in mind that neoliberalism is but one way of managing the uneven dynamics of capital accumulation.

But before discussing what neoliberalism is, it is important to first determine what it is not.

WHAT NEOLIBERALISM IS *NOT*

Much of the confusion around what neoliberalism is stems from a misunderstanding of what it is not, and in particular how it differs from Keynesianism and neoconservatism.

Classic, post-war Keynesianism was characterized by high levels of state ownership and/or management of key sectors of the economy; highly regulated financial, trade and labour markets; corporatist economic planning; protection of domestic industries through tariff and nontariff mechanisms and a focus on the national economy and national state actors (Kriesler and Sardoni 1998, Palley 1998). Keynesianism has changed over the years, however, and is now broadly divided into neo-Keynesianism and post-Keynesianism. The former, according to Palley (2005, 20–22), has adopted many of the neoliberal tenets around labour market flexibility, acting more as of a "forerunner" to neoliberalism than as an active alternative. Post-Keynesianism, on the other hand, "rejects" the idea that markets can equilibrate income distribution and wages, arguing that without state intervention "markets have a tendency to favour capital over labour" (Palley 2005, 28).

Neither of these two schools fundamentally challenges the role of the market, however. There may be heated debates over the emphasis that should be placed on state and nongovernmental institutions to regulate and mediate market failures, but the market is still seen as the primary engine of economic growth, and growth is still seen as the primary route to poverty alleviation. In this respect, Keynesianism shares with neoliberalism a common faith in the ability of the state to regulate the market and to provide equitable and sustainable capitalist growth (Duménil and Lévy 2005, Lapavitsas 2005).

As the lines between Keynesianism and neoliberalism blur it is difficult to know where one set of policies, institutions and ideologies ends and the other begins. This is not to deny that the institutional and policy mechanisms of neoliberalism and post/neo-Keynesianism can differ, with quite important implications for peoples' everyday lives, but the differences are far less significant than they used to be, making our discussions here all the more complex. As neoliberalism in the twenty-first century morphs into a more interventionist, institutional mode to deal with its own internal contradictions and instabilities—as we shall see below—it would appear to take on the institutional and discursive trappings of Keynesianism in an attempt to stabilize new patterns of capital accumulation. In this regard we can turn Seekings' comments on their head, arguing that observers of contemporary South Africa could be forgiven for thinking that postwar Keynesianism has returned.

More obvious, perhaps, are the differences between neoliberalism and neoconservatism, although even here there is much more in common between them than many observers are willing to admit. Certainly there are major differences on social policy, with neoliberal governments generally being supportive of gay rights, abortion rights and a host of other socially progressive reforms, while neoconservative governments oppose them. In this respect, the ANC is not a neoconservative regime, having been at the forefront of progressive social reforms internationally—most notably with its Constitution and Bill of Rights. Despite some deep-seated social conservatism in the country—notably on issues of homosexuality and the death penalty—the ANC government has stood firm in its commitments to progressive social change across a wide range of issues.

But when it comes to economic policy there is generally very little difference between neoconservative and neoliberal positions. Both are fiscally conservative with a commitment to tight monetary policy. Both can take a more (or less) interventionist approach to regulation and industrial policy and can have similar positions on free trade. If anything, neoliberals can be more 'right-wing' on the latter, with neoconservative governments often opting for a more protectionist, nationalist position on trade and liberalization.

WHAT NEOLIBERALISM IS

How, then, do we define neoliberalism? One approach is to identify specific policies: fiscal restraint, privatization, liberalization, inflation targeting, export-oriented growth, tight monetary policies, and so on. But a definitional exercise of this sort has limited analytical value because neoliberalism is in a constant state of flux and never exactly the same in two places.

In this respect, neoliberalism is less of an 'ism' than a process, what Peck and Tickell (2002) call "neoliberalization". It is an "elusive phenomenon" that "must be construed as a historically specific, ongoing, and internally contradictory process of market-driven sociospatial transformation, rather than as a fully actualized policy regime, ideological form, or regulatory framework" (Brenner and Theodore 2002, 353).

Neoliberal projects are also embedded in particular social, economic and political milieus, "produced within national, regional and local contexts and defined by the legacies of inherited institutional frameworks, policy regimes, regulatory practices and political struggles" (Brenner and Theodore 2002, 351). All neoliberalisms are therefore "path dependent" and somewhat different from one another.

In other words, there is no such thing as 'pure' neoliberalism. When it does occur it can take on many different forms and is "neither monolithic nor universal in effect" (Peck and Tickell 2002, 384). As a result, some observers use labels to describe different types of neoliberalism. "Social neoliberalism" (or "neoliberalism with a human face") has been used to describe Sweden's post-welfare reforms, for example (Duménil and Lévy 2005, 12).

South Africa has its own brand of neoliberalism, and it is important to acknowledge the many (potentially) progressive policy elements within it (e.g. the noncontributory old-age pension cited earlier). It is tempting, then, to use a term such as social neoliberalism to describe the post-apartheid ANC but I will avoid the phrase for two reasons. First, it diverts attention from the highly orthodox nature of many neoliberal ANC policies, particularly in key areas such as monetary reform, trade liberalization and cost recovery on services, all of which threaten to undermine progressive policy developments in other areas. Second, the term implies a static condition, diverting our attention away from the more dynamic, creative/destructive tendencies of neoliberalism discussed below.

South African policymaking may indeed have a number of 'social' characteristics at the moment, but will things stay that way? South Africa's neoliberalism is as prone to instability and reformulation as any other country's and is necessarily impregnated with all sorts of policy variants, from the 'social' to the 'orthodox', with the demands of capital constantly putting pressure on any redistributory mechanisms. More importantly, what may appear to be progressive at one moment (e.g. 'free water') may be hiding a deeper dynamic of marketization and commodification, leading to the creation of an even more profound neoliberalization of markets and society than their orthodox counterparts.

It is this shifting, concealing nature of neoliberalization that is central to the discussion here. We therefore turn our attention to a theoretical review of the different 'moments' of neoliberal reform before looking more concretely at how these processes have played themselves out in the (urban) South African context. The challenge is to find a theoretical model that identifies the economic characteristics inherent to all neoliberalisms without obliterating their social, institutional and ideological differences; an approach that does justice to the various shades of neoliberalism but still allows us to "recognise the beast" (Saad-Filho and Johnston 2005, 2).

Two Moments of Neoliberal Reform

I borrow a conceptual device, for this review, developed by Brenner and Theodore (2002) (and developed further by Brenner 2004) in their analysis of "actually existing neoliberalisms" in Europe and North America. After this initial review I examine how it can be adapted to the South African context.

In their review they refer to two "moments" of reform; one that "destroys" the ideological and institutional vestiges of the previous Fordist-Keynesian regimes of accumulation and one that "creates" new and revised modes of neoliberalism, responding in part to the failures and contradictions of the first moment of neoliberal reforms. This first, destructive phase of neoliberalism occurred in the 1970s and 1980s in Europe and North America when there was an aggressive assault on welfarist policies and institutions. What these authors also refer to as "roll back" neoliberalism involved efforts to shrink the size of the state through fiscal restraint, privatization and the rolling back of state powers, as well as efforts to deregulate the economy and reduce the power of unions. This was the neoliberalism of Thatcher and Reagan, with what amounted to the "(partial) destruction of extant institutional arrangements and political compromises through market-oriented reform initiatives" (Brenner and Theodore 2002, 362).

But as the "perverse economic consequences and pronounced social externalities" of these narrow market-driven reforms became apparent and increasingly difficult to ignore (the failures of outright privatization being one example) neoliberal pundits began to change their policy prescriptions, morphing them into more "socially interventionist and ameliorative" forms of neoliberal planning, "epitomized by the Third-Way contortions of the Blair and Clinton administrations" of the 1990s (Peck and Tickell 2002, 388–89).

In this second, "creative" moment of neoliberal reform, policymakers and capital recognize the shortcomings and dangers of the initial, destructive phase of neoliberal dismantling, and scramble to put in place a revised version of economic reform in an effort to secure a more stable platform for economic growth. The underlying agenda remains the same—the "creation of new infrastructure for market-oriented economic growth, commodification, and the rule of capital" (Brenner and Theodore 2002, 362)—but the institutional methods change, with efforts to put a "human face" on neoliberal policy and clean up earlier, messier outcomes.

Peck and Tickell (2002) refer to this as the "roll out" phase of neoliberalism: a reintroduction of state institutions and corporatist planning into the social and economic spheres, without undermining the overall agenda of market liberalization, and with the added advantage of strengthening the state's mediating role in society. "No longer concerned narrowly with the mobilization and extension of markets (and market logics), neoliberalism is increasingly associated with the political foregrounding of new modes of 'social' and penal policy-making, concerned specifically with the aggressive reregulation, disciplining and containment of those marginalized or disposed by the [roll back] neoliberalism of the 1980s" (Peck and Tickell 2002, 389).

"The same politicians, parties, pundits and professors who yesterday mobilized ... in support of 'less government' ... are now demanding, with every bit as much fervor, '*more* government', to mask and contain the deleterious social consequences of [the destructive phase of neoliberalism]" (Wacquant 1999, 323).

It is here that we see the shift from narrow, market policies to more mediated forms of economic change (e.g. a shift from the outright divestiture of state assets to the creation of 'public-private partnerships'; from crude forms of decreased welfare spending to more targeted and invasive forms of indigent policy; from hands-off urban planning to highly regulated urban spaces and extensive security systems).

Ironically, then, the roll out phase of neoliberalism has seen a strengthening of the state not a weakening. Critically, however, this is not the "bloated" and "unaccountable" state of the previous Keynesian period (as neoliberals tend to characterize the Keynesian state model) but a leaner, more efficient, more competent and more market-oriented set of governing bodies, better able to manage the interests of capital and the (inevitable) tensions and contradictions of the market economy, and better able to step aside to let the market deliver the services that the state used to provide (or, in World Bank parlance, having the state "steer" rather than "row" the boat of government).

This phased transition of neoliberalism is not a smooth or necessarily linear process. These destructive and creative moments are "dialectically intertwined" (Brenner and Theodore 2002, 362). There is no single, abrupt time or event at which a society switches from Keynesianism to neoliberalism or from one neoliberal regime to another. There are periods of stop-start, back-and-forth reform as political struggles take place over policy models and as the economy itself shifts.

Nor is this transition to roll out neoliberalism stable in the long run. Even the most 'progressive' forms of neoliberalism cannot resolve the contradictions of its more aggressive predecessors or, most importantly, the inherent contradictions of capitalism itself. Roll out neoliberalism can, at best, ameliorate the worst excesses of uneven capitalist development and help to stave off crises in the short to medium term.

NEOLIBERALISM IN SOUTH AFRICA

Many South African observers have failed to appreciate the complex, shifting and dialectical nature of neoliberalism and have confused the shift toward increased state participation as a move away from neoliberalism. Freund (2002, 27), for example, finds it "surprising" that there is an "increasingly 'strong' state" in the city of Durban. Pieterse (2002, 10) sees this as an indication that the post-apartheid government is Keynesian in its orientation, arguing that the "South African transformation exercise [is happening] in the wake of neo-liberalism's demise as a hegemonic ideology". For Pieterse, the ANC should not be characterized as neoliberal because it is "embracing the importance of the state, the need for forms of regulation, the democratic and economic value of a vibrant civil society, and even the importance of environmental sustainability".

But as I have argued above, it is exactly this "embracing of the importance of the state"—coupled with far-reaching marketization reforms in a wide range of social and economic spheres—that characterize post-apartheid reforms as neoliberal. As we shall see in our investigation of privatization, cost recovery and other forms of social and economic discipline later in the book, market-oriented reforms remain the primary objectives in post-apartheid South Africa and these objectives are being strengthened by roll out forms of neoliberalism, not lessened.

Having said this, South Africa's form of roll out neoliberalism is necessarily different from that of other countries. The most obvious difference is that the welfarism of apartheid was highly skewed along racial (and to some extent ethnic) lines, complicating the moments of neoliberal destruction and creation, with many of these reforms taking place much later in South Africa than they did elsewhere. The fact that most welfarist policies were never (fully) instituted for black South Africans also meant that their destruction was unnecessary, allowing policymakers to move directly to the more formative, roll out phase of neoliberalism.

Nonetheless, apartheid South Africa was, by and large, a Fordist-Keynesianism regime, with whites in particular benefiting from far-reaching welfarist policies. The National Party came to power in 1948 on what was, in large part, an anti–free market, social welfare platform, promising to impose stricter labour regulations to protect (white) workers from the vagaries of (English) capital and to shelter Afrikaner culture from the homogenizing effects of international capitalism (O'Meara 1983). The apartheid state was an "activist state" in the Keynesian sense and would regularly and "often forcibly" intervene in both "social and economic affairs" in contravention of market needs (Marais 2001, 20).

At the level of consumption, apartheid-era government subsidies were extensive, with white South Africans in general, and Afrikaners in particular, being offered extremely generous financial support for housing and other infrastructure. Throughout the 1970s and 1980s, for example, white suburbs received per capita funding for basic municipal services that matched or exceeded that of most European and North American countries (Ahmad 1995).

Even black households received Keynesian-style subsidies in the form of below-cost services and housing (where these services were provided) (Corbett 1992). In some cases these subsidies were provided by default rather than by design, with local authorities continuing to provide subsidized water, electricity and other basic services to township households in an attempt to keep the lid on political unrest. Nevertheless, the effect was the same: state-subsidized consumption.

At the level of production, white South African firms received particularly generous state subsidies under apartheid. Artificially cheap labour, created and maintained by an expensive state military apparatus, was perhaps the most significant (and sinister) way in which these corporate subsidies took place, but there were more conventional corporate welfare systems in the form of cheap raw inputs (water, electricity and steel from state-owned enterprises), cheap state-backed financing, subsidies for marginal firms, protectionist import-substitution policies and government procurement policies designed to benefit local firms (Saul and Gelb 1986, Fine and Rustomjee 1996, Marais 2001).

But, as alluded to in Chapter 2, the transition to neoliberalism in South Africa in the 1990s was in no way preordained, inevitable or smooth. As Bond (1999b, 15) notes in his analysis of this evolution, there was a period of several years after the unbanning of the ANC in 1990 when it seemed that "nearly any kind of political-economic future was possible". There was sufficient ideological hubris within the ANC and its partner organizations—most notably the South African Communist Party (SACP) and the Congress of South African Trade Unions (Cosatu)—to lead observers and participants to believe that the post-apartheid dispensation could be at least strongly Keynesian in its leanings, if not even socialist. The ANC's 1955 Freedom Charter had, after all, promised: "The national wealth of our country, the heritage of South Africans, shall be restored to the people; The mineral wealth beneath the soil, the Banks and monopoly industry shall be transferred to the ownership of the people as a whole; All other industry and trade shall be controlled to assist the well-being of the people".

> The ANC and its partner organizations had long been composed of a broad coalition of forces, and the actual ideological terrain of debate within the alliance was, and remains, a complex one. This fragmentation was exemplified by, and further complicated by, the fact that the ANC "had virtually no economic policy" platform when it was unbanned in 1990 (Hart 2002, 22) and floundered for several years after that with a mixed bag of neo-Keynesian and neoliberal economic policy proposals (Marais 2001, 136–38).

In the end, however, it was "patently neoliberal" thinking that was to prevail in the ANC with much of the residual Keynesianism evident in the early 1990s having been eviscerated from the party's major policy platforms by the time of the 1994 elections (Marais 2001, 136; Murray 1994). The introduction of the Growth Employment and Redistribution (GEAR) framework in 1996—with no consultation with the party's alliance partners and with limited consultation within the party itself—is now seen by many to be a watershed in the ANC's ideological shift.

The ideological trajectory of the National Party during this time was also disjointed. Although the party had begun to move away from its welfarist roots in the 1980s—having introduced a series of roll back–like neoliberal policies during that decade (e.g. efforts to privatize township housing and transportation)—the party was nevertheless still ideologically confused, torn between preserving (white) bureaucratic, corporate and residential privilege and letting the cold winds of market competition rationalize the economy. As a result, economic policy proposals from the National Party while they were still in power in the early 1990s were largely ill-conceived and philosophically inchoate. But neoliberalism was on the ascendancy in that party as well, in line with its commitment to rejuvenating the conditions for capital accumulation along global, nonracial lines (O'Meara 1996).

It was arguably the efforts of domestic and international capital (with the assistance of neoliberal think tanks such as the World Bank) that were most persuasive in the transition to neoliberalism. The sheer volume of advice they provided (the World Bank began sending teams of advisers to work with the ANC on urban policy in the early 1990s), the intellectual coherence of neoliberal policy frameworks (as opposed to the disorganized and often poorly articulated advice that was coming from the left) and the slick presentation styles and resources of neoliberal proponents all combined to make a powerful ideological package (Bond 1999b, 53–89; Marais 2001, 126–30).

The backdrop to this transition was the collapse of the Soviet Union in 1989 and the loss of the only serious potential ally in military, economic and ideological terms for the left wing of the ANC–alliance. Under such conditions, it was no doubt difficult for many in the ANC to imagine a socialist, or even Keynesian, future.

At the heart of this new neoliberal orientation lie the following national-level reforms:

- export-oriented growth;
- trade liberalization (including the signing of trade agreements in the WTO);
- financial deregulation (including the relaxation of regulations over foreign direct investment and the loosening up and eventual elimination of exchange controls);
- fiscal restraint in key social spending areas such as health care and housing;
- lowering of corporate taxes (falling from 27% of tax revenues in 1976 to 11% in 1999, and further still since) and a concomitant increase in personal taxes (from 25% of tax revenues to 42% in the same period, most adversely affecting the poor through regressive mechanisms such as the Value Added Tax);

- a shift to full(er) cost recovery and user fees for a wide range of formerly subsidized services;
- strict inflation targeting via tight monetary policy and downward pressure on the social wage;
- constitutional guarantees on property rights;
- a rejection of nationalization;
- privatization and commercialization of state enterprises and services;
- commitment to market-rated currency valuations;
- constitutional guarantee of Reserve Bank independence;
- labour market flexibility.

It is not possible to discuss the specifics of all of these policy shifts or the institutional differences among them in this chapter. We can, however, look in general terms at the ways in which the neoliberal transition in South Africa is similar to, and differs from, what has taken place in Europe and North America.

Table 3.1 provides a summary of the destructive/creative moments of neoliberalism as it has been practiced in countries in the North (as articulated by Brenner and Theodore 2002, 364–66), followed by a comparison of how these transitions have played themselves out in post-apartheid South Africa. The argument, in sum, is that the South African situation has some important differences from actually existing neoliberalisms elsewhere but the outcome is largely the same.

The most significant difference is that there has been some substantial Keynesian (re)building taking place in South Africa. There has, for example, been Keynesian-style institutional and legislative development to make up for the gross injustices of apartheid (e.g. the strengthening of many central government functions and capacities, the creation of democratic controls over some bureaucratic structures, and an increase in per capita state welfare spending in some areas for black South Africans).

But many of these developments have only a façade of Keynesian reform, being little more than hollowed out shells of state bodies, relying heavily on private sector consultants and private contractors to fulfill their mandates. Other Keynesian initiatives have been built up only to be 'destroyed' soon thereafter by the introduction of roll back neoliberalism, while some reforms have skipped the Keynesian and roll back stages of neoliberalism altogether, moving straight to the roll out neoliberal model.

The shift to neoliberalism in South African is therefore complicated by—and to some extent shrouded by—the 'progressive destruction' of a race-based Keynesian-Fordist system, followed almost immediately by the destruction of Keynesianism more generally; two moments of destruction if you will, with the second being more akin to the types of destructive moments that have taken place in more traditional Keynesian countries in the North. As a result, the dismantling of the institutions and policies of Keynesianism in South Africa has been partial and truncated.

Table 3.1 Destructive and Creative Moments of "Actually Existing Neoliberalism" (at the National Level)—Comparing South Africa to Europe and North America

Site of Regulation	Moment of Destruction	Moment of Creation
Wage relation	• Assaults on organized labour and national collective bargaining agreements • Dismantling of the family wage and the spread of generalized economic insecurity • Downgrading of national regulations ensuring equal employment opportunity, occupational safety, and workers' rights	• Competitive deregulation: atomized renegotiation of wage levels and working conditions combined with expanded managerial discretion • New forms of the social wage and new gender divisions of labour • Promotion of labour 'flexibility'

South Africa: The wage relation for black workers under apartheid was extraordinarily exploitative, leaving little room for further 'destruction' by neoliberalism (although white unions did witness some of the more conventional neoliberal assaults on organized labour described above). After 1994, the ANC introduced a series of progressive labour laws that actually gave (black) labour many of the Keynesian-style benefits that they had missed out on during apartheid, most notably in the form of the Labour Relations Act, the Employment Equity Act and the Basic Conditions of Employment Act, as well as bargaining forums such as the National Economic Development and Labour Council (Nedlac). These laws have benefited millions of workers in the country and have added a degree of Keynesian-style stability to the wage relation that did not exist under apartheid. However, GEAR's calls for 'regulated' labour flexibility and wage restraint, combined with atomized negotiating strategies and increasing casualization and informalization in the labour market have undermined many of these gains, leading to some of the more classically neoliberal outcomes on the 'creation' side of this analysis.

Form of intercapitalist competition	• Selective withdrawing of state support for leading national industries • Dismantling of national protectionist policies • Dismantling of national barriers to foreign direct investment	• New forms of state support for 'sunrise' industries • Extension of global commodities markets through trade liberalization policies codified in the WTO, the IMF, regional trade agreements and other supranational bodies • Establishment of global capital markets through GATT negotiations

(Continued)

Table 3.1 Continued

Site of Regulation	Moment of Destruction	Moment of Creation

South Africa: Here we see a more typical neoliberal development path—though late in the day in global terms and with half-hearted attempts by a still ideologically confused National Party—with the dismantling of most apartheid-era, Keynesian-style subsidies and protectionist policies in the late 1980s followed by selective state support for sunrise industries, heavy buy-in to trade liberalization and international/regional trade agreements and the establishment of global capital markets in the 1990s (including the relisting of major South African firms to the London and New York stock exchanges).

Form of financial and monetary regulation	• Dismantling of Bretton Woods global monetary system and deregulation of money markets • Erosion of national states' capacity to control exchange rates • Dismantling of the regulatory constraints impeding monetary and financial speculation in global markets • Separation of financial and credit flows from productive sources of investment	• Creation of speculation-driven currency markets and 'stateless monies' outside national regulatory control • Expanded role of global regulatory bodies (such as the Bank for International Settlements) in the monitoring of global financial transactions • Creation of offshore financial centres, international banking facilities and tax havens

South Africa: Both the destructive and creative moments of this site of regulation had to await the arrival of the ANC onto the policymaking stage, with the apartheid state seemingly unable to make anything but the most timid of moves in this neoliberal direction. Although some reforms have been introduced slowly in comparative terms (exchange control mechanisms were phased in over ten years, for example), others were introduced rapidly (the constitutionally guaranteed independence of the Reserve Bank), and South Africa now has a highly deregulated financial and monetary system of the 'roll out' form.

The state and other forms of governance	• Abandonment of Keynesian forms of demand management • Dismantling of traditional national relays of welfare service provision • 'Hollowing out' of national state capacities to regulate money, trade and investment flows • De-centring of traditional hierarchical-bureaucratic forms of government control	• 'Rolling forward' of supply-side and monetarist programmes of state intervention • Devolution of social welfare functions to lower levels of government, the social economy, and households • Mobilization of strategies to promote territorial competitiveness, technological innovation and internationalization

Site of Regulation	Moment of Destruction	Moment of Creation
	• Dismantling of traditional relays of democratic control at national and subnational level • Strategies to 'hollow out' the autocentric national economy as a target of state intervention • Erosion of traditional managerial-redistributive functions of national and subnational administrative agencies • Imposition of fiscal austerity measures aimed at reducing public expenditures • Shrinking of public sector employment	• Establishment of public-private partnerships and networked forms of governance • Creation of 'new authoritarian' state apparatuses and 'quangos' that are insulated from public accountability and popular-democratic control • Rescaling of state economic intervention to privilege strategic supranational and subnational spaces of accumulation • Underwriting the costs of private investment through state subsidies • Transfer of erstwhile forms of public employment to the private sector through privatization

South Africa: This is the most complex and 'irregular' of the neoliberal sites of re-regulation in the South African context. Many of the issues highlighted here will be taken up in greater detail later in the book (e.g. public-private partnerships). In general, though, there has been a combination of rebuilding, destruction and creation. There has, for example, been significant Keynesian-style institution and legislation building to make up for the gross injustices of apartheid (e.g. the strengthening of many central government functions and capacities, the creation of democratic controls over some bureaucratic structures, and an increase in per capita state spending in many areas for black South Africans). But this has also been accompanied by both the 'destructive' tendencies of hollowing out state capacity and the 'creative' tendencies of restructuring the state to benefit capital (e.g. the creation of public-private agencies removed from direct public accountability (such as City Improvement Districts); the offloading of (unfunded) mandates to local governments; and the promotion of territorial competitiveness).

| International configuration | • Decentring of the national scale of accumulation, regulation, and sociopolitical struggle
 • Undercutting of regulatory standards across localities, regions, national states, and supranational economic zones | • 'Relativization of scales' as relations among subnational, national, and supranational institutional forms are systematically rearranged
 • Introduction of policies to promote market-mediated, competitive relations among subnational levels of state power |

(Continued)

Table 3.1 Continued

Site of Regulation	Moment of Destruction	Moment of Creation

South Africa: Here again we see a mix of strategies. Although the apartheid government had decentred certain responsibilities to the local and regional level, these efforts were motivated largely by the desire to maintain a racially segregated geography and economy. The post-apartheid state has deracialized these initiatives and even recentred certain functions (e.g. the development of national standards for service delivery, environmental policy, municipal budgeting and accounting controls) but many functions remain decentred and in some cases this decentring has expanded the role of local/provincial governments considerably (e.g. the legislatively mandated obligation of local governments to ensure adequate service delivery to all residents in its area of jurisdiction). But despite the peculiarities of South Africa's 'moments' of destruction and creation the overall effect of rescaling the state has been consistent with neoliberal practice elsewhere, with local governments in particular now expected to compete nationally and internationally for funding and investment.

Site of Regulation	Moment of Destruction	Moment of Creation
Uneven spatial development	• Selective withdrawal of state support for declining regions and cities • Destruction of traditional relays of compensatory, redistributive regional policy (spatial Keynesianism)	• Mobilization of new forms of state policy to promote capital mobility within supranational trade blocs and to encourage capital (re)investment within strategic city-regions and industrial districts • Establishment of new forms of sociospatial inequality, polarization, and territorial competition at global, national and subnational scales

South Africa: The collapse of state subsidies for homelands and townships in the 1980s drew few tears in South Africa, with capitalists and anti-apartheid activists generally united in their opposition to these enormously inefficient and racially skewed attempts to keep the artificial and oppressive institutions of apartheid afloat. However, the death of these racially skewed subsidies also signalled the start of the end to Keynesian-style redistribution mechanisms in general, with neoliberal-type Industrial Development Zones and (re)investment in strategic city-regions having become the policies of choice. The extent to which these strategic interventions have worsened sociospatial inequality and polarization at the national level is a matter of much heated debate, but they have certainly worsened conditions at the city level as will be discussed in later chapters.

Adapted from Brenner and Theodore 2002, 364–66.

It is here that we see the important role of radical theory (and the source of so much misinterpretation by liberal analysts). Taken on their own, the 'destruction' of race-based welfarism and the subsequent/simultaneous introduction of strengthened and democratized forms of national and local government are positive developments. They are not, in and of themselves, inherently 'neoliberal'. But with the insights of theory—and the benefits of hindsight—we can see these developments for what they really are: part of a larger dialectic of neoliberal reform designed to assist with a new capital accumulation strategy in a globalized economy. With these insights we can distinguish the progressive from the regressive, and the strategic class-motivated reforms from the more broadly liberal objectives of improving basic human rights.

With this in mind we turn now to a discussion of *urban* neoliberalism, arguably the most dynamic arena of neoliberal policy formation in South Africa—and internationally—today.

URBAN NEOLIBERALISM

Over the past two decades cities have become strategic sites not just of neoliberal policy implementation but as virtual laboratories of cutting-edge neoliberal innovation. Not only are cities "key politico-institutional arenas within the broader geographies of actually existing neoliberalism", they have become "central to the reproduction, mutation, and continual reconstitution of neoliberalism itself during the last two decades" (Brenner and Theodore 2002, 367, 375). As Hart (2002, 292) notes in the South African context, the local state is "a key terrain on which some of the most intense contradictions of the neo-liberal post-apartheid order are taking shape".

Why is this? The most obvious reason is that cities are so central to the new capital accumulation strategies (and contradictions) outlined in the previous chapter. Capitalism is still very much dependent on rural locations and activities, but urban accumulation is by far the most important site of capital growth today. As a result, cities attract considerable policy attention, with the "overarching goal of neoliberal urban policy experiments [being] to mobilize city space as an arena for both market-oriented economic growth and for elite consumption" (Brenner and Theodore 2002, 368).

Another reason that cities have attracted policy attention is that they can, and typically do, offer more manageable and more easily manipulated institutional and spatial landscapes. It is much easier to envision spatial planning for a city (or city-region) than for a country as a whole, which may help to explain why cities were the first policy focus of South African capital during the crises of the 1970s (with the establishment of the Urban Foundation) and were the site of the World Bank's first major post-apartheid policy interventions with its Urban Missions in the early 1990s (World Bank 1991a,b).

Urban policy in South Africa continues to attract the most concerted attention of neoliberal policy think tanks (e.g. the Centre for Development and Enterprise) as well as that of neoliberal aid and development agencies such as USAID and the UK's Department for International Development (DFID). It is easier for lobbyists to engage with local government decision makers in an attempt to try and shape an institutional/legislative/spatial fix. Local governments in South Africa are less dense, less layered, less powerful, and less resourced than their national counterparts, making them more vulnerable to ideological suasion.

The relatively recent phenomenon of decentralization in South Africa has made this power imbalance all the more significant. This is no coincidence, of course. As we shall see in Chapter 4, decentralization has been part of the broader neoliberal agenda in the country, with a concerted effort to download responsibilities and decision-making powers to local and regional governments. Indeed, many decentralizations are impregnated with neoliberal policy requirements from the start, such as the expectation that they will be oversight bodies rather than actual delivery agencies.

Finally, with cities as sites of some of the most active and regular resistance to neoliberalism, urban policymakers have been forced into a particularly dynamic mode of thinking around neoliberal policymaking (Merrifield 2002, Peck and Tickell 2002). Urban neoliberal policymakers must deal not only with the tensions and contradictions of capitalism and neoliberalism at the national and international level but also with the (ever faster) rhythms of their own internal, urban contradictions and changes. Neoliberalism at the urban level is arguably even less stable than neoliberalism practiced at a national/international level where the contradictions can be slower to surface (in part because they can be more easily moved around geographically) and where it can be more difficult for people to mobilize against them in a coordinated manner.

Despite this, urban neoliberalism remains surprisingly underanalyzed in the academic literature (with some notable exceptions that will be taken up below). Most books and articles that tackle neoliberalism as a concept limit their investigation to national and international policy developments (e.g. the otherwise useful *Neoliberal Reader* compiled by Saad-Filho and Johnston (2005)). The same applies to much of the South African literature on neoliberalism, which tends to focus on national-level policy developments and/or fails to tease out the specifically urban facets of neoliberal policy design and contradictions.

But before examining the urban characteristics of neoliberalism there are two general comments to make. The first is that urban neoliberalism shares the same dialectical, path-dependent and contested processes that characterize neoliberalism at a national and international level. As a set of policies and institutions designed to respond to the cycles and crises of capital accumulation, urban neoliberalism is just as unpredictable and contradiction prone as neoliberalism in general. Urban neoliberalism is a stop-start, uneven and place-specific phenomenon. No two cities experience the exact same set of neoliberal reforms, no two cities are affected in exactly the same way by neoliberal policies and no two cities develop neoliberal reforms at the same time or pace. Neoliberalism is taken up—and resisted—in different ways throughout the urban world.

The second point is that despite its unique geographic and institutional characteristics urban neoliberalism operates as part of an integrated, multiscalar set of neoliberal ideologies and policy and institutional objectives. The privatization and commercialization of municipal services, for example, typically complement national policies of fiscal conservancy. So too does the national state rely on (and sometimes impose) the application of neoliberal policies at the local level to achieve its broader objectives.

This interscalar policy and institutional synchronicity is not automatic, though. There are times when the demands of local institutions and/or local capital are at odds with that of state institutions and national/international capital, making interscalar policy conflicts inevitable. A local government may, for example, want to protect a particular industry, but national macroeconomic policy priorities may be such that these local objectives are undermined through, say, the elimination of sectoral tariffs.

These interscalar stresses are inherent to neoliberalism. Just as neoliberalism is bound to create tensions and contradictions across sectors and over time, so too does it create tensions and contradictions across space. This is neoliberalism's "scalar constitution" (Peck and Tickell 2002, 301; Brenner 2004). In this respect, urban neoliberalism is yet another layer in the dialectical—and sometimes elliptical—process of neoliberalism as a whole, a reterritorialization of the unstable, national-level neoliberal tendencies described above (Brenner 1999, Swyngedouw 1992, 1997).

But we must be careful not to reify scale as an ontological starting point. The urban may very well constitute a unique set of geographic and institutional characteristics, but 'scale', in and of itself, does not have motive or force. The dialectical relationship is not between predefined spatial entities, but rather between distinct but mutually linked sets of social and economic processes that operate *within*, and continually *reshape*, a particular spatial/scalar configuration. The crux is "not whether the local or the global has theoretical and empirical priority in shaping the conditions of daily life, but rather how the local, the global, and other relevant (though perpetually shifting) geographic scale levels are the result, the product of processes, of sociospatial change" (Swyngedouw 1997, 140).

So too can these processes move up, down and across these various scales. What appears to be a strictly urban process at one moment can become national or global in scope, or can 'jump' vertically from one city to another, depending on the nature of the issues and the actors involved. Here we see the value of the (rather inelegant but metaphorically useful) phrase "glocalization" (Swyngedouw 1992) to describe the inherently interscalar nature of all neoliberal/capitalist activity.

The importance of these interscalar relationships has not escaped the attention of non-Marxist analysts either. Mainstream world city analysts ask "at what level of resolution we can best identify and/or theorize the functional dynamics of world cities" (Knox 1995, 11) and posit a range of scales from the local to the global, with heated debates over the extent to which cities are "embedded" or "nested" in their national/regional context (see, for example, the special issue of *Urban Studies* (2003)). This literature also highlights the "networked" nature of world cities and the ease with which capital moves horizontally within this urban scale.

But missing from this world city research is an analysis of the capitalist processes that tie these scalar moments into a theoretically coherent whole. As a result, the interscalar debates in the mainstream world city literature tend to be overly atomistic and/or deterministic in their explanations of how various scales interact, relying heavily on culturalist and/or statist modes of analysis.

URBAN NEOLIBERALISM IN SOUTH AFRICA

Cities in South Africa have also been affected by this dialectical, multiscalar process of neoliberalization. Urban policymaking in the country is driven in large part by national government in the form of Constitutional mandates and a growing mass of legislation that directly or indirectly circumscribes the roles, obligations and, perhaps most importantly, the limitations of local government.

Nevertheless, we must not lose sight of the relative autonomy of local governments in South Africa and the social, economic and political dynamics that lend themselves to local forms of neoliberal policymaking. To assist with this analysis in theoretical terms I turn, once again, to the work of Brenner and Theodore (2002, 369–72) who provide a useful conceptual overview of the moments and mechanisms of "neoliberal localization" (see Table 3.2). Not all of these moments and mechanisms apply to South African cities or to Cape Town but the taxonomy is useful insofar as it provides a reference point for how urban neoliberalism in South Africa is both similar to, and different from, that of "actually existing" urban neoliberalisms elsewhere in the world.

To better illustrate these comparisons I have added comments under each row in the table to describe how these dynamics have manifested themselves in South Africa, with the most notable differences arising under "moments of destruction". As with our discussion of neoliberalism at the national and international scale (Table 3.1), many of the specifically *urban* moments of Keynesian-Fordist 'destruction' must be seen to have occurred

Table 3.2 Destructive and Creative Moments of "Neoliberal Localization"—
Comparing South Africa to Europe and North America

Mechanisms of Neoliberal Localization	Moment of Destruction	Moment of Creation
Recalibration of intergovernmental relations	• Dismantling of earlier systems of central government support for municipal activities	• Devolution of new tasks, burdens, and responsibilities to municipalities; creation of new incentive structures to reward local entrepreneurialism and to catalyze 'endogenous growth'

South Africa: Here we see the simultaneous 'destruction' of race-based systems of central government support for municipal activities with the 'creation' of new types of central support for deracialized and restructured municipalities. The central-local relationship therefore remains an important one (e.g. intergovernmental fiscal transfers, institutional support). With regard to the devolution of tasks, municipal authorities in South Africa have long had a high degree of service responsibility and fiscal independence (approximately 90% of municipal expenditures have been raised though local revenue sources) but the post-apartheid transition has seen two important shifts in this regard. The first is a quantitative one: local authorities are now responsible for ensuring the delivery of services to all residents of (significantly) enlarged jurisdictions, but with relatively little in the way of additional funding on a per capita basis (hence the expansion of 'unfunded mandates'). The second is a quantitative shift, in line with that outlined in the 'creation' column above: the creation of new incentive structures to reward entrepreneurialism and endogenous growth.

Retrenchment of public finance	• Imposition of fiscal austerity measures upon municipal governments	• Creation of revenue-collection districts and increased reliance of municipalities upon local sources of revenue, user fees, and other instruments of private finance

South Africa: As noted above, intergovernmental fiscal transfers remain an integral part of central-local relations but the actual amount of money transferred fell dramatically in real, per capita terms in the 1990s (by as much as 85%) and has only begun to recover since 2003. These increases are woefully inadequate, however, for the scale of service infrastructure and delivery that is required in low-income areas and have disproportionately benefited upper-income areas via the direct and indirect allocation of these funds to former suburban areas. The simultaneous 'creation' of user-fee mechanisms such as cost recovery on basic services and the introduction of private financing for service delivery has served to further undermine the role of public finance in basic needs service areas.

(Continued)

Table 3.2 Continued

Mechanisms of Neoliberal Localization	Moment of Destruction	Moment of Creation
Restructuring the welfare state	• Local relays of national welfare service-provision are retrenched; assault on managerial-welfarist local state apparatuses	• Expansion of community-based sectors and private approaches to social service provision • Imposition of mandatory work requirements on urban welfare recipients; new (local) forms of workfare experimentation

South Africa: Once again we see the 'destruction' of race-based systems with the simultaneous 'creation' of expanded, deracialized managerial-welfarist type systems (e.g. old age pensions, 'free' basic services). But the Keynesian qualities of the latter have been largely hollowed out by the relatively stingy levels of funding made available for these welfarist reforms, the introduction of community-based welfare provision in the name of 'participation', the use of indigent policies that separate the poor from the very poor, and the increasing use of the private sector in the delivery of these services. The use of mandatory work requirements for the receipt of welfare is also an increasingly central aspect of post-apartheid reforms (e.g. the Expanded Public Works Programme).

Reconfiguring the institutional infrastructure of the local state	• Dismantling of bureaucratized, hierarchical forms of local public administration • Devolution of erstwhile state tasks to voluntary community networks • Assault on traditional relays of local democratic accountability	• 'Rolling forward' of new networked forms of local governance based upon public-private partnerships, 'quangos' and 'new public management' • Establishment of new institutional relays through which elite business interests can directly influence major local development decisions

South Africa: Apartheid South Africa had one of the most bureaucratic, hierarchical and fragmented forms of local government in the world. This was due in part to the militarized nature of local government management but also to racially and ethnically segregated local authorities (Cape Town had more than 60 local authorities in what is now one metropolitan government). Dismantling this system was therefore a necessary part of deracializing and democratizing local government and was a universally welcomed 'moment of destruction'. At the same time there have been ongoing efforts to create local forms of democratic accountability that never existed for black urban residents and were of limited scope for whites. Neither of these developments should be seen as inherently

Mechanisms of Neoliberal Localization	*Moment of Destruction*	*Moment of Creation*

neoliberal. However, the nature of this transformation has been such that policymakers have essentially jumped to the 'creation' stage of 'rolling forward' neoliberal institutional reforms such as public-private partnerships and new public management, with a strong role being played by local business elites in major local development systems. Efforts to build institutions and processes for direct community participation have largely failed (e.g. RDP and IDP forums, Ward Committees).

Privatization of the municipal public sector and collective infrastructures	• Elimination of public monopolies for the provision of standardized municipal services (water, electricity, public safety, recreation, etc.)	• Privatization and competitive contracting of municipal services • Creation of new markets for service delivery and infrastructure maintenance • Creation of privatized, customized, and networked urban infrastructures intended to (re)position cities within supranational capital flows

South Africa: Before 'destroying' public monopolies the post-apartheid state first had to restructure them along deracialized lines and to create the legislative and institutional means to introduce more equitable standards of service delivery. These required considerable Keynesian-style reforms. However, these efforts have been largely accompanied by 'roll out' forms of neoliberalism in the shape of privatization, commercialization, contracting out, public-private partnerships and corporatization in virtually all local government service areas, many of which are aimed specifically at helping reposition South African cities within supranational capital flows (e.g. sea ports, IT infrastructure).

Restructuring urban housing markets	• Razing public housing and other forms of low-rent accommodation • Elimination of rent controls and project-based construction subsidies	• Creation of new opportunities for speculative investment in central-city real estate markets • Emergency shelters become 'warehouses' for the poor • Introduction of market rents and tenant-based vouchers in low-rent niches of urban housing markets

(Continued)

Table 3.2 Continued

Mechanisms of Neoliberal Localization	*Moment of Destruction*	*Moment of Creation*

South Africa: Although post-apartheid public sector housing delivery has been much lower than anticipated the state has nonetheless provided subsidies and assisted with the construction of several million new homes since 1994. However, subsidies only allow for small and generally underbuilt houses on the outskirts of cities with few amenities and a low level of municipal service delivery (with the latter being a product of the give-people-what-they-can-afford-to-pay-for mentality of neoliberal service delivery). The private sector has been slow to provide private financing to low-income communities and has been responsible for much of the substandard building quality. Meanwhile, the state has provided subsidy mechanisms for speculative investments in central-city real estate, and upper-income housing markets have exploded since the late 1990s with price increases of 30% or more per annum in some parts of Cape Town.

Reworking labour market regulation	• Dismantling of traditional, publicly funded education, skills training, and apprenticeship programs for youth, displaced workers, and the unemployed	• Creation of new regulatory environment in which temporary staffing agencies, unregulated 'labour corners' and other forms of contingent work can proliferate • Implementation of work-readiness programs aimed at the conscription of workers into low-wage jobs • Expansion of informal economies

South Africa: Again we see the simultaneous 'destruction' of apartheid-era training and education programs with the 'creation' of post-apartheid nonracial programs designed, first and foremost, to benefit the previously disadvantaged (e.g. the Sector Education and Training Authorities). These have been important, Keynesian-style initiatives. However, they are strategically targeted for the new flexible, global economy, with the Local Government Water and Related Services Sector and Education Training Authority (LGWSETA) being a good example of neoliberal ideological and institutional bias (see Chapter 6).

Restructuring strategies of territorial development	• Dismantling of autocentric models of capitalist growth • Destruction of traditional compensatory regional policies • Increasing exposure of local and regional economies to global competitive forces	• Creation of free trade zones, enterprise zones, and other deregulated spaces within major urban regions • Creation of new development areas, technopoles, and other new industrial spaces at subnational scales

Mechanisms of Neoliberal Localization	*Moment of Destruction*	*Moment of Creation*
	• Fragmentation of national space-economies into discrete urban and regional industrial systems	• Mobilization of new 'glocal' strategies intended to rechannel economic capacities and infrastructure investments into 'globally connected' local/regional agglomerations

South Africa: Here we see a more conventional form of neoliberal destruction and creation (with the exception, once again, of the preliminary destruction of apartheid-era regional policies—most notably the efforts of the apartheid state to create economic nodes in the former homelands). The destruction of autocentric models of capitalist growth was quickly followed by the creation of strategic spatial development initiatives for export-oriented growth, technopoles and 'glocal' strategies of connecting cities to the global economy more generally.

| Transformations of the built environment and urban form | • Elimination and/or intensified surveillance of urban public spaces • Destruction of traditional working-class neighbourhoods in order to make way for speculative redevelopment • Retreat from community-oriented planning initiatives | • Creation of new privatized spaces of elite/corporate consumption • Construction of large-scale megaprojects intended to attract corporate investment and reconfigure local land-use patterns • Creation of gated communities, urban enclaves, and other 'purified' spaces of social reproduction • 'Rolling forward' of the gentrification frontier and the intensification of sociospatial polarization • Adoption of the principle of 'highest and best use' as the basis for major land-use planning decisions |

South Africa: Much of the 'destruction' of universally accessible public space and working-class neighbourhoods was accomplished by the apartheid state as part of its race-based urban planning. Forced relocations in the 1960s and 1970s served to eliminate 'unwanted' elements from the urban landscape while providing 'purified' spaces of social reproduction. These were not done for neoliberal reasons, per se, but they did serve to benefit capital through the creation of cheap pools of urban labour and opportunities for speculative

(Continued)

Table 3.2 Continued

Mechanisms of Neoliberal Localization	Moment of Destruction	Moment of Creation

investment in those residential and commercial areas that blacks were forced to move out of (small fortunes were made by real estate firms in Cape Town during this time, with the gentrification of places such as Mowbray and Wynberg when coloured residents were moved to the Cape Flats). In this respect, the dirty work of destroying a heterogenous spatial configuration had already been largely completed by the apartheid state, allowing post-apartheid neoliberal reformers to jump directly to the entrenchment of these spatial inequities through the intensification of surveillance, new spaces of elite consumption (e.g. Cape Town's Waterfront) and the increasingly gentrified nature of strategic urban locations.

Mechanisms of Neoliberal Localization	Moment of Destruction	Moment of Creation
Interlocal policy transfer	• Erosion of contextually sensitive approaches to local policymaking • Marginalization of 'homegrown' solutions to localized market failures and governance failures	• Diffusion of generic, prototypical approaches to 'modernizing' reform among policymakers in the search for a quick fix for local social problems (e.g. place-marketing, zero-tolerance crime policies, etc.) • Imposition of decontextualized 'best practice' models upon local policy environments

South Africa: The 'destruction' of homegrown apartheid policymaking was not necessarily a neoliberal phenomenon, but the subsequent adoption of international 'best practice' and generic models of 'modernizing' reforms—at all levels of government in South Africa—illustrated a willingness on the part of post-apartheid policymakers to uncritically accept neoliberal reform packages. The extensive use of urban institutional modeling from the World Bank and private sector consulting firms such as KPMG and PricewaterhouseCoopers amongst urban policymakers exemplifies the marginalization of local, context-based and ideologically alternative policymaking options.

Mechanisms of Neoliberal Localization	Moment of Destruction	Moment of Creation
Re-regulation of urban civil society	• Destruction of the 'liberal city' in which all inhabitants are entitled to basic civil liberties, social services and political rights	• Mobilization of zero-tolerance crime policies and 'broken windows' policing • Introduction of new discriminatory forms of surveillance and social control • Introduction of new policies to combat social exclusion by reinserting individuals into the labour market

Mechanisms of Neoliberal Localization	*Moment of Destruction*	*Moment of Creation*

South Africa: Rather than the destruction of civil liberties, social services and political rights, post-apartheid South African cities have witnessed the introduction of some of the most progressive legislative and constitutional developments in the world. But lest we get lost in the progressive aspects of these changes, we must also keep in mind the simultaneous rush to re-regulate the 'liberal city' with neoliberal reforms such as heightened surveillance mechanisms (many of which are privatized), exclusive 'public' spaces, the expansion and tightening of indigent policies, and so on. Once again, then, we see the simultaneous destruction of old, apartheid-era restrictions accompanied by new neoliberal-era restrictions, determined in large part by the size of one's wallet rather than the colour of one's skin.

Re-presenting the city	• Postwar image of the industrial, working-class city is recast through a (re)emphasis on urban disorder, 'dangerous classes' and economic decline	• Mobilization of entrepreneurial discourses and representations focused on the need for revitalization, reinvestment and rejuvenation within major metropolitan areas

South Africa: Under apartheid, the 'dangerous classes' were black township residents who, according to the official rhetoric of the day, would swarm into the white suburbs in their rampaging masses if influx controls were lifted (the infamous *swaart gevaar* that played on the minds of so many white urbanites). There are still strong residues of this racist rhetoric—even amongst some Coloured Capetonians who, for years under apartheid, were told by the National Policy that their enemy was African—but the dominant discourse now is a deracialized, class-based rhetoric more typical of neoliberal discourse elsewhere. The threats to the South African city today are the 'idle' masses, the 'inflexible' trade unions, the 'inefficient' civil service and the 'ultra-leftists', all of whom undermine South Africa's attempts to modernize its economy and create economic growth for poverty alleviation.

Adapted from Brenner and Theodore 2002, 369–72.

simultaneously with, or shortly before, the more 'progressive' realization of roll out neoliberalism in the mid- to late 1990s.

There are also nonmarket mechanisms at play that should be highlighted in our review of Table 3.2. These political 'flanking mechanisms' form a substantial part of the urban neoliberal arsenal, intended to both control and limit the scope of acceptable behaviour while at the same time legitimating and valorizing neoliberal reforms—e.g. heavy state control over 'community participation' in the name of decentralization; video surveillance of 'crime' in the name of security; the promotion of 'international best practice' in the name of imposing market-oriented performance incentives.

The establishment of these institutional practices has been an integral and necessary part of dealing with the failures and contradictions of roll back urban neoliberalism. This social regulation goes beyond the merely institutional and policymaking aspects of reform to deeper "strategies of rule" that "encourage people to see themselves as individualized and active subjects responsible for changing their own well being" and not relying on the state (Larner 2000, 13).

Here we see the "disciplinary" effects of neoliberalism (Abrahamsen 2000, Dolgan 1999), or, in Foucauldian terms, its "governmentality" (Burchell et al. 1991, Barry et al. 1996, Larner 2000), an extra-economic set of control mechanisms that serve to entrench and enforce the ideology of neoliberalism.

This governmentality is exemplified in the neoliberal focus on creating 'partnerships' between the state, private capital and community organizations in an attempt to deliver 'better' municipal services such as water and refuse collection. Ostensibly democratic and innovative, these partnerships serve to conceal the overarching objectives of commercialization.

These partnerships are often more democratic than the exclusionary, top-down processes of decision making that preceded them (under liberal Keynesian-Fordist regimes as well as more autocratic regimes such as that of apartheid) but the class objectives remain: "The neoliberal project of institutional creation is no longer oriented simply toward the promotion of market-driven capitalist growth; it is also oriented toward the establishment of new flanking mechanisms and modes of crisis displacement through which to insulate powerful actors from the manifold failures of the market, the state, and governance" (Brenner and Theodore 2002, 372).

The specific, concrete nature of these flanking mechanisms will be taken up in detail in subsequent chapters. The point to emphasize here is a conceptual one: in its attempts to create the conditions for renewed economic growth, capital has also created a new set of urban institutions and institutional arrangements which, on the surface, may appear to be more democratic and progressive than those which preceded them—and less destructive than roll back forms of neoliberalism—but which, at their heart, are intended to protect and expand the accumulation opportunities of capital and which fail to address the inherently unequal and uneven development path of capitalist growth. Neoliberalism may have taken on a progressive façade in terms of some of its policies and institutions, but when these are examined in detail—and understood against the backdrop of unstable capital accumulation—it is possible to see the deeply unequal and unsustainable ways in which they operate.

CLOSING THE CIRCLE

We have now come full circle in our theoretical review. Beginning in Chapter 1 with an examination of Cape Town as a world city we saw that the mainstream academic literature on the subject provided an excellent description of the primary dynamics, institutions and policy foci of world cities, but failed to offer a sufficiently coherent theoretical framework for explaining the emergence of these globalized urban centres or for understanding the inequities that appear to be inherent to them. We needed, in Chapter 2, to turn to a review of the more radical literature on uneven development to see the links between capitalism and the emergence of new urban spatial economies as well as their inherently unstable and inequitable nature. In that discussion we saw Cape Town as a capitalist city, prone to the same crises of overaccumulation and reconfiguration as other market-oriented urban economies.

This current chapter has argued that the overaccumulation crisis of (urban) South Africa has led to the development of a new accumulation strategy, driven by neoliberal policies and institutions. The hubris of racial Fordism was discarded in favour of a set of ideological and institutional reforms at the national and local level that fit broadly into a (dynamic) model of urban neoliberal change.

What remains is to see how these neoliberal initiatives have played themselves out in concrete terms in the city of Cape Town. Chapter 4 looks at the reorganization of local government and how this decentralization and concentration of authority has made for a stronger local state and one that is better able to put in place the kinds of policy reforms needed for renewed accumulation growth. Without these political reforms it would have been very difficult for Cape Town to compete in a global marketplace.

This is followed in Chapter 5 by a look at the physical restructuring of the city, with a focus on infrastructure such as roads, airports and tele-communications. Here we see a classic 'spatial fix', with the local state ensuring that the facilities that (service-oriented) capital needs to compete internationally are in place. There has also been significant investment by the local and national state in low-income township areas, but this pales in comparison to the investments in commercial infrastructure.

More importantly, investments in all urban infrastructure have been shaped by neoliberal policies of privatization (broadly defined) and cost recovery, creating a multi-tiered effect of world-class services for elites, and substandard (and often unaffordable) services for the poor. It is here, in Chapters 6 and 7, that we see the true nature of roll out neoliberalism, with ongoing revisions to the nature of private sector involvement in service delivery and increasingly devious ways of squeezing payments out of the poor (while continuing to provide corporate subsidies to industry).

Chapter 8 looks at the disciplining effects of neoliberalism and how it limits effective participation in decision making on the part of the marginalized poor, while Chapter 9 looks at the ways in which corporate interests have served to expand and entrench the ghettoization of Cape Town's African population.

The overall picture is one of dynamic, and increasingly entrenched, forms of neoliberal policy operating in the interests of an urban transnational elite in an effort to establish, and further the potential for, renewed capital accumulation.

Part II

4 Respatializing Cape Town (I)
Local Government Restructuring

The battle for a new South Africa will be fought at the local level.... We are only at the beginning of this process of change.

Thabo Mbeki, June 1995, speaking in Cape Town as Deputy Vice-President, Government of National Unity

In the literature on the post-apartheid transition in South Africa enormous attention has been paid to the restructuring of national government and the deracialization of national laws and institutions. Considerably less attention has been paid to the physical and legislative restructuring of local government. And yet it is at the local level where some of the most far-reaching political, institutional and geographic changes have taken place in the country.

The current city of Cape Town, for example, was previously composed of 25 racially segregated municipalities and some 69 decision-making authorities. Although some of these municipalities escaped the process of amalgamation—a point we will return to—most of the 'white local authorities' were merged with 'black local authorities' in the mid-1990s to create a new, metropolitan Cape Town. Universal, multiparty local government elections were held for the first time in the city's history in 1996.

This restructuring involved a long, drawn out and politically charged process of redrawing the physical and political boundaries of local governments throughout the country, as well as determining the role of local governments vis-à-vis provincial and national authorities. The result is a city of Cape Town that is dramatically 'respatialized', having gone through more change in the past decade than many cities go through in a century.

But just how different is this new spatial entity and how does it relate to Cape Town's status as a neoliberal city? We look in this chapter at the political and institutional reforms that have taken place in Cape Town since the early 1990s and how the potential for progressive change has been largely captured and distorted by local capital and policymaking elites. While efforts to deracialize and decentralize local government have opened the doors to a wide range of possible reforms—and were not necessarily neoliberal (or even pro-market) in their conceptualization—these political and institutional changes have nevertheless come to serve the interests of capital and middle-class ratepayers and are constitutive of the capital accumulation strategies discussed in Chapters 2 and 3.

In short, local government reforms have helped set the stage for a capital investment strategy that is biased toward the creation of 'world-class' business nodes and areas of elite consumption at the expense of poverty alleviation and township upgrading. Townships in Cape Town have certainly received improved levels of investment when compared to the apartheid era, but these are a far cry from the heady expectations of the early days of local government reform and pale in comparison to the resources (both public and private) that are being poured into meeting the infrastructural needs of capital and transnational elites.

This chapter looks solely at the political and institutional respatialization of the city and illustrates how this restructuring process has helped set the stage for a new capital investment strategy. Chapter 5 looks in detail at these infrastructural investments in the built environment and how they have been shaped by fiscal restraint and stingy intergovernmental fiscal transfers.

My argument here is that local government restructuring in Cape Town has created a local state that is 'weak' in the sense that it has limited political and institutional strength to institute the kinds of redistributory mechanisms that were part of the ANC's original vision of local government reform. At the same time, however, restructuring has created a local government that is 'strong', in the sense that it now has the capacity to implement and enforce a hands-off, neoliberal approach to local governance, with the state overseeing a more business-like approach to running municipal services and acting to keep a lid on pressures for more radical fiscal change.

This is the paradoxical character of the neoliberal state which, far from being emasculated or impotent, is in fact capable of pushing forward a policy agenda that requires considerable technical capacity, ideological commitment and political will. Though not uncontested in its emergence, nor monolithic in its form, this new local state represents a radical shift from the managerialist racial-welfarism of the past and plays a major role in the repositioning of Cape Town as a competitive world city.

We start our examination of this process with a look at the debates around the deracialization of local government and the drawing of new urban boundaries. We then examine the debates around decentralization and the powers of local government. In each case we explore the rationale for these broad policy initiatives and how they had the potential of suiting a wide range of interests. It was, in fact, this potential to please almost everyone that was the key to moving forward with the restructuring process in the first place, at a time of great uncertainty.

We then explore the actual outcomes of local government negotiating in Cape Town. Here we see the promise of progressive reform stifled by class interests and an entrenched bureaucracy, with many of the potential redistributional powers of city council being stripped away by reactionary suburban ratepayers, new institutional boundaries and political compromises on the part of the ANC.

Not all of this can be read in narrow class terms, however. There are important racial overtones to the restructuring process as well as gendered aspects to this reform that have preserved the largely white, male-dominated culture of local government decision making and entrenched many of the gender-biased spaces that make the daily lives of so many (black) girls and women in the city so difficult. We touch on some of these points below, and again in Chapter 9.

DERACIALIZING CAPE TOWN

As noted above, the greater metropolitan area of Cape Town was divided into 25 municipalities at the end of the apartheid era. Eighteen of these municipalities were what were known as White Local Authorities (WLAs), which encompassed white, coloured and Asian residents. Seven were Black Local Authorities (BLAs), which were designated for Africans only. There was, in addition to this, a Regional Service Council (RSC) set up to administer the urban and peri-urban areas that did not fall within any of the existing local authorities. If one adds ratepayer associations, management committees, and other local agencies involved in local government, there was a patchwork of 69 decision-making bodies.

These municipal jurisdictions had varying degrees of access to resources—largely but not entirely based on race—and had varying degrees of communication with one another. Forty years of racial planning and neo-apartheid reforms had led to one of the most fragmented and inequitable forms of local government anywhere in the world (Lemon 1991, Smith 1992).

In 1994, the newly elected ANC national government established Provincial Demarcation Boards in each province tasked with the responsibility of redrawing local government boundaries to create nonracial, unified towns and cities. The guidelines for this restructuring were provided in national regulations and informed the demarcation process throughout the country. The criteria for these boundaries included a range of political, economic and geophysical factors (see Table 4.1) but the actual decision making was done at the local level in what was expected to be a wide-ranging consultative process (for a detailed discussion of the demarcation process in Cape Town see Cameron 1999).

The primary objective of the demarcation process was to create urban areas that were contiguous and economically and politically functional and viable (and ideally having some geophysical relationship to watershed boundaries).

Table 4.1 Criteria for the Demarcation of Nonracial Post-apartheid Local Authorities

Topographical and physical characteristics of the area concerned
Population distribution within the area concerned
Existing demarcation of areas pertaining to local government affairs and services
Existing and potential land usage, town and transport planning, including industrial, business, commercial and residential usage and planning
Economy, functionality, efficiency and financial viability with regard to the administration and rendering of services within the areas concerned
Development potential in relation to the availability of sufficient land for a reasonably foreseeable period to meet the spatial needs of the existing and potential residents of the proposed area for their residential, business, recreational and amenity use
Interdependence of and community interest among residents in respect of residency, work, commuting, and recreation
The integrated urban economy as dictated by commercial, industrial and residential linkages

Source: RSA 1994a, Section 11.6.b.

A secondary objective was to create standardized classifications of these newly redrawn municipalities, which would take into account their potential to perform the duties and responsibilities of post-apartheid local governments. Large metropolitan areas such as Cape Town, Johannesburg, Pretoria and Durban were considered to have the most capacity and were eventually classified as Category A municipalities with full powers over their jurisdiction. Category B and C municipalities consist of smaller towns and regional municipalities in rural areas where duties are sometimes shared across municipal boundaries and where local government's capacity to perform its duties is much more restricted due to such limitations as weak managerial capacity and limited revenue generation opportunities. I will restrict my discussion to Category A municipalities.

The reasons for this local government restructuring are numerous. The first, and most obvious, is the fact that local government had to be in tune with the larger, national changes taking place. With the deracialization of all other aspects of South African life it was imperative that local government be changed as well. Local government had been one of the most visible and concrete expressions of state apartheid. This is true of Cape Town, which, despite its reputation as a 'liberal' city and its relaxation of certain petty apartheid laws in the 1980s, actually enforced spatial segregation in ruthlessly efficient and often brutal ways (van Heningen 1994, Western 1996, Marks and Bezzoli 2000). The continuation of racially defined municipal authorities and legislatively enforced spatial segregation was entirely inconsistent with national-level constitutional changes and had to be reformed.

One aspect of this reform was to create democratic and representative local government. The introduction of universal franchise provided for both proportional representation and constituency-based representative democracy, with multiparty elections being held throughout the country in 1995 and 1996 (although the 'transitional' phase of local government from 1995–2000 allowed for racially skewed representation, as we shall see below).

Local government was also made more transparent with deracialization. As with all apartheid-era institutions, the internal operations of racialized local government were shrouded in secrecy. BLAs were particularly opaque and unaccountable. Established by the National Party in 1982, ostensibly to provide a form of self-government for urban Africans, the BLAs were expected to be financially and administratively independent of WLAs and to provide a complete range of services to African residents. BLAs were immediately rejected by township residents as a form of neo-apartheid, however, and voter turnouts at BLA elections were so low (often less than 5%) and resistance to these puppet administrations so high that provincial governments soon had to give up the charade of representation and simply appoint white administrators to run them (Shubane 1991).

But it was not just BLAs that operated in the dark. WLAs were subject to measures of 'national security' as well, with policing and other security functions being hidden from public purview. Nor was there consistent or transparent policy on the relationship of WLAs with other tiers of government. Even across WLAs there were different levels of intergovernmental financial transfers, with extensive hidden subsidies and fragmented funding formulas that made it virtually impossible to compare funding levels across municipal authorities.

And then there was the ambiguous status of coloured and Asian townships under apartheid. Falling under the jurisdiction of WLAs, and receiving demonstrably better levels of services than Africans in neighbouring BLAs, coloured and Asian residents of Cape Town were nevertheless in a state of political limbo. Having been taken off the municipal voting roles in Cape Town in 1961 they had no direct representation on local government (Cameron 1991). "Management Committees" were created in the 1970s to allow coloured and Asian representatives to make decisions about recreation facilities and other minor service functions, and additional funds came into coloured and Asian townships via the House of Delegates that was formed in 1984 as part of the neo-apartheid Tricameral Parliament at the national level. But neither the Management Committees nor the House of Delegates gained much credibility on the ground and the level of resources and real access to power available was in the hands of white councillors and administrators.

This uneven and fragmented urban system was made worse by the fact that local authorities within a contiguous urban area had very little contact with one another. WLAs situated next to one another would have little, if any, formal communication, making it impossible to know what was happening at a city-wide level. Cape Town, with its jigsaw puzzle of WLAs and BLAs, never compiled metropolitan data during the apartheid era because there was no consistent record keeping across municipalities and no political or legislative imperative to do so. Beyond rough estimates of population and bulk water and electricity consumption, little was known about the city as a metropolitan entity until the reconfiguration of local government in the mid-1990s. Even the Local Government Demarcation Board, a committee that had access to records from every municipality, found it "extremely difficult to obtain accurate financial data regarding the current position and development needs of local communities within existing local authorities" (LGDB 1995, 30).

This byzantine system was driven in large part by the rationality of racial segregation but was also the product of political differences across WLAs (central Cape Town was typically more 'liberal' than many of its neighbouring WLAs, for example) as well as ethnic tensions (English versus Afrikaner-dominated municipalities). But there was also the sheer momentum of an institutionalized culture of myopia. I was amazed when I first began to interview municipal bureaucrats in Cape Town in 1993 how little awareness they had of the happenings beyond their municipal boundaries. It was not unusual to see maps on the walls of senior managers with blank spaces beyond the municipal border (despite the fact that the municipality would be surrounded on all sides by built-up urban areas) and I would typically receive blank stares if I asked questions about their relationship with the neighbouring local authority. Only a handful of senior managers in the metropolitan area at that time were able to articulate any sense of the bigger picture of local government in the city, and even this was severely limited by data availability, deep-seated prejudices, party politics and crude forms of turf protection (with battles between the Regional Service Council and the former City of Cape Town municipal authority being the most significant of these struggles).

The fragmentation of municipal authority also led to a tremendous waste of valuable municipal resources—prompting the World Bank to call apartheid-era Cape Town "one of the most inefficient cities in the world" (as quoted in WCEDF 1993, 11). Duplication of staff and equipment was rife: white municipalities next to one another would have their own complement of urban planners, road engineers, and accountants, as well as their own refuse collection equipment, mechanical workshops and sewage treatment plants. There were no attempts to amalgamate human or capital resources and no one knew for sure exactly what resources other municipalities had. Additional inefficiencies were to be found in land-use planning, public transportation and a host of other important metro-wide services, with independent local authorities spending millions of rand researching locations for dump sites or maintaining sports and recreation facilities oblivious to the needs and constraints of neighbouring municipal authorities—be they white or black. Industrial zones were often located upstream or upwind from an adjacent municipality (particularly if that municipality was black) and residential developments would proceed without any analysis of their impact on larger watershed boundaries.

As a result of these inefficiencies it was anticipated that "substantial productivity gains" would be made with the rationalization and amalgamation of municipal authorities into fewer, more administratively coherent post-apartheid units (RSA 1994b, s5.8.1). Although the exact value of such a reorganization could not be determined when the ANC first published its Reconstruction and Development Programme in 1994, it was anticipated that local government rationalization could free up a "substantial amount of financial and human resources" for RDP efforts (RSA 1994b, 15–16).

It should be noted here as well that the discussion over efficiency gains was informed to some extent by a larger international debate about whether single-tier or two-tier metropolitan systems would be more efficient (Cameron 1999, 36, 48), but there was widespread agreement about the general potential for considerable efficiency gains with the deracialization of local government.

An important corollary to the efficiency argument was the potential for a redistribution of municipal resources. Efficiency gains were expected to allow for a redirection of existing personnel, finances and equipment to areas most in need. Although no one assumed that these efficiency savings would be sufficient on their own the ANC did state that they expected the "largest portion of RDP proposals [to] be financed by a better use of existing resources", particularly at the local government level (ANC 1994, 142). This was the so-called "peace dividend" of apartheid and was expected to provide a cost-free way of upgrading and expanding services in the townships and/or minimizing tax increases and cross-subsidization tariffs in middle-class suburbs.

Finally, it was envisioned that the restructuring of local government would allow for the creation of a single tax unit for a metropolitan area and a more equitable revenue collection and spending system. By the end of the 1980s most BLAs in the Cape Metropolitan Area were effectively bankrupt. There were no major commercial or industrial centres in the BLAs with which to generate municipal revenue, and high levels of African unemployment and low wages for those who did work meant that African ratepayers were unable to contribute to BLA municipal income (WCEDF 1995, 10, 16). These BLA incomes dropped even further with the escalation of rent boycotts in the mid-1980s as Africans refused to pay for the few, poor services they received as part of the resurgent anti-apartheid movement at the time. In the BLA of iKapa for example—an area that included the townships of Langa, Gugulethu, Nyanga and Crossroads—it was estimated in January of 1994 that the municipality was receiving less than 1% of its operating costs from local service and rates revenue.[1] To keep these neo-apartheid institutions afloat the Cape Provincial Administration (CPA) and several WLAs began to subsidize operations, but this did little to improve the quality of services and only served to worsen the financial problems of the city.

By contrast, white local authorities had virtually all of the commercial and industrial activity in their jurisdictions and benefited from these tax revenues. The fact that the wages earned by black South Africans were also spent in shops in white municipalities contributed further to the reverse-Robin Hood style of local government taxation, whereby "the apartheid local government finance system facilitated the redistribution of local resources from the poor African areas to the rich white areas" (Swilling et al. 1991, 176).

REDEFINING THE ROLE OF LOCAL GOVERNMENT

At the same time that the demarcation process was taking place there was a parallel process of redefining the roles and responsibilities of deracialized local government vis-à-vis other "spheres of government" (the term "sphere" was adopted in the 1996 Constitution to emphasize a cooperative rather than hierarchical relationship between local, provincial and national authorities (Reddy 1999b, 31)).

Although there had long been legislation governing the duties of local government these rules were highly differentiated during the apartheid era across BLAs and WLAs and were constantly changing in practice as the country moved in and out of 'states of emergency' and as neo-apartheid reforms were introduced. There were also variations across WLAs in the actual implementation of their responsibilities depending on their financial and managerial capacity and their ideological commitment to enforcing apartheid. The fact that some WLAs raised more than 90% of their operating and capital revenues at the local level (as high as 97% in the case of Cape Town (Ahmad 1995, 51)), while other WLAs and all BLAs were more dependent on central government funding, created additional discrepancies and added to the lack of consistent and transparent intergovernmental relations.

The objective of these reforms was to establish a nationally consistent set of rules and regulations governing the operation of post-apartheid local government. Although this is still an ongoing process of change—and will likely remain so for many years to come given the highly dynamic nature of change in the country—the general parameters of these redefined roles and responsibilities have been laid out in the new Constitution and in subsequent legislation such as the Municipal Structures Act and the Municipal Systems Act.

In a nutshell, local government has been handed the responsibility of managing and delivering some of the most important basic services in the country, such as water, electricity and sanitation, as well as the implementation of housing delivery, some health care functions, amenities such as parks and recreation and a host of planning and regulatory functions (see Table 4.2 for a complete list of powers and duties for metropolitan municipalities, although it should be noted that additional responsibilities can be assigned by national and provincial governments if it is determined that "the matter would most effectively be administered locally" and if "the municipality has the capacity to administer it" (RSA 1996a, s156.1.4)).

This is an impressive and extensive list of responsibilities, prompting Jay Naidoo, the former Minister responsible for the Reconstruction and Development Programme, to refer to post-apartheid local government as

Table 4.2 Schedule Two Powers and Duties of a Transitional Metropolitan Council

1. Bulk supply of water
2. Bulk supply of electricity
3. Bulk sewerage purification works and main sewerage disposal pipelines for the metropolitan area
4. Metropolitan coordination, land usage and transport planning
5. Arterial metropolitan roads and storm water drainage
6. Passenger transport services
7. Traffic matters
8. Abattoirs
9. Fresh produce markets
10. Refuse dumps
11. Cemeteries and crematoriums
12. Ambulance and fire brigade services
13. Hospital services
14. Airports
15. Civil protection
16. Metropolitan libraries
17. Metropolitan museums
18. Metropolitan recreation facilities
19. Metropolitan environment conservation
20. Metropolitan promotion of tourism
21. Metropolitan promotion of economic development and job creation
22. The establishment, improvement and maintenance of other metropolitan services and facilities
23. The power to levy and claim—
    a) a regional services levy and the regional establishment levy [currently collected from Regional Service Councils];
    b) levies or tariffs from any transitional metropolitan substructure in respect of any function or service referred to in items 1–22; and
    c) an equitable contribution from any transitional metropolitan substructure based on the gross or rates income of such transitional metropolitan substructure
24. The receipt, allocation and distribution of intergovernmental grants
25. The power to borrow or lend money, with the prior approval of the [provincial Premier], for the purposes of or in connection with the exercise of any power or duty

Source: RSA 1994a.

"the hands and feet of the RDP" and a "key institution" in the successful implementation of the state's development agenda (RSA 1994b, 18).

Equally important is the fact that local government has also been tasked with the responsibility of "ensur[ing] that all members of the local community have access to at least the minimum level of basic municipal services" (RSA 2000a, s73.1.c). This responsibility, at the stroke of a pen, multiplies the responsibility of post-apartheid local governments manyfold, with local authorities now responsible for ensuring that everyone in their jurisdiction—not just those within a limited WLA or BLA—be provided with services. What exactly constitutes a 'minimum level' of services, and what determines a "prudent, economic, efficient and effective use of available resources" to realize these rights (RSA 1998a, s73.2.b), is a matter that will be taken up later in the book. The important point to highlight here is that local government has an enormous, and enormously important, role in post-apartheid South Africa, having been tasked with nothing less than the improvement of people's everyday lives.

Also, with the introduction of wall-to-wall local government—such that every square inch of the country now falls within the jurisdiction of a local authority, capturing some of the poorest (rural) parts of the country within the ambit of local government for the first time—the duties of local government have been expanded even further in quantitative terms.

Decentralization

Does this reconfiguration of local government responsibilities represent a 'decentralization' of powers and duties? Yes and no. No, in the sense that local governments in South Africa have long been responsible for a wide range of services (far more, in fact, than local governments in most other 'developing' countries). Some observers have even argued that the list of powers and responsibilities of post-apartheid local governments represents a "watering down" of the role of large local authorities in the country (Reddy 1999b, 206).

But it can also be argued that there has been considerable decentralization. The sheer scale of responsibilities of post-apartheid local government and the expansion of these responsibilities to all municipalities in the country represents a much broader form of decentralization than was the case under apartheid.

The term "decentralization" may be something of a misnomer in the South African context, however, suggesting as it does that powers and responsibilities are being devolved and decentred for the first time. Nevertheless, the phrase can be used to acknowledge that the roles and responsibilities of local government have been reconfigured in qualitative and quantitative terms and that this redefining of local-national relationships represents a new and important organization of post-apartheid political and economic power, making local government much more important overall today than it was under apartheid.

This is not to say that the idea of decentralization, or the specifics associated with it, went uncontested during the post-apartheid negotiating process. In many respects, decentralization ran counter to the "centralizing tendencies" of the ANC (Beall et al. 2002, 65). Many in the ANC fought to reign in local government power for fear of losing political and economic control to local power bases and/or ratepayer associations. As a result, it has been argued by some observers that decentralization has occurred in post-apartheid South Africa more by "stealth" than by design, with negotiations over local government powers unfolding in ways that were not anticipated by—or necessarily desired by—the ANC (Beall et al. 2002, 85).

While I would agree with these analysts that there was some "reticence" on the part of the ANC to devolve post-apartheid reconstruction and development powers from the national level it is also clear that the party made local government restructuring a key focus of its transition efforts and opted early on to strengthen, build and revitalize local government—a point that is amply illustrated by then-Deputy Vice-President Thabo Mbeki's quote at the opening of this chapter. This shift to support a devolution of powers to the local level did not occur overnight—and to some extent is still a matter of debate within the ANC—but it cannot be denied that the party has put considerable effort and resources into creating strong local government authorities since the early 1990s.

It is also true that the ANC insisted on clauses in the Constitution that allow for direct and indirect control of local government from the national (and to some extent provincial) level. Despite Constitutional language recognizing the independence of the different "spheres" of government, national government can set standards and minimum requirements for service delivery, establish monitoring processes, and even make laws in areas that are technically part of the powers and duties of local government. Legislation restricting the scope of local government—such as the legal requirement that municipalities not be allowed to pass a deficit budget— add to a situation where national government's power to regulate local government is considerable.

More important to our discussion here, however, is the rationale for reconfiguring the role of local government. As with deracialization there are numerous reasons for the restructuring of intergovernmental relations. The first, and perhaps most significant, of these was the belief that local authorities had the capacity (or could get the capacity) to deliver on their mandates. Small towns/cities and rural municipalities have proven to be a challenge in this regard, with many still undercapacitated, but large metros like Cape Town were seen to have the institutional, administrative and fiscal capacity to deliver.

Fiscally, metropolitan areas already collected about 90% of their revenues locally (as compared to 60–70% in most European and North American cities (Lemon 2002, 22)) and had the technical and administrative capacity to expand these fiscal systems to township areas. It was also anticipated that the local state could redistribute the efficiency gains from amalgamation, put in place improved tax collection systems (such as updated property valuation systems) and utilize increased funding from national and provincial government, creating financially viable local authorities.

Most municipalities also had the bulk infrastructure in place for essential services—albeit geared for white residents—allowing for an easier upgrading and expansion of household-based infrastructure in un(der)serviced areas. Bulk water supply systems, electricity grids, roads, dump sites and sewage treatment plants, for example, were typically of high quality and often allowed for relatively easy expansion to township areas.

All of this required skilled bureaucrats of course, and here, once again, local government in South Africa was in a relatively strong position to deliver. It has been estimated, for example, that over half of all the civil engineers on the African continent lived in South Africa in the mid-1990s, and there is a strong network of municipal engineers in the country (see, for example, *The Official Journal of the Institute of Municipal Engineers of Southern Africa*). There were also impressive numbers of accountants, biologists, demographers, and urban planners within the former white local authority structures. The overwhelming majority of this personnel was (and still is) white and male, and there remains a potent streak of conservatism and racism in the municipal civil service, but there was a pool of skills available to local government in South Africa in the early 1990s that made the rapid expansion and upgrading of services in the townships seem very possible.

There was also a considerable pool of talent in the NGO and CBO sector to draw on. Nongovernmental organizations such as the Development Action Group and PLANACT were staffed with highly skilled urban planners and architects, many with years of experience working with communities as well as city officials. These groups made up a small fraction of the overall skills base at the time, but they were a prominent and well-organized voice on the urban restructuring scene and promised to add to the capacity of local government. (Many did indeed become major players on the local government scene, often as proponents of neoliberal reform (Bond 2006a).)

Finally, there was a culture of local government in place in the country that made it easier to introduce new roles and responsibilities. Though obviously racially skewed across WLAs and BLAs (and even within WLAs, as the virtual exclusion of coloureds and Asians from local government in Cape Town illustrated) there was nonetheless a familiarity with local elections, local taxes/tariffs and local dialogue that made it easier for post-apartheid local governments to initiate decentralized reforms.

Ironically, the efforts of the anti-apartheid movement to make townships ungovernable in the 1980s, and the attention paid to civic formation and grass-roots community building at that time, also served to strengthen the potential of post-apartheid local government by creating a culture of local political action in township areas and by strengthening the institutional capacity of community organizations to interact with local authorities (Shubane 1991, Mayekiso 1996). While much of this civic culture and capacity was to melt away remarkably quickly after local government elections in the mid-1990s, at the time of deciding the roles of local government it appeared to be a positive force for democratic change.

Which brings us to the more conventional arguments used to promote decentralization in South Africa: that it brings government closer to the people; that it makes government more responsive to people's needs and more accountable to their demands; and that it allows for direct participation in decision making at the local level (Howe 1987, Eaton 2004, Coaffe and Johnston 2005). These were the "local governance" arguments that had become prominent in the mainstream international literature on decentralization in the late 1980s and early 1990s and were being pushed aggressively by development agencies such as the World Bank (1989, 1992; see also Hyden and Bratton 1992, McCarney 1996, Swilling 1996, CCT 2006e, 60).

One could argue that the ANC was blindly adopting mainstream rhetoric from international funders in an attempt to curry funding favour. There may be some truth to this argument but there were clearly other good reasons for wanting to make local government in South Africa more accountable, more responsive and more participatory. The actual modes and culture of decentralization were a long way from being finalized with a wide range of possible outcomes.

This last point highlights the extremely ambiguous character of local government reform at the time. It was impossible to determine with certainty what the actual outcomes of the decentralization process might be, and it was certainly not clear that a neoliberal outcome was inevitable.

It was, in fact, precisely because anything was possible that the restructuring of local government was able to move forward so quickly, having, as it did, the potential of suiting a wide range of interests. For capital, local government restructuring had the potential of ending civil unrest in the cities and creating a more efficient, more transparent and more responsive and accountable local government that could help to expand, improve and reconfigure urban infrastructure. For middle- and upper-income ratepayers there was the promise that service levels in the suburbs would be largely maintained (or that local government would at least be forced to be responsive to their demands and would be more transparent and accountable than in the past). There was also the promise of better efficiency with the potential for minimizing cross-subsidization to the townships via increased taxes. According to Mabin (1995, 10), the concept of nonracial cities did little to "threaten the identity" of white suburbanites and offered the "promise of peace to counter the threat to the pockets of WLA taxpayers".

For the democratic movement there was the promise of massive upgrades and new infrastructure and service delivery in the townships, either with new funding or through redistributed resources. The townships would also benefit from more responsive, more democratic, more participatory, more accountable and more transparent local government (none of which had been practiced in the past in the BLAs).

On the surface of things, then, the deracialization of local government and a reconfiguration and standardization of its relationship with other spheres of government presented an apparent win-win situation, with possible benefits for everyone. As a result, early debates over the reconfiguration of local government moved along quickly and with relatively little controversy.

By October of 1990—a mere eight months after the unbanning of the ANC—a major local government conference had taken place in Johannesburg, and local government negotiating fora were quickly established in over a hundred towns and cities in the country (CDS 1991, Mabin 1995, 25). A rash of books on post-apartheid urban restructuring was also quickly published (Tomlinson 1990, CDS 1991, Swilling et al. 1991, Lemon 1991, Smith 1992) and several journals and magazines began to feature local government restructuring debates (e.g. *Urban Forum*, *Work In Progress*).

With the exception of certain Conservative Party strongholds, a "growing consensus" soon emerged on the need for unified towns and cities in the country (Mabin 1995, 9). By the time the first round of negotiations for a new federal constitution was under way in 1991, virtually every local authority and political party in South Africa had agreed on the "one city" principle—i.e. nonracial, democratically elected local governments with a common tax base and a commitment to improving the quality of life of all its residents. This discourse met with "little to no challenge" in the initial stages of negotiations and quickly dominated the local government negotiating agenda (Mabin 1995, 10).

More detailed decisions on new municipal boundaries, powers and assets would eventually have to be made, however, and multiparty consensus on the principles of local government reform soon gave way to heated debates over what these new local governments would actually look like. The mood of reconciliation had been enough to bring opposing sides to the local government negotiating table but it would not resolve the very tangible problems of urban neglect. Difficult decisions would have to be made on new, nonracial boundaries, the election of councillors, the collection of taxes, and the (re)distribution of metropolitan assets.

In small towns these decisions were relatively straightforward. The central part of municipalities (typically white residential areas where (white) businesses were located) would simply be amalgamated with the one or two outlying black townships into a single local authority. This is not to say that the decision-making process in small towns was free of tension, or that representatives from these small White Local Authorities did not try to negotiate themselves out of the unification process, but given the hegemonic nature of the one-city discourse in the country there was no feasible political option but to amalgamate.

In large cities the decisions were much more complex. In the Cape Metropolitan Area, with its eighteen WLAs, seven BLAs and Regional Service Council spread over a fifty-kilometre radius, it was not immediately apparent which authorities would be included in a metropolitan council and which might be left to form smaller local authorities. It was also unclear how municipalities within a new metropolitan area would be divided into "metropolitan substructures".[2] Because there had never been a metropolitan government in Cape Town (or elsewhere in South Africa for that matter) there were no local precedents upon which to base these decisions.

NATIONAL LOCAL GOVERNMENT NEGOTIATING FORUM (NLGNF)

With the formation of a National Local Government Negotiating Forum (NLGNF) in 1993—part of the multiparty Kempton Park negotiations for a new federal constitution—national guidelines were developed for local government negotiations (Cloete 1995). The Local Government Transition Act (LGTA) of February of 1994 formally legislated the negotiation criteria and the "political hegemony of the one city discourse ... was [officially] enforced" (Mabin 1995, 25). The amalgamation of black and white local authorities became a constitutional requirement and the soon-to-be-elected provincial Governments of National Unity were granted the right to amalgamate black and white local authorities—against their will if necessary.

But the LGTA was a flexible piece of legislation open to a number of legislative changes and provided for three distinct phases of local government restructuring. The first, "pre-interim", phase of restructuring covered the period from the publication of the LGTA in 1994 to the first nonracial local government elections (May of 1996 in Cape Town's case). During this period it was expected that broadly representative negotiating teams would be established in each town and city, that nonracial municipal boundaries would be determined, and that the powers and duties of new local authorities would be decided upon.

Decisions made in the pre-interim phase were then carried through to the second stage of the transition, the "interim phase"—a period lasting from "the day after the elections are held for transitional local councils ... and ending with the implementation of final arrangements to be enacted by a competent [local government] legislative body" (RSA 1994a, 2). Consequently, there was no guarantee that local government legislation would not also be changed. Everything from municipal boundaries to the powers of metropolitan government were open to renegotiation and could be fundamentally altered in the third, and by no means final, phase of the post-apartheid local government transition, which began with the second local government elections in December 2000.

Participation in local government negotiations was based on the LGTA principle of "inclusivity and representivity" (RSA 1994a, 32–34). Schedule One of the Act stipulates that negotiating fora must be composed of two equally represented groups: "statutory" members on one side (local government bodies and political parties officially recognized under apartheid—e.g. White Local Authorities, coloured Management Committees, previously recognized political parties); "non-statutory" members on the other (any group other than a statutory group with a "vested interest in the political restructuring of local government"—e.g. civic organizations and previously banned political parties such as the ANC and the Pan African Congress (PAC)).

Ratepayer organizations were not included in this initial statutory list, but they made such a "clamour" to be admitted that they were eventually permitted to participate on the statutory side—despite the fact that these ratepayers were already represented by the WLAs (Mabin 1995, 26). Bodies such as the local chambers of commerce and industry as well as supplier boards such as Eskom (electricity) were granted "observer status".

The fact that 50% of the negotiating seats (and therefore 50% of the negotiating votes) went to statutory bodies was a major concession on the part of the ANC–alliance negotiating the LGTA. In most towns and cities in the country Africans outnumbered whites by a wide margin—as many as twenty to one in some cases. Fifty percent representation therefore gave whites (and those otherwise officially represented by statutory bodies—Asians and coloureds) a significant bargaining advantage. But it must be remembered that the LGTA was part of a larger deal for nonracial democracy in the country as a whole and as such was fraught with the same kinds of compromises and settlements that were made to pave the way for peaceful, multiparty national negotiations and elections. In the interests, therefore, of "promoting reconciliation at the local level" and, more ominously, in recognition of "the need to offer concessions so the white right-wing would become part of the transition process rather than resort to lawlessness and terrorism", the nonstatutory bodies negotiating at the NLGNF agreed to give white South Africans equal representation at local government negotiating fora (Mayekiso 1994, 20).[3]

Ironically, this compromise had the reverse effect in the Western Cape—the one province where the National Party retained power after the 1994 national/provincial elections—where Africans made up less than 15% of the population at the time. Although coloureds constituted more than half of the population in the province, coloured townships were situated within White Local Authorities under apartheid and were therefore officially represented by statutory bodies at the negotiations. The result was that whites and coloureds in the Western Cape received far fewer seats at negotiating tables than they would have otherwise been entitled to on the basis of proportional representation, while African residents have received a much higher number of seats. In the small towns and villages of the province where Africans sometimes made up less than 5% of the population this was a significant negotiating advantage.

But this twist of constitutional fate had its problems as well. For those who had hoped that local elections would provide an opportunity to heal the deep wounds that had developed between coloured and African communities in the CMA (Cape Metropolitan Authority), the fact that coloured and African residents sat across the table from each other—rather than beside one another—served to undermine the credibility and legitimacy of representatives from oppressed coloured areas and created new political rifts (Mayekiso 1994, 21).

Moreover, 50% representation at the negotiating table did not guarantee 50% of the negotiating influence. The nonstatutory side in Cape Town, as elsewhere in the country, had to run on a shoestring budget for most of the pre-interim phase of negotiations and many of its key members were involved in a myriad of other important activities that took away from the time they could devote to local government meetings.[4] Nor was there a united front amongst nonstatutory members. In the Cape Metropolitan Negotiating Forum (CMNF), for example, the nonstatutory side included representatives from the Inkatha Freedom Party and the Western Cape United Squatters' Association—organizations that were openly hostile to the ANC–alliance.[5]

Moreover, 50% representation does not mean that the nonstatutory side had 50% of the negotiating resources. Although nonstatutory groups received some funding from municipalities and other levels of government, as well as help from local NGOs, these resources did not come close to those available to the statutory side. The fact that almost all of the professional municipal staff in the CMA was situated in the offices of the White Local Authorities, and representatives from these authorities had easy access to municipal information and equipment (photocopiers, vehicles, computers), gave the statutory side in Cape Town a distinct negotiating advantage.

In addition, many of the nonstatutory representatives had little experience in the kind of formal negotiating required under the LGTA. Skills that were developed in the anti-apartheid movement in the townships in the 1970s and 1980s were not quickly or easily transferable to formal, wood-panelled council chambers. Statutory representatives on the other hand were familiar with the physical and social environments of the boardroom and were well-versed in the art of municipal politicking.

Compounding this problem of representivity in the Western Cape was a clause in the LGTA that granted the provincial Premier and the Minister of Local Government, both of whom were long-time collaborators in the apartheid system[6], the power to appoint people to the two most influential local government negotiating committees—the Provincial Committee for Local Government and the Local Government Demarcation Boards.[7] The LGTA stated that these committees must be "broadly representative of stakeholders in local government" (Section 3.2) but it also made provisions for the Minister or Premier to remove members from a committee if they so desired (Section 11.5)—a prerogative that was exercised by the Minister when one of these committees made a recommendation he did not agree with.

The nonstatutory side negotiating the LGTA also compromised on rules governing the election of local government officials. In order to placate white fears that the large number of black voters would overwhelm any hope of electing white officials it was agreed that only 40% of councillors would be elected on a proportional representation basis and the rest would come from elections in wards. Of the 60% of councillors elected from wards, half would have to come from the ex-WLAs, half from the ex-BLAs—effectively guaranteeing white South Africans at least 30% of the seats in local government.

Again, this imbalance worked in favour of the African townships in the Western Cape on a numerical basis because coloured townships fell under the WLAs, but on a political level this arrangement served to aggravate, yet again, coloured/African tensions in the province.

NEGOTIATIONS IN CAPE TOWN

This next section describes local government negotiations in Cape Town up to and including the first local government elections in May 1996. The focus here is on the division of powers and duties between the various levels of local government and how this affected the potential to rationalize and redistribute municipal resources and implement the kinds of equitable service delivery systems that the more progressive architects of local government restructuring had planned for.

The results of the interim negotiations were such that the transitional metropolitan council was largely stripped of its ability to redistribute municipal resources. The formation of a Unicity in 2000 corrected some of this institutional imbalance but the nature of the interim phase of local government (1996–2000) was such that it served to entrench much of the apartheid-era distribution of resources and set in train a culture of political compromise and neoliberal thinking that pushed the notion of *redistribution* on to the back burner (where it remains to this day).

Of particular importance was the weakening of the metropolitan tier of government in Cape Town and a concomitant decline in the ability of the local state to effect a redistribution of municipal resources. Two events are particularly noteworthy in this regard and are featured below.

Determining the Outer Boundaries of the Cape Metropolitan Council

The first blow to a strong metropolitan authority came with the exclusion from the Cape Metropolitan Council (CMC) of several important satellite towns. The municipalities of Paarl, Stellenbosch, Franschhoek, and Wellington—home to many of the intellectual and financial elites of Afrikanerdom—managed to bargain their way out of a metropolitan Cape Town and the associated responsibilities of urban upgrading. These former WLAs are responsible for helping to upgrade townships in their own jurisdictions but the financial liabilities of these areas were minor in comparison to the badly degraded townships and sprawling informal settlements of the CMC. African townships constituted less than 10% of the population of these satellite towns as compared to almost 30% in the CMC, and both coloured and African townships in these towns tended to be in much better shape in terms of infrastructure than those closer to Cape Town.

The decision to exclude these authorities from the CMC was made by a provincially appointed, sixteen-member Local Government Demarcation Board (LGDB). This Board was expected to base its decision on criteria outlined in Schedule Six of the LGTA for metropolitan boundaries (as listed in Table 4.1 above) as well as from written and oral submissions from statutory and nonstatutory bodies in the greater metropolitan area. The process took several months to complete and final recommendations were sent to the provincial Minster of Local Government for approval.

Statutory representatives from these peripheral municipalities argued that their towns were not sufficiently "urbanized" in terms of the criteria laid out in the LGTA and not economically reliant on Cape Town proper, and that their inclusion in the metropolitan area would bring about a loss of cultural and financial "autonomy" (LGDB 1994, 2–10). Comments such as, "A rural area will be discriminated against in a metro Council simply because they are rural", and "The power must be with the people", were typical of the statements made by these statutory representatives (LGDB 1994, 44–50). One business owner went so far as to say that the wine industry, which makes up a significant part of the fringe area's economy, "was self-contained and had greater links with France and Australia than Cape Town" (LGDB 1994, 28, 50).

Several other outlying WLAs also tried to disengage themselves from the CMC, but were unsuccessful. A National Party representative from the town of Somerset West argued that the "Helderberg basin [where Somerset West is located] has a character of its own that differs widely from that of the metropole". The Gordon's Bay Business and Ratepayers Associations argued in a similar vein that local government "should be close to the people" and not be given to a CMC, which they consider to be a distant and unwieldy "monster" (LGDB 1994, 34). In fact, there was not a single statutory body from the outlying municipalities that did not make a case for its own distinct cultural, economic and political status and the need for its independence from a metropolitan Cape Town.

Opponents[8] of this exclusionary vision of metropolitan government maintained that these satellite towns did in fact fit the criteria for inclusion in a metropolitan area and were economically dependent on the CMC. Only a large metropolitan authority, it was argued, would be capable of financing the massive urban upgrading required in the townships and of effectively managing urban growth. Splitting what was considered to be a single metropolitan area into two or more completely separate municipal authorities would lead to capital flight from the city to the fringe, driving taxes up in the CMC and further weakening the ability of a metropolitan government to address the enormous backlog of services in the townships. "Wealthier individuals and companies", according to a representative from the World Bank who backed the opposition views, "[would then be driven to] relocate outside the metropolitan boundary to escape higher metro taxes and fees" (LGDB 1994, 44).

Loss of autonomy for these fringe municipalities was not considered a problem by these opposition groups, because "effective democratic participation in government is dependent in the main on the system of representation and on the strength of civil society, not on the area of jurisdiction of an authority" (LGDB 1994, 17). Fringe municipalities would have elected representatives in lower tiers of municipal government located directly in their jurisdictions as well as representatives elected to a metropolitan government.

In the end, however, a majority of the Local Government Demarcation Board (thirteen of sixteen members) decided in favour of excluding the satellite towns, despite their own admission that these fringe municipalities "spent lavish sums of public money on consultants to prepare arguments against inclusion in the metropolitan area while virtually no assistance was given by these bodies to the respective non-statutory groups who differed from them" (LGDB 1994, 82). A majority of the Board members were apparently unconvinced by the arguments forecasting capital flight from the centre of the city and were determined that these small, outlying towns must have their own political autonomy. As Cameron (1999, 114) points out, "technical considerations were ultimately overshadowed by political considerations when it came to the final boundary decision".

The Board's point about the need for political autonomy was a curious one though, given that turnouts at public demarcation hearings in these areas were extremely low. Of an estimated population of 51 000 in Stellenbosch, for example, only nineteen oral submissions were made at three public Demarcation Board meetings held in the town hall and public attendance was fewer than forty people a day on average (LGDB 1994, 132). If public participation was this low for what was arguably one of the most important and historic local government decisions in the town's long history, on what grounds did the Demarcation Board argue that residents in these towns want to be able to participate in government that is "closer to the people" (LGDB 1994, 3–4)?

Powers, Duties and Boundaries Within the CMC

The second major blow to a strong metropolitan authority in Cape Town came with a substantial devolution of metropolitan powers and duties to the metropolitan substructures. As noted earlier, ANC approval of decentralization was tempered by the desire for a certain degree of centralization. Consequently, the party fought for strong metropolitan government in the National Local Government Negotiating Forum. Schedule Two of the LGTA recognized these desires by appointing certain duties and powers to metropolitan-level authorities (as opposed to their substructures). In general, it was decided that metropolitan-level authorities would be granted the right to collect metropolitan-wide taxes in order to address the taxation imbalance in cities and to coordinate activities considered of importance to the city as a whole (e.g. waste management, bulk water supply). Metropolitan substructures, meanwhile, were expected to handle services and functions considered to be more local in nature (e.g. parking tickets, street cleaning).

In contrast, most statutory representatives wanted to *minimize* the power of metropolitan governments, with the National Party, local chambers of commerce and suburban ratepayer associations consistently arguing against strong, centralized municipal governments in favour of strong, decentralized substructures and ward councils. To accommodate these concerns, a clause was inserted in the LGTA (Section 7.1) that stated that "any transitional metropolitan council may, in its discretion, decide not to exercise any power or duty" listed in Schedule Two, and may hand any or all of these responsibilities over to a metropolitan substructure, effectively opening the door to a deeper decentralization of powers than that desired by the ANC.

The outcome of the CMNF Agreement was a "relatively weak Transitional Metropolitan Council and strong substructures" (LGDB 1995, 23). Sections 11, 12 and 13 of the Agreement outline the powers and duties of different levels of local government and state very clearly that "any or some" of the responsibilities assigned to metropolitan governments in Schedule Two of the LGTA can be transferred to the substructures (CMNF 1994, 13) with the responsibility to "provide, restore, extend and upgrade services in disadvantaged areas" transferred early on (CMNF 1994, 14).

Most important was the clause in the Agreement that granted substructures "maximum control over local decision-making and implementation" of duties (CMNF 1994, 15). In other words, not only were substructures able to decide where and how municipal services should be delivered in the city, they were also able to determine the level of taxation used to support these services. More specifically, elected representatives from the wealthier parts of the city (with at least 30% of councillors coming from white, suburban ward councils) were able to insist on a tax ceiling: section 12.3 of the CMNF Agreement stated that the responsibility to "provide, restore, extend and upgrade services in the disadvantaged areas" shall not force a metropolitan substructure to "impose inordinate increases in any of its taxes and charges" to ratepayers (CMNF 1994, 14).

The Local Government Demarcation Board also suggested that "the principle of ward council autonomy be applied in cases where substructures feel the need to decentralize their activities" even further. Sensing continued resistance from statutory groups to unification, the Demarcation Board hoped that by pushing control of the municipal purse strings down to the level of the ward it might help to "persuade communities who resist amalgamation with other communities to accept such amalgamation" (LGDB 1995, 64).

Nevertheless, the Demarcation Board was aware of the need to ensure financially sustainable and capable municipal substructures and attempted to balance its far-reaching decentralization with the creation of substructures that had the financial and administrative capacity to deal with this devolution of powers and duties (LGDB 1995, 23). On a financial level it was determined that "substructures should have an equitable share in the commercial and industrial base of the Metropolitan Area" and that the financial capacity of a substructure should be matched "as far as possible ... with its population and development needs". Hence, "richer local authorities with strong tax bases should assume greater financial responsibility by incorporating densely populated poorer areas", leading to a "reduction in the [total] number of local government bodies in the [CMA]" (LGDB 1995, 4–5, 21–24). Efforts were also made to take into account topographical features in the demarcation process (e.g. watershed boundaries) and there was a desire to link, as far as possible, local authorities closest to and most economically dependent on one another.

Another demarcation principle which "influenced the Board's decisions was its conclusion at an early stage of its deliberations that it was not possible to subdivide the community of Khayelitsha [or the townships of iKapa] into two or more units". Although keeping these BLAs intact meant a large "developmental burden" for whichever White Local Authority became responsible for them, it was felt that attempts to cut the townships up "resulted in highly artificial boundaries [with] detrimental effects on an organic community" (LGDB 1995, 5). Although there was a concern at first that large substructures would be "bureaucratic, remote and inefficient", the decentralized nature of the CMNF agreement led the LGDB to conclude "that substructures should be somewhat larger than initially anticipated" (LGDB 1995, 20). In the end, the Board decided that "two relatively large substructures with sufficient capacity and resources should take the major responsibility" of upgrading the most disadvantaged areas (LGDB 1995, 20).

The first of these was called the Central Substructure and brought together the largest and most powerful WLA in the metropolitan area—the predominantly English-speaking Cape Town City Council (CCC)—with the African townships of iKapa and several coloured townships on the Cape Flats. The second large substructure was called Tygerberg, and brought together the predominantly Afrikaans-speaking northern suburbs of Bellville, Durbanville, Goodwood and Parow with the coloured townships of Elsies River, Bontheuwel and Belhar and the Black Local Authority of Lingelethu West (i.e. Khayelitsha). Four other substructures were created with significantly less upgrading responsibility in absolute terms, but with a similar financial load in per capita terms.

There were other boundary proposals considered by the Demarcation Board but these were rejected on the grounds that they were "contrary to the objectives of the Local Government Transition Act" (LGDB 1995, 23). In one of these proposals, the Cape Town City Council was expected to assume responsibility for upgrading virtually all of the African townships in the CMC. Both the Cape Town City Council and the Demarcation Board felt that such a "disproportionately heavy burden ... could have serious financial consequences, such as capital flight to neighbouring municipalities" (LGDB 1995, 25) and the Board stuck to its inner-boundary mandate to try and spread the burden of upgrading as evenly as possible throughout the city.

Most of the statutory groups in the CMC did not appreciate the Demarcation Board's commitment to efficiency and equity, however. With the notable exception of the Cape Town City Council—or, more correctly, certain key individuals in that Council[9]—virtually every statutory group making a presentation to the Demarcation Board on inner metropolitan boundaries argued for their own political and economic autonomy (in direct contrast, it should be noted, to their criticism of the same arguments being made by the peripheral municipalities, as discussed earlier).

Representatives from the wealthy WLA of Bellville argued, for example, that they were "fully committed to non-racialism" but there has been "no sense of community between Bellville and Khayelitsha" and therefore the Demarcation Board should not "force change" on residents in either area. Representatives from the even wealthier WLA of Durbanville argued that "apartheid did not shape development [in the city], and therefore it wishes to be retained as a separate substructure" (LGDB 1995, 115–16). The other white municipalities included in the Tygerberg substructure (Goodwood and Parow) suggested that Khayelitsha simply be left "as a local authority on its own with funding from the Transitional Metropolitan Council" and that they would assist the coloured townships in their areas instead (LGDB 1995, 117, 125).

Statutory groups from the southern suburbs also rejected the idea of large substructures, arguing that the southern suburbs have "more in common with [each other] than the rest of Cape Town" (LGDB 1995, 130). Critical of the Cape Town City Council for being "too big" and not "consulting its ratepayers about its constitutional proposals", at least sixteen statutory bodies supported a proposal by the South Peninsula Initiative to have "the Simon's Town Magisterial District [designated] a separate Transitional Metropolitan Substructure" (LGDB 1995, 127–28). One statutory group from this area—the Red Hill Landowners Conservation Group—went so far as to argue that they live in "an important [nature] conservation area ... [with] needs, problems and management requirements [that] are completely different from those of urban areas" and that they should therefore have a "Southern South Peninsula Rural/Conservation Substructure" of their own (LGDB 1995, 129).

Nonstatutory groups, on the other hand, were fully behind the proposals of the Demarcation Board for financially balanced substructures. The nonstatutory delegation to the CMNF cited as a "non-negotiable tenet" that "black local authorities must be amalgamated with white local authorities that are able to provide administrative support and other infrastructure necessary to aid the development of these areas". Large substructures are the "preferred model", it was argued, because "they can provide a wider range of services, they are better equipped to implement the Reconstruction and Development Programme ... [and they are] more diverse, including a mix of different communities and races, rich areas and poor areas" (LGDB 1995, 120).

The Demarcation Debacle

All of this otherwise democratic decision making was brought to an abrupt halt when then-Provincial Minister of Local Government Peter Marais declared the Demarcation Board's recommendations null and void shortly after they were released in February of 1995. The Minister then replaced two ANC–allied members of the Provincial Committee for Local Government with two National Party supporters and went on to submit his own inner boundary proposals to the six-member committee for consideration.

Marais insisted that the (Afrikaner-dominated) northern suburbs and the coloured townships in the Tygerberg substructure were unable to support urban upgrading in Khayelitsha and he unilaterally drew up substructure boundaries that attached all of the major African townships and squatter camps to Cape Town City Council—almost exactly the same proposal that had been rejected by the LGDB at the beginning of boundary negotiations because it laid most of the upgrading requirements in the African townships on the Cape Town City Council. Not surprisingly, residents in the (English-dominated) southern suburbs of the Central substructure were up in arms over these proposals with local papers predicting "massive rates increases" if the National Party plan went ahead, placing a burden of taxation on southern suburb residents that is "both illogical and unjust" (*Southern Suburbs Tatler*, June 8, 1995).

The ANC and other nonstatutory bodies were also infuriated with the Minister's moves, not just because they undermined the financial and administrative viability of the Central substructure to upgrade the townships, but because of the highly undemocratic nature of the decisions. The Demarcation Board had committed itself in writing to "transparent and open decision making" (LGDB 1995, 22) and the Minister had violated any sense of democratic protocol. The Government of National Unity was quick to step in to investigate these events and, with the support of several prominent National Party members of cabinet (including Roelf Meyer, then the federal Minister for Constitutional Affairs), threatened to declare the Provincial Minister's moves unconstitutional.

Marais did back down on his original proposal but then submitted an equally objectionable plan to twin the Tygerberg substructure with the townships of iKapa and the Central substructure with those of Khayelitsha—a proposition that the leader of the ANC for the Western Cape called "economic and geographical nonsense" (*Cape Argus*, June 24, 1995). The controversy eventually went to Constitutional Court, paralyzing demarcation negotiations in the city and delaying local government elections in metropolitan Cape Town until May 1996. The original substructure boundary proposals were eventually adopted in December of 1995 as a result of the court injunction, but the acrimony and underlying tensions remained. Marais was considered a "local hero" in the precincts of white Durbanville (to where he moved) and in the coloured townships of Bishop Lavis and Elsies River (from whence he hailed). Moreover, the National Party was able to report at the height of the demarcation standoff that the incident was "swelling both its support and its coffers" in the province (*Weekly Mail*, June 15, 1995).

Several media commentators suggested that the inner boundary dispute represented political gerrymandering on the part of the National Party to win a majority of ward seats in the Tygerberg substructure; others suggested old-fashioned racism. But the incident also clearly illustrated the stark economic interests at play in local government restructuring. It was clear that it was going to cost a lot of money to upgrade the townships and informal areas of the city, and affluent Capetonians wanted to shelter themselves from these costs as much as possible.

Weak Metropolitan Government

In the end, local government negotiations resulted in deracialized institutions that were clearly more democratic and more transparent than before but that were largely incapable of effecting major redistributional change. Municipal substructures in Cape Town during the interim period operated, in many respects, in the same way as their myopic municipal predecessors, with political tensions between ANC–controlled and National Party–controlled substructures adding to the difficulty of effecting metropolitan-wide changes.

Continuous pressures from business and ratepayer associations, and agreements that the metropolitan substructure would not "impose inordinate increases in any of its taxes and charges", added to the difficulty of effecting significant change. Attempts to introduce more progressive cross-subsidization measures were generally met with stiff resistance from ratepayers and local business. Similar actions were taken in other cities in the country, with Johannesburg experiencing a crippling rates boycott in the wealthy suburb of Sandton (costing the city over R220 million in lost revenue (Allen et al. 2001)) and the metropolitan authority in Durban lacking the power to redistribute resources in the face of resistance from wealthy ratepayers (Khan 1997).

All this was despite the glaring inequalities in resource distribution in cities and towns across the country. On average, ten times the money had been spent per capita on residential infrastructure in the WLAs (roads, drainage, sanitation, etc.) as compared to the townships during the apartheid era, and this rate continued into the early 1990s. In some cases, per capita expenditures in the WLAs were greater than those of cities in Europe and Australia. In the Central Witwatersrand for example, an average of US$550 per person per year was spent on residential infrastructure in the 1980s as compared to only US$300 per person per year in Stockholm, Munich, Melbourne and Singapore over the same time period (Ahmad 1995, 51), and it is likely that similar or even higher figures were spent in the suburbs of Cape Town where water pipes, sewerage mains and electrical lines have quite literally been carved into the side of Table Mountain and reinforced with expensive soil retention barriers and ongoing maintenance.

A more concrete illustration of these inequities can be seen in data that I collected in early 1994. Questionnaires were sent to the Town/City Engineers of all 25 municipalities in the Cape Metropolitan Area requesting data on human and capital resources in a number of key service areas (the only data to my knowledge that was collected at this microlevel at the time). Figures vary somewhat from municipality to municipality but in general the physical and human resources that were available to WLAs for basic operations such as refuse collection far outweighed those of the BLAs. Table 4.3 illustrates the refuse collection capacity of two typical former WLAs (Bellville and Parow) and one former BLA (Mbekweni) from the Cape Metropolitan Area.

The large difference in per capita expenditures between Parow and Bellville in Table 4.3 can be explained in part by the fact that Parow was composed primarily of white residents while Bellville had a large coloured population that would have been relatively underserviced, bringing down the ratios. It should also be noted that the plant and equipment in the BLAs were generally in very poor condition and the numbers provided here did

Table 4.3 Refuse Collection Capacities of WLAs and BLAs in the Cape Metropolitan Area

Cleansing Department Information	Parow	Bellville	Mbekweni
Years for which data were provided	1993–94	1992–93	1993
Estimated population of municipality	19,100	117,500	33,500
Annual operating expenditure/capita	R165	R46	R5
Number of residents/manager	1193	5875	33,500
Number of residents/labourer	222	1632	2791
Number of compactor trucks	7	6	1
Number of auto mechanics	3	2	0

not reflect the frequent breakdowns, which limited the number of vehicles available for service functions.

In the former BLA of iKapa, for example, there were twelve compactor trucks available for cleansing operations but only six of these were working at any given time. Of these six, one or two were usually out for repairs (iKapa had no mechanical workshop of its own), leaving four or five vehicles to service almost half a million people.[10] To make matters worse, roads in the African townships were in bad condition and refuse vehicles had to travel through closely quartered shacks on rutted, muddy streets, making it much more difficult and time-consuming to collect refuse. The figure of R5 per capita per year for refuse collection in Mbekweni—where over 50% of residents were living in shacks—does not take in account these additional challenges.

To use another example, in the former Cape Town City Council (CCC) there were over 16,000 employees for 1.1 million residents (CCC 1991, 4). Conservatively estimating that 60% of these human resources were allocated to the white suburbs meant that there was approximately one municipal employee for every 30 suburban residents. This compared to an estimate of one municipal employee for every 472 people in iKapa.[11]

Significantly, there was no call for metropolitan-wide audits of this sort at the time of local government negotiations or, for that matter, during the entire interim phase of local government from 1996–2000. The Demarcation Board did make broad estimates of the resources available within substructures but this aggregate accounting said nothing about the detailed depot-by-depot, suburb-by-township assessments of the distribution of resources and spending patterns that drove the day-to-day reality of service delivery, despite the widely anticipated "productivity gains" that would free up a "substantial amount of financial and human resources" for RDP efforts.

The lack of change during the interim period is illustrated by data collected in 2000, shortly before the formation of the Unicity and the second round of local government elections in December of that year (McDonald and Smith 2002). Although partial in terms of the range of services researched (water and solid waste management), the figures represent the only depot-level data available for that time period and illustrate in concrete terms what was widely being reported by township activists and municipal workers in more anecdotal form.[12]

Table 4.4 provides a breakdown of the personnel and equipment available for residential waste management in the CMA in mid-2000, four years after the first post-apartheid local government elections.[13] The figures refer to the number of people per piece of equipment and per municipal employee, with lower numbers indicating higher levels of resources per person. The 33 waste depots have been divided into those that predominantly

Table 4.4 Distribution of Waste Management Resources in the CMA by Depot (1999–2000)

Equipment	Suburbs	Townships
	(number of residents per piece of equipment)	
Containerized vehicles	12,315	27,445
Bakkies	30,684	47,906
Tractors	n/a	101,600
Compactor trucks	13,408	43,160
Front-end loaders	35,500	70,763
Grab trains	30,150	95,000
Long-wallers	30,750	n/a
LDVs	45,690	62,350
Mechanized sweepers	51,428	25,000
Water trucks	40,125	54,966
Refuse trucks	19,650	52,112
Trailers	37,500	140,000
Green machines	45,750	55,944
Push-carts	11,850	78,000
Wheelbarrows	10,312	43,562
Human resources	*(number of residents per employee)*	
Managers/supervisors	6833	24,847
Labourers	1027	1659
Administrators	22,014	67,820
Shift workers on-site	9012	13,888

service suburban areas (e.g. the Claremont depot) and those that service predominantly African and coloured township areas (e.g. the Langa and Bontheheuwel depots) and have been aggregated for the metropolitan area as a whole. The former represented approximately 800,000 residents and the latter some 1.7 million residents. It should be noted, though, that there was overlap in some of the areas serviced by the depots. As a result, the figures provided here should be seen as indicative of resource distribution and not an exact allocation. Nevertheless, they do illustrate considerable resource differentials along race/class lines.

Even more striking are the direct comparisons of particular depots. Table 4.5 provides a comparison of the waste depot in Durbanville (an upper-income and predominantly white suburb) with that of Khayelitsha (an extremely poor and predominantly African township). These two depots have been chosen for comparison in part because of their race/class divide but also because they were part of the same municipal substructure (Tygerberg) from 1996–2000 and demonstrate the limited transformation that took place during that period.

In every category the Khayelitsha depot has significantly lower levels of resources than that of Durbanville. Even in the area of capital expenditures the Durbanville depot received ten times more money on a per capita basis than Khayelitsha in fiscal year 1999–2000.

The same is true of water services. Table 4.6 provides a comparison of human, capital and financial resources available to the Durbanville and

Table 4.5 A Comparison of Resources in Waste Depots in Khayelitsha and Durbanville (1999–2000)

	Khayelitsha	*Durbanville*
Approximate population serviced	450,000	36,000
Operating expenses (rand per resident)	R57	R194
Capital expenses (rand per resident)	R0.56	R5.55
Value of office supplies and equipment in stock (rand per resident)	R0.01	R0.97
Value of materials and tools in stock (rand per resident)	R0.16	R0.55
Number of residents per piece of heavy equipment	18,750	2403
Number of residents per manager/supervisor	45,000	5150
Number of residents per labourer	3261	1288

Table 4.6 A Comparison of Resources in Water Depots in Khayelitsha and Durbanville (1999–2000)

	Khayelitsha depot	Durbanville depot
Approximate population serviced	450,000	45,000
Operating expenses in 1999–2000 (rand per resident)	R11.56	R86.67
Cumulative operating expenses from 1996–2000 (rand per resident)	R28.89	R177.78
Capital expenses in 1999–2000 (rand per resident)	R0.67	R100.00
Cumulative capital expenses from 1996–2000 (rand per resident)	R22.22	R122.22
Value of office supplies and equipment in stock (rand per resident)	R0.44	R1.78
Value of materials and tools in stock (rand per resident)	R0.17	R0.67
Number of residents per piece of heavy equipment	28,125	4500
Number of residents per manager/supervisor	56,250	9000
Number of residents per labourer	90,000	2368
Average monthly water consumption per person per month (in kl)	4.0	13.8

Khayelitsha water depots. In this case, data on cumulative operating and capital expenditures from 1996–2000 were also available and illustrate a strong bias in favour of Durbanville during that four-year period, with five times more being spent on a per capita basis in Durbanville than Khayelitsha on capital investments.

Once again, these data represented the first attempt to collect metropolitan-wide statistics on municipal resources in the CMA in the interim phase, despite legislation requiring such audits and despite repeated requests from organized labour in Cape Town for information on resource distribution in the city. That such data had not been collected almost five years after the first post-apartheid local government elections helps to illustrate the lack of commitment on the part of city politicians and bureaucrats to the transformation and redistribution of publicly owned resources. As the data show, the potential for creating a more equitable and efficient public sector with *existing* public resources was still considerable in 2000 and could have been used to help alleviate, or perhaps even eliminate, the assumed need to rely on private capital and cost recovery to expand service delivery in township areas.

THE FORMATION OF A UNICITY

The creation of a Unicity in Cape Town in December 2000 gave rise to a stronger, more coherent form of metropolitan government. Flowing out of the recommendations of the Green Paper on Local Government in 1997, and enshrined legislatively as a governance option in the Municipal Structures Act of 1998, the creation of a Unicity in Cape Town and five other metropolitan areas in the country was a direct result of concerns with the lack of redistribution that was taking place in urban areas and the recognition during the interim phase that "the mere existence of a metropolitan government did not guarantee the existence of a single city ... or a single tax base" (Wooldridge 2002, 131).

Substructures still exist and still have considerable control over service functions and decision making in Cape Town, but the Unicity model grants much more authority to the metro-level government. Despite this, there still have not been detailed, metropolitan-wide audits of municipal resources. The city's 2003 Restructuring Grant (CCT 2003a, Appendix 6A) admitted as much, three years into the Unicity's mandate, stating that "the reduction, rationalization and redeployment of excess staff and management following the amalgamation of the seven administrations has not been realized" (note here the document's concern with the "reduction" of "excess" staff rather than the "redeployment" of workers to parts of the city where they could be usefully employed). And, in an interview with a senior advisor to the Mayor of Cape Town in late 2004 I was informed that the city does "not have any aggregate figures on what the total capital investment needs of the city are. We do it sectorally but not on an aggregate basis" (personal interview, David Schmidt).

This is not to deny the fact that significant amounts of money have been spent in township areas since 1996, but when one compares the investments in townships versus suburbs and business nodes—as we will do in detail in Chapter 5—and when the actual distribution of existing municipal resources is examined, as it has been in this chapter, it becomes clear that the anticipated "peace dividend" of post-apartheid local government has not been remotely realized.

The fact that the ANC lost the 2000 local government elections in Cape Town to the Democratic Alliance (a merger of the New National Party and the Democratic Party of the time) did not help matters. Any potential plans on the part of the ANC to flex the new metropolitan muscles of the Unicity government were put on hold while the reactionary and fiscally conservative Democratic Alliance (DA) acted to protect suburban ratepayers from cross-subsidization efforts and began to implement an even more neoliberal vision of administration.

Floor-crossing legislation introduced by the ANC at a national level in 2002 changed this situation, with a sufficient number of New National Party (NNP) councillors crossing the chamber floor in Cape Town to join the ANC later that year, allowing the ANC to take control of city council once again. A subsequent merger of the NNP and the ANC at a national level served to formalize this coalition and the party held power for the rest of that term of office (losing control to the DA again in local government elections in March 2006).

This political gerrymandering left many with the impression that the ANC was more interested in securing power than in the difficult and controversial task of creating a more equitable distribution of municipal resources and spending in local government.

Despite its newfound metropolitan powers from 2002–2006 the ANC did little to enact a more significant redistribution of local government resources while in power in Cape Town, focusing instead on making the city more competitive in the global marketplace. As Watson (2002, 1) notes in her review of debates over urban restructuring in the city, the focus has moved from "an approach to planning aimed at urban integration and redistribution ... to a view of planning as integral to 'global positioning' and 'entrepreneurial' government". The only overall planning framework developed to date—the Metropolitan Spatial Development Framework (MSDF)—has been effectively shelved, with (progressive) urban planners having been marginalized in favour of financial advisors and engineers (Watson 2002, chapter eight), though the city continues to point to the need for better integrated spatial development policies (CCT 2006e, 25–31).

The continued influence of apartheid-era bureaucrats has also been a problem. Although most of the top management positions in council have changed since 1996, one need not scratch too deeply to find the same (white male) bureaucrats making decisions today that were enforcing apartheid legislation in the 1980s and/or resisting change to local government in the 1990s. In interviews with municipal managers in the mid-1990s I heard shockingly racist comments such as: "They [blacks] like to live that way" and "Trying to teach an African about the environment is like trying to teach a baboon". One manager suggested that the proper thing to do was to "sterilize the retarded ones ... [because] they can really breed, eh", while another said that "Hitler wasn't necessarily right, but he did have a point [about getting rid of certain elements of the population]" (see McDonald 1997).

Not all managers made racist comments at that time, however, with many going out of their way to reject the racial policies of the past. This was especially true of the most prominent senior managers interviewed, mirroring the trend in senior civil service circles at that time toward a more (neo)liberal approach to social and economic policy (Hendler 1991, 201).

Some of these racist managers have left the civil service since 1996 and some may have changed their attitudes toward black South Africans. Nevertheless, white males still dominate the upper ranks of decision making in city council, making up 162 of a total of 236 senior managers in the Unicity in 2003 (CCT 2003a, Appendix 4B02).

BOTH "WEAK" AND "STRONG"

In general, then, we see the emergence of a relatively "weak" local government in Cape Town in terms of its institutional capacity and political commitment to a redistributional framework but a relatively "strong" local government in terms of its dedication to a neoliberal agenda of supporting transnational capital and pushing for trickle-down development. On this ideological front we see an increasingly united position across all political parties and in the civil service. To the extent that there remain vestiges of Keynesian-style redistribution within policymaking circles in the city this commitment is far outweighed by a new, hegemonic vision of business-minded, outward-looking, fiscally conservative local government.

Backing up this neoliberal ideology is a vast array of technical skills. In the same way that apartheid bureaucrats were able to use their technical expertise and access to municipal resources to shape the negotiations of a post-apartheid dispensation, so too can these technical and resource strengths be turned now to implement and enforce neoliberal policies and institutions. Although there has been a significant downsizing of municipal employees from approximately 28,000 in 1996 to about 23,000 in 1996 (CCT 2006d, 100) there were still some 4000 technicians and professionals in 2003 providing the city with an array of managerial and scientific skills, a level of urban capacity that is impressive by any standard (CCT 2003a, Appendix 4B02).

Certain city departments have seen a significant downsizing and demoralization of their skills base since 1996—particularly urban planning—but the city's capacity to generate information, develop policy, implement planning strategies, collect taxes and police and punish those who disobey the rules is considerable. Arguably, the city's bureaucratic capacity is stronger than any other metropolitan area in South Africa and far outweighs that of local governments in other parts of the continent. The creation of a metropolitan-funded police force in 2001 (in addition to the national government–funded South African Police and countless private security firms in the city) adds an additional dimension to the city's enforcement ability.

Cape Town, along with other cities in the country, has also been spending lavishly on training its councillors and civil servants, with officials being sent to courses on everything from accounting to learning how to make the city more competitive internationally. The formation of the South African Local Government Association (Salga) and the South African Cities Network (SACN) has added additional networking resources, and there has been generous funding for local government capacity building from funders such as the World Bank, USAID, DFID and the United Nations Development Programme (UNDP).

There is also considerable research and policy support from national government agencies such as the Municipal Infrastructure Investment Unit (MIIU), the Human Sciences Research Council (HSRC), the Financial and

Fiscal Commission (FFC) and the Water Resources Council (WRC), to name but a few providing direct and indirect assistance to local government in the country. That most of this advice is neoliberal in its orientation only serves to strengthen the increasingly narrow set of skills being developed at the local level.

Far from being an impotent observer unable to effect change, then, the Cape Town bureaucracy and city council have emerged as powerful political actors, capable of developing, implementing and enforcing quite dramatic transformation. The fact that it is a smaller bureaucracy than 10 years ago should not obscure the fact that local government in Cape Town is much better equipped to govern (in terms of personnel, legislative authority and fiscal resources) than it has ever been.

So too is political party power becoming more concentrated. The DA and the ANC have emerged as the two dominant parties (though the Independent Democrats (DI), formed in 2004, managed to capture 11% of the vote in local elections in Cape Town in 2006). More importantly, the two parties are virtually indistinguishable in policy terms. The DA, as I will argue in Chapter 6, is more aggressively neoliberal than the ANC (and than the DI) but a close examination of the policy platforms of all three parties, and actual terms of office of the DA and the ANC, reveals little in the way of different philosophical positions.

The governance of Cape Town may be contested by more than one political party but there is little to distinguish these competing forces in ideological terms, with neoliberalism now the dominant (and truly hegemonic) post-apartheid political orientation of the city. The top-down, centralized cultures of the DA and, especially, the ANC have also meant that there is little dissent within the party ranks, with rebel voices being dealt with swiftly and aggressively when they criticize the party line.[14]

CONCLUSION

In the end, whatever momentum or commitment there may have been for a major redistribution of resources in the Cape Metropolitan Area in the early 1990s (and there was considerable commitment at that time amongst individuals and organizations in the ANC–alliance) is now an opportunity lost and will not recur without a dramatic shift in the institutional makeup and ideological character of the local state. These changes would also require massive policy and ideological changes at the national level, a slim prospect at this point in time.

What we see now in Cape Town is a post-apartheid local government that is fundamentally altered in terms of its geographic and political boundaries, and ideologically transformed from race-based welfarism to business-minded neoliberalism, but where spending and investment patterns in middle- and upper-income suburbs and business nodes have changed very little. What remains for the next chapter is a closer investigation of the fiscal implications of this neoliberalism at the national and local level and how, combined with an ideological commitment to making Cape Town a world city, this has resulted in a dramatic physical transformation of the city. Massive investments in the built environment geared toward elite consumption and business growth have altered the city's spatial configuration, but in ways that serve to entrench rather than alleviate the inequalities of the apartheid era, and that have created further impetus for the privatization of services and for aggressive cost recovery from the poor.

5 Respatializing Cape Town (II)
Investments in the Built Environment

Neoliberal austerity is conjuring up the ghosts of apartheid in familiar spatialized form.

Gillian Hart (2002, 248)

The previous chapter explored the institutional and geographic respatialization of Cape Town, looking at the deracialization and decentralization of local government. From this discussion we saw that local government in Cape Town (and throughout South Africa) is much more transparent, democratic and rational than it was under apartheid, with the potential to redistribute resources and wealth more equitably. However, the actual process of local government reform in Cape Town was such that wealthy ratepayer associations and local capital controlled much of the decision making and in doing so constructed physical and institutional boundaries that severely restricted the ability of the local state to implement the kind of redistributional agenda that had been originally envisioned by progressive elements of the ANC and other democratic movement organizations.

In the process, the ANC became caught up in a game of political and ideological compromise, which has further diminished its potential to better equalize services and investments in the city, effectively handicapping a more aggressive redistributive agenda. In this respect, local government in Cape Town is "weak": unable and/or unwilling to implement a stronger vision of urban equality.

But the local state in Cape Town is also "strong", capable of developing, implementing and enforcing a new neoliberal agenda of accumulation, limiting the redistribution of wealth and assets while at the same time rolling out massive investment projects for capital and transnational elites. This agenda requires a muscular and sophisticated—although streamlined in cost terms—local state. Engineers, software specialists, accountants, lawyers and front-line clerks all form part of a civil service that is impressive in both South African and 'developing country' terms, and is capable of managing a 'world city'.

In this chapter we go further to look at the *physical* respatialization of Cape Town—changes in the built environment since 1994—and how these public and private investments have shaped the major infrastructural features of the city: roads, railways, housing, offices, telecommunications and other basic services. This is not the only requirement for being a world city, but these infrastructures are an essential part of a new capital accumulation strategy.

My central argument here is that although the local and national state have made significant infrastructure investments in the townships of the city—having spent billions of rand on new low-income homes, water, electricity and other basic services since the first democratic local elections in 1996—these investments will not lift the majority of Capetonians out of poverty, let alone create equality. Thousands of people have seen some improvements in their daily living conditions, but the level and rate of investment in the townships is nowhere near what is required to deal effectively with homelessness and the poor quality of service delivery in low-income areas.

By contrast, much more public and private money is being spent on the suburbs and business nodes of the city, in strategic sectors and nodes aimed at improving the competitiveness of Cape Town in a global economy. As South African capital becomes increasingly globalized, demanding (and receiving) world-class infrastructure, township residents are left to get by on 'basic' services.

Here, then, is the strategic 'spatial fix' discussed in Chapter 2, with capital—or at least certain, internationally linked factions thereof—and elite policymakers driving a reinvestment strategy aimed at rejuvenating (urban) capital growth. Elite residential areas in the business cores, first-rate transportation and telecommunication infrastructure, world-class entertainment and convention facilities, and guaranteed access to cheap water and electricity are the hallmarks of this urban renewal strategy. For local and national neoliberal policymakers, investments to "optimize logistic pathways (transportation, ports and harbours, airports, etc)" are deemed essential to the "enhance[ment] of local business competitiveness" (SACN 2004, 167).

"Growth", as the business-friendly *Financial Mail* (October 29, 2004) noted in its review of major new infrastructure plans announced by the ANC in late 2004, "is at the heart of this [investment] strategy". National government has plans to increase public sector investment spending over the medium term in railways, ports, electricity and other core infrastructure, with expenditures on capital investments (at all levels of government) expected to grow by an average of 15.6% a year, from an estimated R73.54bn in 2004–05 to R113.54bn in 2007–08 (a total of 6.55% of GDP).

The Minister of Finance, Trevor Manuel, has said he would like to spend even more on infrastructure to boost economic growth but feels that he is "constrained" by an "alarming and unsustainable" growth in social grant spending, particularly for disability and foster grants (*Financial Mail*, October 29, 2004, 20), going so far as to blame the poor for limiting his investment options: "People must learn to work instead of living on handouts".[1]

Here we see the true neoliberal character of the ANC's infrastructure investment strategy. Rather than a redistribution of wealth or resources, government simply wants to build a bigger pie: a supply-side strategy of investing in the infrastructure needed for capital growth in the hopes that these benefits will trickle down to the urban poor in the form of job creation and an enlarged public sector budget. As the Centre for Development and Enterprise (an offshoot of the Urban Foundation) has argued: "While any local authority in the new dispensation must be concerned about redress [in the townships] this must not in any way lead to a deterioration in the quality of administration and services as they impact on wealthier neighbourhoods. While this balance cannot be justified on a moral basis [sic!], it is a practical imperative and an essential precondition for the investment and employment creation which will eventually benefit the poor much more than in the longer run than administratively-driven redistribution in the short run" (as quoted in Hart 2002, 236).

President Thabo Mbeki has made similar remarks: "Nationally we have spoken of two economies within one country. We have said that we need to do everything possible to ensure that the First Economy, which is developed and integrated into the world economy, grows, prospers and helps to address the task of achieving the objective of a better life for all" (speech to a Salga conference in September 2004, as published in the *Sunday Independent*, October 3, 2004).

Not surprisingly, the same trickle-down thinking has been adopted by the ANC in Cape Town, with former ANC Mayor Nomaindia Mfeketo commenting in her 2003–04 budget speech that, "The budget seeks to strike a balance between the massive development challenges of poor areas, especially the informal settlements, and the need to maintain our CBDs and the world-class infrastructure in established areas" (CCT 2003c, 1). In other words, investments and upgrades in the townships must not undermine international competitiveness in the suburbs and business nodes of the city.

It is not surprising that some observers see this development strategy as a form of Keynesianism. And in some respects they are right. Massive government-led investments in public works programs look like the Keynesianism of old, intended to kick start the economy. But, as a close review of these investments in Cape Town will illustrate, the bulk of government spending is going toward the 'haves', not the 'have-nots', with little evidence of trickle-down benefits.

Instead, we see the entrenchment of a physically segregated city with an increasing polarization of wealth and social services. Cape Town is typical of world cities in this regard: a highly networked urban core with world-class infrastructure and gated, elite residential areas, supported by a large pool of underemployed workers with 'basic', but not adequate, levels of services.

The first part of the chapter illustrates, in empirical terms, the skewed nature of these urban infrastructure investments in Cape Town and draws direct comparisons between the townships and the elite residential and commercial sections of the city. This is not an exhaustive review of infrastructure in Cape Town but it is an indicative summary of key sectors (housing, transportation, electricity, water and telecommunications).

The data presented here serve to illustrate the overwhelmingly unbalanced and uneven nature of public sector investments in elite residential and business areas of the city versus the townships. I have also included private sector investments in infrastructure in some of these examples because they help to illustrate the overall scale of unequal development in the city and because they represent a pool of resources that could potentially be tapped into with more progressive forms of taxation and cross-subsidization. That much of this private sector money is also being backed or matched by public sector funding, government-sponsored tax breaks and/or government-sponsored loans, serves to further illustrate the state's bias toward elite capital investments.

I close the chapter with a review of intergovernment fiscal transfers (from national to local government). After a decade of shrinking transfer payments, grants to local government have begun to increase, but it would appear to be a case of too little too late, with local authorities widely in agreement that they do not have the funding they need from national government to fulfill their service delivery mandates. A good case in point is the Municipal Infrastructure Grant. As generous at it seems at first blush, it will neither address the short-term infrastructure crises in the townships nor offer the sort of long-term operating and maintenance support that will be required to ensure the sustainability of these services in poverty-endemic areas.

This leads us to the catch-22 of infrastructure investments in low-income areas in Cape Town: even if the city were to have adequate capital resources to invest in higher levels of infrastructure in these areas it does not have the operating budget to support the delivery of anything more than the most basic, lifeline level of services, contributing to the downward spiral of unequal service delivery in the city and to the related neoliberal policies of cost recovery and privatization that serve to reinforce and legitimize inequalities in service standards. These are the knock-on effects of fiscal austerity, creating a self-reinforcing loop of neoliberal inequity.

EVIDENCE OF SKEWED INVESTMENT PATTERNS

I start the discussion with a review of the 'good news' and remind readers once again that the South African state—at all levels of government—has invested considerable resources in infrastructure upgrades and expansions in low-income urban and rural areas throughout the country. This is not a purely instrumental, capital accumulation strategy. As critical as basic infrastructure is to the reinvigoration of capital growth, it must be acknowledged that most senior policymakers in Cape Town and elsewhere in the country—particularly those from the ANC and other progressive parties—genuinely want to see service improvements in low-income areas for purely humanitarian reasons. Many of these politicians and civil servants dedicated their lives to the fight against apartheid and see basic services as a core commitment of this struggle.

So too has there been considerable effort put into providing basic services in Cape Town over the past decade. The city's annual budget is one indication of this scale of change. In 2004–05 the operating budget was R11.3bn and the capital budget R1.53bn (CCT 2004a). In 2005–06 the operating budget rose to R13.97bn and the capital budget to R3.8bn for a total all-time high of close to R18bn (note, however, that that year's budget was distorted by a large one-off grant from national government for a housing project—discussed below—and that the "true growth in the size of the operating budget" was only about 6.2%) (CCT 2005a, 15).

Over a three-year period (2004–07), then, the city will have spent R4.5bn on capital expenditures and R35.7bn on operating costs. This is, without a doubt, "a significant expenditure for a City of this magnitude" (CCT 2004a, 8). Planned expenditures were expected to raise these numbers further, with the ANC–led council "committed to spending approximately R8 billion on capital and R40.6 billion on the operating budgets" through to 2007–08 (CCT 2005a, 17). The DA–led council elected in March 2006 seems committed to these expenditure levels as well, with an overall budget of some R17.1bn in 2006–07 and capital expenditures of about R8bn through to 2008–09, though it would appear that carry-forwards on unspent capital funds may be distorting these figures somewhat (CCT 2006a,b).

Nevertheless, the sums are large. To put them in perspective, the 2005–06 budget translated to approximately US$3bn at exchange rates at the time, more than four times the budget for the entire country of Lesotho (at US$0.72bn for the same fiscal year), three times larger than the budget of Swaziland (at US$1bn) and even slightly larger than Tanzania's 2004–05 national budget of US$2.8bn for a population of more than 35 million people (as opposed to Cape Town's three million people) (GKS 2004; Mramba 2004; Thahane 2005, 19). In 'developing' country terms, then, Cape Town has a large and impressive resource base.

These figures are less impressive when compared to world cities in the north, of course. At US$49.7bn, New York City's 2006 budget is the biggest municipal budget in the world, and about five times larger than Cape Town's on a per capita basis. Perhaps a better comparison is the City of Toronto which, with about the same municipal population as Cape Town,

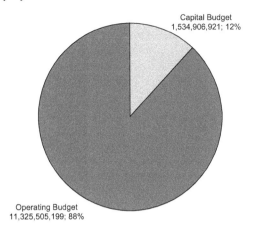

Figure 5.1 Total Budget for Cape Town in Rand (2004–5). Source: CCT 2004a, 17.

had a budget of approximately US$6.4bn in 2005–06 (of which about US$0.8bn was for capital expenditures).[2] Though still twice the per capita budget as Cape Town, the comparison shows that Cape Town is nonetheless a significant player in global municipal spending terms.

It is also useful to see how the city's budget breaks down by revenue and expenditures to get a sense of how the municipality sources its money and on which general categories it spends its money. Figures 5.1–5.4 provide pie charts of this budgeting using figures from 2004–05 (due to the fact that that year was more indicative of city revenue and spending patterns than the 2005–06 budget with its inflated grant figures).

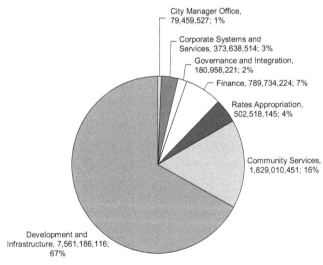

Figure 5.2 Operating Expenditures for Cape Town in Rand (2004–5). Source: CCT 2004a, 20.

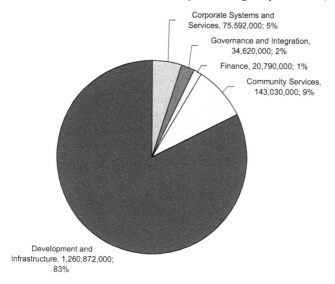

Figure 5.3 Capital Expenditures for Cape Town in Rand (2004–5). Source: CCT 2004a, 18.

Figure 5.1 illustrates the operating versus capital spending ratio. Figures 5.2 and 5.3 show how the lion's share of this spending went toward new and improved infrastructure (67% of operating costs (R7.59bn) and 83% of capital costs (R1.03bn)), making it by far the single most important feature of the city's budgeting.

On the revenue side, more than half of the city's income comes from "property rates" and "user charges" (57%), highlighting the sensitivity of the city's budget to local revenue sources and changes (Figure 5.4)—a point we will return to in our discussion of cost recovery in Chapter 7.

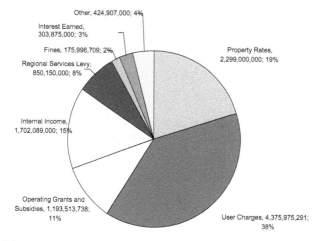

Figure 5.4 Revenue Sources for Operating Budget in Rand for Cape Town (2004–5). Source: CCT 2004a, 17.

Where has the city spent all this money? Some of it, as I have indicated, has been poured into improving and expanding infrastructure and services in townships and informal areas. It is not possible to list all of the poverty-related projects that the city has undertaken since 1996 but a few recent developments indicate both the scale and the scope of activity.

By far the biggest project to date is the R2.3bn, nationally funded, N2 Gateway project with plans to build up to 22 000 households along the N2 highway corridor in the township of Langa, leading into the city centre. How realistic these goals are given the housing delivery record of the city to date remains to be seen but the project does represent a major, integrated housing initiative designed to fit with a larger transportation plan for the metropolitan area.

In addition to the housing grant, R234m is being spent in other areas of the city with new low-income housing to upgrade roads and to provide recreation facilities and other basic amenities (CCT 2004a, 9; 2005b, s8). Plans include the "Uluntu Plaza/Dignified Places Programme", with the creation of new landscaped squares (with paved surfaces, trees, seating, lighting, and facilities for traders and local small businesses). The projects are located at structurally significant places, including public transport interchanges, community facilities, and places where there are large groups of traders and busy pedestrian routes.

Investment has also gone into the central business districts (CBDs) of numerous townships via the nationally funded Presidential Urban Renewal Programme. Some of the anchor projects here include the Mitchell's Plain CBD transport interchange and market and similar developments in the Khayelitsha CBD (with a planned long-term investment of R500m), with 34 projects having been completed in these two nodes by mid-2005 (CCT 2004b, 21; CCT 2005b, 16).

Basic services (water, sanitation, electricity, refuse removal) have also received considerable investment, with Cape Town being able to claim the best level of overall service provision in the country (with "basic" being defined as a water tap within 200m from household tap with no less than one tap for every 25 dwelling units, a toilet ratio of five dwellings per toilet (except for dry sanitation, which has a ratio of one dwelling per toilet), an electricity supply point for every dwelling unit, weekly door-to-door solid waste collection for formal households and informal households on Council land and communal "skip" refuse collection for informal households on private land) (CCT 2005b, 54).

This level of provision is largely a result of the legacy of apartheid-era investments in coloured townships (given the 'preferential' treatment of these areas by the National Party) and the fact that the largest African township in the city—Khayelitsha—is relatively new (built in the mid-1980s) with concomitantly new-ish bulk infrastructure. However, older African townships such as Langa and Guguletu have much older and poorer quality infrastructure and have proven to be much more expensive to maintain and upgrade.

In total, it is estimated that 96% of households in the city have access to at least basic levels of water, 91% have access to at least basic levels of sanitation, 99% have access to weekly refuse collection, and 89% have access to electricity (CCT 2005b, 53). The city has also expanded basic service level provision to all informal areas of the city with "Operation Do or Die", resulting in emergency basic services being provided to all accessible settlements, with water provided to 95% of settlements, sanitation to 91% of settlements, and refuse collection to 99% of settlements. "The great obstacle to achieving 100% [service coverage]", according to the city, "was obtaining the permission of the owners of private land to put in the services. Many were cooperative but some were not and it remains an on-going task" (CCT 2005a, 4).

STILL NOT ENOUGH

But as impressive as these aggregate figures are, they hide many of the quantitative and qualitative differences in infrastructure investments and service levels between the townships and the suburban/business areas of the city. In fact, a closer look at the city's capital budgets over the years reveal an actual decline in capital spending, despite the growing backlog in housing and other basic needs.

In 2003, for example, it was estimated that the cost of "upgrading" informal settlements in the city was R1.25 billion over a five-year period (2003–08) (although the specifics of what constituted "upgrading" were not provided). The city announced its intention to spend R645 million of its own funds to pay for the upgrading, with R227 million more coming from external sources. But even the city admitted this was not enough, declaring that, "without further support from national government, the envisaged five-year programme will take considerably longer" (CCT 2003a, Appendix 2A).

In 2004, the city announced a much more ambitious program to spend R4.5bn on capital investments from 2004–07, yet immediately qualified this by saying that even this amount was "inadequate if we are to address all our challenges in the short to medium term" (CCT 2004a, 8). There were also concerns that the city was engaged in the practice of "asset stripping", putting off needed maintenance work to use funds for new infrastructure and/or other operating expenses, with only 15% of the capital budget going toward "maintenance" (CCT 2004a, 8, 19).

In 2005, even with the large injection of capital funding from national government for the N2 Gateway housing project, city council still felt obliged to note that, "While there have been significant investments and successes in the past decade, these have not succeeded in fundamentally shifting Cape Town's development path" (CCT 2005b, 14).

We must also keep in mind that recent increases in capital spending in the city have come after years of shrinking capital budgets, at least since 2000 (it is difficult to determine overall capital expenditures before that time due to the fragmented nature of record keeping during the "interim" phase of local government). In total, the Cape Town capital budget decreased by 27.2% in nominal terms and more than 40% in inflation-adjusted terms from 2000–01 to 2004–05, and is only projected to be at 2000–01 levels again by 2006–07 (see Table 5.1). The blip in 2005–06 spending is due to the one-off N2 Gateway housing project.

Over this eight-year period, therefore, the city's capital budget will have dropped by approximately 35% in inflation-adjusted terms, and this in a city where service needs are expanding every day with in-migration and population growth. On an aggregate level, then, the city is spending far less on basic service infrastructure than is required to address poverty.

Making matters worse is the fact that the city is not spending its entire capital budget. In 2003–04, the city spent only 60% of its capital funds (*Cape Times*, July 8, 2005) and there have been underspending problems every other year since 2000. This is due in part to capacity problems on the delivery side—exacerbated by political squabbles over resource allocation—and partly due to bad planning. Whatever the reasons, the end result is that the city has not spent nearly as much money as it needs to improve people's lives in the townships.

How much should the city be spending? This is a difficult question. As a former City Manager commented to me in an interview, "How long is a piece of string?" (personal interview, Wallace Mgoqi). The answer, of course, depends on one's definition of an adequate level of service delivery, how fast the city is growing, and what the potential is for a redistribution of resources from other, wealthier parts of the municipality. But as we saw

Table 5.1 Capital Budget Expenditures by the City of Cape Town (2000–2008)

Year	Capital budget
2000–01	R2.106bn
2001–02	R2.221bn
2002–03	R1.913bn
2003–04	R1.785bn
2004–05	R1.534bn
2005–06	R3.806bn
2006–07	R2.077bn (projected)
2007–08	R2.118bn (projected)

Sources: CCT 2003a, Executive Summary; CCT 2005a, 52; CCT 2005b, 42.

in Chapter 4, the city has never compiled an estimate of its total infra-structure needs or where resource reallocation could come from, making it impossible to estimate the length of this particular piece of string.

We can, however, look at a handful of key service and infrastructure sectors to get a better sense of the quantitative and qualitative levels of provision in Cape Town and how they compare among townships and the suburbs/business districts of the city.

I will start with housing and related commercial buildings. Given that housing is the single most important infrastructural gap in the city, and that business office space and elite residential areas play such an important role in the new accumulation strategies of capital, a comparison of these investment areas is particularly revealing.

INVESTMENTS IN HOUSING AND COMMERCIAL BUILDINGS

There are approximately 3.1 million people and 875,000 households in the city of Cape Town (CCT 2006e, 44). It is estimated that about 48,000 people arrive in the city each year from other parts of the country—and to a lesser extent from other parts of the continent and world—requiring between 14,000 and 18,000 new homes a year (CCT 2004b, 78; CCT 2005b, 11). Not all of this growth is due to in-migration, however. Some is due to population growth within the city and some is due to households splitting into smaller units to take advantage of the availability of subsi-dized housing and/or new spaces for informal housing structures.

Of these 875,000 households approximately 655,000 are "formal" homes, with the housing backlog in the city in 2004 estimated to be around 260,000 units. Of these, there were an estimated 96,200 "shacks" in some 70 informal settlements, 28,600 shacks on serviced sites, 75,400 shacks in backyards and some 59,800 households that were considered "over-crowded" (CCT 2006d, 12). In late 2006 these housing backlog estimates were raised dramatically to more than 350,000 units—more than a third of the city's population (*Cape Argus*, November 7, 2006). To put this growth in perspective, there were approximately 150,000 informal housing units in 1998.

Whether this growing housing backlog is an "imminent urban time bomb", as provincial MEC for Local Government and Housing Marius Fransman once put it (*Cape Times*, October 5, 2004) is a matter of debate, but the magnitude of the problem makes it Cape Town's largest infrastruc-ture challenge. The growing backlogs also create a situation that is akin to "running to stand still", with massive housing efforts required simply to maintain the current housing backlog, with the city admitting that "there is little chance of formalising these [informal] settlements in the near future" (CCT 2005b, 9).

In this regard, the housing challenge in Cape Town must be seen in the larger national context. As unemployment and diminishing opportunities in smaller towns and rural areas drive people to the larger urban centres urbanization rates have increased throughout the country. In 1996, census figures showed that 53.7% of the South Africa's population was urbanized; by 2001 it was 57.5% and this is expected to keep rising.

There has also been a decline in the average number of people per household, from 4.5 in the 1996 census to 3.8 in the 2001 census, with the total number of households across the country increasing by 23.7% during that period from 9.1 million to 11.2 million. Thus the South African government finds itself having to provide many more houses than originally anticipated in the 1990s, and this is true of Cape Town as well.

Funding for housing comes from national government but local governments are responsible for actual housing development. Here is the first major bottleneck to improved infrastructure for the poor: although national government provided 1.6 million "housing opportunities" from 1994 to 2004, helping to house some nine million people, and allowed 500,000 families to secure titles on old publicly-owned housing, there is still an estimated backlog of 2.4 million homes nationally, for about eight million people. Much of this is due to the fact that insufficient funding has been allocated to housing projects by national government, with "deep cuts in the housing budget in the late 1990s, during the GEAR era, which have still not been overcome" (Cosatu 2004).

Originally the expectation was that housing would constitute 5% of the national budget, but even with increases since 2001 this has only averaged about 1.4% (with only R4.5bn being allocated to housing subsidies by national government in 2004–05) (RSA 2004a,b). As a result, plans to build 350,000 housing units per annum in the country have floundered, averaging fewer than 200,000 housing "opportunities" a year.

What is being done to address the housing problem in Cape Town? Statistics vary but the following figures are indicative of the incredibly slow pace of low-income housing delivery. The 2004 Integrated Development Plan (IDP) states that 11,000 "housing opportunities" are being created each year (CCT 2004b, 9) but the City Manager stated a figure of 8000 per year in my interview with him in December of that year.

In total, it is estimated that the city has created some 50,000 "assisted household opportunities" since 1995 (CCT 2004b, 79). Notably, most of these "opportunities" consist only of "serviced sites", housing upgrades and subsidies to secure existing public housing stock rather than actual new homes. Of the 4000 "housing opportunities" created in 2003–04 only 342 were actually new homes (speech by David Schmidt, senior advisor to the Mayor, Elsies River Town Hall meeting, November 22, 2004).

At this rate, the city cannot even address the annual *growth* in housing backlogs, let alone meet the overall housing backlog. The N2 Gateway project will go some way to addressing this shortage but even this megaproject is moving very slowly (with only 750 homes built by February 2006 and none of them occupied (*BuaNews*, February 17, 2006). See Figure 5.5 for an aerial photograph of this project in 2006, with the N2 highway on the right side of the picture)). And with a construction boom in other (wealthier) parts of Cape Town driving up building costs and making access to building materials and equipment difficult it will be even harder for the city to address its housing problem with its existing budget allocations.

The city is aware of these problems and council has set itself a "medium-term" goal of "ensuring that less than 5% of the city's population lives in

Figure 5.5 N2 Gateway Housing Project, Cape Town. Photo: Courtesy of City of Cape Town.

informal settlements" (CCT 2004b, 19) and with plans to "gear up capacity for the delivery of 8000 to 20,000 housing opportunities per annum (CCT 2006d, 59). There are also plans to develop high-density, mixed-income housing along different transportation corridors to reduce per-unit build-ing costs, improve transport networks and to create what Acting Head of Housing for the Western Cape province Laurie Platzky once referred to as "vibey places that are safe at night" (*Cape Times*, October 5, 2004). But without the funding and capacity to build these homes these objectives will remain pipe dreams.

Private banks also a play part here, effectively redlining low-income areas in terms of the provision of housing loans. Only recently has national government taken the banks to task on this, applying pressure to create loan opportunities when the Department of Housing released its "Breaking New Ground" policy paper in September 2004 (RSA 2004b). Critics have argued that these initiatives represent too little, too late, with Cosatu and the SACP accusing banks of using black economic empowerment (BEE) initiatives as proxy for contributions to "development", diverting attention away from the fact they are not investing in the riskier home loan market for low-income families (*Sunday Independent*, October 10, 2004). The fact that these banks have been making enormous profits from the housing boom in upper-income suburban areas further demonstrates their biased role in housing finance.

But it is not just the lack of housing that is at issue here. The low-income homes that have been built are generally of poor quality and in poor loca-tions. As Cosatu (2004) notes, "much of the new [low-income] housing in the country is far from city centres and employment opportunities, small in size and sometimes poor in quality". Even the Cape Town city council admits that "low income housing continues to be located on cheap land far from economic activity" (CCT 2004b, 11) and that "urban growth since 1994 has tended to reinforce apartheid spatial patterns with its skewed distribution of opportunities (CCT 2006d, Annexure E, 6).

Despite stated desires by planners and policymakers for more compact cities (CCT 2006e, 25–31), all urban areas in the country have witnessed this peripheral de-densification of housing. The South African Cities Net-work (SACN 2004, 129, 133) goes so far as to say that "South African cities are less integrated today than they were 10 years ago", putting the blame on the developer-driven housing approach since 1994, which has "in some instances ... ended up reinforcing" the spatial patterns of apartheid rather than eliminating them.[3]

These are enormously unappealing locations aesthetically as well. Defined by highways, railway tracks, industrial zones, sewage treatment plants, refuse dumps and the like, the vast majority of new housing devel-opments in Cape Town are on the Cape Flats, a low-lying sandy area prone to stifling heat in the summer and cold and floods in the winter, with the highest incidence of tuberculosis in the country. Even the new flagship N2

Gateway project is built downwind from a sewage treatment plant and a waste transfer station and beside the busiest highway in the city.

National government has said it will push its housing densification strategy harder, promoting "mixed-income" housing developments. But no sooner was this September 2004 housing strategy paper released than irate suburban homeowners and estate agents in the country complained about the potential for such a strategy to bring down the value of suburban homes. DA housing spokesman Butch Steyn caught the mood of his constituents, arguing: "One cannot have a Reconstruction and Development Programme (RDP) scheme right next door to a R3 million home.... People move in different social spheres and it won't work. But putting a R70,000 home near one worth about R400,000 could work" (*Sapa*, September 5, 2004).

Government officials retreated the next day, with the Minister of Housing at the time stating that government has no intention to build a "low-cost house on the doorstep of a R3-million house.... There is no reason for the [housing] department to negatively affect the high-income market. The high- and low-income markets need each other to survive." Another Housing Ministry spokesperson said that no "right-thinking government would build low-cost homes next to those costing millions.... South Africa is not a 'banana republic'" (*Sapa*, September 6, 2004).

Whether mixed-income, densification plans in Cape Town can move forward in the face of this kind of pressure from suburban ratepayers and suburban developers remains to be seen, but experience thus far in the city shows that there is little political will and few resources to bring low-income housing closer to the CBD or to the more physically attractive and environmentally healthier parts of the city.

The situation in middle- and upper-income areas of the city, by contrast, could not be more different. There has been a dramatic construction boom in the city centre and suburbs since the mid-1990s, with more than R8bn worth of building plans being approved in 2004 alone, up from R5.5bn in 2003 and R4bn in 2000. The city hired 45 people in 2004 just to fast-track these building applications and the ANC Mayor at the time made the reduction of building plan approval time a priority in her budget speech. Addressing the South African Property Owners' Association of Cape Town later that year, Mfeketo said that the building boom was exciting news for the economy of the city and that she was "committed to making it even better" (*Cape Times*, October 14, 2004).

According to City Planning Director Japie Hugo, building plans were being submitted at the rate of "one plan every three minutes of every working day" and building in the city was taking place at such a frenetic pace that the city was running out of building supplies such as bricks, cement and cranes in 2004 and 2005. Hugo also noted that these investment figures considerably underestimate the actual value of new building development because builders tend to submit lower values to reduce the building

Table 5.2 Value of Building Permits Approved in Cape Town (2000–2004)

Approval Year	Value (rand)	Type
2000	1,098,098,116	Commercial
2000	3,145,396,400	Noncommercial
2001	1,097,032,996	Commercial
2001	3,359,397,930	Noncommercial
2002	1,148,021,659	Commercial
2002	4,002,031,253	Noncommercial
2003	1,047,852,124	Commercial
2003	4,426,407,398	Noncommercial
2004	1,868,054,777	Commercial
2004	6,464,229,924	Noncommercial
TOTAL	27,656,522,578	

Source: Personal interview, Japie Hugo.

fees they have to pay to the city, which are a portion of total costs (personal interview, Japie Hugo).

Not all of this growth is in housing, but 78% of the building plans in 2004 were for noncommercial developments, a 105% increase since 2000 (see Table 5.2). These investments include everything from renovations to new apartment towers. Condominium developments in the Waterfront and flat conversions in old office and warehouse buildings in the CBD have been particularly popular. One example of the latter is the Mandela Rhodes Place (the name itself a telling indication of the post-apartheid political compromise), a collection of five buildings in the CBD that have been converted to 163 residential lofts selling for R2.5–5m each, 80% of which sold within four months of going on sale (*Cape Times*, November 11, 2004). There have also been expansive developments of new, gated communities in the northern suburbs and new housing growth in virtually every suburb in the city where there is still vacant land.

Some of this elite residential development has been subsidized by the state. In October 2004, the National Treasury announced a tax break designed to stimulate the refurbishment of dilapidated buildings in older CBDs in the country and, more generally, to promote private sector investment in run-down parts of city cores. Parts of the "east city" in Cape Town are being developed under this subsidy plan and other efforts are being made to attract "young professionals" to the urban core.

At a Cape Town Partnership conference entitled "East City Investment and Development" in late 2004, the ANC Mayor at the time stated that "housing for ordinary people, especially the youth should be a priority. What if we build, say, 300 apartments [in the city centre] with a starting price of about R350,000—the kind of housing that young professionals can afford.... Is it not possible, should the city provide the land on a 99-year lease at a nominal charge, for us to talk of social capital?... [This is] the kind of housing that offers a real choice for our young people who otherwise end up living with parents or on the outskirts of the city.... [This is] a definition of 'world class' which includes the ordinary needs of life" (*Cape Times*, October 14, 2004).

Ordinary indeed. Meanwhile, a third of the city's population are living below the poverty line in shacks and are expected to enter the housing market with a one-off housing grant of about R20,000 that will, at best, get them a tiny house on the periphery of the city. So much for integration.

The building boom in the suburbs and city centre has also meant that housing prices in these areas have skyrocketed, with suburban house prices across the country jumping by an average of 30% in 2004 (as compared to a 2.2% appreciation in equity prices and a 9.3% rise in the All Bond Index over the same period). In Cape Town the jumps were even more dramatic, with average nominal house prices more than doubling from about R410,000 in 2002 to about R820,000 in 2005 (a figure that takes into account township homes) (SACN 2006, 34).

The reasons for these price rises are various: increased demand from an emerging black middle class (although this has not been a major factor in Cape Town, as we shall see in Chapter 10), foreign interest in coastal resort areas (which *has* been a major factor in Cape Town), and a switch by small-scale investors from other asset classes to real estate. Not surprisingly, private banks have been happy to finance this particular investment surge.

Housing prices in the townships, on the other hand, have actually decreased on average by about 0.5% since 1994. Some middle-income coloured townships in Cape Town have seen modest value increases but for the most part the price surge has been restricted to the formerly white suburbs.

This appreciation in the value of residential properties has also created significant gentrification pressures. Observatory, Woodstock, Kalk Bay and Muizenburg—to name a few formerly working-class residential areas experiencing significant gentrification pressures—are seeing rapid changes in demographics and housing prices.[4] So too are parts of the CBD. Long Street is witnessing the disappearance of small, owner-run shops and long-time residents to make way for upmarket stores, restaurants and tourist accommodation. The Bo-Kaap, a particularly important historic part of the central city settled by freed slaves in the early 1800s and long one of the most vibrant and culturally distinct parts of Cape Town, has been experiencing this gentrification pressure as well, with residents selling homes to take advantage of high prices and/or because they cannot afford the new, market-value rates increases. Alex Borraine, the Chief Executive Officer of the Cape Town Partnership—the public-private venture responsible for driving much of this inner-city revitalization—ironically laments this change in the Bo-Kaap, saying that it is "taking away some of the colour and character of the city" (Anon. 2004, 4).

Having said this, the largest gentrification pressures in Cape Town actually took place during the apartheid period. As Western (1996, Chapter 7) outlines in detail in his important review of Cape Town during that time, forced removals of coloured, African and Asian residents from the central suburbs in the 1960s, '70s and '80s created enormous opportunities for estate agents and developers to scoop up properties at cheap prices, renovate them as "Chelsea cottages" and sell them at enormously inflated prices (with price increases as high as 120% and averaging 25% in the 1960s and early 1970s). Some of the most expensive areas of the city currently—Constantia, Claremont and Rondebosch for example—all experienced these forced gentrification pressures and have seen their values increase substantially further since.

In this respect, contemporary neoliberalism in Cape Town is benefiting from the dirty work of apartheid. What Smith (1996, 26–27) has coined the "revanchist" city, whereby "[g]entrification portends a class conquest of the city ... [with] the new urban pioneers seeking to scrub the city clean of its working-class geography and history", largely took place in South Africa during apartheid. The gentrification tensions being experienced today in New York, London, Toronto, Tokyo and virtually every other world city (Sassen 2001, chapter nine) are eerily reminiscent of the political, social and economic tensions of forced removals under apartheid, sometimes leading to violent confrontations between low-income residents and developers or police in those cities.

That Cape Town went through its most revanchist period under apartheid is another of the city's 'competitive advantages' in terms of attracting a transnational elite. Property developers and estate agents are not faced with the sometimes ugly task of pressuring low-income residents out of frontier neighbourhoods in the way that they are in cities in the north. There is little need for yuppies to rub shoulders with the working class and the unemployed in fringe neighbourhoods (though places like Woodstock and Salt River still experience these dynamics). 'Unwanted' groups were largely moved long ago by the Group Areas Act.

The fact that many Capetonians have forgotten that their property wealth was created by forced removals is also a point worth making, as Pape (2002) has demonstrated in his perceptive account of selective memory in the ultra-wealthy suburb of Constantia. So too are foreign buyers largely ignorant to the history of the suburbs that they buy into, with estate agents choosing to disregard the sordid history of racial exclusion and forced removals when selling prime property.

Finally, there is the Victoria & Albert (V&A) Waterfront development. Located on gated, reclaimed land around the working port of the city, the Waterfront is a mix of commercial and up-market residential property that has exceeded all investment expectations since breaking ground in the late 1980s, with a seemingly insatiable appetite for growth and with more land-fill being added to expand the site.

Begun under the apartheid regime, the V&A Waterfront had seen some R1.428b in investments as of late 2005, with nearly R900m of this coming from state-owned Transnet and its pension fund. A further R1.6b has been budgeted for projects over the next five years (van Zyl 2005), though the purchase of the property in late 2006 by deep-pocketed investors from Dubai will likely push these figures even higher.

Located near the CBD, the Waterfront is like any other waterfront development in the world: brand-name shops, glass-filled hotels and condominiums with themed post-modern architecture. Linked to the CBD by a canal and a massive convention centre (completed in 2003 with "more than R500 million" in public funds being spent on its development (CCT 2005b, 38)), the Waterfront adds to the contiguous set of privileged spaces in an agglomerated urban core.

Former ANC Minister of Environmental Affairs and Development Planning for the province of the Western Cape, Tasneen Essop, noticed this spatial dynamic emerging as well and has worried aloud about whether the city is creating a "playground for the rich" (as quoted in McKenzie 2004, 30). City planners are aware of the problem also, noting in the 2005 Integrated Development Plan that "the CBD's recent development history shows patterns of consolidating segregation. Over the past two decades ... there has been little investment for the benefit of ordinary citizens in the Cape Town CBD" (CCT 2005b, 38). The best the city can do to "break down this exclusivity", it would seem, is to increase access for "ordinary people" in institutions such as museums, squares and churches (CCT 2005b, 38).

Plans are in place to create inner-city accommodation for low-income households, but little has happened on this front since 1996. The redevelopment of District Six, with its 40 acres of prime land just south of the CBD, is the only concrete development to date, but has been very slow. After 10 years of working on the project, and widespread political support for reinstating people in the neighbourhood from which they were evicted in the 1960s and 1970s, only nine houses (out of a planned 4000) had been built in the area by early 2005.

We can conclude, then, from this brief review of housing and commercial building investment patterns in the city, that market-driven development strategies combined with neoliberal constraints on public spending have served to reinforce apartheid-era residential segregation, encouraging and protecting massive investments in the suburbs and CBDs while forcing low-income families to live in poor quality housing on the outskirts of the city and/or its busy highway corridors. The future, it seems, is one of increased exclusivity and segregation in Cape Town.

WATER AND SANITATION

The next area of infrastructure investment we look at is water and sanitation. In a relatively "water scarce" region of the country, capital investments in this sector make for an interesting comparison of spending priorities. Given water's importance to both the productive and consumptive side of the economy, it plays a critical part of any city's attempts to attract both business and residents.

We saw in the previous chapter the vast differences that have existed in water and sanitation investments at the depot level in Cape Town in terms of capital and operating expenditures. Here we look more closely at the city's claim that it has provided water and sanitation to virtually all of the city's residents.

While it is true that most Capetonians have some form of access to safe, potable water and sanitation it is also true that only 69% of residents had water inside their dwelling as of the 2001 national census, down from 79% in 1996 (SACN 2004, 187). This decrease was due in part to population growth and the splitting of households—the aforementioned problem of "running to stand still"—but it also indicates the woefully inadequate levels of funding being applied to water and sanitation in low-income areas.

In-dwelling services have improved since the 2001 census (with approximately 83% of households having in-house services in 2004), but there are still some 45,000 households without access to water on site (SACN 2006, 3–36). The latter depend on communal taps, which are expected to be within 200m of a household in order to satisfy the nationally established criteria of "basic" services, with no more than 25 housing units per tap, but this is not always the case, forcing tens of thousands of low-income households to carry water long distances and after dark.

With regards to sanitation, over 95,000 Cape Town households were using pit latrines "or less" in 2001 (SACN 2006, 3–38). While this had been reduced considerably by 2004 to fewer than 10,000 households, many pit latrines are being shared by more than the required maximum of five dwellings. The same is true of many in-house flush toilets, with some hostel dwellings still having as many as 15 families sharing a single washroom. As in other parts of the country, these communal facilities are "associated with the worst humiliations of abject living conditions" (Beall et al. 2002, 157)—a sad perpetuation of the kind of sanitation conditions described by Ramphele (1993) in her review of hostel accommodations in Cape Town during the 1980s. And there are still some 45,000 households in the city without access to even this "basic" level of sanitation (CCT 2006d, 43).

But perhaps the single most damning indictment of ongoing inequity in water and sanitation services in Cape Town is the continued existence of "bucket toilets"—plastic pails used in informal settlements, situated in the back of shacks or in informal latrines, and collected by municipal workers.

The bucket system is the most unpleasant and demeaning form of municipal sanitation of all—both for those forced to use it and for those who must collect the buckets for disposal. And yet there were still some 1800 households forced to use buckets in Cape Town as of January 2006, servicing several thousand people (CCT 2006d, Annexure D).

Part of the problem, once again, is a lack of adequate investment. In 2004, for example, the city had a capital budget of R257.8m for water services but reported that this was "insufficient for expansion ... delay[ing] development in key areas of the City". The blame was laid on "insufficient national funding", forcing the city to revise its entire Water Services Development Plan due to "major reduction in capital and operating budgets" (CCT 2004b, 77–78).

Just how much money is needed for water and sanitation in the city? There are no city-wide estimates but the provincial government estimated in 2004 that there was at least R2bn of "urgent" work required in sewage treatment facilities alone in the province, suggesting that Cape Town's immediate requirements for all water and sanitation services are significantly larger than the R257m allocated to it in 2004 (*Cape Times*, October 13, 2004), made worse by the previously noted concerns about "asset stripping".

The suburbs and commercial areas of the city, by contrast, have 'world-class' water and sanitation services, with much of the infrastructure having been carved out of the mountainside, making for extremely expensive operating and maintenance costs. In these areas of the city there is 100% in-dwelling water and sanitation coverage, with most suburban homes having more than one flush toilet.

There is also enormous water consumption in the suburbs, with high-end households consuming as much as 50kl of water per month (or 415 litres per person per day for a household of four), twice the city average and more than eight times that used by a typical township household (Anderson 2004, 7). Suburban households consume almost half of the city's water, with 35% going into the watering of gardens (as reported in the *Cape Times*, September 30, 2004).

Swimming pools are another example of skewed consumption patterns. With an estimated 68,000 pools in the city (virtually all of which are in the suburbs), each using 50,000 litres of water a year on average, these pools consume as much water as about 47,000 low-income households per year.[5]

Golf courses are also massive water consumers, averaging between one and three million litres per day. If we assume, conservatively, that the average golf course uses 1.2m litres of water a day (some use twice this much), and multiply this by the 82 golf courses in the Western Cape (at least 10 of which are located within the city boundaries and many of which are within the city's broader watershed), golf courses in the province consume the equivalent supply of close to 500,000 low-income households per year.

To make matters worse, golf courses are regularly exempted from water restrictions (e.g. during the drought of 2004), despite fairly stringent cutbacks in other parts of the city and the continued disconnection and restriction of water services in low-income households unable to pay their water bills.

But rather than addressing these massive inequities in consumption and investment the city has opted to build a new dam (having convinced the Department of Water Affairs that it had done all it could to manage water demand in the suburbs). The Berg Water scheme will be the largest concrete-faced rock fill dam in South Africa (60m high) with a storage capacity of 130 million kilolitres, boosting Cape Town's water capacity by 18% beginning in 2007. The Trans Caledon Tunnel Authority (TCTA), a "state-owned specialized liability management body" for bulk water supply development set up to manage the project in 2004, received R1.5bn in long-term funding from private banks from South Africa and Europe and the state-owned Development Bank of Southern Africa, to be repaid from revenue from water sales. Interestingly, the TCTA is described as a "unique public-public partnership", "providing financing for bulk infrastructure with the private sector, off government's balance sheet without any government guarantees, financed solely on the strength of the projected cash flows" (*Business Report*, September 23, 2004).

ELECTRICITY

Similar patterns of skewed investment can be seen in the electricity sector in Cape Town. Despite claims by the city's "Energy Strategy" unit that "relatively few urban dwellings are currently without electricity" (CCT 2003b, 6) the 2001 census showed that more than 85,000 households did not have access to electricity (up from just under 83,000 in 1996), with about 12% of city households not having access to the electricity grid (SACN 2004, 187).

This is considered "relatively good" compared to other cities in the country, with Cape Town's unserviced population being about half that of the national urban average, but it still indicates a massive underinvestment problem when one considers the number of new households being created in the city each year. Records show that only about 8000 new connections were being installed per annum in low-cost and informal housing areas of the city from 1991–2006. These investments peaked at about 13,000 connections in 2002–03 (the only year there was a major investment in "informal settlements") and then dropped off again dramatically to 6000 connections in 2004–05 (RED 2006, 30). How the city (in collaboration with the Regional Electricity Distributor) will manage to connect about 30,000 low-income and informal households to the grid each year from

2006–09 as they say they will (RED 2006, 31), without a massive injection of new capital, remains to be seen.

Moreover, the quality of services for those who are connected to the grid is not always good. Many household connections in the townships and informal settlements are dangerously flimsy, with a dozen or more households connected to a single service pole, with wires regularly being blown down in strong winds, creating spot blackouts and leaving dangerous live wires in flood-prone areas. There are no official statistics on these qualitative aspects of electricity provision, but a drive through any informal settlement or older township in the city reveals an endless entanglement of wires a few feet above makeshift roofs of shacks and old, dilapidated council housing (see Figure 5.6).

For those households that do not have electricity—or cannot afford to consume as much electricity as they would like—paraffin, candles and wood make up the bulk of the energy source (making up about 85% of energy consumption in low-income areas of Cape Town) (CCT 2003b, 6). Every year thousands of children across the country are poisoned by accidentally consuming paraffin (Malangu 2005) and more than "40,000 households are affected by paraffin-related fires each year", causing more than R1.3bn worth of property loss and as many as 1100 child deaths a year (Jiji 2005, de Swardt et al. 2005).

Cape Town is no different in this respect, with shack fires destroying hundreds of households at a time on a regular basis, such as the fire

Figure 5.6 Electricity Connections in an Informal Settlement in Cape Town. Photo: Courtesy of the City of Cape Town.

that destroyed at least 1000 shacks in December 2004 near Stellenbosch. Miraculously, no one was killed in that fire but seven people were killed in other shack fires that same weekend (*Cape Times*, December 13, 2004) with close to 4500 shacks being damaged or destroyed that year in Cape Town—a more than two-fold increase since 2001 (CCT 2006d, 336).

But it is not just fire and kerosene poisoning that cause problems. Respiratory illnesses from inhaling paraffin fumes and smoke from biomass is also a major health concern in the city, with the Medical Research Council noting in a report that about half of all South African households are exposed to indoor air pollution from the use of cooking and lighting fuels, contributing to elevated levels of acute respiratory infections (*Cape Times*, December 9, 2004).

Once again, the contrast with the suburbs is stark. Universal electricity provision with well-maintained electricity lines and trees regularly trimmed back from wires are the norm, part of what former ANC Councillor Saleem Mowzer proudly pointed to as an illustration of Cape Town's status as a "world-class African city" in his Foreword to the council's energy strategy document (CCT 2003b, 2). Now Chief Executive Officer of the city's recently established Regional Electricity Distributor (RED), Mowzer's "vision" of the RED is one that will lead the city on a "journey towards the provision of world-class consolidated electricity distribution and related services" (RED 2006, 13).

Supply problems in Cape Town in late 2005 and early 2006 raised concerns about the ability of Eskom (the state-owned electricity generator that provides Cape Town with its bulk electricity supplies) to provide reliable services—with rolling blackouts and brownouts to suburbs and townships alike—but Eskom has committed to building two gas turbine power stations in nearby Atlantis and Mossel Bay by July 2007 at a cost of R3.5 billion and to strengthen the supply capacity at the nearby Koeberg Nuclear Power Station to ensure regular service provision (*Mail & Guardian*, December 23, 2005).

Unlike water, however, the bulk of electricity is consumed by industry, with households using only 15% of the city's 10,200GWh a year (CCT 2003b 6). "Severe data shortages on household energy use in Cape Town" make it difficult to know for sure what the distribution of this residential consumption is (CCT 2003b, 6) but the city has estimated that "consumers in informal settlements typically use 120kwh per month" (CCT 2004a, 67), well below the 600kwh per month that the city uses as its cutoff point for "low consumption" in its tariff structure, suggesting that average suburban consumption is much higher.

We do know that per capita energy consumption in the country as a whole is extremely high when industry use is factored in, averaging 3745kwh a person per year in 2000 (DBSA 2003, 234). This figure was almost nine times the average for sub-Saharan African countries in the same year, making South Africa the third largest per capita producer of greenhouse gases in the world (*Business Day*, December 10, 2004).

But rather than address over-consumption and skewed distribution patterns in the city, the state has plans to dramatically increase electricity production. After almost three decades of excess production capacity Eskom anticipates that the country will need to generate some 5000MW more electricity a year to meet immediate demand and wants to invest some R200bn in new capacity over the next 25 years, replacing all of its current generating plants (some with the controversial pebble-bed nuclear technology).

Between 2005 and 2009 Eskom plans to spend R110.3bn on electricity infrastructure across the country: R74bn on generation, R11.8bn on transmission and R15.9bn on distribution (*Business Day*, February 24, 2005; a significant increase from the R84bn in Eskom spending announced in September 2004 by the Department of Public Enterprises, adding another R26bn to this sector, more than five times the national housing budget for 2004–05). An additional R23bn in spending is expected to come from the private sector in the form of new power generation plants, with the first tenders having gone out in 2005 for power plants expected to cost approximately R6bn (*Business Day*, April 28, 2005).

This is part of a larger infrastructure spending package by national government of approximately R159bn of public funds (up from R123bn in September 2004) to be invested in a range of bulk infrastructure in the country, including ports and rail (discussed below). The initial announcement was met with delight by the business community, with the *Financial Mail* (October 29, 2004) hailing the investments in electricity generation in particular as coming "Not a moment too soon". Writers in the *Business Report* (October 24, 2004) expressed "amazement as spending turns to expectations of growth", with Public Enterprises Minister Alec Erwin having "invited the private sector to come to the party". All in all, "a reason for serious excitement" according to the paper's editorial.

These investments represent the single largest outlay on bulk infrastructure by national government since 1994 and exemplify the central thesis of this book: that the state is spearheading a restructuring of the space economy of the country via strategic investments in the built environment that may benefit the poor but are aimed primarily at creating the conditions for capital to compete effectively in a global economy. Rather than attempting to reduce electricity consumption by the rich or redistribute production more equitably, the state has taken a supply-side approach to increasing production and effectively subsidizing industry with electricity prices that are often below marginal cost and always below the larger social, health and environmental costs of coal-fired and nuclear energy production.

TRANSPORTATION

Planned investments by Transnet (the parastatal unit responsible for rail, road and port services in South Africa) are equally impressive in quantitative terms but once again reveal the corporate bias in public spending. In

2004, national Cabinet approved investments of R37bn over five years in Transnet infrastructure (increased to R49bn in early 2005) with the possibility that government could approve a further R58bn over 5–10 years for "blue sky" developments such as new railway lines and new container ports, with the investments indicating "government's desire to play a strategic role in lowering the freight costs chain through more hands on ownership and direction of public entities" (*Business Report*, October 22, 2004). Maria Ramos—former Director General of Finance and appointed CEO of Transnet in January 2004—commented that these new investments must be seen as "adding a competitive advantage ... underpinning South Africa's efforts to become globally competitive" (as quoted in Christianson 2004, 37).

Approximately R20bn of the Transnet funds will be spent on ports. The National Ports Authority (NPA) will spend R14bn and the South African Port Operations R5bn, with R7.2bn of these funds earmarked for Durban's port—by far the largest in the country—and R2.3bn for Saldhana Bay just north of Cape Town (for the export of steel). These investments are intended to "reposition NPA as a key facilitator of South Africa's global competitiveness", according to NPA spokesperson Donald Kau (as quoted in *Business Report*, November 29, 2004).

The plan is to keep the ports "public", but the National Ports Authority Bill indicates that the department wants to "corporatize" the Authority and Minister Alec Erwin has said that there will be private operators at the ports, "with competition between terminals" (as quoted in *Business Day*, October 25, 2004).

Cape Town's port is not nearly as large (or as central to the city's economy) as Durban's is, but it has been noted by Cape Town officials that a lack of investment in the port has led to "infrastructural gaps that constrain the productivity of the city. The Cape Town Port has had no significant capital investment for the past 25 years. As a result the port is currently inefficient with delays in on and off-loading ships imposing heavy costs on shipping companies and resulting in lost export orders, thus reducing the global competitiveness of local export industries" (CCT 2004b, 10).

There are plans, as a result, to use some of the Transnet funds to expand the Cape Town harbour, starting with R700m to upgrade the main electrical feed and expand the container stacking area by reclaiming 300 meters from the sea (*Business Report*, November 29, 2004). Whether these investments create new jobs remains to be seen, but it should facilitate local capital's interface with the global economy.

On the rail side, Transnet will upgrade rail links from Sishen to Saldhana for iron ore export (done as a public-private partnership (PPP) with mining company Kumba Resources), build a new high-speed freight line between Gauteng and Durban for the automotive industry (as a PPP with car manufacturers), and Spoornet will spend R14bn on infrastructure and new locomotives, also involving private partners.

But according to the railway unions, the Transnet announcements will do little to improve the transportation crisis for low-income rail commuters. R820 million was committed to overhaul 498 Metrorail coaches for passenger traffic in 2004–05, but this was considered insufficient: "This is not even beginning to deal with the crisis", argued Ezrom Mabyana, president of the South African Transport and Allied Workers Union (Satawu). This view was supported by Cosatu Regional Secretary for the Western Cape, Tony Ehrenreich, who noted at the time: "Billions of rand are spent on planes and no money on improving the rail system. Is it because the rich elite travel by air while working class families use trains?" (as quoted in Bell, 2004, 2).[6]

The commuter train situation in Cape Town is no different from the national situation, with overcrowding and safety concerns endemic on all of the township lines. As a result, ridership is dropping, down to 673,500 daily passengers in 2004 from 780,000 in 2002, largely because "the rail service has been in decline over the past two or three decades". Buses take 19, 000 passengers daily (up from 119,000 in 2002) and 'taxis' carry about 325,000 passengers a day (CCT 2004a, 47, 83; CTRCCI 2004b, 67). There are an estimated 7500 taxis operating in the city, of which 43% are deemed to be operating without a licence (CCT 2006e, 50).

What has the city done to improve the train situation for township residents? "Fuck all", according to one long-time urban planner in the city whom I interviewed. There are plans underway to improve the train system, with two new stations having been added to the Khayelitsha line and improvements to many of the existing platforms, but these investments pale in comparison to the investments in the rail system discussed above for big business. Or, as two other city planners put it in their assessment of the situation, "We can only hope that one day a good public transport system will happen [in the city] against the syndrome of much talk and no action" (Mammon and Ewing 2006).

It is not just trains that are in disarray. The city acknowledges that public transport as a whole "is currently in a severe state of decline" (CCT 2004a, 47). Buses may be the worst off, with an average age of about 15 years, as compared to a policy ideal of six years (Christianson 2004, 33), but so too is the taxi industry a major problem. Cape Town's taxi fleet—the ubiquitous 16-seater vans that emerged in the 1980s as part of the National Party's plans to privatize the public transport sector for black South Africans (Khosa 1992)—carry about a third of daily commuters in the city, but these are the most dangerous forms of transport as safety standards have proven difficult to monitor and enforce and as 'taxi wars' have resulted in occasional gun battles between taxi owners. There have even been incidents of taxi drivers shooting at buses in Cape Town as part of these turf battles, with several passengers having been killed in 2001.

The national state has plans for a R4bn recapitalization program in the taxi industry to upgrade and buy new, safer vehicles, but despite many years of proposals nothing has happened. Part of the problem is that full recapitalization (replacing 16-seater taxis with 18- and 35-seat purpose built vehicles) would cost at least R20bn for the estimated 80,000 to 140,000 taxis currently on the road and the state has balked at the price tag (Christianson 2004, 42).

Another problem lies with institutional fragmentation: national government is responsible for rail, provincial government is responsible for bus and taxi services and local government is responsible for local bus and taxi facilities. The city of Cape Town has attempted to address this with the establishment of a Metropolitan Transport Authority in 2005, but without the funding necessary to upgrade and expand these services it will be difficult for any authority to realize significant improvements in public transportation in the city.

Road quality is a concern in the country now as well, largely due to the emphasis that has been placed on trucking. Before 1982, subsidized public rail made it difficult for trucks to compete. Since the 1982 National Transport Study the emphasis has been on private trucking and the ANC has continued in this vein. The private trucking industry has now taken on virtually all new growth in commercial transport (Christianson 2004, 31), with 80% of all land commerce dependent on roads in South Africa (Thale 2004, 121). Truck overloading, by an average of about 20% by weight, is now largely blamed for deteriorating road quality.

Certain roads, however, have been seeing major investments. Toll roads, constructed in conjunction with the private sector, have seen the largest post-apartheid attention. The N4 Maputo corridor road was built in this way to promote trade with Mozambique and to move goods to and from the port in Maputo. The N3 toll road was also a public-private partnership, costing an estimated R3.5bn. Both have made it more efficient for capital but more expensive for low-income commuters.

Roads in business nodes and suburbs in Cape Town have also seen considerable investment since 1994, particularly in the central CBD and the Claremont CBD, with the city investing R24m in the latter on roads, taxi ranks and sidewalks as part of a larger R1bn investment in upmarket housing and commercial real estate in that part of the city (CCT 2004a, 9). So too are the N2, N1 and M3 highways in excellent condition in Cape Town, critical as they are for intersuburban vehicular traffic and for access to the airport.

Roads in the city's townships, by contrast, are in much worse condition on average. There have been some road improvements and some road expansions since 1996 (notably the M5 extension) but potholes, blown sand, litter and other obstacles remain a constant problem on all township roads and they are not nearly as well maintained as their suburban counterparts.

Storm water drainage presents a particularly serious problem for township traffic, with clogged and broken storm water systems creating regular flooding. One such incident occurred in Langa in August 2004, flooding 4200 people from their homes. Xolile Gophe, a ward councillor in Langa at the time, blamed council for the blocked drains, accusing the city of ignoring residents' appeals for stormwater drains to be installed. "I am very angry", he said, "This should never have been a disaster.... The city wants to say that this is a city for all and that it wants to bring dignity to people. But if they allow people to live like this, how can they say they are giving people dignity?" (as quoted in *Cape Times*, August 9, 2004).

A final comment on transportation relates to Cape Town's international airport. Though not a municipal responsibility, the airport plays a critical role in linking Cape Town to the global economy and has seen considerable investment since 1994. The airport is managed by the Airports Company of South Africa (ACSA), which owns and operates South Africa's nine principal airfields. Their mission, according to their website, is "to manage and develop world-class airports for the benefit of all stakeholders." Until April 1998 ACSA was fully owned by the state, after which Aeroporti di Roma, an Italian airports management firm, bought 20% of the company's shares. An additional 4.2% of shares is owned by five South African empowerment consortia.

Cape Town International Airport has seen remarkable expansion from its backwater days as DF Malan airport during apartheid. It is now South Africa's second largest airport attracting more than 60,000 aircraft and 6.5 million passengers a year, with 14 million passengers a year expected by 2015. ACSA has announced another R1bn expansion plan in late 2004 to deal with this growth in Cape Town, part of which is intended to prepare for the World Cup of soccer in 2010 (*Financial Mail*, October 29, 2004).

In fact, the World Cup seems to be drawing enormous sums of public funding, with an anticipated R1.3bn being spent to upgrade Cape Town's Green Point Stadium, and a staggering R242bn being committed by national government to "guarantee" to FIFA that all infrastructure required for the event will be in place in time (*Cape Argus*, March 30, 2006). Yet more public money for the benefit of capital and a transnational elite.

TELECOMMUNICATIONS

The last sector we will look at is telecommunications. Given its importance to global connectivity it is important to have a sense of investment patterns and priorities in this sector in Cape Town.

In general, telecommunication connectivity in South Africa is considerably higher than all other sub-Saharan African countries. Table 5.3 illustrates the difference, with South Africa having 7–10 times as many phones, mobile phones and personal computers as the average person in sub-Saharan Africa, making up close to half of all Internet users on the continent (with an estimated 3.8 million users by 2004 (Goldstuck 2003)). South

Table 5.3 Access to Telecommunications in South Africa versus Sub-Saharan Africa (as at 2001)

	South Africa	Sub-Saharan Africa
Telephone mainlines per 1000 people	112.5	14.1
Mobile phones per 1000 people	251.9	26.8
Personal computers per 1000 people	68.5	9.9
Internet users ('000)	3068.0	5299.9

Source: DBSA 2003, 234–35.

Africa also has more than 90% of all Internet service providers (ISPs) on the continent.[7]

In global terms South Africa is considered to be in the "middle tier of ICT [information and communication technology] development" (CCT 2002a, 4), and is ranked among the top 20 countries in the world in terms of the number of Internet nodes. The Economist Intelligence Unit ranks countries according to the extent to which their business environment is "conducive to Internet-based commercial opportunities" and in 2001 described South Africa as an "e-business follower" that has "begun to create an environment conducive to e-business, but has a great deal of work still to do." In 2002, South Africa was given a score of 5.45 and ranked 33rd internationally (as compared to Turkey (40th), Brazil (34th), Malaysia (32nd), United Kingdom (3rd), and the United States (1st) (CCT 2002a, 17).

South Africa is connected to the international telecommunication hub via a number of satellite connections and submarine cables (the latter carrying about 80% of all overseas telecommunication signals). The most recent submarine connection is the SAT-3/WASC/SAFE fibre optic cable along the west coast of Africa from Portugal to Cape Town and continuing on to India and Malaysia—the first of its kind—that became operational in 2002. The cable can handle 120Gb/s of data and 5.8 million simultaneous phone calls at what its developers say is a faster, more reliable, and clearer signal than satellite. The project has been driven by the South African telecommunications giant Telkom—previously state owned but now partially privatized—in collaboration with 36 other countries at a cost of US$600m.[8] Another planned submarine cable, the AfricaOne project, will further connect Europe and the Middle East to South(ern) Africa.

Investments in satellite ICT have also been significant in South Africa. Cell phone use in the country has grown dramatically from its inception in 1994, to a total of 17.4 million subscribers in January 2004 (*The Star*, November 3, 2004). There are now three main satellite phone companies with plans for a fourth service network operator, attracting billions of rand in investment. The DBSA (2003, 238) estimates that private sector investment alone in South Africa in the telecommunications sector (in what they call "socially useful projects") was US$1.1bn from 1990–95 and US$8.54bn from 1996–2001. Most of this investment was in satellite phones. Telkom invested another R4.2bn in 2004–05 to boost capacity in new-generation technology, particularly wireless broadband (*Business Day*, November 17, 2004).

In terms of bulk infrastructure, therefore, South Africa is well-serviced in ICT in international terms, with Cape Town being fully connected to the "global grids of glass" that are deemed essential to the competitiveness of world cities (Graham 1999, 2002). But as Graham (2002, 71) points out, this infrastructure is typically highly skewed in "world cities":

> On the one hand, seamless and powerful global-local connections are being constructed within and among highly valued spaces ... to the doorsteps of institutions. On the other hand, intervening spaces—even those that may geographically be cheek-by-jowl with the favored zones within the same city—seem to be largely ignored by telecommunications investment plans. Such spaces threaten to emerge as "network ghettos", places of low telecommunications access and social disadvantage.

Cape Town is a perfect example of this geographical unevenness. Although 70% of households in Cape Town have a telephone in their home and 27% of households have a computer (SACN 2004, 187), this access is highly skewed along race/class/geographic lines, as Table 5.4 illustrates for the nine major cities of the country as a whole.

There is an affordability problem here as well. Although Telkom has connected 2.8 million new land-based phone lines across the country since 1996—mostly in low-income areas as part of its roll out obligations with the state when it was partially privatized in 1997—there has been a massive disconnection rate (as high as 70%). Telkom blames this in part on the shift in preferences from fixed to mobile telephony, but admits that the bulk of the disconnections were due to nonpayment, largely from those who could not afford the cost (CCT 2002a, 6).

Further evidence of a "network ghetto" is seen in the lack of public access points to the Internet. Research in 2002 found that "community access points [to the Internet in Cape Town] are rare and cover only a small portion of the population. Although libraries, post offices, telecentres, and Internet cafés have shown promise in giving people access to ICT, they have not yet managed to do so to large sectors of the community" (CCT 2002a,

Table 5.4 Access to Telecommunications in Major South African Cities, by Race (%)

	African	*White*	*Coloured*	*Asian*
Telephone in home	18.4	80.1	56.9	75.7
Cell phone	31.0	76.6	40.1	58.8
Computer in home	3.3	50.8	14.5	28.6

Source: SACN 2004, 92.

24). Cape Town's "Smart Cape Access Project" was set up to address this problem in 2001, with plans to install computers in the city's 107 public libraries for free Internet access by June 2005 (Moodley 2005, 60), but despite good intentions—and an "Access to Learning" award from the Bill and Melinda Gates Foundation in 2003—only six pilot sites were established as of mid-2005.[9] By contrast, there are Internet cafés in all of the business nodes and shopping malls of the city and in major hotels.

Clearly, the interests of Cape Town's decision makers lie in using ICT to make the city more competitive in global economic terms, as the following quote from the 2006–07 Integrated Development Plan indicates: "Government commits to making major investments in ICT technology including fibre optic and wireless broadband networks in key economic areas. This will be targeted at reinforcing Cape Town's competitiveness in the business process outsourcing and ICT sectors" (CCT 2006d, Annexure E, 11).

This strategic targeting would appear to be working for ICT capital. Telkom has had record revenues in recent years, with operating profits of R11.2bn in 2004–05, up 21% from the year before and up almost 100% from 2003–04, due largely to its cell phone subsidiary, Vodacom (*Business Report*, June 8, 2005). Telkom share values have also gone up dramatically, almost tripling from August 2003 to October 2004 (*Financial Mail*, October 29, 2004). One empowerment group received a windfall profit of R326m from a mere six-month, state-sponsored investment in Telkom in early 2005, while the original American/Malaysian investors sold their 30% share of the company for what has been estimated at a R9bn profit after just seven years (*Business Report*, June 8, 2005).

Given this financial success one has to wonder why more pressure has not been placed on Telkom to address the network gap by reducing prices in township areas, providing free access to ICT points in these areas and not cutting off phone lines. The fact that as many as 30,000 workers have been retrenched by Telkom since 1994 is also troubling in light of these profit figures, although they go a long way to explaining the increase in headline earnings (AIDC 2004, 2; *Business Report*, March 30, 2006).

The only dark spot for capital is the cost of ICT. Although South African telephone and Internet is considerably cheaper than on the rest of the continent, with the cheapest long-distance rates in sub-Saharan African (DBSA 2003, 234), costs are relatively expensive in global terms. The introduction of another network operator, which will break Telkom's network monopoly, is expected to lower costs considerably, however. In anticipation of this competition, Telkom requested permission from government for tariff drops for long-distance calls in late 2004 (*Business Report*, November 17, 2004). At the same time, however, they raised local telephone call prices by 5.5%, which disproportionately impacts on low-income households.

EXPLAINING SKEWED INVESTMENT PATTERNS

In sum, investments in the built environment in Cape Town (and other major cities across the country) have been heavily skewed toward middle- and upper-income residential areas and business nodes. There have been important investments in the townships of the city, with widespread improvements in the daily living conditions of many (including those still living in shacks), but the overall trend has been toward investments that benefit capital and elites at the expense of low-income areas.

Could the city of Cape Town do more to invest in low-income areas if it wanted to? There is certainly potential for a better redistribution of existing municipal-level resources, as we saw in the previous chapter. There is also the possibility of more progressive rates and tariff structures to help cross-subsidize capital and operating costs in the townships (as we will discuss in Chapter 7).

The potential for a more radical redistribution of resources, or for a substantial increase in new capital spending for township infrastructure, is constrained by the limited funding that Cape Town receives from national government. Redistribution is also constrained by national legislation that limits the ability of local government to raise taxes and tariffs above a certain level.

Limited Fiscal Transfers

By far the biggest obstacle to a more rapid expansion of services to low-income areas in Cape Town is the lack of adequate funding from national government. As noted at the outset of this chapter, city council has commented on several occasions that intergovernmental transfers are insufficient to deal with the city's post-apartheid mandate. Even with the one-off R2.3bn injection from national government for the flagship N2 Gateway housing project, city council still feels that the level of funding from national authorities is "limited considering the scope of community needs and development pressures" (CCT 2005b, 52).

Insufficient transfers to local government have been a persistent post-apartheid problem, leading to charges of "unfunded mandates" from local authorities throughout the country. As far back as the early 1990s, under the then-ruling National Party, local government transfers began to shrink. The cutbacks continued after the ANC came to power, resulting in an 85% decrease (in real terms) between 1991 and 1997 according to the Financial and Fiscal Commission (1997).

After the introduction of GEAR in 1996, "the flow of public resources to local government remained static at best" (Whelan 2002, 233), with transfers to the city of Cape Town falling by 55% in real terms between 1997 and 2000 (Unicity Commission 2000a).

Responding to criticisms from local authorities, national government began to increase the levels of intergovernmental support from 2003, with plans to increase conditional grants by an average of 18.9% a year over the "medium term" starting from 2004–05 (DPLG 2004b, 36). These changes include the creation of the Municipal Infrastructure Grant (MIG), which consolidates seven previous funding mechanisms for capital expenditures, simplifying what was an incredibly complex and confusing system of intergovernmental transfers (see Bahl and Smoke (2003) for a review of the complexities of national-local financing in South Africa).

Introduced in August 2004 by the Department of Provincial and Local Government, the MIG is "aimed at providing all South Africans with at least a basic level of service by the year 2013 through the provision of grant finance to cover the capital cost of basic infrastructure for the poor" (DPLG 2004a, 3). Operating and maintenance (O&M) costs are expected to be covered by other funds, such as the Equitable Share, and "capacity building" is to be covered by the Capacity Building Grant.

National government refers to MIG as "one of the biggest capital grants in the world" (DPLG 2004a, 3), and it is indeed a significant amount of money: R15.9bn over three years, from 2004–05 (though this includes funding that was already committed to the Expanded Public Works Programme). The amount of money transferred to any particular municipality is based on a funding formula determined by population, needs, capacity, etc, and will be conditional upon the completion of a municipal IDP. It has also been stipulated that the funding only be used for low-income households.

Compared to many other 'developing' countries, therefore, the South African state is spending a considerable amount of money on its poverty-related infrastructure backlog. But viewed as part of the larger budgetary needs of South African cities the MIG is far from adequate. In 2000, for example, the Department of Provincial and Local Government "conservatively estimated that the total cumulative [infrastructure] backlog [in the country] is about R47-53 billion, with an average annual backlog of R10.6 billion", arguing that it would take much longer than the year 2013 to reach even a "basic" level of services (DPLG went on to note that "if these backlogs are addressed through public sector resources alone, many communities will receive adequate services only in the year 2065") (RSA 2000c).

Transfers to the city of Cape Town will only increase slightly during the MIG period, from an estimated R354m in 2004–05, to R448m in 2005–06, to R504m in 2006–07 (not including the funding for the N2 Gateway project) (PGWC 2004). While not an insignificant amount of money it is still a far cry from what the city needs to deal with its massive housing and infrastructure backlog and makes up only a small fraction of the city's budget. In 2004–05, total transfers from all levels of government made up only

4.52% of the Cape Town's operating revenue[10], prompting the city to ask, "Will there be sufficient funding from the MIG?" (CCT 2005b, 78).

Even Salga (2004a, 27)—the ANC–dominated authority that speaks on behalf of organized local government in South Africa—has also complained (if only cautiously) that the MIG increases are not enough: "There are concerns that the MIG allocations ... are insufficient". So too has the National Council of Provinces (NCOP) "lashed out" at the National Treasury for its frugality. According to the *Business Day* (October 5, 2004), "Treasury officials have faced a barrage of complaints from NCOP members about inadequate budget allocations for everything from houses to water, electricity and land redistribution".

One can also compare MIG funding to other national government expenditures. At R15.9bn the MIG is a mere fraction of the R123bn that the state plans to pour into Eskom and Transnet (as discussed above). It also pales in comparison to the controversial R40-65bn being spent on the purchase of new war ships and fighter jets.[11] A surprise announcement in December 2004 to purchase additional military transport aircraft for R8bn added to the controversy, prompting the editors of the *Mail & Guardian* (December 10, 2004) to note that the planes will cost "twice this year's total expenditure on housing subsidies and six times this year's outlay on land reform.... Does a country of intermediate development like South Africa really need the biggest, best and most expensive on offer?" In total, the state spends about R20bn a year on its Defence budget, four times more than Housing and more than the Health and Education budgets combined (RSA 2004a, Annexure A).

Another controversial area of government spending has been on Black Economic Empowerment (BEE), with billions of rand being spent on "redress[ing] the economic inequalities bequeathed by apartheid by providing historically disadvantaged persons with opportunities to acquire shares in both restructured state-owned assets and private business enterprises" (according to the mission statement of the National Empowerment Fund (NEF)). The NEF was established in 1998 and received an additional R2bn in government funding in June 2004.

But more significant than the public monies that have gone into supporting BEE is the allocation of private sector funding that has been set aside to meet BEE legislation. For example, it is estimated that R166.7bn will be required to meet the terms of the Mining Charter BEE (*Business Report*, April 1, 2004). The Financial Sector Charter, for its part, has committed to financing R50bn worth of black empowerment deals. This is "private" money, but must be seen against the reluctance of capital to "redistribute" its wealth for more poverty-related projects, most notably the redlining of low-income housing.

How much money has gone into BEE over the years? In 2003, the BusinessMap Foundation estimated in its Empowerment Report that there were

62 BEE deals in the country worth R21.1bn. They noted an additional
58 deals where the value was not disclosed, likely increasing values by
another 25%. Ernst and Young, in its thirteenth annual survey of mergers and acquisitions in that same year estimated that there were 189 BEE
deals worth R42.2bn. The most famous BEE recipient—Cyril Ramaphosa
(one-time unionist, then ANC negotiator, then Deputy Presidential hopeful, now a wealthy businessman)—had an estimated "market influence"
of R167bn in 2004 and sits on boards of many major companies (*Mail &
Guardian*, October 12, 2004).

Equally revealing are investments that the state refuses to fund. The
Basic Income Grant (BIG), for example, a monthly allowance of approximately R100 a month to all South Africans, was proposed by the Ministry of Social Development in 2002 but has been regularly rejected by
national Treasury. Finance Minister Trevor Manuel has argued that it will
cost the fiscus R83bn and "bankrupt the country" (*IRIN News*, November
23, 2004). Proponents, on the other hand, argue that the BIG would provide income security to millions of low-income households and only cost
between R24 and R40bn a year (Makino 2004; see also *Social Dynamics*
2002).

Restrictions on Local Government

It is not only intergovernmental fiscal transfers that have limited local government's potential for more dramatic infrastructure spending in the townships. National government has imposed a series of legislative constraints
on local government's ability to raise revenue and there is legislation that
prevents municipalities from budgeting for a deficit (RSA 1996b).

With regard to property rates—approximately 20% of Cape Town's
revenues (CCT 2003a, 57)—national government has put ceilings on the
increases that local governments can levy on (wealthy) property owners.
There is, in fact, a constitutional clause to this effect, which states: "The
power of a municipality to impose rates on property, surcharges on fees
for services provided by or on behalf of the municipality, or other taxes,
levies or duties (a) may not be exercised in a way that materially and unreasonably prejudices national economic policies, economic activities across
municipal boundaries, or the national mobility of goods, services, capital
or labour; and (b) may be regulated by national legislation" (RSA 1996a,
s229.2.a/b).

The national legislation that regulates this clause is the Local Government Municipal Property Rates Act of 2004, which states that local
governments cannot apply taxes at the local level that threaten its own
tax-reducing, fiscally conservative strategy (RSA 2004c, s1.3.20(1)): "The
Minister [of Provincial and Local Government] may, with concurrence of
the Minister of Finance ... set an upper limit on the percentage by which
rates on properties ... may be increased". Suburban ratepayer associations

and the powerful South African Property Owners Association fought hard for these clauses in the legislation.

Local government is also constrained by what the city of Cape Town (CCT 2005a, 15) refers to as National Treasury's "budget growth parameter", a "guideline" that limits operating and capital budget growth to 6.5% per annum (to keep government spending within target inflation rates of 5–7%). It is not clear what legal status this "growth parameter" has but the impact is nonetheless a significant one given that policymakers in Cape Town continue to cap tariff and rates increases "in line with or below inflation" (CCT 2004a, 6).

But even if more money was available from national government (or from local taxation) to fund capital investments it is not clear that city council would want to spend it in low-income areas. As Cape Town city officials noted in a 2003 report to national Treasury: "Capital expenditure leads to increased charges for repayment of capital as well as interest. Apart from that, it adds to operating costs, often requiring expanded staff to run new facilities, and additional maintenance costs. The high levels of capital expenditure in recent years are a key cause of financial distress". As a result, the city felt that it needed to cut what it considered to be "an overly ambitious capital expenditure programme", reducing its capital budget by more than 14% in 2002–03 and with plans for a "much more stringent cutback in the current financial year" (CCT 2003a, 6, 4).

The capital budget did increase again after 2004–05 but only with the injection of special funding for the N2 Gateway project and with increases in the MIG. Nonetheless, the city remains concerned that it may be unable to finance the ongoing operating and maintenance costs of these capital investments and therefore insists on investing in capital expenditures that fall within residents' "affordability levels" (CCT 2004b, 55).

The lack of adequate national funding has also forced local government into borrowing on the open market, with the city of Cape Town spending R1.033bn in 2004–05 to finance its loans (two thirds of the total capital budget for that year), with additional borrowing expected to raise these financing costs to R1.232bn a year by 2007–08 (CCT 2004a, 56; CCT 2005b, 43). The city is also "seriously considering raising loans on the recently rejuvenated bond market", arguing that its "sound financial base, coupled with a favourable long-term credit rating, should allow it to access funds on the capital market at a competitive interest rate" (CCT 2004a, 59).

Unwilling to Challenge National Government

Despite clearly inadequate levels of funding from national government, South African municipalities appear unwilling to challenge Treasury on the matter. Rumblings from Salga and some local authorities occasionally make the news, but there has been no coordinated effort on the part of Salga or individual municipalities to challenge national government in this regard.

Ironically, it was the more overtly neoliberal Democratic Alliance that made intergovernmental transfers a political issue in its attempt to win favour amongst Cape Town's urban poor while electioneering in Cape Town for the December 2000 local elections. The DA promised to push for increased transfers during that campaign and it was flagged as a major issue in the party's election manifesto (something that the ANC election manifesto failed to mention entirely). The DA did not follow through on its promise to push for more transfers when it was elected that year, however. Nor did the ANC take it up as a political issue when it retook control of council in 2002.

ANC officials have told me that they did not push the matter because Cape Town is a "relatively wealthy municipality and we should not deprive other, smaller municipalities of limited government funding. We can afford to provide basic level of services with our own budget" (personal interview, David Schmidt). The real reason, I would argue, is that it is very risky to challenge the fiscal orthodoxy of the national ANC, making for a very short political career (as a number of internal ANC critics have discovered over the years).

Neither party made fiscal transfers a significant part of their election campaign in the March 2006 local elections—with only a brief clause in the DA Election Manifesto stating that they want to "[e]nsure that inter-governmental transfers and grants constitute the main source of funding for eliminating infrastructure and service backlogs and for providing those basic services that have been devolved to local government". Whether the DA actually acts on this remains to be seen. The issue could be used as a way to embarrass the ANC at a national level, but it also runs counter to the party's overall emphasis on fiscal restraint and I expect the party would rather put more emphasis on cost recovery, privatization and "affordable services" to keep the fiscal costs of township development to a minimum.

CONCLUSION

It should be noted, in conclusion, that none of this public spending should be seen as a return to Keynesianism. As large as these sums may be in certain sectors, capital expenditures at the national level have dropped from 10.4% of government spending in 1990 to 4.0% in 2000, while wage expenditures dropped from 23.2% of national government spending to 12.5% in 2000 (DBSA 2003, 256), part of the haemorrhaging of some 100,000 public sector jobs in the country in the 1990s. In total, government expenditure as a percent of GNP over this period dropped from 30.1% to 29.1% (DBSA 2003, 255) and then dropped further to 27.7% in 2004–05 with no expected increases for the next three years (*Financial Mail*, October 29, 2004, 32).

What this public spending really represents is a focused and energetic attempt to invest in the infrastructures most required for the service-oriented, export-driven and elite-attracting areas of the urban economy. The overall pattern of infrastructure investment in the city is wildly unequal, contributing to a paralyzation of the sociospatial inequities of the city, not to their alleviation.

Efforts to commercialize and privatize these infrastructure and service investments in the city have made the situation even worse, a trend that we turn to next.

6   Privatizing Cape Town

> All stakeholders [should] acknowledge the reality that a significant propor-
> tion of local government service delivery responsibilities [in Cape Town] are
> already outsourced, and that this proportion is likely to increase in future,
> particularly in the case of new services.
>
> *Unicity Commission 2000a, 25*

The previous two chapters outlined the spatial reconfiguration of Cape
Town in broad political, institutional and infrastructural terms. It was
argued that the long hoped-for redistribution and equalization of municipal resources in the city has not occurred because the post-apartheid local
government has been unwilling—and to some extent unable—to implement a stronger redistributory agenda.

Fiscal restraint is at the heart of this paralyzation, with government arguing that it cannot overspend in low-income areas because of inflationary
concerns and the need to keep tax and tariff rates competitive for business
and suburban elites. But this is a selective form of fiscal restraint. While
low-income communities receive, at best, a 'basic' level of services—sufficient for improving living conditions and expanding the consumption fund
for a larger, mass consumption society—suburbs and commercial districts
have seen massive public sector spending on a wide range of infrastructure
and services, intended to improve Cape Town's place in an international
network of competitive global cities.

Where does 'privatization' (as I will broadly define it) fit into this neoliberal agenda? There are several arguments developed in this chapter. The
first is that the privatization of services and local government functions
serves to reduce government spending, providing a financial and institutional mechanism for fiscal restraint without abandoning government's
commitment to service delivery to the poor. Second, privatization offers
the possibility of creating multi-tiered service levels for different service
needs: 'basic' services for the townships and 'world-class' services for elites.
Third, privatization creates investment opportunities for local and international capital in sectors that remain largely untapped by market forces,
opening new doors for profit taking and commodification and creating vast

new swaths of service 'consumers' under the disciplinary pressures of the market. These are not the only objectives of privatization, but they are the most pronounced in Cape Town.

My discussion focuses primarily on the privatization of municipal services such as water, electricity, transportation and public spaces, but will also address the privatization of decision-making processes around infrastructure investments, such as the growing reliance on private sector consultants in urban planning.

The chapter begins with a brief terminological and conceptual review of privatization, followed by a discussion of how these fit with 'roll out' neoliberalism and its place in the accumulation strategies of world cities. I then discuss the extent to which municipal services and infrastructure have been privatized in Cape Town, the people responsible for making this happen, and what the future trajectory of privatization looks like for the city. I conclude with a discussion of the implications of privatization for low-income communities—actual and projected—preparing the ground for a discussion of cost recovery in the next chapter.

But before doing this I want to note that none of these privatization initiatives was inevitable. There was nothing preordained about the ANC's post-apartheid emphasis on privatization. After years of talking about nationalizing key sectors of the economy, it was assumed that when the ANC came to power it would at least insist on publicly owned and operated municipal services run along welfarist lines. Inequality in basic services had been, after all, one of the major flash points of the anti-apartheid movement.

To some extent the ANC has stuck to this script. As we shall see, most services in the country, Cape Town included, remain in public hands. The emphasis, instead, has been on the 'corporatization' of public services—the running of publicly owned facilities on private sector principles. The outcomes, however, have been much the same, with the commercialization of a wide range of government functions and a radical transformation of state-citizen relations emerging from this managerial and ideological shift.

But so too has there been a considerable amount of more conventional privatization, from parking services to road maintenance, with an accelerating trend toward the off-loading of municipal services to the private sector. Though complex, and still in the process of unfolding, this general shift cannot be denied, and illustrates—perhaps better than any other single post-apartheid development—the extent to which the city has become neoliberal in character.

WHAT IS PRIVATIZATION?[1]

In its narrowest sense, privatization refers to the sale of state assets to a private company. Over the past 30 years states around the world have divested themselves of airlines, railroads, telecommunications, health facilities and other services. Divestiture, as this form of privatization is formally known, was the model of privatization adopted in the United Kingdom (UK) under Margaret Thatcher in the late 1980s, with entire water systems (from water collection, to reticulation, to sewage treatment), as well as railways and other state-owned services being sold to private firms (Ernst 1994, Schofield and Shaoul 1997, Barlow and Clarke 2002, Bakker 2003). The state—or some parastatal body—typically remains responsible for monitoring and regulating these privatized entities but maintenance, planning and operational responsibilities are those of the private firm.

This kind of privatization falls into the 'roll back' brand of neoliberalism discussed in Chapter 3, and was intended as a radical dismantling of the Keynesian welfarism of the day. But the "shallow neoliberalisms of Thatcher and Reagan encountered their institutional limits as evidence of the perverse economic consequences and pronounced social externalities of narrowly market-centric forms of neoliberalism became increasingly difficult to contest" (Peck and Tickell 2002, 388). In the case of municipal services such as water and electricity these privatizations have often resulted in poor service standards (especially for low-income households), environmental infringements, the redlining of poor communities, and the lowering of health and safety standards for workers (Sclar 2000, CUPE 2002, McDonald 2002b, PSIRU 2005, Chavez 2006).

The consequence of these failures was not implosion but "reconstitution", as the neoliberal project morphed into Third Way alternatives in the 1990s (Peck and Tickell 2002, 388). This newer, roll out phase of privatization has distinguished itself from the roll back phase by foregrounding social issues and placing a stronger emphasis on (re)regulating the private sector. Roll out privatization calls for a more active role for government than the Thatcherite version, as a way "to mask and contain its deleterious social consequences" (Wacquant 1999, 323).

In this respect, roll out privatization represents "both the frailty of the neoliberal project and its deepening"; holding onto the same economic objectives of fiscal restraint, labour flexibility and the creation of new terrains of capital accumulation while simultaneously rolling out new technologies of government and new discourses of reform.

Since this institutional shift there has been relatively little divestiture of municipal services outside of the UK, with virtually no municipalities divesting of their water services in the way that Britain did. Most municipal privatization schemes today do not involve any transfer of state assets, focusing instead on the transfer of operational and managerial functions to private companies (e.g. meter reading, personnel management, and strategic planning, maintenance). Infrastructure and equipment typically remain in public hands—or are transferred back to public ownership after a specified period—and there may be joint responsibilities between the state and a private firm in managing operational functions. This model is used across

the world by leading water and construction firms such as the French multinational giants Suez and Veolia (formerly Vivendi) (Goubert 1986, Hanke
1987, Lorrain 1991).

Formally known as private sector partnerships (PSPs) or public-private
partnerships (PPPs), these institutional arrangements are nevertheless a
form of privatization. There is a clear transfer of crucial decision-making responsibilities from the public to the private sector and an effective
transfer of power over assets to a private company, with qualitatively and
quantitatively different rules and regulations guiding the decisions that are
made and how citizens are able to access information.

PPPs can range from small operations, such as one-person contractors
who collect refuse in an informal urban settlement, to a large multinational company hired to manage the provision of bulk water and sanitation
to an entire city. The size and types of contracts can vary as well, from
short-term, fee-for-service contracts, to 30-year licenses. Although large
multinationals tend to attract the most attention when it comes to service
privatization debates, small firms and 'entrepreneurs' represent a large part
of the privatization thrust, with these microenterprise deals often going
unnoticed by the public. This smaller, 'creeping' form of privatization is as
much a focus of our attention here as efforts by large multinationals to take
over entire service systems.

Less easy to classify are forms of privatization that involve the downloading of service responsibilities to individuals, communities and nongovernmental organizations (e.g. the repairing of roads or the digging of trenches
for water pipes by community groups). Represented in the neoliberal literature as "active citizenship" (Burrows and Loader 1994) and "community empowerment"—a counter to welfare dependency (Wolch and Dear
1989)—this transfer of water service decision making and responsibility
also constitutes a move from the public (i.e. the state) to the private (in this
case an individual or community). Although not necessarily acting with
the same institutional or economic incentives and frameworks as private
capital, the transfer of decision-making power to individuals and communities nevertheless constitutes an abdication of responsibilities on the part
of the state.

Privatization, in other words, is not an either/or situation (either the
state owns and runs a service or the private sector does). It must be seen as
a continuum of public and private mixes, with varying degrees of involvement and exposure to risks by the two sectors (Starr 1988). It is a conceptual and political mistake to pose the market (private) and the state (public)
as binary opposites on this issue.

Moreover, as Bakker (2003, 4, 36) has argued in the case of water privatization in the UK, even the outright divestiture of state assets can, ironically, mean greater state involvement in water services, prompting her to
employ the term "re-regulation" rather than deregulation in regards to legislative changes that allow for greater private sector involvement in water

services: "a process in which the state has reconfigured its role, and in some instances expanded its powers and administrative reach.... the state does not necessarily withdraw, but rather changes the nature of its interaction with citizens and corporations."

The term "privatization" is therefore used here as a generic expression for a range of private sector involvements in service delivery rather than a single state of being. This is done in part because the term is widely recognized in popular discourse (as opposed to public-private partnerships) and in part because it highlights the fact that assets and/or decision-making responsibilities have passed from public to private hands. I will also use the term "commercialization' insofar as it captures the market-driven reforms behind the privatization push.

PRIVATIZATION IN SOUTH AFRICA

Despite early efforts to privatize certain services by the National Party in the 1980s, it was not until the early to mid-1990s that the privatization debate really took off in earnest in South Africa. As a result, the roll back phase of privatization never really took place in the country. By the time the World Bank Urban Missions were active in Cape Town and other South African cities in 1991, the international lessons of divestiture had been learned and the primary funders/advisors to the ANC had already adopted a roll out model of neoliberal reform, with the language of public-private partnerships dominating the discourse of urban service delivery from the outset.

Equally important has been the emphasis in South Africa on introducing private sector operating principles and mechanisms into the public sector. As noted above, the corporatization of municipal services is the most significant policy shift in this regard and it is important to understand how this shift has been linked—mechanically and conceptually—to other forms of privatization and commercialization.

Corporatization refers to a process by which market mechanisms and market practices are introduced into the operational decision making of a publicly owned and operated organization—e.g. profit maximization, cost recovery, competitive bidding, cost-benefit analysis, demand-driven investments and performance targeted salaries (Stoker 1989, Pendleton and Winterton 1993, Dunsire 1999, Leys 2001, Olcay-Unver et al. 2003). This form of operation is in direct contrast to the more traditional public sector operating principles of integrated planning, (cross) subsidization, supply-driven decision making and equity orientation (keeping in mind that there are no 'ideal' or absolute types here—i.e. commercial principals and more traditional public sector management principals can run concurrently, to varying degrees).

In post-apartheid South Africa, integrated municipal services such as water and electricity have been turned into stand-alone 'business units', owned and operated by the (local) state but run on market principles. This partition typically involves two organizational shifts. The first entails financial ringfencing, whereby all resources directly involved in the delivery of a service are separated from other service functions (e.g. personnel involved in electricity are separated out for accounting purposes from personnel in waste management and water). When resources are shared by more than one department (e.g. information technology), the ringfenced entity pays the other unit a full-cost fee for the use of those resources (see Shirley 1999, PWC 1999, PDG 2001, Whincop 2003, Bollier 2003).

The purpose of this financial ringfencing is to create a transparent form of accounting where all costs and revenues related to the service can be identified, along with any subsidies in and out of the ringfenced unit. This is intended to reveal the 'real' costs and surpluses of running a service and allows managers to identify areas of financial loss or gain that may have otherwise been hidden in the intricate accounting schemes and cross-subsidization mechanisms of an integrated service delivery system with centralized accounting. Financial ringfencing also creates an opportunity to introduce financially driven performance targets for managers (i.e. managers are rewarded for meeting loss/profit targets). This approach introduces market-based salaries for managers with the aim of attracting 'world-class' executives who are expected to pay their way by ensuring that the bottom line is positive.

The second aspect of corporatization is managerial ringfencing—the creation of separate business units managed by appointed officials operating at arm's length from the municipal authority. Elected officials still set standards and service delivery goals for a corporatized service unit, as well as monitor and evaluate its activities, but the daily management and long-term planning of the unit are done by the ringfenced management team.

What is the link between corporatization and privatization? First and foremost is the change in management ethos with a focus on a narrow and increasingly short-term financial bottom line. So complete can this shift in management culture be that services fully owned and operated by the state (i.e. technically 'public') can be more commercial than their 'privatized' counterparts, with managers aggressively promoting and enforcing cost recovery and other market principles.

Second, corporatization often promotes outsourcing as an operating strategy and discreet form of cost cutting. A competitive operating environment, in turn, requires deregulating (or re-regulating) monopolistic control of the service and allowing multiple service providers to compete with the ringfenced unit to provide a particular service at cost-effective prices (e.g. meter reading). The removal of subsidies, for instance, forces state-owned enterprises to compete for finance on an equal basis with private firms or other corporatized entities within and across municipalities.

Third, corporatization can act as a gateway for direct private sector investment, ownership or control by making public water services more attractive to the private sector. Private companies are not interested in buying into services with hidden cross-subsidization structures, inflexible and politically integrated decision-making procedures, or anti-market management cultures. Service units that have been delineated from other municipal functions with clearly defined costs and revenue structures, with some form of managerial autonomy, and with market-oriented managers are much more likely to attract interest from private firms.

Not all corporatization efforts are mere preparation for bigger privatization plans, but this is a real—and growing—motivation for municipalities that are adopting the corporatization model internationally. Comments from senior city managers in Cape Town, interviewed in 2000, are indicative of the kind of thinking around corporatization and privatization. One of the most senior managers responsible for service delivery argued that the role local government should play is to ensure that "services are run like stand-alone business units, moving from public utilities then to the private sector". Equally explicit was the admission by a senior water manager that "Lyonnais des Eaux has come knocking on my door on two occasions. These French water companies have become too powerful to resist. The take-over is inevitable. I want to run our services like solid business units to make sure that we negotiate from a position of strength when it does happen" (as quoted in McDonald and Smith 2002, 32).

Commercialization can therefore pave the way for private sector involvement in municipal services or it can simply create publicly owned and operated service systems that behave, for all intents and purposes, like a private sector service provider, mimicking business discourses and practices (Stoker 1989, Clarke and Newman 1997, Dunsire 1999, Taylor-Gooby 2000).

Tying all of this together are the underlying processes of commodification (for an extended discussion see McDonald and Ruiters 2005b, 19–24). Only when a service such as water or electricity is treated as a commodity can it be properly commercialized and, eventually, privatized. Some goods and services lend themselves to deeper and faster commodification than others. There can also be political and cultural differences across countries/regions that affect what is commodified and the rate at which commodification takes place. "Cultures of resistance" and tensions inherent to the shift to commodification can slow the commodification process down and make it uneven (Williams 2002, Williams and Windebank 2003). Thus, although there are powerful pressures to commodify (Harvey 1989a, 2003) commodification is not necessarily a linear or inevitable process.

Nevertheless, we have witnessed a steady expansion of market relations and commodification around the world over the past two centuries, with remarkable acceleration in the past few decades. Commodification may not be complete, and it may not be inescapable, but "the reality of capitalism is that ever more of social life is mediated through and by the market", with far-reaching transformative effects (Watts 1999, 312).

What are these transformative effects? The first is that the social rationale for the production of a service such as sanitation or health care is submerged by a focus on exchange value, with 'public good' service ethics and a commitment to professional values overrun by the necessity of turning a profit/surplus. Second, there is a rationalization of service delivery along industrial lines—i.e. the 'Taylorization' of services—whereby service activities are cut into increasingly smaller, stand-alone functions, with less skilled tasks being conducted by less skilled and cheaper workers and more skilled tasks being increasingly automated. The result is the creation of 'cost centres', with discreet service functions coming under the same product cycle pressures as hard goods such as computers or washing machines (Leys 2001, 84–95).

We see the effects of this commodification in municipal services in the dissection of tasks into smaller and smaller pieces, separated from other service activities and analyzed for efficiency improvements, mechanization (e.g. prepaid meters), outsourcing, and possible downloading (e.g. do-it-yourself sanitation systems in low-income communities).

Here we see corporatization as the logic of commodification *par excellence*: the compartmentalization of all hitherto integrated service functions into stand-alone, cost recovery units; the homogenization of measurement and reward structures; and the increasingly narrow focus on a financial bottom line. Corporatization may not be the same as privatization in the narrow, ownership sense described above, but it does serve to embed market logics into all aspects of the decision-making process in municipal services, resulting in many of the same outcomes.

WHY IS PRIVATIZATION HAPPENING?

Why is privatization happening in Cape Town (and in other cities of the country)? The primary reason is that it assists with the drive to put in place the services and infrastructures required for renewed capital accumulation (airports, roads, electricity systems, etc.). The state—as we have seen—is investing billions of rand in services and infrastructure but this is often deemed insufficient (or not good enough or not fast enough) by capital and urban elites. In these cases there are demands for private sector investment to supplement, or even replace, public sector initiatives. City Improvement Districts are a classic example, with private contractors being employed by local businesses to enhance the municipal services being offered by the city in a specific geographic area (e.g. policing, cleansing, urban planning, etc.).

There is also the belief that the private sector can better respond to the needs of the market, providing a level of service and a quality of service that the public sector cannot offer. Demands for private investments in the rail sector are an example of this. Although state-owned Transnet has committed billions of rand to the upgrading and expansion of rail links and locomotives to assist with exports of minerals and manufactured goods, the private sector still wants to own its own rolling stock and invest as it sees fit for its needs. According to James Lennox, the Chief Executive of the South African Chamber of Business (Sacob), "The purchase of rolling stock [by private firms] ... is a very pragmatic solution to individual company requirements, and it's in line with global trends. Companies make better use of assets than a nationalised industry. It's a different mind set" (as quoted in *Business Day*, November 11, 2004).

The lowering of taxes and tariffs is key here as well, with the private sector (or a corporatized entity) deemed to be more efficient than the traditional public sector, reducing the tax and tariff burden for residents and business, and making the city more competitive internationally.

New investment opportunities for capital are a major issue also. Municipal services such as water and electricity remain one of the last, great untapped markets for capital investments in South Africa and internationally. It has been estimated, for example, that less than 10% of the world's water market has been privatized, providing enormous investment outlets for over-accumulated capital around the world (Barlow and Clarke 2002, Harvey 2003).

Profit opportunities are available through direct investing in privatized services, and also in consulting work related to privatization, with large multinational firms such as PricewaterhouseCoopers and KPMG being very active in commercialization efforts in Cape Town (e.g. PWC 1999, 2000, 2001). A heavy reliance on private sector consultants is itself a telling institutional feature of the ideological transition in the city, with a significant presence and growing influence on the part of multinational as well as local consultancy groups. In fact, much of the municipal documentation related to privatization that will be reviewed in this chapter (e.g. the Unicity reports, the city's corporatization strategies) was written largely, if not entirely, by private consultancy groups, many of which have benefited from their recommendations to commercialize or corporatize by winning additional consultancy contracts, generating something of a self-fulfilling loop of neoliberal prophesy. I have yet to see a private sector consultancy report in Cape Town that has recommended against commercialization.

But it is not just big capital that plays a role here. The development of small enterprises (SMMEs)—particularly for black firms—is critical. Salga, in an eight-page, full-colour supplement in the *Mail & Guardian* newspaper in September 2004, highlighted the need to "fast-track black business entry into development projects" through the private contracting of municipal services, profiling a young African couple who had obtained a R4.5m tender to provide street light maintenance in the Johannesburg area. The contract, Salga argued, has helped the couple to take "huge strides in reclaiming their ancestral heritage", arguing that this kind of contracting will help to ensure that "a lot of black rich people [will] be in the driving seat of the country's economic activities".

Procurement is also targeted as a part of larger-scale black economic empowerment (BEE) program in the country, with billions of rand worth of municipal spending being directed toward black-owned companies. Johannesburg's corporatized electricity division—City Power—spent 60% of its procurement budget on empowerment companies in 2003, and expected to spend R400m on BEE procurement in 2004, with considerable efforts going into helping "to educate black entrepreneurs on how to secure tenders from state-owned enterprises" (*Business Report*, October 8, 2004).

Most important to our discussion, though, is the question of why privatization is happening in the way that it is in South Africa and Cape Town— i.e. PPPs, outsourcing, corporatization—and not as outright divestiture. The simple reason is that outlined above in theoretical terms: local and national governments in South Africa (and their major funders and advisors) had learned the lessons of roll back neoliberalism before they had to make decisions about post-apartheid service delivery and opted for the less controversial and problematic route. With the exception of some relatively minor municipal services such as abattoirs, fresh food markets and natural gas providers, there has been virtually no outright divestiture of major municipal services in Cape Town or elsewhere in South Africa, with publicly owned water, electricity and other essential services remaining in public hands or in some form of public-private partnership.

This is not, I would argue, a result of any fundamental ideological shift away from the neoliberal objectives of fiscal restraint or catering to the needs of capital, but rather a recognition of the failures of outright privatization in ensuring that infrastructure and service investments happen in a rational and strategic way. An increased role for the state in a public-private partnership does not represent a shift back to Keynesian-style politics. It is intended to impose a less risky, more predictable and more manipulatable pattern of investment.

So too do PPPs, corporatization and other roll out forms of commercialization serve as important public relations 'flanking mechanisms' for capital and neoliberal policymakers. Arguing that these forms of commercialization are not the same as privatization, the state (and capital) can claim that they are operating in the interests of all citizens and consumers.

It is remarkable, in fact, how seldom one sees the term "privatization" in South Africa, with the word being effectively purged from government publications. Even the term "public-private partnerships" is seldom used any more, with "municipal service partnerships" (RSA 2000c), and "alternative service delivery models" (CCT 2003a, Executive Summary), being the preferred nomenclature, further diverting attention from the privatized nature of these institutional arrangements.

The term "corporatization" is also increasingly avoided by the state (presumably because of its association with the word 'corporate'). 'Business unit' is the phrase of choice, with Cape Town now also using "transparent service units" (CCT 2004b, 47). The latter is particularly obscurantist, as evidenced by the city's claim that "transparent service units" are "not the same" as corporatization, even though other official city policy documents make a clear link between the two concepts (see, for example, CCT 2004c).

Just how successful this discursive game has been is demonstrated by the way in which the South African press has also taken on, and been convinced by, the new terminology. The editor of the *Mail & Guardian*, for example, argued in a lengthy article in mid-2004 that the "view among social movements and the intelligentsia linked to them is that South Africa has undergone a massive exercise in water and electricity privatization.... [This] is plain wrong, yet is repeated over and over again—as if repeating it often enough will make it true. Only four of 284 municipalities—and relatively small ones at that—have contracted out the management of water.... As for electricity supply—none, none of it has been privatised" (June 11–17, 2004). There is no mention here of the massive and widespread outsourcing of contracts to small operators, the huge build-operate-train-and-transfer (BOTT) programs in rural areas (Bakker and Hemson 2000, Greenberg 2005) or of the almost universal corporatization of core services in the country, all three of which have fundamentally transformed the nature of public sector service provision in South Africa.

ThisDay—the now defunct daily that prided itself on critical reporting—also fell victim to this flanking discourse, arguing: "Many observers believe that the ANC has put privatization on the backburner" (June 17, 2004). Even Zwelinzima Vavi, General Secretary of the Congress of South African Trade Unions, has spoken of "government's shift and rethink on privatization" (*Business Day*, May 28, 2004).

These discursive shifts are not merely defensive, however. Soft language such as 'partnerships' has actually served to undermine the struggle against commercialization, with individuals and communities that might otherwise oppose privatization coming out in favour of PPPs and other forms of marketization in the hopes that they might create jobs. Most successful in this regard have been efforts to convince low-income communities that the outsourcing of small-scale services such as street cleaning and meter reading is a positive, job-creating initiative. At the same time, 'privileged' and 'uncommitted' unionized municipal workers are blamed for denying neighbourhoods the opportunity for this kind of 'entrepreneurial' job creation. The end result is typically conflict between township communities and the public sector workers that service them, fragmenting and confusing organized resistance to this particular form of neoliberalism (more on this below).

Nor should it be forgotten that the roll out phase of neoliberalism is simply that, a 'phase': part of the dialectical choreography of crisis management in a capitalist economy. As the pressures for international competitiveness deepen in Cape Town, as the opportunities for lucrative capital investment shrink, and as the demands for 'world-class' infrastructure and service delivery from a transnational elite increase, so too will the pressures for more explicit forms of privatization rise. The transition from corporatization to direct private sector involvement is perhaps the most obvious future trend but it is also likely that there will be pressures for the outright divestiture of more services and a deepening reliance on private sector capital and expertise across all forms of PPPs.

TO WHAT EXTENT IS PRIVATIZATION HAPPENING?

To what extent, then, is privatization actually taking place in Cape Town? I begin with an overview of the national scene to establish both the legislative and ideological context within which the city of Cape Town is making decisions about service provision, and then discuss the extent to which pro-privatization mindsets have come to dominate policymaking and practice in the city. This is followed by a summary of actual privatization/corporatization initiatives in Cape Town.

Legislation

The Municipal Systems Act (RSA 2000a) governs decision making around the delivery of municipal services in South Africa and determines what, if any, role there is for the private sector and other "external" service providers. Significantly, the legislation leaves it up to individual municipalities to determine service provision mechanisms, guided by a set of rules and procedures.

Section 76 of the Act distinguishes between "internal [service delivery] mechanisms" (which includes corporatized "business units") and "external mechanisms". The latter consists of the following: "another municipal entity or another organ of state; a licensed service provider; a traditional authority; a community based organization or other nongovernmental organization legally competent to enter into such an agreement; or any other institution, entity or person legally competent to operate a business activity."

When making these decisions a municipality "must first assess" the costs and benefits of an internal mechanism, including "the likely impact on development, job creation and employment patterns", the "views of organised labour" and "any developing trends in the sustainable provision of municipal services generally" (RSA 2000a, s78.1). Should the municipality decide, after this process, that an external provider is a better option, "it must (a) give notice to the local community of its intention to explore the provision of the service through an external mechanism; and (b) assess the different service delivery options in terms of section 76(b), taking into account—(i) the direct and indirect costs and benefits associated with the project, including the expected impact of any service delivery mechanism on the environment and on human health, well-being and safety; (ii) the capacity and potential future capacity of prospective service providers to furnish the skills, expertise and resources necessary for the provision of the service; (iii) the views of the local community; (iv) the likely impact on development and employment patterns in the municipality; and (v) the views of organised labour" (RSA 2000a, s78.2-3).

Chapter 11 of the Municipal Management Finance Act (RSA 2003a) reinforces these principles by requiring municipalities to conduct feasibility studies on PPPs. The municipality must then give public notice of the proposed PPP, together with a copy of their report on the feasibility study, to allow communities and other interested parties to comment. They must also consult with Treasury, DPLG and other relevant national departments (e.g. DME, DWAF), although the exact nature of this consultation is unclear in the legislation.

Legislatively, then, municipalities are free to choose different modes of service delivery—public or private—as long as they follow the required decision-making steps. There is no legislative bias—strictly speaking—for or against privatization. The state has simply made it legally possible to privatize municipal services (in all its variants).

There are, however, related political agreements and policy papers that need to be considered. The first is the National Framework Agreement signed between national government and Cosatu in 1998, which makes the "public sector" the "preferred service provider" in the country (notably, the "public sector" includes corporatized business units in this case). The ANC's local government election manifesto of 2000 made similar promises, arguing that "national and provincial governments will keep the public sector as the preferred provider of municipal services".[2]

Interestingly, none of this public sector preference language appeared in the ANC's local government election manifesto in 2006, with only a vague reference to "improving the capacity of all government structures to serve the people". But even if this language did remain, and the party was committed to this policy, none of it is legally binding. In the places where it really matters—legislation and the Constitution—there is no use of the term "preferred options", raising serious questions about the state's commitment to this public sector principle.

The Department of Provincial and Local Government's White Paper on Municipal Service Partnerships attempts to clarify the matter, but succeeds merely in downgrading the public sector option to one that is no more important than private sector initiatives: "While the Government is committed to facilitating the use of MSP [municipal service partnerships] arrangements, this does not mean that MSPs are the preferred option for improving service delivery. It is rather that MSPs should enjoy equal status among a range of possible service delivery options available to municipal councils" (RSA 2000c, 14).

The White Paper on Local Government is equally confusing, arguing: "In assessing the appropriateness of different service delivery mechanisms, it is important to note that the choice is not between public and private provision. Rather, the real issue facing each municipality is to find an appropriate combination of options which most effectively achieves their policy objectives.... Each municipal Council will need to make its own assessment in relation to the strategic direction put forward in the municipal integrated development plan" (RSA 1998b, s2.3).

The legal framework related to service privatization is therefore ambiguous, at best. To better evaluate the actual practice and potential of privatization we must look to the ideological and fiscal pressures that municipalities such as Cape Town find themselves operating under.

Ideological Pressures

The ideological pressures to privatize municipal services are coming from within local government but the strongest and most important pressures are coming from outside (another indication of the multiscalar constitution of urban neoliberalism). One of the biggest influences in this regard is the national Treasury, with long-time Finance Minister Trevor Manuel regularly applauding the commercialization trend in local government: "Our service delivery record has been enriched through PPPs in recent years, and our PPP project pipeline continues to grow, both in numbers and in the innovative value-for-money solutions it contains" (RSA 2004d, Preface). Statements to this effect by President Thabo Mbeki and other senior cabinet ministers further illustrate a pro-privatization bias at the national level: "We will proceed with [privatization] ... the restructuring of state assets", declared Mbeki in Parliament in 2002, in advance of a two-day strike by Cosatu to protest government's privatization initiatives (Reuters, September 20, 2002).

A more concrete example of this ideological bias is found in the nationally run and funded Municipal Infrastructure Investment Unit (MIIU). Established as a government agency in 1997 in collaboration with foreign donors (primarily USAID), the MIIU's mission is "to encourage and optimise private sector investment in local authority services" (MIIU 2000). Activities to be undertaken include "assistance to local authorities in the process of hiring private sector consultants and the management of contracts with the private sector" and "developing project proposals involving private sector investment". These investments can comprise "contracting out of the management of ongoing services, concessions to operate the local authority's assets over a defined period, contracts requiring the private sector to Design, Build, Finance and Operate assets to deliver services for the local authority, and the privatization of assets and services". The MIIU has been active in promoting and financing the privatization and corporatization of municipal services throughout the country, including Cape Town.

The more recent creation of a Public-Private Partnerships for the Urban Environment (PPPUE) office in Pretoria (funded in part by the United Nations Development Programme) is another example of a state-backed initiative for privatizing municipal services.

Notably, there is no parallel organization set up at a national level to promote public sector service delivery or to conduct research on improving and extending public sector services. Plans by the Department of Provincial and Local Government to establish a "Support Unit for Public Provision of Services (SUPPS)" to address this "imbalance" have yet to materialize, despite repeated requests from Samwu for such an organization.[3]

There have been some attempts in South Africa to establish 'public-public partnerships' (PuPs)—as opposed to public-*private* partnerships—which involve different public sector agencies, but these have been few and far between and have generally met with poor results, prompting some observers to question whether these PuPs were perhaps "set up to fail" (Pape 2001, Smith and Fakir 2003, Smith 2005). Others have asked if PuPs have simply become another way of introducing private sector operating principles into the public sector or as a way of preparing the ground for direct private sector involvement, as has taken place in other countries (Hall et al. 2005).

Whatever the reasons, the fact remains that very little has been done financially or institutionally to investigate ways of specifically promoting and improving public sector municipal service delivery in South Africa, despite the ANC's stated commitment to improving the public sector and making it the "preferred service provider".

National government has invested considerable resources into training bureaucrats and councillors with education workshops (spending R220m on "local government capacity building" in 2004–05 (RSA 2004a, Vote 5, 6)), but a qualitative assessment of these efforts reveals them to be primarily concerned with a more business-like approach to running the public sector, with a steady diet of neoliberal principles and assumptions.

An example of this is the Local Government Water and Related Services Sector and Education Training Authority (LGWSETA), designed to "bring about more effective co-ordination of capacity building and skills development initiatives between government departments, local government and water agencies and stakeholders ... to promote leadership, skills development programmes, and other educational interventions to enhance the efficiency and effectiveness of basic services (water and sanitation, housing, clean environment, etc.), governance and administration and to support employment creation" (LGWSETA 2004). LGWSETA has its own substantial funding for this task, spending R262m in 2003–04 alone (LGWSETA 2004, 20, 40).

The Board of the LGWSETA consists of unions (Samwu and Imatu) as well as employers, but according to the National Education Director at Samwu the union's hopes that this body would create opportunities for promoting and improving the public sector have not been met:

> On the whole it is not providing anything new to the majority of work-ers, and if anything has actually undermined areas of training that were relatively well developed such as apprenticeships just at the time that they were escaping from apartheid job reservation.... It is fairly evident that the largest slice of money has gone to upper managers and councillors. Councillors are obsessed with their own training. This has been a major problem. Not to mention all the study visits overseas! This is not to say that lower levels do not receive any training. All in all it is not quantified—which is what we have fought for so that a more rational distribution would be achieved. [4]

When asked to what extent the ideological and pedagogical content of the LGWSETA courses challenges the dominant neoliberal thinking of the day, the Samwu official replied that they had fought for exactly this "criti-cal thinking content":

> [The hope was that people] would not only learn the technical skills of plumbing, but be opened up to critical discourses about society and economics. I realize now this hope was pure naiveté on our part. We managed to adopt an overall system which is clothed in often radical sounding terminology but which at base is essentially about turning out productive units for the global capitalist economy.... To change the content of what is taught is really a struggle over curriculum. What is the 'contextual' part filled with? If it is a water skills development path is this done in a manner that seeks to engender critical debate about questions such as the 'value of water'? Is its human right value high-lighted? Is the debate between full cost recovery versus social needs taken up? No!

Nor is there much hope for critical training from international funding agencies. The World Bank remains pro-privatization (at least in its 'roll out' guise) and continues to fund privatization initiatives in South Africa. The Development Bank of Southern Africa (DBSA), established and operated by the South African government, is also pro-privatization, as demonstrated by DBSA Chairman Trevor Manuel's statement: "More relationships with the private sector are needed in order to improve the lives of the poor and reduce poverty" (DBSA 2004, 1). With an annual budget of about R1.5bn, and with a mandate to improve services and infrastructure in the region, the DBSA is a major service and infrastructure player. The DBSA also has plans to establish an educational "academy ... to support the Bank's knowledge management strategy and its vision for the year 2010 ... consistent with the strategy and overall ethos of the Bank". This would include a "Local Government Resource Centre".

USAID and Britain's DFID are important players in this respect as well. Besides USAID's funding of the MIIU it has also been directly involved in Cape Town's efforts to corporatize its core services (CCT 2003a, Appendix 2A). DFID has been active on this front too, and has, as a result, been criticized for aggressively pushing a privatization agenda in South Africa. George Monbiot of the *Guardian* newspaper (October 19, 2004) has accused DFID of putting inordinate pressure on the South African government to privatize. Quoting British Chancellor Kenneth Clarke before he went to South Africa as the head of a trade mission in 1996, Monbiot points to a clear pro-privatization agenda on the part of the UK government: "Privatisation has been at the very heart of our public-sector reforms in Britain. Can what we have done here in the UK be exported to South Africa? I would argue definitely yes.... British business can help.... Britain can share in the bright future that beckons for South Africa."

Monbiot notes that DFID recently granted "£6.3m to the Adam Smith Institute—the ultra-rightwing privatisation lobby group—for 'public-sector reform' in South Africa ... to disburse as it pleases. By this means, DFID can generate all the support it likes for privatisation and public-private partnerships".

Finally, there is the pressure of private sector service firms themselves. This is done, in part, with promotional booths at conferences (e.g. at the annual Salga National Conferences), full-page advertisements in industry magazines, the financing of pro-privatization conferences and the sponsoring of municipal bureaucrats and policymakers to travel to locations around the world where companies have privatized services (such as the French water multinational, Suez, paying for policymakers from Cape Town to fly to Buenos Aires to see its (ultimately ill-fated) water concession in that city (Loftus and McDonald 2001b)).

What are the implications of this ideological hegemony and institutional bias toward privatization in South Africa? For one, it has proven unwise for aspirant politicians and policymakers to buck the ideological trend. To resist the push toward commercialization in any of its variants can mean marginalization in ANC policymaking circles or outright expulsion from the party, as one ANC councillor in Soweto, Trevor Ngwane, discovered in 2000 with his public criticisms of the ANC's plans to corporatize and privatize services in Johannesburg as part of that municipality's controversial "iGoli 2002" plan. The proportional representation system also means that political parties draw up their own lists of candidates for elections, giving power to the central executive to determine who can become an elected official (although at the local level 50% of councillors are voted in on a first-past-the-post ward basis, allowing, theoretically, for some ideo-logical freedom in municipal councils. In practice, however, ward-based ANC councillors have tended to adopt the party line).

Enormous pressure has also been placed on officials from Cosatu and the SACP to moderate their organizations' criticisms of the ANC's priva-tization record. Just how serious and widespread this pressure has been is difficult to say for sure given that much of it takes place behind closed doors, but both Mbeki and Mandela have publicly (and forcefully) chas-tised senior Cosatu and SACP leaders for their 'ultra-leftist' positions on the matter, dampening some of the earlier anti-privatization language from these two organizations.

There are also instances of community activists being intimidated by ANC–allied organizations for their anti-privatization work in townships, with accusations of unwarranted police harassment, arrests and detentions (an issue taken up in greater detail in Chapter 8). Although a far cry from the brutal violence and intimidation of the apartheid era, the trend toward ideological hegemony and the active marginalization of political opposi-tion by (and within) the ANC does not bode well for democratic debate in the country (Peet 2002).

This intellectual climate has also put a chill on academic research on privatization, with many funding organizations—particularly state agen-cies—reluctant to provide monies to researchers and research organizations that are known to be critical. State research funding bodies such as the Human Sciences Research Council (HSRC), the Water Research Commis-sion (WRC) and the Council for Scientific and Industrial Research (CSIR) have a long track record—stretching back to the apartheid era in some cases—of funding research that is either openly pro-privatization or fails to engage meaningfully with the debates over privatization. The WRC, for example—"the country's water-centred knowledge 'hub'"—has funded millions of rand worth of water-related research over the past decade but has not produced a single report critical of privatization. Indeed, the bulk of the research produced with WRC funding is openly in favour of some form of commercialization and/or supportive of other neoliberal policy measures such as service cutoffs or prepaid water meters.[5]

At the same time, much of the pro-privatization research that is funded by the state (or by state-backed agencies) is of dubious quality. Research on the Nelspruit and Dolphin Coast water concessions conducted by the MIIU, for example, have come in for particularly harsh criticism (Hemson and Batidzirai 2002, Smith et al. 2005) and there are examples of research used to justify privatization initiatives in Cape Town that are equally prob-lematic (discussed below).

Significantly, none of this pro-privatization research comes in for close public scrutiny. In fact, the media generally perpetuates the problem, ignoring or uncritically reporting on privatization initiatives and typically coming out in favour of commercialization (Mayher and McDonald, forthcoming). The two major English dailies in Cape Town, the *Cape Times* and the *Cape Argus*—both owned by the Independent Group, whose proprietor is on President Thabo Mbeki's 'international advisory group'—are overwhelmingly pro-privatization.

In contrast, research that is critical of privatization is constantly challenged by neoliberal policymakers, often in very public and aggressive ways. In some respects this ideological bias is good for critical academics insofar as it forces scholars and activists to be highly rigorous (much more rigorous on average, I would argue, than the pro-privatization research being conducted in the country). It can, however, be intimidating to be critical, especially for new researchers or those reliant on state funding sources, and has definitely contributed to a chill and polarization in the academic community by establishing (false) categories of 'anti–ANC' and 'ultra-leftist' researchers.

Finally, the pro-privatization literature and lobby has made it very difficult for the average person to participate in debates. Legislatively required 'consultation processes' over private sector participation in service delivery have done little to provide community members with the kinds of information they need to make informed decisions. Relatively low levels of literacy and numeracy in the townships make it even more difficult for these residents to participate given the highly technical and legalistic verbiage of official council reports, made worse by the fact that most township residents have difficulty getting to meetings due to poor public transportation facilities and the cost of travelling. Online access to reports is also a major problem.

Even public sector unions struggle to keep up with the flood of pro-privatization initiatives. Samwu, for example, has only one researcher at their national office, and even this person has other responsibilities in the union. Individual Samwu branches often have even less capacity to critically scrutinize privatization proposals that directly affect their membership, resulting in little to no organized resistance in many cases.

So too does the NGO sector have limited capacity. Only a handful of NGOs in the country are directly engaged in privatization debates (e.g. Environmental Monitoring Group, Alternative Information and Development Centre) and their resources pale in comparison to that of pro-privatization government bodies and aid agencies such as the DBSA and MIIU. Throw in the handful of South African academics actively engaged in a critical review of privatization efforts in the country and it is truly a David and Goliath battle of ideas.

Having said that, opposition to privatization certainly does exist in the country, and within the ANC–alliance, and can be extremely dynamic. The massive Cosatu-led strikes protesting privatization in August 2001 and October 2002, involving several million workers, are two concrete examples of this, as was an anti-neoliberal march in Johannesburg at the World Summit on Sustainable Development (WSSD) in 2002, which attracted some

25,000 community and labour activists from South Africa and around the world, with a clear anti-privatization stance.

But it is the daily, grass-roots opposition to privatization and commodification that holds out the most hope for change in South Africa. Groups such as the Anti-Privatisation Forum, the Soweto Electricity Crisis Committee, and the Anti-Eviction Campaign have all been energetic and effective opponents to these kinds of neoliberal reforms. Splits over political strategy have served to factionalize these groups over the years, and there has been a slowdown in protest action since the 2001–02 peak (partly due to the state's acquiescence on some demands, such as free lifeline supplies of water and electricity), but they remain active and some are regrouping to address the flanking mechanisms of the ANC's revised neoliberal strategies (e.g. prepaid water meters) (Buhlungu 2004, Dwyer 2004, Egan and Wafer 2004, Oldfield and Stokke 2004, Naidoo and Veriava 2005).

Fiscal Pressures

There are also very strong fiscal pressures on municipalities to privatize services. As discussed in Chapters 4 and 5, post-apartheid South African municipalities have been handed a massive set of reconstruction and development responsibilities (becoming the 'hands and feet of the RDP') but have not been provided with the resources to fulfill these mandates. Municipal revenues have only increased slightly in real terms since municipal amalgamations in 2000, with only minor improvements expected over the next five years, despite promises of 'massive' transfer increases via mechanisms such as the Municipal Infrastructure Grant.

These unfunded mandates—combined with the legislative requirement of maintaining a balanced budget and not raising municipal taxes or tariffs above nationally determined inflation targets—means that most municipalities in the country are looking to private sector investments to meet their infrastructure and service delivery goals.

As the city of Cape Town noted in a 2003 request to National Treasury to help restructure its finances, "the disposal of non-core [services] is an integral part of the City's [efforts to] strive for cost effective and efficient service delivery ... due to, inter alia, resource constraints that face the City and the increasing demand from residents for needs to be met" (CCT 2003a, Appendix 5E). In other words, the city is saying that it does not have the money to provide all the services it is expected to provide and therefore has no choice but to bring in the private sector.

TO WHAT EXTENT IS PRIVATIZATION
TAKING PLACE IN CAPE TOWN?

To what extent has privatization taken place in the city of Cape Town? I look first at the discursive/policy trends in the city and then turn to the more concrete commercialization initiatives since 1996 to illustrate how this ideological shift has manifested itself in practice.

What should be apparent from this review is the widespread and deep-seated commitment to neoliberal principles across party political lines and amongst a wide range of senior bureaucrats in Cape Town. There may be differences of opinion with regards to how fast and how hard to push for commercialization in the city between the two leading political parties (the DA and ANC), but both parties, and most of the major decision-making bodies in the city, have adopted a roll out neoliberal position on service delivery and infrastructure development.

This analysis directly challenges the opinion of many that the ANC is not neoliberal and that its local government policies are "fundamentally different than that of the DA" (as a senior ANC official has claimed).[6] The two parties have adopted essentially synonymous positions on commercialization in their written and verbal positions on the matter, and certainly in terms of actual policy implementation, with the both the DA and the ANC having held power in Cape Town since 1996.

The degree to which this neoliberal buy-in represents a shift from the (racial) welfarism of the past is also remarkable. Though some old-guard bureaucrats have expressed concern with the new neoliberal management ethos that has taken over the city—having been brought up in the (racialized) welfarism of the past—this is a minority view and would appear to be largely impervious to the political gerrymandering that has characterized local politics in the city since the end of apartheid.

The Discursive Terrain

As discussed elsewhere in more detail (McDonald and Smith 2004), there has been a strong and consistent trend toward neoliberal discourse amongst the ranks of senior bureaucrats and elected officials in the city of Cape Town. Extensive interviews with this cadre of decision makers in 2000 demonstrated strong preferences for private sector involvement in service delivery, with the majority of interviewees having adopted a 'bullish' pro-privatization perspective. This group felt that the public sector in Cape Town is simply incapable of providing services on a sustainable basis and made calls for rapid and widespread private sector investment and participation.

Another group of interviewees took a more 'cautious' approach to privatization but were nonetheless strong proponents of increased private sector involvement. Only four of the senior 61 managers and councillors interviewed were actually opposed to increased private sector participation. Interestingly, almost all of the elected officials that were interviewed came out as bullish on the matter, while managers were split between the cautious and bullish positions.[7]

One area that differentiated the cautious group from their more bullish counterparts was a concern about 'core' services such as water, sanitation, electricity and waste. The cautious respondents saw these as intrinsically public in nature and needing to be provided by local government. One manager argued that "government is better at providing emergency services and sewerage, which is a highly integrated service and where the risk for a contractor is too high". He added that the public sector has better knowledge of these key services due to its long history of running them. Another manager commented: "The result of privatizing an area like sewerage to the private sector is that if payment isn't received, you will end up seeing sewerage running down the street".

There was also a general sense amongst the cautious group of respondents that government should remain in charge of services that are highly subsidized, such as libraries, clinics, community halls and swimming pools, where "customers are unable to pay the full economic value of running services". This concern reflected a broader apprehension about privatizing highly subsidized services and how this might affect the city's capacity to cross-subsidize services in low-income communities.

The general response to these kinds of concerns, however, was not one of less private sector participation but rather one of better regulation. As a senior manager noted: "The key issue is government ensuring that the service gets provided. This doesn't necessarily [mean that government] has to be the deliverer of services. We need to hold the public authority accountable for this in terms of how the private sector engages poor people and builds on their skills."

In contrast, the bullish group of respondents held a one-dimensional view of privatization, arguing that the private sector was able to deliver services more effectively and less expensively than the public sector. Efficiency was the most frequently cited issue in deciding whether core or noncore services should be turned over to the private sector, regardless of equity concerns. As one senior level manager noted, employing World Bank terminology: "The role of local government is to be the ensurer, with services as stand-alone business units moving to public utilities then to the private sector.... Electricity and water are well suited for this line of thinking".

Other respondents were fatalistic in their belief that the private sector was the only service delivery option, with one manager stating "there is no way to restructure the public sector without moving into the private sector and the formation of utilities". Another manager suggested that the "public sector should only be considered once proven that it can beat the private sector with cost-effectiveness".

When asked what municipal services would be better provided by the private sector, one manager responded: "All of them. Services like cleansing, water and electricity could be enhanced if there were greater competition". A senior councillor pushed this idea of competition further, stating that "everything within the public domain should be opened up for competition with the private sector". Another councillor added the following: "The national framework agreement [the document signed between government

and Cosatu which makes the public sector the 'preferred service provider']
has to be discarded. The private sector service delivery will be more efficient than government when it can achieve the proper market situation".

These respondents were unanimous in their belief that the private sector
could provide better services than the public sector, and there was widespread agreement that privatization is an inevitable outcome of post-apartheid restructuring. As one respondent argued: "The disparities in local
government create a climate that makes it more difficult to save on costs.
This makes it difficult to compete with the private sector". In other words,
this group sees privatization as a rational and unavoidable response to the
inefficiencies of apartheid planning and service delivery.

Further evidence of the bias toward privatization comes from policy
documents and discussion papers in the city—the most important of which
were produced by the Unicity Commission (or 'Unicom') as part of its role
in the amalgamation of Cape Town into a single 'Unicity' in 2000. The
Unicom was composed of an equal number of ANC and New National
Party (NNP) councillors (five from each party) and one Democratic Party
(later to become the Democratic Alliance) councillor, as per party political representation in the municipal structures at the time. This group
reviewed and voted on recommendations made by a team of technical
advisors composed of senior bureaucrats from municipalities in the Cape
Metropolitan Area and private sector consultants (with the consultants
conducting the bulk of the research work and writing the final reports, e.g.
PricewaterhouseCoopers).

The Unicom policy recommendations are important for at least two reasons. First, they represented the first-ever policy recommendations to deal
with the Cape Metropolitan Area in its entirety. Second, the two major sets
of policy recommendations put forward by the Unicom—the August 2000
"Discussion Document" and the November 2000 "Strategic Recommendations"—were unanimously (and uncontestedly) approved by all political
representatives on the Commission.

Although the term "privatization" is not used in the Discussion Document (no doubt for the same politico-discursive reasons discussed earlier),
the report makes repeated references to "private sector participation" in a
future Unicity and clearly sees private sector involvement as the path to a
"successful" and "competitive" Cape Town. The most explicit reference is
the call to "move boldly beyond the current emphasis on service provision
issues" to a position where the new Unicity Council "understands its role
as a service ensurer as a guarantor of municipal services rather than as a
primary service provider" (Unicom 2000a, section 3.1). In other words,
local government should act primarily as a regulator of services while the
private sector or a public-private entity provides the services.

By contrast, there is a marked shortage of references in the Discussion
Document to building public sector capacity and/or redistributing existing
municipal resources in a more equitable manner. There is fleeting reference

to the need to improve the "skills base" of city employees (section 9.1) but there are no details as to what this "large investment" might entail financially or how these skills-development funds would be broken down between managers, politicians and labourers. Nor is there any reference to the issue of resource distribution in the Cape Metropolitan Area. In short, the Unicity's Discussion Document failed to explore the public sector option in any meaningful way, situating the private sector—or at least private sector operating principles—as the driving force of service transformation.

The Discussion Document was re-released in November of 2000 as the Unicom's "Strategic Recommendations" to the new soon-to-be-elected Unicity Council. These recommendations were even more explicit in their pro-privatization bias, as demonstrated by the following quote: "All stakeholders [must] acknowledge the reality that a significant proportion of local government service delivery responsibilities are already outsourced, and that this proportion is likely to increase in future, particularly in the case of new services".[8]

The document also made recommendations about the ringfencing of tradeable services such as water, electricity, sanitation and sewerage, as follows:

- That service ringfencing initiatives should seek to foster competitive incentives in service delivery where these are sensible and appropriate.
- That service ringfencing should always assist in revealing true service delivery costs, and that all services should therefore be ringfenced from a financial accounting point of view.
- That the service ringfencing should [be] undertaken on an incremental basis, with increasing levels of decentralisation being balanced by increasing levels of corporate capacity to manage ringfenced services. Lessons from the experiences of Johannesburg and other local governments should be gathered and applied.
- That particular attention be given to addressing those aspects of industrial relations, which inhibit ringfencing initiatives and lead to inflexible and inefficient human resource utilisation.

There have been modifications and new additions to this strategic framework since 2000, but the core recommendations have remained the same through DA, then ANC, then back to DA, governments. The corporatization of core tradeable services such as water, sanitation, electricity and solid waste remains the main priority—with all of these having been set up as separate "business units" of some kind—but other options such as outsourcing and PPPs have been aggressively pursued.

The next major policy statement on privatization was the ANC–authored Restructuring Grant written for national Treasury in 2003, shortly after the party had wrested control of city council back from the DA in 2002 (facilitated by floor-crossing legislation that the ANC had passed at the national level, allowing former NNP councillors to become members of the ANC, giving the latter a majority of seats in council). In this document we see a continuation of the neoliberal themes of the Unicity Commission, with, for example, a commitment to "strive to explore alternative service delivery models in order to determine optimal ways to improve service delivery at an efficient cost" (CCT 2003a, Appendix 5A). Written behind closed doors and not released to the public until pressure from Samwu brought it to the attention of local media in mid-2004, the Restructuring Grant did nothing to alter the pro-privatization agenda of the multiparty Unicity Commission.

This pro-privatization theme continued with the ANC's 2004–05 Integrated Development Plan (IDP) for the city. Intended as a long-term "vision" for Cape Town to the year 2020 (CCT 2004b, 14), that year's IDP strives to give the city "a competitive edge" so it can "compete globally in the 21st century". To accomplish this, it is argued, the city needs to have "private sector investment in social housing", an "enabling business environment", "appropriate partnerships with ... the private sector" and "financially transparent service units", all of which are intended to help the city "ensur[e] full cost recovery" in its service delivery mandate (CCT 2004b, 13, 22, 24, 35, 47, 76). The IDP also highlights plans to "reduce the number of staff and the staff budget as the major cost driver of the operating budget by approximately R800 million over the course of the next four years" (CCT 2004b, 39). The latter has proven to be the most controversial recommendation, attracting considerable protest on the part of Samwu, but the DA-led council continues with its "strategic goal" of reducing the costs of staffing to 28% of its operating budget (CCT 2006d, 101).

In late 2006, the city released its first "State of the City" report, further highlighting the ideological bias toward privatization. The report is forthright about the sociospatial and economic challenges of the city, but "the solution" is to focus on "partnerships" (CCT 2006e, 62). The document is peppered with comments from "experts" who claim that: "It is limited what the public sector can do to achieve economic development in the City"; "Cut red tape and provide infrastructure to support business"; and "It's important that business plays a key role by contributing solutions to the city". The objective is to "minimize any constraints that government activity places on shared growth and development" and to put "more focus ... in developing linkages between the public sector, the business sector and civil society" (CCT 2006e, 40, 41, 61, 63).

Election campaigns are another good indictor of the discursive shifts to privatization. The Democratic Alliance has been the most bullish in this regard, with overtly pro-privatization statements in its local government "election manifestos" of 2000 and 2006. In 2000, for example, the DA (2000, s6) promised that: "In DA–controlled municipalities, cost savings through competitive out-sourcing and privatisation will be instituted in an ongoing drive to provide better value for money. Local and international experience has shown that the introduction of a businesslike approach, competition, and private sector involvement in the delivery of municipal services ... leads to significant savings and improvement in the quality of services delivered."

The manifesto went on to say that virtually all services that municipalities are responsible for "lend themselves to variants of commercialisation, competitive outsourcing and privatisation": "garbage and solid waste disposal, fire protection, emergency ambulance services, maintenance of parks and recreational amenities, public transport systems, certain social services and primary health care, certain planning and zoning functions, water and sanitation, and certain municipal management functions". There is no mention whatsoever of building public sector capacity or looking for public sector efficiency gains through a more equitable distribution of municipal resources (the term "public sector" is not even used in the manifesto).

The party's 2006 manifesto is equally pro-privatization in its tone, calling for "accelerated privatisation", "real incentives for private sector involvement", "commercialised municipal service", "Public-Private Partnerships", "Outsourcing" and even outright "Privatisation", concluding that a "municipality may stand to benefit from relieving itself of certain responsibilities" (DA 2006, s4.1-4.2).

The ANC's election manifestos have been more ambiguous, in line with the party's obfuscating position on privatization at a national level. After an initial statement about making the public sector the "preferred option to provide services" in the 2000 manifesto, the party goes on to say that "where a local government lacks the necessary capacity, it may engage in partnerships with other government institutions, such as state-owned enterprise or other local governments, as well as community organisations and/or the private sector" (ANC 2000, 4).

The ANC mayoral candidate for Cape Town in 2000, Lynn Brown, was equally noncommittal when pressed on the matter at the time, stating at a community forum on privatization held in November of that year that she is "opposed to privatization without proper evaluation and public consultation", but then held out public-private partnerships and other forms of commercialization as "possible alternatives" for service delivery in the new Unicity.[9]

The ANC's 2006 election manifesto was equally coy. Although calling for "compassionate government service" and a commitment to "improv[ing] all public services" there was no indication of what role the private sector would play in this "People's Contract". Nor was there any use of the term "preferred provider" for the public sector—a remarkable omission given the emphasis the party had placed on this rhetoric in its 2000 election manifesto.

One is left wondering, then, what it is that makes the ANC's policies in Cape Town so "fundamentally different" from those of the DA, at least when it comes to municipal services. My answer is that there is no fundamental difference. The DA may be more aggressive (or perhaps just more honest?) in its drive for privatization, but the ANC continues to make verbal and written commitments to the same effect, even if it is clothed in ambiguous language.

One development that may have a small impact on these politics was the success of the Independent Democrats (ID) in the local elections in Cape Town in 2006. Contesting local elections for the first time that year, and led by former Pan-African Congress party stalwart (and coloured Capetonian) Patricia de Lille, the party won approximately 11% of the popular vote, preventing either the DA or the ANC from taking single-party control of council (the end result was 90 seats for the DA on the 210-seat council, with the ANC winning 81 seats and the ID 23 seats and the rest being split amongst smaller parties).

The ID backed the ANC after the election in the hopes of forming a coalition government but the DA narrowly won control of council (and the Mayorship) with the support of the smaller parties and one rogue vote from an ID councillor. This is a tenuous position for the DA, of course, but it does mean that the ANC has lost political control of the city once again (at least until the next floor-crossing window in mid-2007).

These results could mean that the DA will moderate its approach to privatization, opting for a slower and/or more subtle approach to its calls for widespread commercialization, in part because the Independent Democrats were openly opposed to "full privatization" and to "public-private partnerships" in their election manifesto, arguing that both policies have negative impacts on the poor (with the bulk of their support coming from coloured working-class townships). The ID was highly critical of all forms of commercialization, arguing that the state should be investing in "public-public partnerships" and advocating for "service delivery options that entail a more involved and interventionist state". The party also called for large increases in intergovernmental transfers to deal with the unfunded mandates of local government, fairer tariff structures and larger allocations of "free services" to assist the poor (ID 2006, 3–8). De Lille has even stated that Cape Town is "not ready for the liberal market ideology of the DA and ANC" and that "social democracy is the only way forward" (*Cape Argus*, November 7, 2006).

Just how committed the ID is to these policies and ideologies remains to be seen, however, and must be tempered by the party's enthusiastic support for market-led, export-oriented growth strategies at the national level: "The broad trajectory of the [national] government's macro-economic programme (tariff reduction, the reduction of the budget deficit, inflation targeting and stable monetary policy) should be applauded and should continue" (ID 2004). And given that the party has now placed its future in the hands of a possible coalition with the ANC it is unlikely that it is going to be too critical of its bedmate's local government policies. Indeed, De Lille went on in her opinion piece in the *Cape Argus* (November 7, 2006) to say that the poor in Cape Town must "replace their sense of entitlement with hard work"—a neoliberal sentiment if ever there was one.

PRIVATIZATION IN PRACTICE

The real neoliberal test, of course, comes with examining privatization in practice. It is here that we see the truly neoliberal character of local government reform in post-apartheid Cape Town, with both the ANC and the DA having implemented rapid and far-reaching commercialization initiatives while in power since 1996.

In providing a summary of the various services that have been privatized and corporatized in the city it should be noted that there is no single or easy source to draw on. The city does not keep a central record of services that have been privatized, and it is only since the formation of the Unicity in 2000 that there has been any centralized, metropolitan-scale record keeping at all.

What is offered here is a list of the commercialization efforts that I have come across over the years, informed by conversations with policymakers, unionists, researchers and community activists as well as official council documents. It is not a comprehensive list by any means. Much of the small-scale outsourcing and (sub)contracting of services takes place with little, if any, public notice and is very difficult to track. An attempt in mid-2004 by the Cape Town branch of Samwu to compile a list of the services that have been privatized is incorporated here, but this too is far from complete.

I have listed services on a sectoral basis, along with some details on the process by which the privatization/corporatization decisions were possible.

Water and Sanitation

As a "core" service—arguably the most important service the city provides—Cape Town city council has made it clear that it "does not intend to privatise" water and sanitation (CCT 2004b, 47). It has also stated that it does not intend to "corporatise" the service.

And yet the latter is exactly what the city has done. First proposed by the Unicity Commission in 2000, the Democratic Alliance moved quickly after its electoral win that year to push for the corporatization of water and sanitation, electricity, and solid waste management by July 2002. The political chaos of floor-crossing in 2002 contributed to "delays beyond the control of the Internal Business Unit Project" to meet this schedule, but the ANC continued with the DA's plans once it recaptured the Mayoral office in 2002 (CCT 2001a, 2004c; PWC 1999, 2000, 2001; Smith 2005).

Whether council was intentionally trying to mislead Capetonians by saying that the city is not going to "corporatise" these services—opting instead to use more ambiguous terms such as "business units" and "transparent service units"—is not clear. What is clear is that enormous efforts have gone into creating these corporatized entities, with the city having "made more progress in the technical ringfencing of these services than its peers [in other parts of the country]" (CCT 2004c, 5, 8).

Interestingly, one of the "delays beyond the control" of the Internal Business Unit Project was that the original proposal for corporatization had to be withdrawn due to noncompliance with the Municipal Systems Act. The process was put back on track in mid-2001 with the appointment of a consultant to make recommendations to council, but procedural concerns remained. The most significant of these has been the lack of consultation with labour and civil society. There have been no public consultations on the proposed corporatization of water, sanitation and refuse, and very limited consultation on electricity. Interactions with organized labour have also been limited—even confrontational—with Samwu being told after a decision had been made to corporatize water that "[t]his is a lawful decision of Council and we do not have to justify the decisions to the unions".[10]

Equally problematic was the speed at which the city made its initial decisions to corporatize. Claiming to have completed a thorough analysis of all the "human resource, industrial relations, organization design, finance, service operational issues and other internal issues required", the consultancy firm hired by the city for this work produced the first draft of the report in just eight weeks, despite the fact that very little metro-wide data was available at the time (PWC 2001).

One explanation for this extraordinary speed is that the research methodology employed by the consultants was simply imported from other jurisdictions and not necessarily appropriate for Cape Town. With the exclusive use of the "Excelsior Diagnostic Improvement Tool"—an evaluative mechanism "developed by PriceWaterhouseCoopers to assist their global initiative on supporting excellence in the public sector" (PWC 2001, 5)—Cape Town's water, sanitation, electricity and waste management services were assessed against "international best practice" (primarily with cities in Europe and North America). In effect, Cape Town's services were rapidly evaluated on the basis of a quantitative research tool developed in Europe and then compared to corporatized service units in Britain, Canada and other highly industrialized nations, with no reference to the unique post-apartheid service delivery features of Cape Town or comparisons with other 'third world' cities. Nonetheless, city council approved the model, arguing that cost reductions and efficiency gains could only "become possible if the recommendation to implement Business Units is accepted" (CCT 2001a, 13).

But it is not just corporatization that has taken place in this sector. There has been considerable outsourcing and (sub)contracting of water and sanitation services throughout the city. The digging of trenches for pipes, the reading of water meters and maintenance of sewage treatment facilities are examples of the kinds of smaller-scale, creeping privatizations that have taken place. Although the bulk of water services continue to be provided by the state-owned 'business unit', all of the 13 water depots in the city have outsourced activities, with the trend being toward further contracting out.[11]

Solid Waste

Plans to corporatize solid waste management have progressed along the same lines as that of water and sanitation, but would appear to be less advanced. There is also considerably more private sector involvement in this service area, with large multinational firms such as Waste Tech and Waste Man operating alongside small and microenterprise operations, many of the latter being township-based 'empowerment' initiatives.

The larger companies tend to manage waste removal and disposal in commercial/industrial districts and suburbs of the city, with the smaller/ micro firms managing waste removal activities in low-income areas. The contracting out of waste removal to microenterprises in the townships has, in fact, been one of the biggest privatization growth areas in the city, with individual contractors being assigned small sections of a neighbourhood and given responsibility for street cleaning as well as door-to-door refuse collection (the so-called 'one man contracts').

Cape Town's "Community Based Refuse Collection" program gives institutional strength to this privatization trend. The program oversees microcontracts throughout the city and is intended to "ensure effective refuse collections by contracting community based entrepreneurs to deliver services and to educate communities to ultimately take full responsibility for their living environment. The benefits to City are: Satisfied communities and residents; Cleaner living environments; Economic empowerment; and Facilitation of job creation opportunities" (CCT 2003a, Appendix 5C).

Most townships in the city now have some form of microenterprise waste management. In some cases there are larger private firms that act to coordinate these contracts, making a profit out of their brokering role. Billy Hattingh & Associates is one such company in Cape Town, with significant operations in Khayelitsha. These Khayelitsha operations have been controversial, however, with Samwu insisting in the late 1990s that it was not necessary to privatize the service. The Tygerberg municipality (the municipal substructure responsible for the area at the time) ignored requests from Samwu leadership to restructure the public service in the area to take better account of the enormous disparities in existing public sector resources in the different waste management depots, but management refused, driving through the privatization program with no public consultation (Qotole et al. 2001).

These microenterprise schemes have also created considerable political tension between municipal workers and community organizations. In the

Khayelitsha initiative community leaders (many linked to the ANC–allied South African National Civic Organization (Sanco)) were aggressively selling the Billy Hattingh scheme as 'job creation' for unemployed residents, portraying unionized workers as 'fat cat' labourers with no interest in the community (despite the fact that many of the labourers themselves lived in Khayelitsha). The situation degenerated into threats and intimidation of workers from these community leaders and is part of a larger rift that has emerged across the country between labour and municipal unions with microenterprise privatization schemes (Qotole et al. 2001). Not all community members have fallen victim to the neoliberal rhetoric of job creation, however, and the Cape Town branch of Samwu has been somewhat effective at containing the tensions and in creating political alliances with anti-privatization community organizations and NGOs in the city (Lier and Stokke 2006).

Another significant area of privatization is that taking place in the City Improvement Districts, all of which have private waste management firms to collect waste and conduct street cleaning. Coordination of these CIDs is done by the Cape Town Partnership—set up as a PPP with the city in October 2000—which claims that its research "highlighted crime and grime as the two major disincentives to success and growth" in the city. In response, they have allocated a "significant proportion of the CID's budget to additional cleansing". In the central city, the CID pays for a doubling of cleansing services and, "together with the co-operation of the City of Cape Town and business in the City, is making Cape Town a much cleaner and more pleasant place to visit" according to its website. The cleansing is performed by both the city and by privately owned Minizu Cleansing Solutions. Even much of the cleansing in council-owned buildings is contracted out to private firms.

Electricity

Electricity is the third 'tradeable' service to be corporatized by the city. However, original plans have now been changed due to the introduction of regional electricity distributors (REDs), a national government program to reform electricity distribution throughout the country.

The REDs system is intended to rationalize what has been a very fragmented network system in the country, with 187 municipalities, plus state-owned Eskom, distributing and selling electricity. This fragmentation, like so many other apartheid institutional legacies, has created considerable inefficiencies and irregularities.

It is expected that the REDs will improve economies of scale for billing, servicing, cross-subsidization and infrastructure investments through a more centralized organizational system. The restructuring could help cross-subsidize poor, predominantly rural, areas in a more systematic way, as well as rationalize electricity rates. Consumers currently pay significantly different rates in different parts of the country—even within municipalities—and the rural poor tend to pay the highest rates of all (Fiil 2001). The quality of service also varies considerably across the country, with concerns about different terms of employment and different health and safety systems for electricity workers in what can be an extremely dangerous occupation.

Cape Town became the first RED in South Africa in July 2005, after ringfencing its electricity service into a stand-alone, corporatized business unit (Cape Town was chosen as the first RED exactly because it was so far advanced in this direction).

The introduction of the RED raises some serious concerns, however. The first of these is a matter of financial compensation. Cape Town, like most other municipalities in the country, generates a considerable surplus on the electricity it buys from Eskom and sells to residents (approximately 10% of the city's operating budget). These funds have been used to cross-subsidize services that would not otherwise be able to pay their own way, such as libraries and parks. It is still not clear what will happen to these surpluses under REDs, how the city will be compensated or how it will affect capital spending, contributing to tensions between the recently-elected DA and the national government, with the former threatening to pull out of the RED agreement in late 2006.

A second problem is that the management of Cape Town's electricity system is now in the hands of a national body (the Electricity Distribution Industry (EDI)). It is not clear what authority the city of Cape Town will have in future decision making, vis-à-vis the EDI. Will elected city officials still be involved in decisions about tariffs for the poor? Can residents of Cape Town decide what the city's priorities should be for electricity infrastructure investment? Much remains unresolved.

A third, and related point, has to do with the ideological shift associated with the REDs restructuring. Corporatization, as discussed earlier, creates a new kind of management ethos. Rather than decisions being made as part of a municipal whole, the new RED will think much more narrowly about its own financial bottom line and become one more step removed from local, community control. The fact that Cape Town's RED will have to compete with REDs in other parts of the country will make this focus on the financial bottom line all the more central to its decision-making process.[12]

In this drive to be profitable, might there be more electricity cutoffs for those who cannot afford to pay? Might we see job losses in an attempt to make the RED more competitive? Words of warning from the Chief Financial Officer of the Electricity Distribution Industry are ominous in this regard: "[The introduction of REDs] will come with lots of pain. Efficiencies need strong medicines. I am grateful that we have a government prepared to bite the bullet and take unpopular decisions in the short term for long term benefits" (EDI 2004, 4).

There are also concerns about the outright privatization of the REDs once they are up and running. Eskom has already stated that shareholding in the REDs will eventually be broadened to the private sector. The EDI, for its part, says that the REDs are intended to "become world-class assets that international investors may be interested in venturing into". Will Cape Town's RED be sold off to a private company in the future?

Despite these concerns there was virtually no public consultation on the matter in Cape Town. The city had been informed of the request to make it the site of the first RED in early 2004 and yet did not make information available to the public or ask for public input until the end of that year, giving residents a month (over the Christmas holidays) to learn about and comment on the highly complex proposals. Nor did the media pick up on the issue.[13]

City officials cannot be blamed entirely for this lack of consultation. A culture of nonengagement on the issue had been established at the national level, with the EDI attempting to obtain an exemption on Section 78 of the Municipal Systems Act, which requires municipalities to consult with communities and organized labour about major service restructuring initiatives such as the REDs. The EDI's "gripe" with Section 78 was that "it is time consuming and costly" and the organization lobbied the Minister of Energy and Minerals to allow REDs to be introduced without these consultations. Why "spend time and money on a project that everyone agrees with", asked the EDI legal advisor in its October 2004 newsletter, "merely to comply with legislation that is a process all concerned with would prefer to pass?" (EDI 2004, 9).

But as with water, sanitation and waste management, corporatization is not the only privatization threat in the electricity sector. As I have already indicated, there is a strong interest in privatizing sections of REDs in the near future and there are already plans to have private firms build new power stations in the country (including nuclear power plants and "alternative" energy sources such as windmills). There had also been talk of selling the coal-fired Athlone Power Station in Cape Town to a private power company (CCT 2003a, Appendix 5C), though the station has since been decommissioned and mothballed (with the latter creating serious health and safety problems for workers dealing with the asbestos in the building).

On a smaller scale there is considerable outsourcing of electricity services to medium- and micro-sized firms in the city, from the maintenance of street lights to meter reading/installation and electricity (dis)connections. This sector typically requires a higher level of skills due to its inherent safety risks but this has not stopped the rapid spread of small and micro-enterprise contracts.

TRANSPORTATION

Much of the responsibility for transportation services falls outside of the purview of local government in South Africa, with ports, rails, highways and airports being the responsibility of national and provincial authorities. I outlined trends toward privatization and corporatization in these sectors in the previous chapter but it is worth repeating here that all of the major, internationally linked transport infrastructures of the city are now run by private companies or as stand-alone business units, with no direct political or economic accountability to the city.

Cape Town is, however, responsible for all of the roads within its municipal boundaries and for the management of its own vehicular fleet. With regards to the former, the city has outsourced a considerable amount of road maintenance to private companies and has even proposed "a community-based initiative, associated with the upgrading of concrete roads, stormwater provisioning and prevention of flooding ... road maintenance, street sweeping and gully cleaning" (CCT 2003a, Appendix 5A). Similar to the 'one man contracts' in waste management, these responsibilities can now be contracted out to microenterprises in the name of job creation. Fleet management for much of the city's vehicular stock has also been outsourced to a private company, as has the management of a number of council-owned parking lots and street parking areas (much of the latter being controlled now by CIDs).

The city has also sold off its road surfacing facilities, handing this responsibility over to a private company in 2000. So remarkable was the decision-making process around this particular policy that it bears repeating here, illustrating as it does both the highly dubious nature of the privatization processes in the city and the blindly ideological commitment to privatization on the part of senior decision makers. I have condensed a 25-page report to council on the matter to a handful of key paragraphs here (see CCT 2000 for the full text).

The report begins by stating that the bitumen and bitumen-related industries in the Western Cape and many other parts of the country are "dominated by monopolies and cartel type organizations" and highlights this as the primary reason that it is necessary to have a publicly owned premix plant for road building and repairs. The authors saw this as "[a] bulwark against a non-benign monopoly in premix manufacture". In fact, the council's premix manufacturing plant was established in 1979 as a "countermeasure to a non-benign private sector monopoly that would push prices exceedingly high if the Council plant did not exist".

At the time there were only two premix manufacturing companies in the Western Cape, one being Much and the other More asphalt. The first company was part of the Murray and Roberts Group (the second largest construction conglomerate in the country), which controls all of the stone quarries in the Cape Town area, including the supply of stone to the

More factory. According to the report, "it appears that Much has recently achieved a cartel type arrangement with, or control over, More".

The report writers also noted that the existence of a council-owned plant and in-house laying crews and machinery "ensured a better quality of premix and a better standard of laying than was available from the private sector. Voluminous documentation on this exists. The current view is that problems with the quality of the premix supply from the private sector ... would continue to occur if the Council plant closed down".

A third stated reason to keep the service in public hands was "convenience". There are different types of bitumous asphalt premix and these can only be made one type at a time, creating delays if repair crews are waiting for a private company to produce the type of premix the city needs. "Some delays in the Directorate have been up to two days in duration, with crews and machinery standing idle.... Occasionally one is forced to compromise on the quality of premix one accepts ... because private sector premix supply is via virtual monopoly. That monopoly may (and experience proves it does) dictate supply timing and to some extent quality irrespective of what is written in contracts".

Finally, it was indicated that "during the period of the late 1980s and through to the mid-1990s the council premix material prices and costs closely matched or indeed undercut the tendered prices the private sector was offering for this material. However, in 1995 the two local premix companies ... started offering below market prices in their tenders to Council. The prices were about 20–25% below-market. Surprisingly, this large drop in prices was not matched by a similar drop in prices these companies offered to private sector paving contractors.... The reasons for the below-market prices offered to Council are not clear but the only reasonable conjecture is that it was a multipurpose marketing and business ploy used to tempt council to close its plant. This conjecture is supported by precedent in that there have been a number of formal and informal attempts by Much in particular to wrest the plant away from Council and remove it as a competitive player in the Western Cape.... In December of 1998 both firms suddenly stopped offering below-market prices and both increased their tendered prices by the very large amount of 48%.... [This price hike] coincided with unconfirmed statements in the press that the City of Cape Town was going to close its plant. It did not coincide with any increase in crude oil prices." Moreover, there was "no indication that private sector laid surfacing prices are less than the internal laid surfacing costs.... the rate payer is still getting roads maintained via internal resurfacing at the same price or better than the private sector can manage".

A private sector consultant hired in early 1999 then conducted his own investigation of the road surfacing facilities of council, culminating in a draft report in June 1999. The authors of the council report noted that the consultant's report "lacked adherence to any terms of reference making the report jumbled and difficult to follow and also led to the in-house members

of the Works Branch Business Improvement team questioning the correct-
ness of an inordinately high number of assertions, figures and assumptions
contained in the report.... [Moreover] there was no comparative analysis of
in-house versus private sector or of the overall end cost to the ratepayer for
premix laid, complete and in place.... The inclusion of pothole repairs in the
business analysis and recommendations was [also] considered ill advised,
and had certainly not been asked for."

The outside consultant's recommendations were as follows: "Shut down
the [council] plant permanently as soon as possible and effectively remove
all overheads and staff; Immediately call for proposals from the private
sector regarding the disposal of the plant and the land it stands upon; That
the transport and laying components of the existing Surfacing Undertaking
also be closed down as soon as practical and these functions be outsourced
to the private sector [despite the fact that this aspect of roads maintenance
was not part of the consultant's review mandate]."

Remarkably, the council analysts accepted these recommendations and
argued in their own report that council should in fact move to privatize the
service, despite all of their previous objections. The authors do conclude
with a warning, however: "The Business Improvement Team recognized
very clearly that past history and current indications mean that there is a
very real possibility that the manufacturers of premix could exhibit a car-
tel-type façade and attempt to overexploit the needs of Council and indeed
of the future Unicity—i.e. they would push their prices up". They also note:
"Union leadership and representatives have consistently indicated that they
are opposed to this Business Initiative".

In the end, the council's plant was shut down and road surfacing is now
done by the 'cartel' of Much and More, with increasing complaints of quality, price and reliability. Ah, the logic of neoliberalism!

City Improvement Districts (CIDs)

Having made several references to CIDs, I will now explain in more detail
how these operate in Cape Town and how they contribute to the privatization of services and public space in the city.

City improvement districts (or, as they are more appropriately called
elsewhere in the world, business improvement districts (BIDs)) are essentially a partnership between the city and private businesses in a geographically defined area (typically delineated by boundaries such as
streets or open spaces). In Cape Town this arrangement consists of a
Service Level Agreement containing 30 different levels of "guaranteed services". Through this agreement the city is legally bound to perform agreed-upon municipal services at a certain standard. If these
standards are not met subcontractors can be brought in at the City's
expense, including cleansing, security and parking service providers.
Cape Town CIDs are based on what the city refers to as "international

best practice" (CCT 2003d, s1.1), with the Cape Town Partnership's website claiming that "international research proved that the CID model was the best means by which the private and public sectors could make a substantive improvement to the urban environment in partnership with each other."

The purpose of the CIDs is to: "enhance and supplement the municipal services provided by the City; facilitate investment in the City Improvement Districts; facilitate a co-operative approach between the City and the private sector in the provision of municipal services; halt the degeneration and facilitate the upliftment of distressed business and mixed-use areas; and promote economic growth and sustainable development and in this way assist the Council in the fulfillment of its objects and developmental duties" (CCT 2003d, s1.2).

The first CID in Cape Town came on stream in November 2000 in the central business district to much fanfare from city council and local business associations. The city released a multipage, colour broadsheet announcing the benefits of the CID with two of the ANC's top councillors and a senior administrator pictured on the front page striding confidently across an intersection in the centre of the city (the administrator subsequently became the executive director of the Cape Town Partnership). There are plans for as many as 60 CIDs in the city, with 14 having been established by 2005 (Miraftab 2006, 3).

According to the city's by-laws on CIDs (CCT 2003d) the Management Board is made up of unelected property owners and representatives from the city. In practice, however, they are "run entirely by the private sector" (according to the Cape Town Partnership's website). The powers and duties of this Board have also evolved to include virtually every municipal service that the city provides. From cleansing to policing to the monitoring of parking, the CIDs in Cape Town have effectively become private sector enclaves where service levels and rates levies are determined by the property owners association and where public spaces become private enclaves of privilege, with street kids, panhandlers and informal traders pushed out of the demarcated areas by the business and homeowners who control the decision making.

As Nahnsen (2003, 147) notes in her study of CIDs, "Both the Cape Town Partnership and the Central City Improvement District must be understood as vehicles that create an exclusive and powerful network as well as a voice for the established formal business community providing them with the tools to re-construct inner city urban space to their own needs ... with its vision and mission to seek to promote Cape Town as 'the heart of a world class city'". Informal activities such as trading and parking attendance (what the city council refers to as "parking terrorists") are marginalized in the process, as are any other unsuitable people that do not fit the safe, orderly, clean and "civilized" image that business interests want to project (Nahnsen 2003, 149–50).

Even the neoliberal South African Cities Network (2003, 25) admits that the establishment of CIDs "may entail the effective privatization of public space." In some cases, CIDs have taken on the (*de facto*) role of urban planning in their areas, making demands and decisions about open spaces, long-term investments in the built environment, tourism marketing and spatial development strategies. Given that CIDs in Cape Town also cover the most strategic economic areas in the city—i.e. the business nodes—this planning influence is all the more significant (in the central business district CID it has been reported that management hired a Danish design and planning firm to draw up plans for public space).

Whether this takeover of city planning is a 'rational' response to the decline of the city's planning capacity over the past ten years, or whether the CIDs themselves have contributed to the demise of the planning department, is not clear (see Watson 2002 for an extended discussion). What is clear is that the influence of the private sector in municipal functions such as urban planning is growing in Cape Town.

It is also clear that there is considerable support for CIDs from all levels of government and from neoliberal think tanks and policy groups. Despite SACN's concerns about the "privatisation of public space", they nonetheless see CIDs as "particularly successful in the South African context, as they constitute a credible institutional vehicle to support and represent business interests" (SACN 2003, 25).

The ultimate aims of these CIDs are captured by the following quote by the founding director of the Central CID, Michael Farr: "The first objective is the attainment of world-class standards in the Cape Town central city, while the second involves the branding, positioning, marketing and establishment of the central city as a globally competitive city with a globally competitive product offering" (as quoted in Miraftab 2006, 3).

OTHER SERVICE SECTORS

Other service sectors that have either been privatized or for which there are future plans for some form of commercialization in Cape Town include the following:

- Sale of the Epping National Fresh Produce Market
- Sale of the Maitland Abattoir
- Outsourcing of some functions in libraries
- Outsourcing of Parks and Recreation functions and facilities, including "a gradual outsourcing of nurseries" (the nursery in Bellville is now run by Plant Cape), "the development of the City's parks and nature conservation network and programme through partnerships with communities and external service providers", the outsourcing

of its construction unit, and the outsourcing of the city's 18 resorts for "minimising expenditure and maximising income" (CCT 2003a, Appendices 5C and 5F)

- Outsourcing of mechanical workshops
- Outsourcing of creative services
- Outsourcing of tea and coffee services
- Outsourcing of warehousing
- Contracting of water and milk testing laboratories
- Outsourcing of certain IT, human resources and finance functions
- Outsourcing of the maintenance of council housing and buildings
- Outsourcing of mowing of publicly owned lawns
- Outsourcing of traffic summons and traffic cameras
- Outsourcing of removal of animal carcases

Once again, this is only a partial list, but it does serve to illustrate how deep and widespread the privatization agenda has become in practical terms in Cape Town.

PROBLEMS WITH PRIVATIZATION

Having established the fact of privatization in Cape Town, I conclude the chapter with a brief discussion of how it impacts on spatial and socioeconomic inequalities in the city.

Multi-tiered Service Standards

It can be argued that private sector service delivery is inherently unequal insofar as it provides a level of service according to ability to pay. Upper-income residential areas and business associations are able to purchase 'world-class' services and infrastructure while low-income residents must get by on a 'basic' level of service.

But rather than being a problem, this inherent inequality is seen by policymakers in the city as one of the benefits of privatization: "Communities should have some choice and discretion in determining what range of municipal services they want and can afford. It follows that some areas may opt for a higher level of services for which they are prepared to pay a premium, while other communities may opt for lower levels of services for which they should receive a discount" (CCT 2004b, 69).

These multi-tiered service standards are justified by at least two neoliberal arguments. The first is that world-class services are needed by transnational elites and capital if they are to remain competitive in the global economy and if the city is going to attract new investments and skilled personnel. To lower service standards in these areas, it is argued, would be suicidal to the economy as a whole. Hence the assertion by a former ANC mayor of Cape Town that the city "needs to maintain our CBDs and the world-class infrastructure in established areas" (CCT 2003c, 1).

A second neoliberal argument is that by allowing wealthy neighbourhoods and businesses to buy their own services from the private sector it frees up public funds for investments in low-income areas. The city of Cape Town believes that "the private provision of health, recreation and security services for those who can afford it relieves the municipality of their obligation to provide those services to them" (CCT 2003a, Appendix 5B). This is touted as part of the city's "pro-poor" service agenda.

In reality, things are very different. As we have seen in previous chapters, the state (both local and national) continues to pour enormous public funds into business nodes and suburban areas while underinvesting in townships and in infrastructures that benefit low-income residents. In other words, upper-income residents and businesses continue to benefit from public monies while at the same time topping up their service levels from the private sector, further widening the service delivery gap in the city.

There are also many instances of outright 'redlining' by the private sector, with private sector service providers refusing to provide any level of service to a low-income community because they feel they cannot recoup their costs. Redlining for home loans by private banks is an example of this problem. 'Network ghettos' for telecommunications are another. But the problem exists with more mundane services such as waste management, with many of the larger private sector waste firms unwilling to risk a service contract in township areas.

This 'cherry picking' on the part of private companies creates additional problems by leaving the most difficult—and geographically scattered— areas of the city to be serviced by the public sector. This further fragmentation of an already highly fragmented post-apartheid service landscape contributes to a vicious cycle of decay. As areas most in need of services become increasingly difficult to operate in, the public sector becomes less efficient, deskilled and demoralized, potentially driving up public sector operating costs and lowering the standards of service, feeding into neoliberal arguments about the public sector's inability to provide effective services.

Accountability

Another source of inequality is that of accountability. Research has shown that private sector service delivery firms—contrary to what neoliberal proponents argue—tend to be less accountable than their public sector counterparts. There are a host of reasons for this (see Mulgan 1997a, 1997b, 2000 and Roberts 2000 for an extended discussion) but the important point to note here is that this unaccountability tends to be less of a problem for businesses and suburban ratepayers who often have the skills and capacity to monitor service delivery in their areas or to put pressure on the city to monitor and enforce contracts for them. The CIDs in Cape Town, for example, have lawyers and other professionals to write contracts and monitor the performance of contractors and are able to hire and fire private service delivery firms accordingly.

Township residents, on the other hand, typically have no direct role in the decision making process around private sector provision in their areas and generally have no information about the nature of the contract (and may not understand the legal language in any event). Even if township residents are aware of the terms of a contract they have little clout to enforce service standards or to terminate unsatisfactory contracts (though community resistance to privatization can force private companies out, as widespread protests against water privatization in Manila and Cochabamba (Bolivia) have demonstrated, for example). Weaker public sector presence in township areas also means that the state is less likely to properly oversee the performance of private service providers in these areas.

This problem is made worse by the fact that so much of the privatization taking place in the townships is with microenterprises. It is difficult enough to monitor the performance of a large multinational company providing a single service to an entire city. It is another thing altogether to try and monitor dozens of small enterprises operating in small geographic areas with little in the way of administrative infrastructure.

In this kind of scattered supervisory environment, township residents are more likely to be on the receiving end of environmental violations, corruption and noncontracted price increases (to name but a few of the kinds of private sector infringements documented in low-income communities in South Africa and around the world). These are the "hidden costs" (CUPE 2002) of privatization and it is the poor who are most negatively affected.

Labour Conditions

A third way in which inequalities are worsened by privatization is its impact on municipal workers. Although little empirical research has been conducted on wage differentials and working conditions between the public and private sector in Cape Town, or South Africa more generally, there is some evidence in the waste management sector of significant differentials, and considerable anecdotal evidence, to suggest that private sector workers are paid less, have less job security and have worse health and safety conditions than their public sector counterparts (for a discussion of how this is further complicated by gender inequalities see Samson (2003)). There is also evidence from other parts of the world to suggest this is a general trend, as private firms attempt to maximize profits and remain competitive for future contracts (ILO 2000, Samson 2003, Hall 2005).

Health and safety is a particular concern. Municipal workers in Cape Town often work in extremely dangerous and unpleasant conditions, often with little safety equipment. To use two examples, workers who collect the 'night soil' buckets from informal settlements often have little more than a pair of rubber gloves and an apron to work with, despite the fact that buckets can be overflowing with feces and urine and contain communicable diseases. Another example is the collection of refuse from the blue bins located around Cape Town for pedestrians to deposit their trash. There are some 30,000 of these bins in the city (with city managers proud of this 'environmental' initiative) but there is no release mechanism by which to dump the trash out. Workers are forced to reach in to the bin with their hands to pick out broken glass and rotten food, with no more than a pair of gloves. Years of complaints from the union have brought no change to either system.

If these are the kinds of conditions that public sector municipal workers are operating under in Cape Town, with one of the strongest unions in the country to support them (i.e. Samwu), what must it be like for nonunionized workers in private companies, particularly the small start-up microenterprise firms? Similarly, what are working conditions like for volunteers involved in 'community participation' programs who are cleaning streets, digging trenches, and so on? With old car batteries, rancid food and raw sewage a normal feature of the underserviced township landscape, community members may be unwittingly exposing themselves to a wide range of health and safety risks. This is not a problem encountered by suburban Capetonians.

Affordability

A fourth way in which privatization leads to a further polarization of cities is affordability. I have already mentioned the fact that low-income communities are often restricted to the level of services they can afford, but even this 'basic' service provision can be too expensive for households in the townships.

Cost recovery—the practice of charging the cost of delivering a service to a household—often means that low-income families cannot afford the water, electricity and other services they need to use, even if it is just a standpipe in the yard or a low-amperage electricity connection. This lack of affordability has resulted in tens of thousands of households in Cape Town underconsuming on essential services and/or having their services cut off if they cannot afford to pay.

The practice of cost recovery in Cape Town is the subject of the next chapter and will not be dealt with in detail here except to say that it is not just private firms that practice it. The corporatization of municipal services is as much a problem in this regard as the involvement of private companies, with managers from ringfenced 'business units' often acting more like private sector managers than their private sector counterparts. This behaviour may be due in part to the fact that their salaries are increasingly tied to financial performance. It may be because these public sector managers want to prove that they are as business-minded as their private sector counterparts. Whatever the reason, managers of corporatized units in Cape Town have proven themselves aggressive enforcers of cost recovery principles, including the installation of water restrictors and prepaid electricity meters.

Cape Town also appears to be making decisions on infrastructure development and service extensions based on cost recovery rates in the city, with "[p]rioritization [being] given to projects where there is an ... increased level of payment for services" (CCT 2004b, 53). In other words, only those communities that pay the cost of their services will receive these services, effectively holding low-income families ransom to their service bills.

Privatization therefore serves multiple purposes in the South African context: it contains the expectations of the poor; it opens an almost limitless set of service delivery possibilities for the transnational elite; it minimizes the cross-subsidy burden on business and suburban ratepayers; and it provides an investment outlet for large and small capital. Little wonder, then, that it has been so enthusiastically embraced by the new neoliberal policymakers of the city.

CONCLUSION

In conclusion, Cape Town has experienced far-reaching privatization on a wide range of municipal services. Some of these initiatives were begun during apartheid but the real shift to neoliberal service delivery has been since 1996, with the two major parties in Cape Town (the DA and ANC) aggressively promoting and practicing privatization while in power and in opposition.

The emergence of the Independent Democrats at the local level may have some impact on this trend in Cape Town (given the party's explicitly anti-privatization stance), as might the slim margin of victory of the DA in the March 2006 elections, but there is no indication of a seismic shift in ideological attitudes. If anything, the balance of forces would appear to be increasingly in favour of a 'bullish' neoliberal position in council. National government has failed to substantially increase intergovernmental transfers, wealthy ratepayers have managed to resist any attempts at major local redistribution, donor agencies continue to fund commercialization efforts and all of the major services in the city have been corporatized.

It is in this material and ideological climate that efforts to recover the cost of municipal services have been so successful in Cape Town and elsewhere in the country, deepening the neoliberal agenda and further entrenching the inequalities of post-apartheid urban development. We turn to this phenomenon next.

7 Cost Recovering Cape Town

> At the moment I owe the council more than R6000. I must eat and I am unemployed. I do not think I will ever be able to pay my arrears. The council can do what ever they want to do.
>
> *A resident of Khayelitsha, as quoted in Xali (2002)*

The above quote is illustrative of a growing affordability crisis in South Africa, with many low-income families unable to pay the rising costs of basic services. Some are forced to make tragic decisions between buying water, food and clothing, while others have simply thrown their hands up in despair, letting the service bills rack up into massive debt arrears that they can never hope to pay back.

Municipal services that were once provided for free, or at heavily subsidized rates, have now become too expensive for many, contributing to extreme material and psychological hardships and undermining many of the gains made by the infrastructural roll outs of the 1990s and early 2000s.

This chapter describes the phenomenon of cost recovery on municipal services in South Africa since the end of apartheid and looks at how it has manifested itself in Cape Town. I start with a conceptual overview, followed by a discussion of how cost recovery is enforced, promoted and rationalized. The chapter concludes with a discussion of the uneven application of cost recovery in Cape Town and how this has served to entrench inequalities in the city and deepen the commodification of everyday life—yet another piece of the neoliberal, world city puzzle.

WHAT IS COST RECOVERY?[1]

Cost recovery refers to the collection of all, or most, of the costs associated with providing a particular service by a service provider. For publicly owned services this may or may not include a surplus above and beyond the costs of production. For private sector providers it generally entails a surplus (i.e. profit). In either case, the objective is to recoup the full costs of production.

For services that can be accurately measured in volumetric terms (e.g. water, electricity, waterborne sewerage), cost recovery is achieved by charging end-users the short-run marginal cost of production plus a portion of long-term operating and maintenance costs. The cost of providing electricity, for example, would include the expense of connecting the household to the electricity grid, plus a portion of the amortized operating and maintenance cost of the bulk infrastructure required to generate and distribute electricity, and a volumetric rate for the marginal cost of every kilowatt-hour of electricity consumed.

There are numerous ways of calculating these costs (Dinar 2001), but most models incorporate a downward sloping marginal cost curve where, due to economies of scale, those who consume more of a service are charged less per unit of consumption than those who consume less. Historically, this has meant that poor households were penalized on a per unit basis because they consume less than wealthy households and industry.

In response to these equity concerns, progressive block tariffs have been introduced in many countries (including South Africa) in an effort to make the initial levels of consumption (or 'blocks') more affordable, even free, while charging increasingly higher prices as consumption levels rise. This rising block tariff has the added potential benefit of curbing consumption at the top end, thereby introducing conservation incentives.

Block tariffs are not inconsistent with cost recovery, however. The difference with more orthodox pricing models is that block tariffs charge higher than marginal cost prices at upper levels of consumption in order to make up for lower than marginal cost prices at lower levels, effectively cross-subsidizing the poor. Most importantly, they provide individual consumers with a certain level of subsidized consumption.

Not all services can be measured and priced on a volumetric basis though. With services such as refuse collection and dry sewerage (as well as nonmetered water or electricity), it is not possible to accurately or easily measure what an individual household has consumed. In such cases, cost recovery models tend to use a 'flat rate' that covers the average fixed and variable cost of the service. This can be done through a flat charge for individual services or it can be included in a general rates account. Equity concerns can then be dealt with through the application of differential rates, either through household income levels (i.e. income taxation) or via property valuation (i.e. the higher the value of your home, the more you pay, regardless of your level of consumption).

Whether volumetric or flat, all cost recovery models depend on 'ring-fencing'—i.e. the isolation of costs and revenues associated with a given service and the identification (and likely removal) of subsidies in or out of that sector. Ringfencing, as discussed in Chapter 6, requires that human and capital resources not be shared between different service sectors unless they are paid for on a cost recovery basis to the unit that provided them (e.g. the water department would pay the accounting department for the cost of keeping its books). The intention is to ensure that a service provider knows all its fixed and variable costs and is therefore able to apply (marginal) cost pricing to its customers.

In theory, therefore, the full cost of providing services such as water, electricity, refuse and sanitation can be determined and passed on to end-users (with or without cross-subsidization mechanisms such as block tariffs). In reality, the true costs of providing a service are seldom known: costs are complex and difficult to measure; they are constantly changing due to the 'lumpy' nature of infrastructure investments; there are inevitably joint costs that are difficult to apportion; accounting for externalities is constantly evolving, and so on (Renzetti 2001, 130). At best, cost recovery models are an approximation of real costs.

In the end, it is *fuller* cost recovery that is being attempted in Cape Town and elsewhere in the country: charging prices that are as close as possible to the marginal cost in the short term, and to the average cost curve in the long term, with the aim of eventually achieving full cost recovery. Accordingly, I use the term 'cost recovery' in this chapter to refer not only to *full* cost recovery but also to the intermediary stages of *fuller* cost recovery.

HOW IS COST RECOVERY ENFORCED?

For any cost recovery policy to be effective, a service provider must be able to regularly and accurately measure the consumption of a particular service by an individual household, and it must be able to collect payments. For volumetric services such as water and electricity, measurement is relatively easy with the use of increasingly sophisticated meters that measure the number of litres or kilowatt-hours consumed. Without meters it is virtually impossible to apply marginal cost pricing. For those services that are not measurable on a volumetric basis, it is necessary to approximate average consumption and to charge the average cost (with or without differential rates).

But the most accurate measurement and pricing systems in the world mean little if the service provider cannot collect the monies owed for services rendered. Effective administration is important here, including strong accounting and computer systems, financial management and a reliable postal/payment system.

Of equal importance are the punitive measures or threats used to persuade and force consumers to pay their bills. The most common form of punishment in South Africa has been to cut off a service to a household or restrict their access to a service (or merely threaten to do so). Other enforcement tools include legal action, the attachment of assets, and, most controversially in the case of South Africa, the eviction from one's home for nonpayment of services. Cutoffs are more difficult with services such as refuse collection and non-waterborne sewerage, but there have been cases in South Africa of households being denied these services as a penalty for nonpayment of water or electricity (Ruiters 2002).

Cutoffs and evictions are expensive and politically sensitive enforcement weapons, however. As a result, municipalities in South Africa are rapidly moving toward the use of prepaid meters and other forms of service restriction wherever possible. A prepaid meter is a device that not only measures the exact amount of a service that is consumed—allowing for marginal cost pricing—but also forces users to purchase the consumption in advance. 'Units' (be they litres of water or kilowatt-hours of electricity), are purchased at a retail outlet and then entered into the prepaid meter with the use of an electronic 'smart card' (meters are typically located in the household).

Prepaid meters are the ultimate cost recovery tool. They collect money in advance, they do not allow the consumer to go into default, and require no overt—and politically damaging—punitive measures to ensure payment of services. But there have been cases where prepaid meters were tampered with, and the electronic system can be cheated. As a result, service providers and meter manufacturers are actively working to develop more sophisticated metering systems, with South African producers at the forefront of developing these new technologies.

PROMOTING COST RECOVERY IN SOUTH AFRICA

Cost recovery on municipal services is a relatively new feature on the South African political landscape. As noted in Chapter 2, the apartheid state was a welfarist state, and although there were enormous differences between the quantity and quality of services across racial groups, services such as water, electricity and housing were largely and heavily subsidized.

This subsidy model began to erode in the 1980s with the introduction of neo-apartheid reforms by the National Party, with townships in particular expected to pay their own way. But well-orchestrated rates and tariff boycotts in these areas—part of the anti-apartheid campaign to make the townships 'ungovernable'—made it impossible to enforce these new policies, with payment rates for services as low as one or two percent of total billings.

Service standards in the townships dropped even further as the Black Local Authorities that ran them became bankrupt, but the apartheid state continued to prop up these puppet regimes financially, and services were seldom cut due to nonpayment. The National Party knew the situation was already explosive and opted to continue with a *de facto* subsidization of township municipal services into the 1990s. The suburbs, for their part, continued to receive subsidized services, either through direct subsidies from white-run municipalities or indirectly through the unequal taxation systems of apartheid local government.

On coming to power in 1994 the ANC immediately called for an end to rates boycotts and introduced a series of legislative and para-legislative mechanisms for cost recovery on municipal services (Pape and McDonald 2002). In February 1995, for example, national government launched "Operation Masakhane" ("Let's build together"), urging residents to pay for water, electricity, sewerage and refuse collection, and recruiting leading political figures such as Archbishop Desmond Tutu and civic leader Moses Mayekiso for publicity campaigns. Advertising gurus Saatchi and Saatchi were employed to promote the program.

More formally, the state introduced a range of legislation that promotes cost recovery. The Municipal Systems Act (RSA 2000a, s74.2.d), the omnibus legislation for all municipal service delivery, states that municipal services should be as "cost reflexive" as possible. The same applies to policies for specific services such as electricity, water, and sanitation. In the Draft White Paper on Energy Policy (RSA 1998c, 7) it is stated that "Government policy is to ... encourage energy prices to be as cost-reflective as possible". In the White Paper on Water and Sanitation (RSA 1994b, 19), one of the first policy papers written by the ANC, it is argued that "government may subsidise the cost of construction of basic minimum services but not the operating, maintenance or replacement costs".

The subsequent National Sanitation Policy White Paper (RSA 1996c, 4) stated that: "Sanitation systems must be sustainable.... payment by the user is essential to ensure this". The White Paper on Water Policy (RSA 1997a, 4) argues that users should be "charge[d] for the full financial costs of providing access to water, including infrastructure development and catchment management activities".

It is also important to consider the indirect ways in which cost recovery is promoted in South Africa. As discussed in Chapters 5 and 6, there are a series of legislative and Constitutional requirements that limit the ability of local governments to increase tariffs and rates on businesses and in wealthy suburbs. National Treasury has guidelines that limit rates increases to national inflation targets, while the Constitution disallows any rates or tariff increases that could "prejudice national economic policies" (RSA 1996a, s229.2.a), forcing municipalities to recoup a large proportion of the costs of their expanded service delivery mandates from low-income areas.

Intergovernmental transfers have provided little relief in this regard, having been effectively frozen in real terms since the mid-1990s. Even with recent increases in this funding, less than 5% of Cape Town's revenues come from other spheres of government. Nor will Municipal Infrastructure Grant funding be of much assistance, serving to reinforce the cost recovery mandate of the state rather than alleviating it. As the DPLG (2004a, 47) noted in its summary of the MIG in its first year, funding for municipalities will be dependent on "project feasibility studies", which require municipal services to be "sustainable"—i.e. where "all operational, maintenance and replacement costs are covered".

Having said that, most policy documents at the national level also make provision for some form of service subsidization for low-income households in the form of indigency clauses, progressive block tariffs and, importantly, free lifeline supplies of water and electricity. The White Paper on Water Policy (RSA 1997a, 4) is emblematic in this regard, arguing that "provision will also be made for some or all of these [cost recovery] charges to be waived".

The subsequent National Water Act (RSA 1998d, s5.1) took the issue further, stating that the Minister can "establish a pricing strategy which may differentiate among geographical areas, categories of water users or individual water users. The achievement of social equity is one of the considerations in setting differentiated charges". Similarly, the Municipal Systems Act (RSA 2000a, s97.1.c) states that tariffs for municipal services can be differentiated if based on indigency. In other words, the cost recovery policy in South Africa has explicit equity considerations and distinguishes itself in this respect from more orthodox cost recovery models based on simplistic downward sloping marginal cost curves.

But lest we lose sight of the larger cost recovery picture, it must be remembered that progressive block tariffs, indigent policies, and even 'free basic services' are not inconsistent with full cost recovery. As we shall see below, the way in which these policies have been introduced in South Africa and Cape Town is such that they only marginally protect the poor while disproportionately benefiting the rich. Lifelines and block tariffs may serve to round out the roughest edges of the cost recovery agenda but they do not replace it.

COST RECOVERY IN CAPE TOWN

The previous section painted a picture of top-down neoliberalism, with national policymakers forcing local authorities to introduce cost recovery. To some extent this is true, but it would be incorrect to portray local governments as mere victims in this cost recovery game.

Evidence of this is found in municipal policy documents and in policy practice in the city. On the policy front, the city's 2004–05 IDP highlights cost recovery as one of its central policy objectives, noting that all tariffs "should be reflective of the cost of service provision" (CCT 2004b, 53). In the area of housing, the city has introduced a program to "phas[e] in cost recovery rentals" as well as a "tighter collection" of rental payment, "supported by a policy that permits eviction of those who can but won't pay" (CCT 2004b, 22). The city also wants to "ensure full cost recovery" for water services, a "key" to that sector's "sustainability" (CCT 2004b, 76), as well as "the development and implementation of [electricity] tariffs that are cost reflective" (RED 2006, 2). In general, the city's policymakers want to promote an "active payment for services", with the goal of an average cost recovery rate of 96% a year by 2006–07 (up from 83% in September 2003) (CCT 2004b, 53; CCT 2006d, 121).

At the same time, rates increases for businesses and the suburbs will be kept "within national norms and guidelines, ensuring that the national and local economy are not undermined in the process" (CCT 2004b, 54), with rates increases for "both rich and poor not exceed[ing] 5%" (CCT 2004a, 13).

In practical terms, both the ANC and the Democratic Alliance have been keen enforcers of cost recovery in Cape Town, with tens of thousands of households having experienced water and electricity cutoffs over the years and with water restrictors and prepaid meters being rolled out. Equally instructive is the extent to which treatment for transgression on cost recovery is meted out differently across the city, with businesses and wealthy suburban areas being permitted to practice nonpayment in ways that are simply not tolerated in the townships.

Cape Town is not unique in this regard. Municipalities across the country have embraced and enforced cost recovery practices. Increased rates, service cutoffs or restrictions and prepaid service meters are now the norm rather than the exception. The umbrella organization representing organized local government, Salga, has also endorsed cost recovery policies, noting at its 2004 National Conference that all municipalities should "[c]ommit to improve revenue collection systems and to recover the cost of consumption" (Salga 2004b, item 15).

THE RATIONALE FOR COST RECOVERY

What is the rationale for cost recovery on basic municipal services? Officially, there are at least two reasons. The first relates to the ANC's commitment to a fiscally conservative macroeconomic program. Although it subsidizes some of the extension and upgrading of local services—particularly in the poorer, rural municipalities—national government has made it clear that it will not allow subsidization of local services to undermine its broader fiscal strategies.

The rationale here is partly ideological, with cost recovery—as the World Bank (1999, 44) puts it—being "a matter of good public fiscal practice". To deviate too far from this international fiscal norm could undermine confidence in the ANC's overall commitment to neoliberal reforms.

But it is also argued that revenues from cost recovery are essential to sustain municipal services on a long-term basis. Without cost recovery, the argument goes, the state could not generate the funds necessary for future service upgrades and extensions. This is the argument developed in the Water Supply and Sanitation Policy White Paper (RSA 1994b, 23), with government arguing subsidization of services will result in a "reduction in finances available for the development of basic services for those citizens who have nothing. It is therefore not equitable for any community to expect not to have to pay for the recurring costs of their services. It is not the Government who is paying for their free services but the unserved".

The message here is that cost recovery is 'pro-poor', ensuring that everyone will receive basic services. As Brook and Locussol (2002, 37) put it: "When a public sector utility does not recover the costs of providing a service, it is often unable to extend the system—leaving poorer, marginal areas unconnected to the grid". Cost recovery therefore not only makes good fiscal sense, it is the correct, moral thing to do.

A second argument used to justify cost recovery is that it helps reduce the consumption of precious natural resources such as water and energy. Subsidization, it is argued, promotes wasteful consumption of environmentally sensitive services because people do not feel (sufficient) financial pressure to reduce what they are consuming (or throwing away). Rising block tariffs are considered ideal in this respect because they penalize higher levels of consumption: the more you consume the more you pay per unit of consumption. Water shortages in Cape Town are frequently cited as a reason for full cost recovery, as are problems with landfill sites and greenhouse gas emissions.

Some of these goals are laudable, of course. Ensuring that resources are available for extensions and long-term maintenance is central to any prudent form of public management. So too is it necessary to look for ways of reducing what can only be described as enormously wasteful and hedonistic consumption of resources such as water and electricity in many of the wealthier parts of Cape Town and the country as a whole.

The problem is the way in which cost recovery has been implemented and the highly uneven and unjust mechanisms that have been developed to enforce it. But before we look at these it is worth reviewing the 'unofficial' rationale for cost recovery: the generally unstated motivations for cost recovery that help to explain why it has been so unfairly implemented and why it is so central to the competitive placement of a city like Cape Town in the broader world city system.

Reducing the Fiscal Burden on Capital and Elites

The first point to make is that cost recovery in South Africa is primarily intended for low-income areas. The rationale here is not so much 'pro-poor' as it is to reduce—possibly even eliminate—the cross-subsidization burden of service expansion on upper-income residents and businesses. By having low-income residents pay all, or most, of the costs of their services it will keep tariff increases in wealthier areas to a minimum. This in turn will attract and retain upper-income residents and businesses to the municipality. As one senior manager commented in an interview in 2000, "We do not want to kill the goose that lays the golden egg".

Businesses recognize local government's weakness in this regard and have begun to play municipalities against each other on tariff structures. The Durban Chamber of Commerce and Industry, for example, has "expressed the concern of its members regarding the increasing cost of doing business in the Durban Unicity area. The cost of water is one of the major components of the total infrastructural cost, over which our members have no control.... The prime concern of the Chamber is ensuring that the trading environment in the Unicity area contributes to the national and international competitiveness of its members in both commerce and industry". The Chamber went on to complain that the "expensive rural water schemes" in the newly formed Unicity have "exacerbated the financial implications of possible solutions [i.e. put pressure on business to help pay for the costs of these water extensions]" and says that they will work to maintain "acceptable" bulk water tariffs (DCCI 2002, 9).

Both national and local spheres of government are aware of the potential for an intermunicipal pricing war to be disruptive of larger macroeconomic planning and have begun to rationalize water and electricity tariffs across the country (this is one of the reasons for the introduction of the Regional Electricity Distributors (REDs)). But national and local governments are unable to control international price wars, with cities such as Cape Town and Durban having to compete with other cities around the world on the price of basic services. A revealing quote in this regard comes from the former Director General of the Department of Constitutional Development (the forerunner to the DPLG) in which he stated: "If we increase the price of electricity to users like Alusaf [a major aluminium exporter], their products will become uncompetitive."[2] In other words, if a city/country expects to be internationally competitive, attracting and retaining private capital and professionals, it must reduce or minimize the cost of services for the wealthy and boost cost recovery for the poor.

Justifying Differential Service Levels

Another rationale for cost recovery is that it allows wealthy residents and capital to buy the services they want, justifying a system of differential service levels in which 'you get what you can pay for'. Lower-income households are provided with a 'basic' level of services while elites are given the option of paying for 'world-class' standards. The overall objective is still one of cost recovery, and there is still a potential for cross-subsidization from rich to poor, but the underlying objective becomes one of satisfying the 'needs' of capital and transnational elites rather than a more equitable distribution of resources.

The following quote from the city of Cape Town's 2004–05 IDP is instructive in this regard:

The services all communities receive must be affordable on aggregate for the City as the whole and for individual households. It follows that only services that can be built, operated and maintained sustainably can be provided. Communities should have some choice and discretion in determining what range of municipal services they want and can afford. It follows that some areas may opt for a higher level of services for which they are prepared to pay a premium, while other communities may opt for lower levels of services for which they should receive a discount (CCT 2004b, 69).

The end result is a system of cost recovery in Cape Town (and virtually every other city in South Africa) in which the poor are expected to "opt" for a lower level of services and the wealthy are given the legal and moral authority to purchase services far above that of their low-income counterparts. The notion that low-income households would voluntarily "opt" for low levels of services is of course misleading and disingenuous, conflating household affordability with household needs and desires. So too is it disingenuous to suggest that the choice of upper-income residents and businesses to pay for "premium" services is fiscally neutral. In reality, the payment of premiums draws off resources that might otherwise be available for the improvement of services in township areas, effectively denying the city a source of public revenue. The result is lower standards in low-income areas and heightened pressures for cost recovery.

Promoting Commercialization

A third, though largely unacknowledged, rationale for cost recovery is that it promotes the privatization and commercialization of municipal services. At the heart of this process is the ringfencing of services. As discussed earlier, the separation of all cost and revenue streams related to a particular service, and the creation of stand-alone 'business units' to manage these cost structures, is a prerequisite to the application of marginal cost pricing.

The ringfencing of services also sets in train a series of managerial and ideological practices that promote the commercialization of service activities, with public sector managers often forced to act like private sector administrators, focusing on the financial bottom line and driving down costs to improve 'profitability'. Not all corporatization processes lead to this kind of behaviour but international experience has shown that the focus tends to be on narrow financial criteria within the corporatized entity rather than on the broader public service mandate of the local state.

This commercialization philosophy is evident in how the city of Cape Town sees its cost recovery systems operating, noting in its application for a Restructuring Grant from Treasury in 2003 that: "Ringfencing of business units is another alternative to reduce costs.... Should the business operate at a loss, the ringfencing concept will encourage the business unit to curb expenses" (CCT 2003a, Appendix 5A). Elsewhere in the application it is stated: "Ringfenced accounting will improve the management of income and expenditure and ... significantly improv[e] cost reflective tariff modelling" (CCT 2003a, Appendix 2A).

In other words, cost recovery has been introduced in Cape Town in order to run municipal services 'more like a business'. Balancing the books (or even generating a surplus) and maintaining a fiscally conservative platform is still the ultimate objective, but altering the ideological foundation of public sector service delivery is also a central objective of the cost recovery agenda.

It can even be argued that cost recovery is introduced to encourage the outright privatization of municipal services. Once made financially viable, 'business units' can then be sold off to the private sector (or at least told to operate as PPPs).

Disciplining the Poor

Another (unstated) rationale for cost recovery is that it is an excellent way for the state to discipline the poor. Most obviously, there is the legal arsenal available to local governments for this, such as cutting off or restricting people's access to basic services for nonpayment of bills. The Municipal Systems Act even grants local authorities the power to "seize property" for nonpayment of services (RSA 2000a, s104.1.f), leading to the eviction of hundreds of thousands of low-income families from their homes across the country over the past ten years (McDonald 2002c, 170).

Equally powerful are the moral pressures applied by the state, with national and municipal authorities going to great lengths to separate out the 'can't pays' from the 'won't pays'. The latter are demonized for undermining the ability of the state to roll out services to those in need. As the Director of Housing for Cape Town, Seymor Bedderson, stated with regard to housing in the city: "There are people who won't pay even though they can pay. We will take a hard line on these people" (CCT 2004d, 6).

But even the 'can't pays'—those too poor to be able to afford services above and beyond the lifeline supplies—are made to feel guilty, with regular references to a "culture of non-payment" and "bad [payment] habits" in city documents (e.g. van Ryneveld et al. 2003, 41), despite the fact that most low-income households would appear to be very anxious about the fact that they cannot afford the services they use (McDonald and Pape 2002, Xali 2002). The use of moral heavyweights such as Desmond Tutu and Nelson Mandela in the *Masakhane* campaigns to encourage people to pay the full costs of services must only increase the levels of anxiety and guilt.

This morality of cost recovery is also inscribed in the South African Constitution via the Bill of Rights. In classic neoliberal fashion, South African citizens have the "right" to services such as "sufficient food and water", refuse removal, sanitation and housing (RSA 1996a, s24, s27.1b), but they also have the "responsibility" to pay for it. The Department of Water Affairs and Forestry regularly reminds people of these "rights and obligations," insisting that "paying your bills for services rendered" is the central responsibility of all water "customers".[3] The Municipal Systems Act (RSA 2000a, s5.2b) universalizes these financial obligations, stating that municipal residents have the "duty" to "promptly pay service fees, surcharges on fees, rates on property and other taxes, levies and duties imposed by the municipality".

The problem here is not so much the principal of reciprocal expectation for service delivery but rather the narrow financial terms on which this state-citizen relationship is expressed. Municipal 'customers' become atomized units on a financial balance sheet, valued primarily for their ability to pay. Ringfenced financial and managerial systems are once again at the centre of this new institutional and ideological relationship, with managers forced to think in terms of profit/surplus in vertically segregated business units.

But there is something even more profound about a neoliberal cost recovery regime, transforming as it does the very nature of the way in which we value things. Only by paying the full cost of a service, it is argued by neoliberal advocates, can one appreciate its 'true' value. Receiving a service for free, or having it heavily subsidized, distorts not only its exchange value but its use value as well. According to the World Bank (1999, 44), only "a fee reflecting the costs will encourage users to correctly value the service they receive ... help[ing] to reverse the 'entitlement mentality' that has been the historical result of subsidising public services".

The notion that a service such as water could have a use value without an exchange value—i.e. a 'right' without a 'financial responsibility'—is an alien one to the commodity-oriented cost recovery literature. Inculcating this commodified ideology has taken on almost missionary zeal in South Africa, with private capital, politicians and bureaucrats keen to educate township and rural residents to the 'real' value of the services they receive, with extensive education campaigns, posters, billboards and radio advertisements.

Finally, cost recovery serves to discipline residents by effectively lowering their service expectations. If residents receive the level of services they can afford then there is both a financial and moral basis upon which to argue that low-income households should not expect the same level of services as those who can afford to pay for more. Keeping a lid on these demands is central to the capital accumulation strategies of the new ruling elite.

PROBLEMS WITH COST RECOVERY

Having outlined some of the more abstract concerns with neoliberal models of cost recovery, I turn now to a more concrete discussion of how these have manifested themselves in the city of Cape Town. I address two specific themes. The first relates to the structure of tariffs and municipal tax rates and how they continue to privilege elites. The second relates to the fact that cost recovery is dealt with differently in different parts of the city, with business and upper-income residential areas getting away with significant payment transgressions while low-income households can have their services cut off or restricted, or even be evicted from their homes, for relatively minor offences. The 'stick' of cost recovery is an uneven one indeed.

This discussion is followed by a review of recent policies designed to mitigate some of the most unequal aspects of cost recovery: 'free' basic services, prepaid meters, indigent policies and arrears write-offs. I argue that these mechanisms can help to alleviate some of the worst excesses of cost recovery but fail to resolve the underlying tensions of affordability and fairness, with some of these policies actually serving to deepen the contradictions of neoliberalism.

Tariff and Rate Structures Favour Elites

I look first at the structure of tariffs for water, electricity, sanitation and waste management. These are the most essential services provided by the city and make up the bulk of household service costs.

The central question here is the shape of the tariff curve. Tariff curves that are flat or downward sloping are essentially regressive, taxing low-volume users (i.e. low-income households) at the same or lower rates as high-volume users. 'Progressive' tariff structures, by contrast, are upward sloping, charging more per unit consumed as consumption rises. The objective here is to generate financial surplus at the upper end of the consumption band in order to subsidize lower-level consumption (while at the same time curbing overuse of resources at the high end).

Figure 7.1 outlines the general principles of a stepped, progressive cost structure for a volumetric service such as water or electricity. Curve A is the short-run marginal cost curve for an entity providing the service (i.e. the costs per unit of production). Note how this curve falls as production increases due to economies of scale. Curve B is the price that would be charged if pricing were done on a 'pure' neoliberal cost recovery model (i.e. cost plus a markup for profit). In this case, prices parallel costs, falling as consumption increases, negating both of the objectives of progressive tariff pricing.

Curve C is the 'progressive' block tariff, which, in the case of water and electricity in South Africa, includes a free lifeline (the first block of

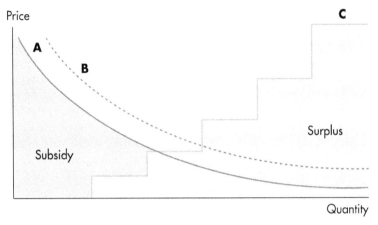

Figure 7.1 Cost and Price Curves for Services. Source: Bond 2005.

consumption on the horizontal axis). The shaded area on the right shows the surplus generated by charging above the marginal cost (used to subsidize prices on the left side of the chart, which are below marginal cost).

There can also be subsidies from other municipal services or from other government revenue sources that are not shown in this graph. Alternatively, excess subsidies can be transferred out to other sectors. Cross-subsidization does not necessarily have to be a closed (i.e. ringfenced) system.

The key to these progressive tariff structures is just how 'progressive' they really are. The price and size of the first block of consumption is the most critical, with most South African municipalities now offering a certain amount of water and electricity for 'free' (more on this below), but the second and third blocks are also important because they can undermine the affordability of the first block if a household needs to consume in this second or third category (which is often the case in South Africa) and cannot afford the rates.

So too are prices at the top end important because they determine the amount of money generated for cross-subsidization and the financial (dis)incentives for reducing high-end consumption. Mainstream analysts will argue that if these prices are too high it will have a negative effect on low-income households, reducing high-end consumption to the point that the monies available for cross-subsidy are diminished as well as driving residents and businesses away to municipalities with cheaper service rates.

The biggest problem with tariff structures in South Africa is that they are not progressive enough. Cape Town has some of the best pricing structures in the country but the overall impact on household incomes is still far too negative. Meanwhile, tariffs for well-to-do suburbanites and private businesses are far too low to generate sufficient cross-subsidization or to significantly reduce overconsumption.

Table 7.1 Domestic Water Tariffs in Cape Town in 2004–05 (price per kiloliter per household)

Amount (kl)	Price as at September 2004 (R per kl)	Price as at October 2004 (R per kl)	Price increase (%)
0–6	0	0	0
7–12	2.15	2.32	7.9
12–20	4.30	6.15	43.0
20–40	5.48	10.41	89.9
40–60	6.67	13.34	100.0
> 60	8.60	17.20	100.0

Source: City of Cape Town website at www.capetown.gov.za/water

An examination of recent water, electricity and general tariff rates in Cape Town illustrates this point.

Water Tariffs

As per national guidelines, the first six kiloliters (kl) of water per month is free for each household in Cape Town. After that the price per kiloliter increases in five blocks, as outlined in Table 7.1. Two things are immediately evident from this Table. The first is the significant price increase that took place in late 2004 (largely as a result of the severe water shortages at that time but also because of pressures to make the tariff structure more progressive). Prior to these changes city officials were able to boast that Cape Town offered the cheapest domestic water in all of South Africa (ACNielson 2003). Now it has some of the most expensive water in the country (at least at higher levels of consumption).

The second feature is the way in which the tariffs changed. In the second block prices went up by only 7.9% per kiloliter (slightly above inflation) but higher blocks went up by as much as 100% per kiloliter. Combined, these two developments have created what is probably the most progressive water tariff structure in the country for domestic water use. These residential and commercial tariff structures remained in effect in 2006, with only inflationary-tied increases expected (*Cape Argus*, March 29, 2006).

Table 7.2 shows the total costs to a household consuming a particular amount of water. If, for example, a household were to consume 15kl of water a month they would pay R32 (up from R26 in the previous tariff format). Households consuming 60kl would pay R538. Once again, the percent of price increases at the top end are much higher than that at the lower end, reflecting the relatively progressive nature of Cape Town's tariff structure as compared to other cities in the country (see McInnes (2005) for a comparison).

Table 7.2 Domestic Water Tariffs in Cape Town in 2004–05 (price per total amount consumed)

Total amount of water consumed (kl)	Price as at September 2004 (R)	Price as at October 2004 (R)	Price increase (%)
6	Free	Free	0
12	13	14	7.6
15	26	32	23
20	47	63	34
25	75	115	53.3
30	102	167	63.7
35	130	219	68.5
40	157	271	72.6
50	224	405	80.1
60	290	538	85.5
80	462	823	78.1
100	634	1226	93.4

Source: City of Cape Town website at www.capetown.gov.za/water

But as progressive as these new tariff rates may seem at first glance (particularly when compared to the hugely regressive tariff pricing structures of the 1980s and 1990s) they do not deal adequately with the underlying inequities of the city. In fact, they continue to perpetuate inequalities despite the pro-poor rhetoric the city uses to describe its tariff policies.

To illustrate, a household consuming 15kl of water a month would pay R32. A household consuming the city average of 26kl a month (Anderson 2004, 7) would pay about R125. While this may seem cheap for middle- and upper-income families it represents a sizeable portion of the household budget for the more than one million people living below the household subsistence level of R1600 a month in Cape Town (CCT 2006d, 179).

In the African townships this can be a budget-breaking expense. A comprehensive study of Khayelitsha and Nyanga found that 52% of residents have no wage income at all and 64% of all adults are unemployed (de Swart et al. 2005, 102). Even with government grants factored in—i.e. the state spending that Seekings (2002, 14) insists makes South Africa a "social democracy"—a full 86% of households "still fall below the food poverty line" (de Swart et al. 2005, 104).

With grants averaging about R600 per month per household in these two townships, R125 for water is 21% of household income. Add to this the cost of electricity, rates, clothing, school fees, food and health care, and it is easy to see why so many Cape Town households struggle to pay their 'progressive' water tariffs. The result is a pricing structure that effectively forces low-income households to limit their consumption to a predefined 'basic' need of 25 litres per person per day, regardless of their actual water requirements.

Suburban residents, by contrast, have little trouble paying their water bills. For that one third of Capetonians who earn more than R10,000 a month, a R125 water bill makes no material difference to their lives at all. Filling a swimming pool might force some suburbanites to think twice about the new tariff structures but the sheer number of pool companies in the city would suggest that even this is not a make-or-break item (a recent version of the Cape Town Yellow Pages had some 27 pages worth of pool company advertisements).

Revealingly, a senior advisor to former ANC Mayor Nomaindia Mfeketo admitted in an interview that the city's new tariffs have a "progressive dimension" but their effect is limited: "They do not really impact on upper-income households ... and limit our ability to redistribute [resources] in the city" (personal interview, David Schmidt).

There have also been limits placed on upper-end tariffs for water so as not to scare away wealthy residents. There is, for example, a price limit on sanitation charges. In 2004–05 the city capped this at R250 a month "for properties valued at over R2 million" in order to "mitigate the effect of this rate on higher value properties" (CCT 2004a, 66). A low-income household producing 15kl of sewage, by contrast, would still have to pay a disproportionately heavy rate of R22 on top of their water bill.

Not surprisingly, few suburban households would appear to be aware of the price of water in the city. Though not a scientific survey, the vast majority of middle- and upper-income South Africans that I have spoken to over the years could not tell me what they spend on water on a monthly basis, what the tariff rates are, or whether they thought it was an appropriate amount. Many expressed concerns with overall water "shortages" in the city, but are typically just as quick to point the finger at "wasteful" township water users who "do not understand the real value of water because they have never had to pay for it".

Low-income households, in reality, usually have an intimate knowledge of service costs, with many household heads knowing exactly how much water they consume each month and what it costs them. Detailed research has shown that township residents keep meticulous records of their water and electricity bills, some going back 10 years, and know exactly how much they are spending—generally because it is such a significant part of their monthly budget (Fiil 2001, Khunou 2002, Xali 2002).

Another major concern with the tariff structure for water in Cape Town is the fact that commercial water users pay a flat rate of R6.59/kl (and R2.68/kl for sanitation). This flat rate means there is no incentive to conserve water use and no progressive form of cross-subsidization (EMG 2005, 19), despite the fact that 72% of businesses surveyed in Cape Town in a study by ACNeilson (2003) said that a higher tariff would encourage them to conserve water.

At these rates a Cape Town business using 15kl of water a month pays more than a domestic consumer (R98 versus R32) but a business consuming 100kl a month pays considerably *less* than a domestic consumer (R685 versus R1226). With commercial users making up about 40% of water consumption in the city this is a real concern, especially as many businesses have been partially exempted from water restrictions.

Electricity Tariffs

The situation with electricity is even worse. Although there have been some improvements in the past ten years, pricing structures introduced by the new Cape Town Regional Electricity Distributor in July 2006 have largely perpetuated pricing disparities. There are now two domestic price structures: a high-consumption package (for households that use more than 600kwh/month) and a low-consumption package (for households that use less than 600kwh/month). Households in the high-consumption category pay R0.305/kwh and a "daily service charge" of R1.99. Low-consumption consumers are charged a flat rate of R.4065/kwh and no daily service charge (CCT 2006c). The only other difference is that low consumption users receive their first 50kwh/month of electricity for free, as part of the "free basic services" package of the city designed to ease the cost of services for the poor.

The intent with this pricing structure is to save low-consumption users (mostly township households) the daily service charge, but they still pay more per kilowatt-hour. Estimates of actual electricity usage in Cape Town households are difficult to come by, but suburban consumers would appear to average about 775kwh/household/month (CCT 2003b). Township households typically consume less (as little as 120kwh/month/household on average in informal areas) but research has shown that electricity consumption of 500kwh/month in the townships is not unusual (Fiil 2001). Using the pricing structure outlined above, a high-consumption household consuming 700kwh of electricity would pay R263.50/month (an effective rate of R0.376/kwh) while a low-consumption household using 500kwh of electricity would pay R182.93/month (taking into account the free 50kwh allocation). At these rates of consumption, the poor pay about 8% more per kilowatt-hour than wealthy suburbanites.

If we look at these charges relative to household incomes, the pricing inequalities become even more stark. At 700kwh, electricity costs make up only a small percentage of a suburban household's income (even with other energy-related expenses added, total energy costs are estimated to be only 3–5% of monthly incomes in suburban areas (CCT 2003b, 6)) while the R182 charge for 500kwh in a township household would make up 23% of an R800 income (not uncommon in households relying on pensions and grants). Little wonder, then, that these households either underconsume and/or cannot pay their electricity bills.

The introduction of user fees for installations and repairs has had an additional negative impact on the poor. According to the city's 2004–05 pricing schedule, it costs R184.21 for an inspection of an electricity connection, R662.68 to have a prepaid meter installed and R1429.83 to have a "tariff, quality of supply or load profile investigation requiring equipment and personnel". There are also steep charges for disconnection and reconnection if a household tampers with their meter or attempts to connect illegally: R482.46 for disconnecting an illegal connection; R991.93 to have it reconnected (R1885.97 for second-time offenders); and R57.02 for the city to "deliver a notice of impending disconnection of supply for non-payment of account".

These charges have effectively barred many households from having their electricity systems upgraded or repaired, and have prevented some households from reconnecting to the grid. The city has recognized this problem and has introduced a system whereby costs can be paid on instalments via the prepaid metering system, but in this case a surcharge is added to every unit of electricity purchased to pay for the fixed costs, creating an even more expensive kilowatt-hour charge.

Industrial rates for electricity contribute further to the uneven nature of cost recovery in the sector. Commerce and industry make up 60% of electricity consumption in the city but they pay much less on average than domestic consumers, with 'large power users' paying R0.1649/kwh and a daily service fee of R9.68 (as of July 2006). At a monthly consumption of 10,000kwh this translates to an effective charge of R0.194/kwh, almost two and a half times lower than rates paid by low-income households.

It is unclear, then, how the city can claim: "Consumers with low consumption ... are subsidized by the other electricity consumers" (CCT 2006c). There are some fixed charges for commercial users that may contribute marginally to cross-subsidization, but the calculations provided here suggest a flat and regressive pricing structure that benefits industry and wealthy suburbanites while penalizing the poor.

Nor is there any incentive for surburban households or industry to consume less: as the city's own investigation into electricity tariffs demonstrated in 2003, mid- to high-income households "are very high energy consumers", but because "electricity is relatively cheap and extremely convenient for these households there is little incentive to implement energy efficient measures" (CCT 2003b, 7) (one of the reasons that South Africa has the third largest per capita production of greenhouse gases in the world (*Business Day*, October 12, 2004)). With even cheaper and more regressive electricity rates for industry, where is the incentive to conserve?

The reason for these electricity pricing schemes? It "helps to build Cape Town's competitive advantage" (CCT 2004a, 67). The city's "Energy Strategy" document is blunt on the matter, arguing that Cape Town should be a city where the provision of electricity "supports economic competitiveness and increases employment ... and where energy prices remain competitive" (CCT 2003b, 5).

General Municipal Rates

Municipal services for which there are no volumetric measurements are either charged through a special service fee (e.g. waste removal) or through the general rates account (e.g. road maintenance), or some combination thereof. In Cape Town the general rates account is calculated on a market-value assessment of property: the more expensive the market value of your home the more you pay in rates and service fees. In 2004–05 the market-value residential rate was R0.007924 to the rand. This meant that if your home was worth R100,000 you paid R792 in rates for that fiscal year. If your home was worth R1.5m you paid R11,886 in rates.

The property tax system in Cape Town is therefore a flat tax, once again generating an essentially regressive taxation system, minimizing cross-subsidy potential and placing a disproportionate rates burden on the poor. There are rates and service charge discounts for households valued at less than R125,000, and there is a sliding scale rebate for households with incomes below R2600/month, but these only benefit the poorest of the poor, leaving many other lower-income households struggling to pay their rates. The South African Cities Network notes that this fails to deal with the extent of the poverty crisis, estimating that "roughly half" of all residents living in large South African cities "cannot afford to live in accommodation that attracts even low levels of ... rates charges" (SACN 2004, 91).

The introduction of market-based rates assessments was intended to help address this problem, but met with fierce resistance from wealthy rate-payer associations, forcing policymakers to water down the already weak redistributive elements of the rates legislation (RSA 2004c) despite the fact that there had not been a major revaluation of the property tax system in cities like Cape Town since the 1970s, with most suburban homes enormously undervalued in taxation terms. Although the introduction of a market-value assessment represents an advance on the outdated apartheid-era taxation model, it fails to provide the kind of pro-poor taxation structure that the city council claims it promotes.

The biggest concern for city council in Cape Town would appear to be keeping rates increases in the wealthy residential and commercial/industrial areas to a *minimum*. As city officials noted in their Restructuring Grant application to National Treasury in 2003: "The City has designed the restructuring plan to use rate and tariff increases as a measure of last resort to generate revenue. In this way the competitiveness of the City's services will be maintained, and investment in commercial and residential enterprises may be maintained" (CCT 2003a, Appendix 7B). Any potential for a more progressive form of municipal taxation has been lost in the process.

Harsh and Uneven Treatment

The second broad area of concern I want to highlight here with respect to cost recovery in Cape Town is the harsh and uneven way in which punishment has been meted out to low-income households that are unable/unwilling to pay for services or rates, as opposed to suburban, commercial and industrial areas. I look at two areas of concern in particular: service cutoffs and housing evictions.

Service Cutoffs

As discussed earlier, there were very few instances of the state cutting off supplies of water or electricity to township homes during the apartheid era, despite the fact that there was widespread practice of nonpayment in the townships as part of the political struggle to make apartheid financially unstable. Apartheid authorities recognized that cutting off service supplies would only inflame an already explosive situation.

After coming to power in 1994 (and particularly after local government elections in 1995 and 1996), ANC officials had no such qualms about cutoffs, arguing that residents now had a moral and financial obligation to pay for the services they received from legitimate and democratically elected governments. Nonpayment was perceived as an attack on the viability of the state and an undermining of the development agenda of the ANC.

It is not clear when widespread disconnections began in South Africa, but by the late 1990s most municipalities were practicing it, as were parastatal service suppliers such as Eskom and Telkom. Water and electricity were the services most targeted, largely because it was easy to determine who was not paying and because disconnections to individual households could be done relatively easily.

The extent of the problem has been the subject of much heated debate. In 2002 I argued that at least 5.5 million people, and as many as 9.8 million people, had been affected by water and/or electricity cutoffs over a seven-year period from 1994–2001 (McDonald 2002c, 170). Based on a statistically representative national survey of approximately 2500 people, this was the first systematic attempt to gauge the scale of the cutoff problem.

There was other evidence to back up these claims. The DPLG had been tracking service cutoffs in its "Project Viability" program for several years. These data have never been made available to the public, and did not cover the entire country, but a leaked report from 2001 showed that there were 256,325 electricity disconnections and 133,456 water disconnections in the last three months of that year alone (DPLG 2002, 30–31). Not all of these disconnections were domestic but a conservative estimate showed that these figures translated to almost one million people having been affected by electricity cutoffs and half a million people having been affected by water cutoffs during this three-month period in 2001 alone. These figures did not include cutoffs by Eskom, which had been disconnecting as many as 20,000 households a month in Soweto in early 2001 for nonpayment (Fiil 2001).

Ronnie Kasrils, the then-Minister of Water Affairs and Forestry, publicly attacked these figures a year later, announcing in Parliament and in an op-ed in a national newspaper that the estimates of water cutoffs were an attempt to "deliberately lie with statistics" in order to "mislead working people" (Kasrils 2003). DWAF subsequently engaged in closed-door discussions with officials from the Human Sciences Research Council (HSRC), the organization that had conducted the 2001 survey, insisting that they complete a follow-up study in January 2004.

The methodologies and results of this second survey have never been fully released to the public, but the figures that have been released reinforce my original argument that millions of people have experienced cutoffs due to nonpayment. In an op-ed article on this data (*Mail & Guardian*, June 6, 2004) the Director General of DWAF admitted that 275,000 households had had their water cut off for nonpayment in 2003 (translating to 1375 million people, using an average household size of five), but this figure excluded some 5.6 million people who had their water cut off that year and did not know why. It also excluded about 2.3 million people who were disconnected that year for less than one day. While not necessarily life threatening, the latter is nevertheless another indication of the scale of the cutoff problem; and all of this more than three years after the introduction of the 'free water' program in the country.

It is not my intent to resolve this numerical debate here. It is a tricky methodological question and there may be different interpretations of the nature and length of service disconnections. My argument remains, however, that the scale of the cutoff phenomenon since 1994 has been enormous, affecting millions of low-income South Africans, forcing them to suffer through the inconveniences, indignities and health and safety risks of having essential services shut down. The fact that many of these cutoffs lasted for weeks and sometimes months, and in some cases involved the outright removal of infrastructure from a household, has created serious health and safety risks.

What has been the cutoff situation in Cape Town? Unfortunately, the city does not make information on service cutoffs readily available (if indeed it keeps a reliable record of this data), making it difficult to track the situation. The only information I have been able to gather is from research on water cutoffs conducted with Laïla Smith in 2000 (McDonald and Smith 2002) and then again in interviews I had with senior city officials in late 2004.

The research in 2000 involved two municipal substructures that were controlled by the ANC (Tygerberg and the City of Cape Town), with data submitted to us by city officials. This data showed that during 1999–2000 more than 75,000 households had their water cut off for nonpayment of services, representing some 375,000 people. A moratorium on water cut-offs was eventually passed by council in 2002, but it is not clear how many cutoffs took place between 2000 and 2002 or how many took place in other parts of the city.

Nor is it clear that the city has stopped cutting off water supply in residential areas. In an interview with the former City Manager in late 2004 I was told that the city would still cut domestic services if there were an illegal connection. Otherwise a 'trickle meter' or 'restrictor' is put in place (a point we return to shortly).

I have not been able to find a record of electricity cutoffs in Cape Town, but there is no reason to believe that the experience has been any different than that of other parts of the country. Although most households are now on prepaid meters, homes with credit meters are still cut off if they do not pay their electricity bill. As of late 2004, 200 domestic consumers were being disconnected each month in the city (affecting some 5000 people a year) and the City Manager at the time expected this to increase to 500 households a month once the "debt management activity [of the city] is fully functional". Up to 1500 disconnection warning letters are served each month.

Housing Evictions

The ultimate punishment for nonpayment of services is to be evicted from one's home. In the 2001 HSRC survey referred to above, three percent of the national sample said they had experienced an "eviction from [their] home for failure to pay for water or electricity" and two percent said they had experienced a "seizure of property for failure to pay for services".

There are no statistics for Cape Town specifically, but once again there is no reason to believe that the city has handled this matter any differently than other municipalities in the country. The formation of the Anti-Eviction Campaign (AEC) in Cape Town in 2000 is one indication of the scale of the problem, with branches being formed throughout the Cape Flats. There have also been numerous protest actions by the AEC in the courts and in the streets to resist forced removals, with some families coming home to find their belongings unceremoniously dumped on the streets by city officials (or by privately owned security firms contracted by the city).

Some of these anti-eviction protests have become violent, with police using rubber bullets and dogs to confront protestors. Protests in late 2001 in Tafelsig in Mitchell's Plain were particularly explosive, with tires burning in the streets and a five-year-old boy being shot in the back with a rubber bullet by police (*Cape Times*, September 27, 2001). Luckily there have been no recorded deaths as a result of these protests in Cape Town, but similar campaigns elsewhere in the country have had more tragic results (e.g. the shooting death by police of Harrismith student Tebogo Mkhonza during a service-related protest on August 30, 2004).

Cape Town's current policy on evictions is that low-income households (those earning less than R800/month in this case) must apply for 'indigent' status, which, if they are accepted, allows them to apply for rental payment relief in council-owned homes for a period of six months (there is no policy for homes purchased with a private bank loan). According to the former City Manager this policy has allowed the city to "limit the number of evictions as a result of issues of affordability", stating that there had been no evictions for nonpayment of bonds/services in 2004 (personal interview, Wallace Mgoqi).

Members of the Anti-Eviction Campaign challenged this claim, however, stating in a separate interview in 2005 that they had had a steady case load of evictees that year and continued to see people on these matters. A high-profile case in October 2004 in Atlantis, a northern part of the city with high unemployment rates, is a case in point. Police used rubber bullets and stun grenades in this instance to deal with several hundred people attempting to prevent the eviction of neighbours who claimed they were unable to afford the R250–650/month in bonds for their "shabby" council-owned homes (*Cape Argus*, October 20, 2004).

Not surprisingly, it has been low-income households that have been targeted for evictions and cutoffs, despite the fact that the bulk of nonpayment in Cape Town has occurred in the suburbs and in commercial and industrial areas (making up approximately three quarters of the city's payment arrears). Despite this, the city has never published a list of these big-ticket defaulters—as some municipalities in South Africa have done, to shame them into paying—and has never publicly chastised these organizations in the way that it has individual township dwellers.

The duplicity of this practice is even more remarkable when one considers the scale of the payment differences. In 2002 city officials were evicting township people from their council-owned homes for arrears as low as R250[4] while at the same time allowing the Newlands cricket ground—the premier destination for 'world-class' cricket in the city—to run a deficit of some R4 million in service arrears. The city was even considering offering the stadium tax rebates at the same time.[5]

New "Flanking Mechanisms"

As these policies of cutoffs and evictions have become increasingly violent and politically problematic for the city there have been efforts on the part of neoliberal policymakers in Cape Town to develop new, less conspicuous modes of cost recovery. In Chapter 3 I referred to these policy revisions as "flanking mechanisms", an integral and necessary progression of neoliberal policymaking in an attempt to deal with its own internal contradictions. Flanking mechanisms are policies that appear to be new and progressive, attempting to iron out the rougher edges of previous practice while at the same time winning political support, but in the end represent only a minor variation on the same accumulation theme.

In this final section of the chapter we look at four of these flanking mechanisms as they relate to cost recovery in Cape Town: service 'restrictions', prepaid meters, free basic services and indigent policies. It is argued in each case that these new policies and technologies are more restrained and potentially less damaging than service cutoffs and evictions—and are therefore more 'progressive' in the narrowest sense of the term—but they do not fundamentally alter the uneven and unfair manner in which cost recovery is pursued. They also serve to deepen the neoliberal vision of commodified state-citizen relations.

Service Restrictions

One of the initial ways in which the city of Cape Town responded to the political tensions over service cutoffs was to introduce a policy of restricting people's services rather than cutting them off completely. For water, this involves placing a small device called a 'restrictor' (or, to use the classicly neoliberal terminology employed by city council, a 'water limiting enabler') in the pipe leading into the home or in the water meter so as to limit the rate of water flow and/or the total amount of water.

Although better than outright cutoffs, water restrictors nevertheless incur their own set of risks, inconveniences and indignities. It can take all day, for example, to fill the cistern on a toilet or to fill a bucket at a yard tap, creating hygiene problems and wasting people's valuable time. Supplies can also run out at inconvenient or dangerous times, forcing people back into modes of operation practiced during complete service cutoffs (e.g. drawing water from unsafe sources).

Once again, it is low-income households that bear the brunt of this cost recovery strategy, with some 830 restrictors having been placed in township homes in Cape Town in 2004, affecting several thousand people (personal interview, Wallace Mgoqi) and many more since.

Prepaid Meters

Even more insidious has been the introduction of prepaid electricity meters, with trials for prepaid water meters having been attempted as well. In this case consumers must purchase a set amount of water or electricity from a licensed vendor before they can consume it (although some meters are preset to allow the 'free' monthly allocation of water or electricity before shutting off). In Cape Town this involves the use of 'tokens' or 'smart cards', which electronically record the amount of a service purchased. Consumers then enter this information into their household meter or swipe a card or drop a token in a prepaid meter at a communal water tap. Recently, companies have been designing meters that combine water and electricity prepayment.

The city's rationale for prepaid meters is fourfold. First, and most importantly, the city is attracted by the fact that prepaid meters eliminate costly arrears and improve the city's cash flow. By paying for services in advance households are unable to fall into debt. The city also benefits from the fact that there is no longer any need to read meters on a monthly basis or to incur the administrative expenses of billing.

Second, prepaid meters avert the financial and politically costly exercise of sending in police and/or municipal employees to cut people's services off. Households effectively cut themselves off, discontinuing consumption at the point they can no longer afford to consume more.

Third, prepaid meters serve as a way to introduce metering more generally. As noted at the outset of this chapter, cost recovery on volumetric services is only possible where there are meters to determine how much is consumed. In places where meters do not exist, the introduction of prepaid meters has given the city all the more incentive to do so, effectively speeding up the general goal of universal metering.

Finally, the state promotes prepaid meters as "pro-poor", arguing that they allow low-income households to budget their service expenditures more effectively. David Erleigh, a senior city councillor responsible for trading services under the DA, said of prepaid meters in 2002 that they would "enable" users to see exactly what their needs were and reduce waste: "The principle here is one of technology with a human touch. It is pro-poor and nonconfrontational. The meters will empower people to manage their own consumption" (*Cape Argus*, March 13, 2002). A former ANC-appointed City Manager concurred, arguing: "Consumers become aware of the cost of [their services] and can manage these to a level that suits their lifestyle and circumstances".

The Chairperson of Salga has been—perhaps unintentionally—a little more circumspect in this regard, but generally sees prepaids as a positive development as well: "We might be appearing quite insensitive and inhumane as some of us introduce prepaid water and electricity systems when in fact these, especially the electricity ones, generally benefit our communities" (Salga 2004c, 11).

How widespread is the use of prepaid meters? Nationally, prepaid electricity meters are most prevalent, with Eskom estimating that 3.2 million had been installed across the country from 1992–2003 (as many as 1500 meters per working day, most of which were installed in new housing developments and newly electrified homes).[6] Prepaid electricity meters are in most, if not all, of the 284 municipalities in the country, with one company—Syntell—operating prepaid electricity meters in over 100 local authorities.

It is not clear how many prepaid water meters have been installed in South Africa, though there are far fewer than for electricity, in part because the technology has been introduced more recently. Some municipalities, such as Johannesburg, have been aggressively introducing prepaid water meters (in this case with the financial support of the French government) while other municipalities have been slow to do so (such as Cape Town). It is clear, however, that more municipalities intend to introduce prepaid water meters in the future, with Salga being broadly supportive of their introduction.

It should also be noted that South Africa is a leading international manufacturer of water and electricity prepaid meters. Durban-based Conlog is the largest producer of prepaid meters in the country and one of the largest in the world, able to boast (on its website) that it has "an installed base of over two million electricity pre-payment meters world wide" with export orders throughout Africa, Asia and Latin America. In 2001 the company sold 300,000 prepaid electricity meters to Khartoum, one of the poorest cities in the world.

Conlog was also the first company to introduce prepaid water meters in South Africa, an event that was attended by then-Deputy President Thabo Mbeki and one of Conlog's investors, former Defence Minister Joe Modise (Nelson Mandela has attended other Conlog functions). Conlog has since been purchased by French multinational Schneider Electric and there are other international firms involved in the prepaid market in the country.

In Cape Town, it is prepaid electricity meters that are the most widely used, with more than 420,000 units installed since 1993, making up 60% of domestic electrical connections—the largest base in South Africa (CCT 2006d, 122). Most commercial and industrial users, as well as homes in established suburban areas, do not use prepaid meters, however, despite the fact that they consume the bulk of the city's electricity and generate the bulk of its electricity revenues (more than 75%) (CCT 2003b, 12; CCT 2004a, 70). This revenue balance will shift, though, as all new homes must be built with prepaid meters and the city is moving toward replacing all credit meters with prepaid technology.

Water meters have had a slower and rockier start in Cape Town. Pilot tests were conducted in various parts of the city starting in 2001, with expectations of a major roll out in 2003 and again in 2005. Former ANC Mayor Nomaindia Mfekto put an abrupt stop to this in mid-2005, however, arguing: "Access to water is a critical right for our people and no measures which will have a negative social impact on our communities will be implemented by this administration as long as I am mayor" (*Cape Argus*, August 31, 2005).

It is possible that the Mayor was genuinely concerned about the impacts of prepaid meters on the poor, but the change in policy was more likely due to the fact that prepaid water meters had begun to be met with considerable resistance in other municipalities around the country (most notably in Johannesburg) and had proven to be very unpopular with most township residents. Local government elections were approaching and it is possible that the ANC did not want to be in the middle of a controversial roll out of prepaid water meters in advance of this. The fact that a Constitutional court case was being mounted to try and have prepaid water meters ruled unconstitutional (as they have been in the UK (Drakeford 1998)) may also have factored into the decision making.

Whatever the reasons, the withdrawal would appear to be more pragmatic than ideological with the city still implementing its water restrictor policy and its unfair tariff structures. It is also possible that the DA council elected in March 2006 could revisit the prepaid water scheme, though it may be too controversial for them as well given their tenuous political coalition.

Problems with Prepaids

What are the problems with prepaid meters? Although by no means an exhaustive list I will summarize some of the most pressing concerns here.

By far the biggest concern relates to the issue of 'self-disconnections'. Because low-income households buy only as much water/electricity as they can afford—as opposed to what they actually need—it is not uncommon for them to run out of supplies before being able to purchase more. Alternatively, households may reduce their daily consumption of a service to a level that is below their actual needs so as not to run out before the end of the month.

In either case the actions constitute a self-imposed cutoff in ways that might not occur with a credit meter (although the fear of cutoffs, restrictions and evictions can have the same effect with the credit meter system). This has been the primary rationale for the legal challenges against prepaid water meters in the UK and South Africa.

A second problem relates to the price of water and electricity with prepaid meters. Prices tend to be higher with these meters because municipalities are attempting to recoup the costs of installing them (Eskom estimated in 2003 that it cost approximately R2500 to install each prepaid meter, including labour). Since most low-income households are unable to pay these capital costs up front they are amortized as part of the per-unit price of the service, increasing tariffs in low-income areas.

In Cape Town these costs have been factored into the price of prepaid electricity across the board and do not, therefore, necessarily bias against the poor. But the fact that these capital costs are being recovered from the poor at all is another indication of the unfair, and ahistorical, way in which cost recovery is being pursued.

Cape Town also uses prepaid meters as a way to collect on debt that already exists. For households that are in electricity arrears, 20% of every electricity purchase is redirected toward paying down that debt. Indebted households have no choice in the matter, driving up the effective cost of electricity for low-income families.

Third, there can be technical problems with the meters. The electronic circuitry in prepaid meters, and the electronic connections between the meter and the centalized computer system, can and do fail, sometimes leaving households without services for lengthy periods of time. These mechanical glitches have been especially problematic with the delivery of free water/electricity, with anecdotal evidence that meter manufacturers have been slow to develop new meters and/or reconfigure older models to ensure the flow of these essential quantities.

A fourth problem relates to buying services. Although generally convenient in suburban areas for residents with vehicles or Internet connections, purchasing prepaid water and electricity in township and informal areas can be extremely time-consuming and expensive. Licensed retailers are less readily available and seldom open 24 hours a day, meaning that homes may be stuck with no water/electricity for a night or a weekend if they run out in the evening. Nor is it easy for single parents and female-headed households to purchase supplies, and moving around in townships after dark can be very dangerous, especially for women.

Finally, there has been little to no consultation on the introduction of prepaid technology in Cape Town (or elsewhere in the country for that matter). The installation of prepaid electricity meters in Cape Town began in the 1990s with no public discussion, and there has been no public debate over the city's ongoing policy of installing prepaid meters in new homes.

With the pilot tests for prepaid water meters, participants were simply "notified of the switch", according to the City Manager at the time. There was no broad-based consultation about the selection of the pilot sites with residents. Nor was there any debate in council on the matter. When asked if there were any concerns about the introduction of prepaid meters the head of the Mayor's office at the time told me: "It has not been a big issue or debate" (personal interview, David Schmidt).

Cape Town is not unique in this regard. The city of Johannesburg has been criticized for its heavy-handed implementation of prepaid electricity meters, with the overwhelming majority of residents interviewed for a major study in Soweto saying that they did not want a prepaid meter and were never consulted on the matter. The first time many of these consumers were informed about prepaid meters "was when Eskom employees actually came to install them" (Nefale 2004, 15). Similar problems have occurred with prepaid water meters in the townships of Soweto and Orange Farm (CAWP 2004, Fiil-Flynn and Naidoo 2004).

Nor have there been any public opinion surveys conducted by government on attitudes toward prepaid meters. Local and national authorities appear to be relying on the neoliberal assumption that low-income households like the prepaid system because it helps them to budget their use of a service. As a result, it is impossible to say with any academic certainty what the general public attitude is toward these meters. More extensive and rigorous studies are urgently needed on this critical issue.

Free Basic Services

A third neoliberal flanking mechanism related to cost recovery has been that of 'free basic services'. In late 2000, shortly before the local government elections of that year, the ANC announced that all South African households would be provided with six kilolitres of free water a month (based on 25 litres/person/day for a household of eight) as well as 50kwh of free electricity a month. The free water was later expanded to include a free allocation of sanitation charges, which has not been standardized nationally but has been set at 4.2kl a month in Cape Town.

Initially, Cape Town only offered 20kwh of electricity for free, then 30kwh and finally 50kwh from July 2004. But this was only provided to households in the "low consumption" category, meaning that if a household consumes more than 500kwh/month (increased to 600kwh in 2006) they would lose their free allocation (CCT 2004a, 67).

There has also been some effort to extend free services to nonvolumetric sectors such as refuse collection. In Cape Town, this is done through a rebate on rates, with informal settlements on council-owned land being offered refuse collection for free, and homes valued under R125,000 receiving "subsidized" refuse collection (CCT 2004a, 67).

Why were free basic services introduced in South Africa? One reason is the ANC's long-standing commitment from the 1994 RDP to provide "lifeline" services. But there would appear to be other, more cynical, reasons as well. One is that the ANC was using the announcement in 2000 to boost its popularity in advance of the December local government elections. Another is that it was simply administratively cheaper for municipalities to offer a free allocation of water to households that were already consuming at the low end than it was to administer the billing and cutoff/reconnection systems. DWAF's (2000) reference to Durban's introduction of free water is instructive in this regard:

> The City of Durban has taken the logical—and socially just and equitable step—of making the first lifeline amount of water (6000 litres per household per month) free-of-charge. Thereafter, the more you use, the more you pay. This constitutes a significant saving in administrative and postage costs. It is a win-win situation for all.... In poor rural areas

... we can simply provide water supplies without charging for them, which will be undoubtedly simpler.

Motivations aside, there are other reasons to be critical of the free services policy. The first is that millions of South Africans have not benefited because they still do not have the infrastructure in place to consume water and electricity (itself a product of neoliberal fiscal restraint, as discussed in Chapter 5). Despite the investments in infrastructure from 1994, an estimated 2.3 million households still did not have access to potable water as of 2006 (i.e. within 200 meters of the house), 4.3 million households did not have adequate sanitation, and 2.9 million households did not have access to electricity. There are also an estimated 2.4 households living in shacks, many of which have no reticulated services at all (Hemson and O'Donovan 2006, 22–30). With an average household size of five to six people in low-income areas this is a sizeable proportion of the South African population not benefiting from free services, despite the glowing national and international media attention that has been given to this 'progressive' policy.

To make matters worse, many municipalities are not providing free services to households even if they have the required infrastructure. As of late 2004, it was estimated that more than 20% of municipalities in the country were not delivering free water and about 60% were not providing free electricity (with many municipalities providing less than the recommended 50kwh/household/month) (Salga 2004c, 11).

Cape Town would appear to be better than most municipalities in this regard (with better infrastructure and a stronger bureaucracy) but it must be remembered that there are still thousands of households in the city without a basic level of services, that many have had their water or electricity supplies cut off or restricted, and that many only have a communal water tap, making water collection difficult even if it is for free.

Another concern for low-income households in Cape Town is the quantity of free services. For water, the free allotment of 25 litres/person/day simply does not cover basic needs. To put things in perspective, it takes 10–15 litres to flush the average toilet in South Africa and as much as 200 litres to fill a bathtub. Many township homes also rely on home gardens to feed themselves and/or for additional income, which has led the South African Municipal Workers' Union to estimate that the real daily needs of low-income households are more in the order of 100 litres/person/day (see Table 7.3).

It should also be noted that average daily domestic consumption of water in Cape Town is about 200 litres/person/day (CCT 2006d, 321) (Johannesburg's daily domestic consumption is even higher at 255l/p/d (*Cape Times*, August 25, 2004)). This includes low-income households, suggesting that suburban per capita consumption is considerably higher. I am not suggesting here that all Capetonians be as wasteful with water as the average

Table 7.3 Minimum Estimated Daily Water Needs in South Africa (per person)

Water Use	Estimated amount of water required (litres)
Wash basin (instead of shower or bath)	10
Toilet (2 flushes)	26
Handwashing	8
Drinking	5
Food preparation	1
Washing of dishes	3
Washing of clothes	7
General housecleaning	3
TOTAL	63
Shower (instead of washbasin)—3 per week @ 100 litres per shower	42
TOTAL (Minus washbasin)	95
Bath (instead of washbasin)—2 per week @ 200 litres per bath	57
TOTAL (Minus washbasin)	110

Note: The above calculations exclude the special water needs of the very young, the old and the sick. They also make no allowance for the water needs of subsistence fruit and vegetable gardens.
Source: Data provided by Jeff Rudin, Research Officer, Samwu, July 10, 2005.

suburbanite, but rather that these figures serve to illustrate the enormously unequal distribution of water resources and the relatively miserly allocation of free water to the households that need it most.

The free electricity allocation is even more problematic. At 50kwh per household per month this is only enough power to run two 60-watt light bulbs for four hours a day, forcing low-income households to use paraffin and candles to heat, light and cook with, creating serious health and safety concerns.

A third concern with free services relates to the way in which tariffs are structured after the initial free block. Prices in the second and third block can effectively erase the benefits of the free allocation, forcing families who consume in these quantities to pay considerable sums of money for what are their actual basic needs. In some municipalities, if you consume one drop more than 6kl there is a fixed monthly fee charged that many families cannot afford to pay.

In this sense, 'free services' are not free in the decommodified sense of the word. They are, rather, part of a larger cost recovery schema, with the first (meagre) portion of consumption being provided at no cost but with subsequent (and necessary) levels of consumption being charged at fiscally conservative cost recovery rates. As DWAF's 2003 Strategic Framework for Water Services put it with regards to water:

> The adoption of free basic water policy has not negated … the principle of user pays. On the contrary, the free basic water policy strengthens the principal in that it clearly requires consumption in excess of the free water supply service to be paid for (DWAF 2003).

Nor has the state allocated much in the way of financial resources to assist with the free services policy. In fiscal 2004–05, for example, national government allocated a mere R500m for free electricity and R1467m for free water, sanitation and refuse collection, all of which was part of the Equitable Share that already went to local authorities (FFC 2004, 27). This worked out to approximately R11/person for electricity and R33/person for water, sanitation and refuse collection: a proverbial drop in the bucket.

For Cape Town, the city's Equitable Share allocation for 2004–05 was R196.3m, or about R65/person (personal interview, Wallace Mgoqi). Only a small portion of this transfer was allowed to be used for funding free services, however, highlighting once again the enormous pressures local governments in South Africa face in trying to finance 'progressive' programs with their own resources. Even Salga has noted that Equitable Share allocations "are still inadequate to subsidize the costs of providing free basic services" (Salga 2004b, 33).

DPLG has made a small amount of funding available to municipalities for free services, but this was only R29m in 2004–05 rising to R39m in 2006–07 (DPLG 2004b, 35).

Indigent Grants

A fourth and final neoliberal flanking mechanism to be reviewed here is the development of indigent grants. Designed to assist the poorest of the poor by providing additional payment relief on municipal services, rates and housing rentals, municipalities are free to decide if they want to develop an indigent policy and, if so, what the terms of this policy should be.

Cape Town's draft indigent policy (van Ryneveld et al. 2003)—yet to be officially implemented—is unusual in that it recommends against "means testing"—i.e. tests to determine whether an individual or household is poor enough to qualify for additional poverty relief. Instead, it advocates for a "universal" approach to financial assistance, arguing that it is better to let residents "self-select" themselves as poor rather than test if they are poor.

The thinking on this is twofold. First, it is argued that "the cost of administering means testing would so substantially reduce the benefits as to make the whole City indigent policy undesirable and impractical" (van

Ryneveld et al. 2003, 19).[7] Second, it is argued that the city's current policies on free services and progressive tariff structures are such that everyone can receive a 'basic' level of services for free or at a very low rate and that there is no need to provide additional financial assistance except in special circumstances.

In this way, "the poor are given a choice in how they manage their [own] resources". As long as they "are guaranteed that they will have a basic level of service free, they can maximise additional services by regulating their consumption in order to take advantage of the pricing structure that favours lower consumers". By "reducing water consumption to low but acceptable levels", for example, "households can reduce their water account to very little or nothing. This is a choice which low-income households are likely to make, but high-income households will not" (van Ryneveld et al. 2003, 37, 45).

But what this 'pro-poor' policy actually does is perpetuate uneven and inequitable service delivery in the city, justifying a 'basic' (though wholly insufficient) allocation of services to the townships while giving suburbanites the 'choice' to continue with their wasteful levels of consumption. There is no discussion in the policy document about the inadequacy of free water and electricity allocations or the impact that tariffs in the second and third blocks of tariff pricing are having on the ability of households to afford the level of services they might actually need.

Nor is there any discussion of whether upper-end tariffs sufficiently penalize the rich or generate sufficient cross-subsidies. In fact, the policy does the exact opposite, arguing that that the "small" number of wealthy people in Cape Town must not be chased away by overtaxation: "Where cross-subsidization results in very high tariffs to other users this results in resistance to payment from such users, and in some cases, even hardship. Overly high tariffs charged to business reduces profitability and constrains the local economy, which in turn leads to reduced jobs and incomes and pressure on payment levels.... An approach which seeks to cater for the special needs of the vulnerable in a manner which impacts unreasonably on the interests of any other segment of the city is not supported" (van Ryneveld et al. 2003, 39, 5).

This reluctance to actually spend money on an indigent grant is reflected in the city's 2004–05 budget, which set aside a mere R185m for this purpose—about R185 per person for the one million or so Capetonians living in poverty and represented a mere 1.6% of the city's total operating and capital budget (slightly more than what the city paid in car allowances to city managers and politicians that same year) (CCT 2004a, 77).

The policy also advocates harsh punishment for payment violations—calling for "severe sanctions such as sales-in-execution and evictions"—as well as a rapid roll out of prepaid meters, arguing that the latter will help the city deal with payment arrears (van Ryneveld et al. 2003, 40, 47).

CONCLUSION

As progressive as it may seem at first glance, Cape Town's approach to indigent grants, free services, block tariffs and other forms of cost control for the poor is anything but. The city has developed a strategy of squeezing maximum payment from the townships while allowing upper-income residents and industry to benefit from state-subsidized services at relatively low rates with few, if any, penalties for nonpayment.

Moreover, these differential rates are being used to justify a multi-tiered service delivery system in which elites can pay for the level of services they want while low-income households are restricted to basic, lifeline amenities. As a result, Capetonians are increasingly defined by their ability to pay as opposed to any legal or residential relationship to the city, with social relations being defined increasingly by what a resident can afford to buy.

Price is not the only mechanism of social control in this neoliberal world, however. As we shall see in the next chapter, the management of civic engagement and the repression of political opposition are also important mechanisms of neoliberal discipline, ensuring that Cape Town provides the kind of social, spatial and economic conditions necessary for renewed capital accumulation.

8   Disciplining Cape Town

In the last three chapters we have seen how neoliberal policymaking in Cape Town has served the interests of capital and suburban elites. Integral to this restructuring has been the imposition of a new set of disciplinary codes, which serve to restrict the life opportunities of the urban poor and impose new, and uneven, behavioural expectations. For the poor this means living with a 'basic' level of services and learning the 'true' (i.e. monetary) value of the services they consume. Businesses and suburban ratepayers, meanwhile, have been told that they can demand, and receive, almost any level of goods and services they are willing to pay for, with minimal (if any) cross-subsidization penalties.

Implicit in this discussion has been the argument that neoliberal tools of governance are more than just managerial strategies. They are, in effect, ideological tools that "encourage people to see themselves as individualized and active subjects responsible for enhancing their own well being" (Larner 2000, 13). What were once matters of 'collective consumption', to be dealt with through the mediating structures of the state, are now presented as questions of individual choice, effectively draining them of social meaning outside of market norms.

Prepaid meters, self-selected standards of living, and user fees for services force residents to think in narrow, individualized terms, obscuring the larger political significance of these technologies and dampening the potential for resistance to market reforms. Neo-Foucauldian scholars refer to this as the "governmentality" of neoliberalism, where institutions and individuals are governed "not directly from above, but through technologies such as budget disciplines, accountancy and audit" (Larner 2000).

In this chapter I explore the more direct forms of discipline associated with neoliberalism. When indirect control breaks down—as it inevitably does, given the inherently unequal and contradictory nature of neoliberalism—the state finds itself in need of more 'old-fashioned' forms of discipline: the manipulation of public participation; the marginalization, harassment and jailing of vocal opposition; and, most problematically, the use of physical violence to deter critics of the regime. As Robins (2005, 13) notes, "the urban poor [in South Africa] continue to be exposed to extraordinary levels of everyday violence. This post-apartheid urban scenario falls short of the normalising, disciplinary surveillance state that Foucauldian critics are so concerned about."

This kind of control, surveillance and aggression was not supposed to happen in post-apartheid South Africa. The ANC had long committed itself to a model of governance that promised nonviolence and broad-based participation by people from all walks of life. In some respects they have delivered on this statutory pledge. After coming to power in 1994 the ANC introduced a plethora of legislation on public participation and 'consultation', both of which continue to be an integral part of all new policy development. There have also been many practical successes along these lines, with widespread participation of individual citizens, community groups, NGOs, organized labour and others in public hearings and policymaking processes, helping to shape and influence decision making.

On the whole, however, public participation in post-apartheid decision making has been largely instrumentalist in nature, serving to protect and reinforce neoliberal policy objectives rather than to openly debate their merit. Sometimes subtle, and not always intentional, the practice of policymaking in South Africa has been one that pays lip service to consultative decision making while moving forward with a largely predetermined policy agenda, prompting even sympathetic observers to "declare the emperor nude" when it comes to public engagement (Chipkin 2004).

Much the same dynamic applies to Cape Town. There have been successes—with hundreds of public forums and community meetings having taken place in the city over the past ten years on issues ranging from public transit to housing—but for the most part public participation has failed to be institutionalized in a meaningful way and there has been little effort to create a culture of critical engagement.

The first term of democratic local government (1996–2000) was particularly problematic in this regard, marked more by its *lack* of public engagement than for any particular attempt to manipulate it. There were public forums but these tended to be focused on specific, neighbourhood issues—be it on the development of a new bus depot or an acute problem such as gang violence. There was virtually no broad-based public discussion of the city's overall policy plans and directions during these years. The much-vaunted RDP Forums—intended to provide a medium for community organizations to have an input on general development priorities—never materialized in any meaningful way in Cape Town in the 1990s and there was virtually no coordinated, city-wide public engagement on issues such as commercialization, service cutoffs or the city's desire to become 'world-class'.

It was only when the contradictions of these neoliberal strategies began to surface—generating heated debate and open resistance in the early 2000s—that the local state began to take participation more seriously. But rather than creating open-ended and critical dialogue, public participation in Cape Town has morphed into an exercise of control management in an attempt to shape public opinion and muffle opposition.

Particularly noteworthy has been the suppression of the Anti-Eviction Campaign (AEC), which has been demonized and attacked not only by the local state but also by mainstream media in the city. Equally problematic has been the marginalization of organized labour in Cape Town—particularly the South African Municipal Workers' Union—sometimes in direct violation of legislation that requires engagement with municipal unions. I look at the experience of these two organizations in this chapter, along with other participation initiatives by the city.

My objectives here are twofold. Empirically, I hope to demonstrate that the rhetoric of participatory democracy in Cape Town has not been met in practice and in fact constitutes the exact opposite: an attempt to contain public engagement rather than enhance it. Second, I hope to demonstrate that this manipulation of the participatory process is an inherent feature of neoliberalism, a necessary addition to the more subtle forms of disciplinary governance discussed in previous chapters.

I begin with a review of the formal legislative mechanisms for public participation in South Africa. Here we see an impressive range of opportunities for civic involvement—arguably one of the most conducive legal structures in the world to public participation—making the failure of this promise all the more remarkable.

This is followed by a review of mainstream explanations for the failures of participatory governance in the city, some of which have little to do with neoliberalism *per se* (e.g. participatory fatigue, the highly technical nature of many policy matters). I argue that there is merit in each of these interpretations but that we must ultimately see participatory failure in Cape Town as part of a larger effort to implement and enforce the neoliberal policies necessary for a new regime of capital accumulation—a phenomenon akin to what Abrahamsen (2000, 122–35) calls "exclusionary democracies".

The remainder of the chapter is an empirical review of key participatory developments in Cape Town in an attempt to illustrate these points concretely. I focus in particular on the Listening Campaign, the introduction of Ward Councils and the city's engagement (and lack thereof) with Samwu.

LEGISLATION AND PUBLIC PARTICIPATION

"All people shall be entitled to take part in the administration of the country!" So states a clause from "The People Shall Govern!", a section of the ANC's Freedom Charter of 1955. For at least 50 years, then, the ANC has championed a vision of government in which ordinary citizens would be able to participate in the management and decision making of the country.

Local government is seen as central to this participatory objective. As noted in Chapter 4, one of the stated goals of decentralization in South

Africa has been that of bringing government "closer to the people", with local government legislation "shot through with the language of 'participation'" (Hart 2002, 261). Beall et al. (2002, 85) point to the "imperative" of participatory planning at the local level and note that it is so legally entrenched that it is "technically impossible for development to occur without community input and engagement with the local authorities." "For the first time in South Africa's history", according to the ANC's Reconstruction and Development Programme White Paper (RSA 1994b, 18), "local authorities must work with community-based organizations and NGOs to establish minimum conditions of good governance and to implement effective development projects".

The White Paper on Local Government further prioritized public participation, most notably by insisting that there be community involvement in the design of Integrated Development Plans (IDPs) (now mandatory for all municipalities in the country). Local governments, it is argued, "should develop mechanisms to ensure citizen participation" in the IDP process (RSA 1998b, section B). Section 7.5.1 of the White Paper also states: "Provincial Governments should encourage the establishment of sub-regional and/or local forums which will consist of representatives of all the stakeholders in the areas".

The Municipal Systems Act (RSA 2000a, s16.1) has made it clear as well that all "municipalit[ies] must develop a culture of municipal governance that complements formal representative government with a system of participatory governance, and must for this purpose encourage, and create conditions for, the local community to participate in the affairs of the municipality". It is expected that this participatory process will take into account the special needs of people who cannot read or write, people with disabilities, women, and other disadvantaged groups.

Further examples of this commitment to participatory governance at the local level include the Development Facilitation Act, which calls for community participation in land-use planning decision making and in the preparation of Land Development Objectives (LDOs), and the Municipal Infrastructure Grant (MIG) program, which requires "community participation and awareness plans" if municipalities are to receive funds from national government for infrastructure development (DPLG 2004a, 43). Even the Constitution (section 152.1e) states that one of the objectives of municipalities is "to encourage the involvement of communities and community organisations in the matters of local government".

But as numerous authors have now argued, legislative commitment has not been followed up by governmental practice. From Johannesburg (Bremner 1998, Beall et al. 2002, Bond 2003, Heller 2003) to Durban (Freund and Padayachee 2002, Desai 2002, McKinley and Veriava 2005, CCS 2006) to Cape Town (Chipkin 2004, McDonald and Smith 2004, Miraftab 2003, 2004) and beyond, there is widespread concern amongst academics, unionists and activists that when it comes to public participation in local government decision making in South Africa the emperor is indeed nude. In the words of one observer, drawing on ten years of research in the Nelson Mandela Metropole (formerly Port Elizabeth), the state has "missed the boat" in implementing the "radical participatory strategy envisaged in the RDP" (Cherry 2004).

Heller (2003, 170) is critical of the "largely top-down" nature of public engagement, a process that has been "dominated by technocrats [and] has afforded few, if any, opportunities for meaningful participation". He goes on to say that "interviews with civic leaders in Johannesburg paint a picture of increasing exclusion from the planning process.... Not a single civic official claimed to have made effective use of participatory structures"; a rather damning indictment of a city that has a formal Public Participation Policy and prides itself on civic engagement (as each Annual Report that the city publishes is keen to proclaim).

Even more damning is Buur's (2005, 253) claim that "the state and the ANC have tried to both undo and capture those forms of organisation that played an important role in the struggle against apartheid and upon which the new democracy was going to be based". "Radical forms of democratic organisation" that "gained the reputation of being impossible to control", and worked so well for the ANC in previous decades, have now become the enemy.

EXPLAINING THE FAILURES

How do we explain this failure of participatory governance? Several theories have been put forward. Each has something to offer our understanding of the situation, but none has adequately captured what I argue to be a more direct and instrumentalist attempt to control the nature of public debate in the interests of capital.

Perhaps the most common argument is that of "participatory fatigue" (e.g. Beall et al. 2002, 85). After years of anti-apartheid protest and civic action, and the intense transition years of the early to mid-1990s—all of which required massive and exhaustive efforts on the part of civil society—it is argued that many people are simply tired of political engagement and want to get on with their lives, particularly now that the political party they fought for is in power (a point we return to below).

While there is considerable truth to this argument it is also true that many South Africans still engage the state and want to participate in decision making. There is a new generation of activists in the 'young lions'—largely black youth in urban townships—and many of the most active citizens at the local level are the 'grannies' and 'aunties' of the anti-apartheid struggle who continue to fight for justice on a wide range of issues (Desai 2002, Bond 2003, McKinley and Veriava 2005). The Soweto Electricity Crisis Committee in Johannesburg and the Concerned Citizens Forum in Durban are both heavily populated with this latter demographic. And yet, if anyone has a right to feel 'fatigued' in post-apartheid South Africa it is this group of elderly women. Burnout no doubt affects many from this generation, and others much younger, but the notion of participatory fatigue fails to explain the existence and dynamism of these organizations.

A second theory relates to the practical aspects of participation and the logistical difficulties people face when trying to take advantage of participatory opportunities. Public transportation in Cape Town, for example, is expensive, time-consuming, sometimes very dangerous and often not available after working hours, making it difficult for low-income residents to attend public meetings. Improvements have been made over the years by holding meetings in township areas—rather than expecting people to come to the city centre—but these initiatives are limited by the fact that public hearings are typically held on a single evening in a single venue. In a sprawling township such as Khayelitsha most people live a considerable distance from the community centre and public transportation *within* townships is even worse than transport to the city centre, while travelling at night is particularly risky, especially for women.

A third argument is that community engagement tends to be designed and managed by white, male bureaucrats with little understanding of township cultures and expectations. This world view, it is argued, fails to understand perspectives that are very different from their own, creating a truncated participation process and/or turning people off participation altogether. Gotz and Simone (2003, 146) argue that bureaucratic municipal authorities in South Africa have largely been unable to understand and/or accommodate the highly complex and often tenuous ways in which township civil society operates and continues to evolve. The challenge to local government, they argue, is to develop a governance system that "respects and confirms multiple existing urban identifications" and to work with these differences to develop participatory systems that are more appropriate to the new, "fluid" urban realities.

A related point is the technicist bent of the engagement process. For people with low literacy and numeracy skills, understanding and engaging in complex policy debates and research evidence can be difficult. Efforts have been made to produce lay material in the vernacular but these initiatives are few and far between in Cape Town and can still require a high degree of technical knowledge about accounting, engineering, etc. This is not a problem unique to South Africa (Meer 1999), but it remains a major barrier to effective participation by the poor. The knowledge gap is made worse by the fact that so many skilled civic leaders from the townships have been drawn off to the public and private sectors since 1994 and are no longer deeply engaged in community participatory initiatives (in some cases they have become the ones trying to limit these initiatives!).

It is also true that it can be very difficult to get access to technical information, even for those who do understand it. This has been a problem for many civic organizations in Cape Town where access to some of the most basic municipal data can prove impossible. Cape Town is not alone in this regard. A study in 2004 by the Open Democracy Advice Centre found that more than half of all requests for information to national government were ignored, despite the introduction of the Promotion of Access to Information Act in 2000 (the first of its kind in Africa and one of the most progressive bills of its kind in the world). The report identified the departments of defence, education, finance and environment and tourism as being particularly unresponsive, and noted that Eskom was the "worst performing" agency of all. The report also noted that if denied access to information the appeals process is "lengthy, expensive and inaccessible to many South Africans" (*Business Day*, September 28, 2004).

A fourth theory is that much of the local government consultative process is being farmed out to private consultants, many of whom are even less well equipped—and less motivated than elected officials—to engage with low-income communities. Some firms have recognized their weaknesses in this regard and subcontract the public engagement components of their work to consultants that specialize in participatory practices. Although this may provide better opportunities for participation it means that the participatory process is removed yet another step from the elected officials making policy decisions. The fact that this participatory information is also filtered through the ideological lenses of the consultancy firms involved—many of which are large multinationals such as PricewaterhouseCoopers and KPMG, which have been instrumental in pushing for the commercialization and privatization of services in Cape Town and around the world—makes the indirect consultative process all the more problematic.

In some cases, public engagement in policymaking is managed entirely by the private sector, with no formal involvement by the state at all. City improvement districts typically operate in this way, engaging residents and businesses in a limited geographic area and forwarding their recommendations to city council. This effective privatization of the decision-making process occurs outside the formal, participatory structures demanded by legislation, with far-reaching implications for decisions on issues such as basic service delivery, tourism marketing campaigns and city policing.

One last theory put forward is that many ANC–aligned individuals, NGOs and CBOs feel that they now have a representative voice in government and no longer need to engage with the state. Experience in other countries has shown that it is not unusual for social movements to demobilize after a political transition if the new government is perceived to be working in their interest, and it is possible that many township-based civics in South Africa "have explicitly abandoned the politics of contention in deference to the authority and legitimacy of the ANC" (Heller 2003, 156).

The problem with these explanations is that they assume (implicitly or explicitly) that better institutional mechanisms and cultural awareness will make for better participatory processes. More locations for meetings, better access to information and more cultural- and gender-sensitive moderators are expected to dramatically advance South Africa's participatory potentials.

While improvement on these fronts can make a significant difference to the ways in which policymaking is conducted and implemented (see, for example, Gotz and Simone's (2003) description of the relatively successful ways in which the Inner City Office of Johannesburg has engaged with residents of the CBD over a new taxi rank, or Chipkin's (2003) description of the way in which Cape Town's former DEVCOM unit conducted its participatory processes) these procedural perspectives overlook or ignore the larger structural and ideological features of capitalist crisis in urban South Africa. It is not just the cultural blinkering of white, male bureaucrats or the technicist bent of policy decisions that are to blame for the highly circumscribed nature of civic participation. It is the necessity of ensuring that systems and behaviours are in place to secure the implementation of a particular set of policy reforms (i.e. privatization, cost recovery, etc.).

It is these direct, Machiavellian methods of handling participatory processes in Cape Town that I will focus on in the remainder of the chapter: namely, the selective ways in which participatory mechanisms are employed, the aggressive marginalization of 'bad' civil society, and hamfisted labour relations. All serve to illustrate how participatory processes have been directly and aggressively circumvented by the local state.

PUBLIC PARTICIPATION IN CAPE TOWN

Selective Engagement

Perhaps the most significant example of 'selective engagement' with the public is the lead-up to the policy recommendations made by the Unicity Commission in 2000, in advance of the first metropolitan-wide local elections in December of that year. The Unicity Commission (as discussed in detail in Chapter 7) was a multiparty committee established to review and vote on recommendations made by a team of technical advisors composed of senior bureaucrats and private sector consultants. The latter conducted the bulk of research and policy advising work and consisted of large multinationals and smaller, local consulting firms (one of which was tasked with the responsibility of coordinating the day-to-day activities of the Commission and was staffed by individuals who remain closely tied to policy development in the city).

The Commission's policy recommendations were critical for several reasons: they were the first policy frameworks in the history of the city to address the Cape Metropolitan Area in its entirety; they were unanimously (and uncontroversially) approved by all of the political parties represented in Council; and they have set the tone for policy development in the city ever since.

Yet few Capetonians knew about the existence or operations of the Unicity Commission, let alone had direct interaction with it. There were limited public hearings shortly before the Commission's final recommendations were released in November 2000 (less than a month before local government elections), and there were limited opportunities for individuals and organizations to interact with the Commission on particular policy questions during its mandate that year, but neither of these opportunities was widely advertised and none of the public hearings was well-attended (with most only attracting a handful of people). Nor was the Commission's report made widely or easily available to the general public.

Was this a case of culturally insensitive bureaucrats not knowing how to engage with Cape Town's citizens? Were Capetonians too tired of politics to go to meetings? Were the times and locations of public hearings not suitable for low-income residents?

Perhaps. But it is also clear that the Unicity Commission had a strongly neoliberal policy agenda, one which broke dramatically from the statist policies of the past and for which there was little apparent interest in debating with the public. Much of this can be put down to the growing hegemony of neoliberal thought amongst the various political parties that made up the Commission and their desire to 'get on with the business of running the city', but there would also appear to have been concerted attempts to shield information from close public scrutiny.

The South African Municipal Workers' Union was most overtly affected by this tactic and was consistently sidelined by the Commission. As noted in a previous chapter, the union was only "informed" of changes being recommended by the Commission rather than being consulted, a strategy that the subsequent elected Council took to heart, telling Samwu on at least one occasion that "we do not have to justify the decisions to the unions"[1] (for an extended review of labour-management relations in the City of Cape Town see MSP (2000)).

Nor has the situation changed. Samwu is still fighting with city officials to participate in the major restructuring initiatives of the city and very few Capetonians could tell you about the nature and extent of these original restructuring initiatives. Complex though they are, the corporatization and commericalization of essential services can (and must) be debated by the general public in open and frequent public forums, with information being provided in accessible, lay terms. More importantly, there should be mechanisms for debating the relative merits and demerits of the different strategies proposed, with opportunities being provided for critics to voice their opinions and explain the links between corporatization, privatization and cost recovery. None of this has been done in Cape Town.

In the end, the restructuring of Cape Town's essential services into stand-alone, cost-reflective 'business units', and its efforts to attract international capital with 'world-class' amenities, have been implemented with virtually no public input or debate.

Managing Engagement

These examples of selective engagement do not, however, fully capture the extent to which participatory governance has failed in Cape Town. There is an even deeper, systemic problem with the city's efforts to 'manage' engagement. Two initiatives illustrate the problem: the Mayoral "Listening Campaigns" (begun by the ANC in 2003), and the creation of "Ward Committees" in 2004.

The Listening Campaigns began "as a means to obtain broad input from residents and other stakeholders" on a wide range of issues and to "test" the City's strategic agenda. It is claimed that over 12,000 people participated in the process in the first year, "through meetings and various communication channels, providing valuable direction to our strategic planning and budgeting process" (CCT 2003a, Appendix 2A).

During the second Listening Campaign in 2004 the Mayor admitted that the first round had not been as successful as she had hoped, noting: "We have not really listened to what people want. We simply build things but do not really hear whether this is what communities want or need" (speech given at the Elsies River Town Hall meeting on November 22, 2004).

Has the situation improved? Subsequent meetings in 2004 and 2005 did give people a better opportunity to voice their opinion but once again there was little effective or meaningful engagement. By and large the meetings consisted of 20–30 municipal officials seated on a stage at the front of a town hall, presenting a slick PowerPoint overview of the Integrated Development Plan (already effectively finalized), followed by an hour of questions/comments from the audience. This was repeated each night over a two-week period at two separate times.

Interestingly, meetings in the townships drew questions/comments that were largely critical in nature and related almost entirely to matters of basic service delivery (stormwater drainage, street lighting, refuse collection, arrears, cost of services, etc.). Critical comments from the floor were typically followed by loud bouts of clapping and cheering from the audience.

Responses to these questions/comments from city officials were largely evasive, with little in the way of concrete explanations for why service delivery had been so slow to arrive or so poorly maintained or so expensive. Nor were any firm commitments made on action. Officials also appeared to have little patience for critical remarks. At a meeting in the predominantly coloured township of Elsies River on November 22, 2004, for example, the ANC Mayor at the time reprimanded the audience for not doing enough for themselves ("unlike the people in Khayelitsha"). She claimed: "There are mischievous people who come to meetings like this and say there is no service delivery. They say we want to retrench workers but we have not made those decisions yet. We are very responsible leaders.... It is the city officials [bureaucrats] you must challenge for not spending their budgets, not the [elected] executive".

By contrast, meetings in the (predominantly white) suburbs saw officials and councillors acting in a much more accommodating manner in responding to questions/comments from the floor. This conciliatory tone was due in part to the fact that comments and criticisms were largely trivial in nature (e.g. "Why do we not have an attendant at the toilet in the park anymore?") and/or prefaced by profuse thanks to the Mayor for having provided an open forum for the public to speak (a novelty for most white Capetonians as well) and/or congratulatory of the kinds of material improvements that had been made to their districts such as new roads, CIDs, and so on.

The suburban meetings were also dominated by representatives from ratepayer associations and other organizations with prepared memorandums on the demands they were making of the city. Well-resourced and well-organized, these suburban groups were much more difficult to ignore or chastise, at least in public. The Mayor went so far as to congratulate some of these organizations, thanking the Claremont Improvement District at one meeting for "doing a wonderful job".

In the end, individuals and organizations whose comments fit with the city's vision of development were listened to intently, while those critical of the regime received little in the way of encouragement or advice. "Leave it to us to take care of things", was the subtext, " ... and stop complaining". Little wonder, then that at the township-based meetings for the Listening Campaign the majority of people left early.

The much-vaunted Ward Committees have been little better. Legislatively provided for in the Municipal Systems Act, their purpose is to facilitate and enhance democracy at the local level. In practice, however, Ward Committees have been "evolving rather slowly" (Salga 2004c, 20). Cape Town is no different in this respect, with Ward Committees only becoming operational on a city-wide basis in late 2004.

More important, however, are their configuration and reporting structures. Although there are Ward Committees in every ward in the city, members are elected by "interest groups" that must be "identified" and approved by a centralized Electoral Body. The ward councillor then chairs the Ward Committee.[2]

The responsibilities of the Ward Committee are: to make recommendations on matters affecting the ward to the ward councillor; to actively seek to understand the needs of the community and report these back to the Committee; to act as "the formal mouthpiece for the residents in that ward ... to contribute to improved service delivery through monitoring and reporting"; and to assist council in conducting public participation on matters such as the IDP, budget and policy formulation.

On paper, this is a marked improvement from the selective engagement models outlined above, but the Ward Councils have also turned out to be a highly controlled and circumscribed participation exercise. The state effectively selects the candidates it wants on the committee, endorses their membership and then chairs all meetings; hardly an independent, robust and inclusive form of civic participation as envisioned by the ANC in its RDP and Freedom Charter discussions, and nowhere near as participatory as the engagement processes taking place in parts of Latin America and elsewhere (Baiocchi 2003, Chavez and Goldfrank 2003).

Even if they were more democratic, Ward Committees have no power other than to "make recommendations" to their ward councillor, who may or may not champion the cause in Council (and will, at any rate, have to compete with all of the other councillors trying to have their voices heard). According to Roland Langley, Chairperson of the Cape Town Civil Society City Wide Forum (CTCSCWF), Ward Committees are just "tea parties for hand selected people. They have no real power. The real power lies with other parts of the city" (personal interview). Even President Mbeki has been forced to comment on the gap between democratic pretence and actual participation, chastising senior city officials in Cape Town in 2005 about the need for better public engagement (Benton 2005, 1).

It would also appear that city officials see Ward Committees as a way to muffle critics. As one ward councillor from Nelson Mandela Metro explained to a journalist (with no apparent irony): "One of the main successes [of the Ward Councils] is that the toyi-toyis and demand for the urgent delivery of services has stopped. As a councillor since 1994 I have really felt the pinch. People used to knock at the door demanding housing and water right away. Now we have educated them on the delivery process, and they understand. Now they don't mind paying for services because they understand. They even take ownership of municipal businesses.... They are fully aware that these things are hitting the taxpayer" (Mkokeli 2005, 65).

But this dampening of demands from the poor does not seem to have calmed the fears of middle-class ratepayers. In late 2004, as a Ward Committee was being established in the affluent Cape Town suburbs of Fish Hoek and Simon's Town, white residents were up in arms about this new form of broad-based engagement, fearing that "[s]treet kids will have [a] say on ward committees", creating "unrealistic" demands on the municipality (according to a front-page headline of the October 14, 2004, issue of the *False Bay Echo*). Residents also complained about the fact that the first Committee meeting had been switched from the suburban town hall in Simon's Town to a venue in Ocean View (a predominantly coloured township about five kilometres away) to better accommodate township residents who did not have transportation—a location that suburban residents claimed was "inconvenient" and dangerous.

Marginalizing Critics

A third feature of participatory discipline in Cape Town is the active and sometimes aggressive marginalization of individuals and organizations deemed problematic. Although present in my examples of the selective and managed engagement processes described above, there are more explicit examples of how city officials actively ostracize and demonize specific groups of people.

The treatment of the Anti-Eviction Campaign is emblematic in this regard. Since first organizing in 2000, AEC members have been continuously harassed by police during their protests against evictions and/or service cutoffs. Dogs, guns (with rubber and real bullets), stun grenades and tear gas form a regular part of the police arsenal in these confrontations.

Two prominent AEC activists describe their experience in Mandela Park on the Cape Flats:

> In September 1999 the sheriffs came to Mandela Park with dogs and teargas and guns. On the first day they came to confiscate our goods. On the second day they came back to evict us from our homes. There were a lot of police, in Caspirs and in small vans. It was as if they were at war. They cordoned off one street at a time and started to evict people. The whole area came out, as well as neighbouring areas, to try and prevent the evictions. We stood up to them. No one told us to resist—it was spontaneous. People were beaten with batons, shot at with rubber bullets and bitten by police dogs. Teargas blew everywhere. A lot of people were injured and it is lucky that no one was killed (as quoted in Desai and Pithouse 2004, 841–42).

Activists such as these have been arrested and jailed, often to be released days, weeks or even months later with no charges being laid. The goal of this harassment, as Desai and Pithouse (2004, 841) put it, is to "make political life almost impossible" for these individuals, robbing their organizations of leadership, draining them of energy and resources in never-ending legal battles, and scaring off current and future membership (see also McKinley and Veriava 2005 for a damning report of state repression of social movements in Cape Town and other parts of the country).

The mainstream media, not surprisingly, tends to side with the state and employ the same rhetoric, referring to groups such as the AEC as "dangerous" and "trouble makers". The effect is to divide community groups into those that are 'good' (i.e. those willing to engage in the formal structures set up by council) and those that are 'bad' (i.e. those operating outside of the formal structures offered by the city, directly challenging city officials on key policy directions, reconnecting water/electricity supplies without permission, and so on).

This divide and conquer strategy is illustrated by the strategic revitalization of the South African National Civic Organization (Sanco) by the ANC in the early 2000s. Largely moribund by the end of the 1990s the ANC reestablished and refinanced Sanco in 2003 in an attempt to counter the growing number of critical community-based social movements that had sprung up around service cutoffs, evictions and privatization. Although still weak on the ground, and widely recognized as a front for the ANC, Sanco nonetheless continues to play an important role in splintering community allegiances at the grass roots level and acting as a gatekeeper in township politics (Zuern 2004).

Nor is Sanco the only front for the ANC. As Patel (2005) argues in the case of the township of Bayview, in Durban, the ANC simply established its own 'grass roots' civic (The Concerned Flatdwellers of Bayview) when the existing civic in that area (the Bayview Flats Residents' Association) became too vocal and too critical of ANC policy. "Like neoliberal governments around the world", argues Patel, "the African National Congress isn't fond of democracy—it's too difficult, dangerous, and unguaranteed. Governments prefer to have a tamed version of dissent, a civil society it can control, a snivel society that bows and scrapes, but never raises its voice".

CONCLUSION

Are there grounds for optimism here? Certainly the potential for meaningful civic engagement has improved dramatically since the nasty days of apartheid when there were virtually no opportunities for broad-based engagement and when 'discipline' often meant arrest, detention, torture and even death. As bad as things are today, legislation is in place for participatory governance, there is public awareness of these possibilities, municipalities are creating opportunities for engagement, and violent repression is nowhere near what it was under apartheid. In this respect, one can point to many positive gains.

But the disciplining effect of this new democracy is complex, sophisticated and powerful, creating a truncated form of participatory governance that shapes and curtails public opinion, allowing the local (and national) state to hide behind a façade of public engagement, legitimizing neoliberal policymaking and practice. The result, in the end, is the construction of a "snivel society" that operates within the parameters deemed acceptable by capital and a policymaking elite while at the same time helping to marginalize and silence more radical critics, creating an inevitable conflict between 'good' and 'bad' civic organizations.

This is not a sustainable strategy, of course. As the inequities of neoliberalism deepen, and as the false promises of pro-government community organizations fail to materialize, low-income Capetonians will recognize the disciplinary effects of neoliberal democracy (regardless of the political party behind it) and join the ranks of thousands of other citizens already resisting neoliberal reforms.

9 (De)Africanizing Cape Town

One day, the remaining whites of Africa may be clustered only in the Western Cape, in their heavily fortified compounds at the very tip of the continent.

Jason Cowley, writing in The Observer (London), April 16, 2006

One of the most remarkable features of Cape Town is how un-African it can feel. There are, of course, the ubiquitous reminders of 'being in Africa' at tourist locations, and there are black faces on the streets and shops of the central city. But unless one spends time in the African townships of Langa, Nyanga and Khayelitsha, or in the innumerable informal settlements in Cape Town, it would be easy to forget that this is a city on the African continent.

This is due in part to the fact that Cape Town is less than one third African by population (half the city is coloured and about 20% is white). But there is more to it than that. As the quote at the opening of this chapter attests to, Cape Town has become a redoubt of sorts for whites fleeing the rest of the continent. And even though whites make up an (ever-dwindling) minority of the city's population, it has a distinctly white—almost apartheid-era—feel to it. Going to a restaurant or an entertainment venue or a park can feel like stepping back in time, where almost all the patrons are white and the staff are black, largely hidden from view.

Johannesburg and Durban share the same racialized socioeconomic structures as Cape Town but these two cities have much larger African populations (and African middle classes) and are not as highly polarized geographically as Cape Town is by its white/coloured/African layout. Nor is there the same palpable sense of trying to sustain the illusion of Europe in these two cities as there is in Cape Town.

Perhaps it is the Mediterranean climate that lends itself to this political and cultural fantasy in Cape Town. For the most part, however, it is a strategic—if sometimes unconscious—attempt by the city's decision makers and developers to maintain a sense of 'whiteness', in part to distinguish the city from Johannesburg and Durban. More importantly, it is a tactical—

and, I would argue, inevitable—part of Cape Town's efforts to be a 'world-class city': an attempt to create a networked place of urban capitalists that looks and feels familiar to a (largely white) transnational elite.

There is an inherent tension that goes with this, however. At the same time as the city resists Africanization it is also Africanizing at a rapid pace. Internal migration from rural areas in South Africa, and cross-border migration from other African countries, is transforming the city's demographics and Cape Town will likely have a predominantly African population within a generation. Also present are the political pressures of pan-Africanism at the national and local level and the desire on the part of many South African politicians to integrate the city and country with the rest of the continent.

Ironically, much of this pressure to integrate is coming from capital, keen as it is to see more trade, resource extraction and foreign investment in the rest of the continent, as well as having access to cheap(er) labour (skilled and unskilled). World cities depend on these trade and migration links and Cape Town is no different in this regard. As Simone (quoted in Nyomnjoh 2006, 80) notes, "Migration confirms South Africa's relative economic transformation".

But it is not just demographics that are at play here. More important than the mere number of people are the city's sociospatial characteristics. In the second part of this chapter I outline why it is that Cape Town can be seen to be 'deAfricanizing' despite its demographic trends. Drawing on the lessons of previous chapters I point to the ways in which neoliberal policies force low-income black people to the periphery of the city—largely out of sight—and how this spatial patterning is exacerbated by Cape Town's own brand of racism. The more recent phenomenon of xenophobia—particularly that aimed at black migrants from other countries in Africa—adds to this ghettoizing trend, leading to the acceleration, not the diminution, of racially and ethnically defined housing clusters throughout the city. Cape Town may be becoming more African demographically but it is becoming less African in integrated, sociocultural terms.

There is a profound tension inherent in all of this. On the one hand, urban capital needs a reserve army of unemployed (African) labour. On the other, urban elites want to control this population influx, minimizing the number of poor Africans on the streets, shops and beaches of the city. Large numbers of unemployed African migrants 'committing crimes' and 'scaring away investors and tourists' is not good for business.

How will this tension be managed? The answer, it would seem, is to have cheap labour without having to live with it or subsidize it. This has been done to some extent already, as we have seen, though the off-loading of development costs via privatization and cost recovery. These indirect means of control are supplemented by the direct involvement of the city's police forces (public and private), detentions and deportations of undesirables by the Department of Home Affairs, and by local community organizations who can help determine who becomes an active citizen of the city.

All of this is supported by a strong—and perhaps even growing—current of racism and xenophobia, justifying and exacerbating the kinds of exclusionary outcomes created by neoliberalism.

This cannot continue forever. In the end, Cape Town will become a much more African city by sheer weight of numbers, and the social, political and economic fortressing of whiteness will be increasingly difficult to sustain. Just how this tension will resolve itself is too early to say, but the inequities of neoliberalism coupled with the indignities of racism and xenophobia make for an explosive mix.

We can also see in this dynamic another example of the multiscalar constitution of neoliberalism, whereby local governments are forced to deal with issues of national and international migration with no legislative authority to deal with them and limited resources to cope with these phenomena.

Remarkably, little research has been conducted on the urban nature of this cross-border migration into South Africa. There are numerous case studies examining the lives of cross-border migrants in specific urban contexts and/or with regard to particular issues such as housing or employment (Rogerson and Rogerson 1997, Morris 1998, McDonald et al. 2000, McDonald 2000a, Reitzes and Bam 2000, Hunter and Skinner 2001). There are also a handful of papers calling for more research in the topic (Kihato 2004, SACN 2004, Landau 2005), including a report by the United Nation's High Commission on Refugees, which makes an urgent call for an "urban refugee policy review" in South Africa (UNHCR 2006).

But despite these calls there have been no systematic studies of the overall impact that cross-border migration is having on the social, economic and political fabric of South African cities or the ability of South African cities to manage these demographic and socioeconomic shifts. Municipalities themselves, as we shall see below, either bury their heads in the sand or turn a blind eye to violent actions on the part of South Africans toward foreign migrants within their municipal borders. The South African Local Government Association has not taken a position on the matter either, choosing instead to inflame the issue with anti-foreigner rhetoric and/or simplistic claims of not having sufficient resources to manage the inflow of people. As Landau (2005, 2) points out, local governments in South Africa have "typically reacted to the presence of foreign migrants by implicitly denying their presence, excluding them from development plans, or allowing discrimination throughout the government bureaucracy or police".

We begin, then, with a review of the demographic trends in Cape Town, highlighting both the internal and cross-border migration patterns that are making it a much more African city. This is followed by a discussion of the deAfricanizing trends outlined above and how these inherent tensions may play themselves out.

AFRICANIZING CAPE TOWN

For much of Cape Town's history, Africans have made up only a small fraction of its population. Bantu-speaking peoples that had migrated to other parts of contemporary South Africa from the fourth century AD onward had not yet settled permanently in the Cape when the Dutch arrived in the 1650s. It was largely local indigenous groups (Khoi/Khoe and San) that the Dutch encountered and enslaved at the time, quickly supplementing this local labour force with slaves from their colonies in the East Indies.

It is the descendants of these indigenous peoples and imported slaves, plus the offspring of mixed-race relationships, that came to form the so-called 'coloured' population of Cape Town (a term first introduced by the British in the 1840s and formally codified under apartheid). Although whites made up the majority of the city's population for the first two centuries, by 1865—the year of the first modern census in South Africa—whites and coloureds were roughly equal in numbers (15,118 and 13,065 people respectively, with only 274 Africans being enumerated). By the late 1940s, however, coloureds were the largest population group in the city and by 1975 outnumbered whites by almost two to one (Western 2001, 623). Today, coloureds are still the largest population group in the city, constituting just under half of the Cape Metropolitan Area's residents (see Table 9.1).

Nationally, however, coloureds make up less than 10% of the country's population. The high proportion of coloureds in Cape Town, and in the Western Cape more generally, is due in part to the inertia of original settlement patterns but also because of laws enacted by the National Party under apartheid. In 1954 the state declared the then-Cape Province to be a "Coloured Labour Preference Area" and set about removing thousands of African workers and their families, resettling them in remote and underserviced rural Bantustans in present-day Eastern Cape. Housing development for Africans ceased in Cape Town at this time, though single-sex hostels for male African workers would eventually be built to handle the inevitable demand for cheap African labour. There was also a mushrooming of informal settlements as hostel accommodation became too crowded or too expensive, and families (illegally) joined these workers (Berstein 1978).

Efforts to keep the Cape a coloured preference area continued late into the apartheid era, with an estimated 70,000 African workers and their families being forcibly removed from the city by the mid-1980s, along with the destruction of a number of informal African settlements. But with the end of 'pass laws' and the growing realization on the part of the neo-apartheid state that cheap labour was required to grease the wheels of urban industry and commerce there was a dramatic rise in the number of Africans in Cape Town from the late 1980s onwards.

Today there are more than one million Africans in the city—making up about a third of the city's population—and it is estimated that this number

Table 9.1 Cape Town's Population Profile—1996 and 2001

Population Group	Cape Town's population (no. of people)		Percent of Cape Town's population		Percent of South Africa's population		Population growth rates (national, %)
	1996	2001	1996	2001	1996	2001	2001
African	702,034	916,520	26.2	31.6	76.7	79.0	1.05
Coloured	1,313,131	1,392,656	48.9	48.1	8.9	8.9	1.21
Asian	36,717	41,490	1.4	1.4	2.6	2.5	-0.02
White	630,985	542,580	23.5	18.8	10.9	9.6	0.96
Unspecified	N/A	N/A	N/A	N/A	0.9	N/A	N/A
TOTAL	2,682,866	2,893,246	100	100	100	100	N/A

Source: Statistics South Africa, Census 1996 and 2001.

is growing by as many as 48,000 people a year (CCT 2004b, 78). Most of the latter is due to in-migration of low-income individuals and families from the Eastern Cape, though natural birth rates and cross-border migration are an important component as well, all of which will likely make Africans the majority population group in the city within a few decades.

Equally significant from a demographic point of view is the absolute and relative decline of whites in Cape Town: from just under a quarter of the population in 1996 to less than a fifth in 2001, with what would appear to be a reduction of some 90,000 people (see Table 9.1). The latter is, no doubt, part of a larger phenomenon of 'white flight' from South Africa, though there are indications that this exodus is not as extensive or as permanent as commonly thought, with most whites seemingly intent on staying in South Africa and increasing numbers returning to the country after having left in the 1990s (McDonald and Crush 2002).

It is also true that Cape Town has been attracting white immigrants (permanent and temporary) from Europe and North America, and these numbers would appear to be on the increase with the easing of immigration regulations for skilled personnel (more on this below).

One final point of demographic interest is that there are very few Asians in Cape Town. At 1.4% of the city's population this is half the (already small) national average for this population group. Although largely middle- to upper-middle income in socioeconomic terms, Asians play a small part in the overall political economy of the city.

FUTURE DEMOGRAPHIC TRENDS

Future demographic trends in Cape Town will depend largely on three factors: natural birth rates and life expectancy, in-migration from other parts of the country, and immigration from outside the country.

Natural Growth Rates

With regards to natural population growth rates coloureds are experiencing the fastest growth nationally, with Mitchell's Plain—a large, predominantly coloured township in Cape Town—experiencing the fastest 'baby boom' in the country according to a 2004 survey by the Bureau for Market Research, at about 5% a year (as compared to the 1% national average) (as reported in the *Cape Times*, September 30, 2004).

Population growth rates for Africans are a close second, but are dampened considerably by deaths from AIDS. HIV-prevalence rates are high in South Africa at about 10% of the national population, affecting close to 4.5 million people, the vast majority of whom are African. Although HIV is not expected to have a significant impact on fertility rates relative to other factors, it is having a disastrous impact on life expectancy (SSA 2005).

Expectations are that there will be an overall decrease in population in South Africa as a result of HIV/AIDS in the short to medium term, taking the country from a projected population of 47.7 million in 2006 to 47.4 million in 2012. It is anticipated that there could be as many as 9.31 million AIDS–related deaths by 2020 (SACN 2005, 120).

Although information on the impact of HIV on cities is "sketchy", urban areas in South Africa are "unlikely to escape this demographic tragedy". In fact, cities may be even more seriously affected than rural areas, as "late-stage AIDS sufferers, unable to secure meaningful care in overcrowded urban health centres, return to [rural] homesteads to be cared for by extended family" (SACN 2004, 43).

The South African Cities Network, in conjunction with its member municipalities (including Cape Town) have been attempting to monitor and address the HIV crisis at the urban level, but resource constraints, the ongoing stigmatization of HIV/AIDS, and uneven political commitment from national government have made this difficult. As a result, the demographic impact of HIV on South African cities remains poorly understood and municipalities are weakly equipped to deal with the growing crisis (on the latter point see IHRG and Samwu 2005). One fact that is known in Cape Town is that HIV prevalence in the African townships (e.g. Guguletu, Khayeltisha) is as "as high as or higher than the national average" of about 28% (CCT 2006e, 33).

Internal Migration

It is in the area of internal migration (i.e. from other parts of South Africa) that Cape Town will see its largest growth in African residents in the near future. Although not the largest destination point for internal migrants (Johannesburg, Ekurhuleni and Tshwane receive the lion's share of this population movement) Cape Town is nonetheless a major net recipient of residents, with the city having received approximately 258,000 in-migrants (as compared to about 65,000 out-migrants) from 1999–2004, the majority of whom are young (18–31 years old), unemployed Africans from the Eastern Cape with a relatively low skills base (SACN 2004, 195; SSA 2005).

It is important to see these trends in historical context, however. South Africa's largest cities experienced large population influxes from 1991–96, during the initial post-apartheid phase, with urban growth rates of 6.05%, slowing to 2.01% in 1996–2001 (SACN 2004, 37). These figures are reflected in the overall urbanization growth rates of the country as well, moving from 53.7% of the South African population in 1996, to 58% in 2001, to a projected 64% in 2030. Though significant, these growth figures suggest a slowing off of the urbanization trend in the country and a much slower rate of urbanization than that projected for elsewhere in sub-Saharan Africa (from 34% in 2003 to about 53% in 2030 for the latter) (SACN 2004, 37).

Nor is urban primacy as much of a concern in South Africa, with the largest cities growing at a slower rate in the 1996–2001 period than secondary cities (3.5% as compared to 5.1%). Cape Town had one of the slowest growth rates during that period at about 2% (slightly above natural national population growth rates), consistent with the national urbanization patterns of the 1970s and 1980s (SACN 2004, 39), and considerably lower than growth rates of almost 4% per annum in the 1960s and 1970s (SACN 2006, 3–4).

Nevertheless, the city's population is growing considerably, with municipal authorities seemingly unable, or unwilling, to keep up with the facilities required to keep people adequately housed and serviced with amenities, health care and education: the 'running to stand still' phenomenon discussed in previous chapters.

Another key question is the extent to which in-migrants are permanent or temporary. While some analysts have argued that circular labour migration to cities has ended or declined since the end of apartheid, Posel (2003) has argued—convincingly in my opinion—that "temporary labour migration within the country appears to have increased, driven particularly by the rise in female labour migration". Statistics South Africa concurs, arguing that "a large proportion of [the movement of people to urban areas] were temporary migrations" (Lehohla 2006), as does the South African Cities Network (SACN 2004, 40), noting that "the apartheid migrant-labour pattern of rural youth moving to urban areas, only to return whenever urban opportunities are closed off, or when a store of capital has been built up to invest in rural homesteads, seems to be continuing". The fact that this migration occurs strategically, to "maximise family and household livelihoods by diversifying sources of household income and risks" comes as no surprise, and is consistent with internal and cross-border migration patterns in the region and around the world (Lehohla 2006; see also Crush and McDonald 2002, SACN 2006, 2–16).

The extent to which migration has been feminized and temporalized in Cape Town in particular is difficult to say with certainty, though there is no reason to believe that it is very different than elsewhere in the country. There may be slightly less (or less frequent) circular migration from Cape Town due to its relative isolation and concomitantly higher transportation costs vis-à-vis the Eastern Cape and elsewhere in the country/continent, but this distance does not appear to fundamentally alter the pattern of circular movement.

Other pressures driving this temporary migration may be growing levels of urban unemployment. Though better, on average, than other cities in the country, and vastly better than most rural areas, unemployment in Cape Town has nonetheless grown considerably and could act as a serious deterrent to permanent migrant settlement. Between 1996 and 2001 the absolute number of unemployed in the city went up by 87%, from approx 210,000 unemployed to 390,000 (SACN 2004, 49), with an estimated unemploy-ment rate of 26% in 2005 (CCT 2006d, 21).

There are other factors determining the nature of migration as well, such as access to basic services/amenities and quality of life, though even the most crude and unreliable services in Cape Town may be seen to be better than (nonexistent) services in rural areas.

It is here, perhaps, in the meagre lifestyle improvements and scarce opportunities for employment that we see the continued draw to South Africa's cities from rural areas. As bad as conditions may be in Cape Town for unskilled rural Africans, they can be immeasurably better than the overcrowded, socially repressive and entirely jobless scenarios people have come from in the countryside and small towns.

Efforts to improve the livelihoods of rural South Africans are ostensibly part of the urban reconstruction and development plans of the ANC gov-ernment, but as we have seen thus far in the book resources are woefully inadequate to provide even the most basic of services to rural South Afri-cans and millions remain off the services grid. As a result, some large cities have attempted to address the source of migration on their own, such as the agreement that has been signed between the city of Cape Town and O.R. Tambo District Municipality in the Eastern Cape. Designed "to minimise migration to Cape Town" by creating jobs and better infrastructure at the source of the city's migratory cycle—with former ANC Mayor, Nomaindia Mfeketo, arguing at the time of signing the agreement that "the squatter settlements won't stop if thousands of people are migrating to Cape Town each year" (cited in *Cape Argus*, September 29, 2004)—the inevitable fail-ure of this venture is inherent in its very structure: two underresourced municipalities attempting to make up for their underresourcedness.

As a result, hundreds of thousands of rural Africans have chosen to make Cape Town a (semi)permanent home and the trend is likely to con-tinue for many years to come.

Cross-border (Im)migration

Far less well documented and understood is migration into Cape Town from other countries (both temporary and permanent). The most concrete infor-mation on this dynamic comes from the 2001 national census, which col-lected data on "country of birth" and "citizenship" from respondents (see Table 9.2 for a breakdown of these statistics for the city of Cape Town).

Of note here are the large numbers of migrants who have come to Cape Town from other African countries. Specific source nations are not identi-fied in the census data, but case study material suggests a broad spectrum of migrants from Southern, Central, Eastern, Western and Northern Africa (with at least one individual claiming to have walked all the way to Cape Town from Somalia (Western 2001; see also Dodson and Oelofse 2002,

Table 9.2 Citizenship and Country of Birth of Cape Town Residents—2001

Country of Birth	Persons	Citizenship	Persons
South Africa	2,805,819	South Africa	2,859,316
Other SADC country	29,266	Other SADC country	7775
Rest of Africa	5683	Rest of Africa	3733
Europe	41,803	Europe	17,684
Asia	5414	Asia	2122
North America	1874	North America	1161
Central and South America	2433	Central and South America	965
Australia and New Zealand	955	Australia and New Zealand	490

Source: Statistics South Africa, Census 2001.

McDonald 2000a, Sichone 2003)). Angola and Namibia are probably the two largest source countries of cross-border migrants in the city—with significant concentrations of fishers from those two nations located in Hout Bay—but large numbers of Congolese, Zimbabweans, Ghanaians, Malawians and others are present in the city as well, often clustered in tight geographic pockets.

The census data are incomplete, however, due to the large number of undocumented migrants from other parts of Africa, many of whom would be understandably reluctant to be interviewed by census personnel or to admit to their immigration status, especially knowing the harsh and summary way in which thousands of migrants from other African countries have been detained and deported by South African authorities since the loosening up of cross-border traffic in the mid-1990s (Crush 1998, Human Rights Watch 1998). There are undocumented migrants from Europe, Asia and the Americas in the city as well, but these numbers are likely much lower than that for other African countries given the proximity of African states and the fact that most overseas visitors are forced to pass through official immigration channels at air- and seaports.

It is impossible, therefore, to know exactly how many foreign migrants are living in Cape Town. The only thing that can be said with certainty is that the actual number is likely significantly higher than official statistics indicate.

Equally true, though, is that the numbers are probably much *lower* than the media would have us believe. Hysterical newspaper headlines claiming that "Africa is flooding the Cape" are indicative of a wave of fear-mongering and exaggeration that has caught the psyche of journalists and policymakers alike, creating a public impression of a cross-border migratory tidal wave that has proven difficult to dislodge despite growing evidence to the contrary. Estimates from the mid-1990s of as many as nine million 'illegal immigrants' in the country continue to be cited by zealous journalists and politicians, despite these figures having been proven to be methodologically flawed and wildly off base (Minaar et al. 1995).

Most critical observers now put the figure of undocumented migrants in the country at somewhere between 500,000 and one million people—about 1–2% of the country's population (Landau 2005, 3). Most of these undocumented migrants appear to be settling in urban areas, which would suggest a larger proportion of foreign-born residents in big cities. If we were to (generously) estimate the figure to be 5% of Cape Town's population then there may be as many as 150,000 Africans from elsewhere on the continent living in the city.

It is possible, however, that the proportion of foreign migrants in Cape Town is considerably lower than that for other major cities in the country, with the bulk of cross-border African migration (documented and otherwise) seemingly focussed on the Gauteng region—particularly Johannesburg and surrounds. Census data from 2001 for Johannesburg, for example, showed 127,120 SADC-born residents living in that city, as compared to just 29,266 in Cape Town. This is probably due to the proximity of Johannesburg to other SADC and African countries, the better transportation networks into Johannesburg, and its stronger manufacturing economy—though it may also have something to do with the social climate of Cape Town, as will be discussed below.

If not 'flooding' the city, then, migrants from elsewhere on the continent are nevertheless a significant and growing presence in Cape Town, contributing in important ways to its 'Africanization'. More importantly, they are contributing to a pan-Africanization of the city that is remarkably heterogeneous and very different from the kind of domestic African migration discussed above in cultural, political and economic terms.

There are also several different categories of migrants that add to the complex makeup of cross-border migration. The smallest group are skilled professionals, including doctors, engineers, professors and others that have been hired by the public and private sectors in Cape Town to work in a wide range of organizations. Though small demographically—and scattered throughout the city in middle- and upper-income neighbourhoods—this group plays an important economic and political role, helping to keep the wheels of industry, commerce and education turning, and representing a considerable 'brain drain' to their home countries (though, like professionals leaving South Africa, many plan to return home and are not entirely happy in their adopted country/city) (Mattes et al. 2000). Most, if not all, of these migrants are legal residents or citizens of South Africa, though obtaining work permits and permanent residency has not always proven to be easy for professionals from outside of the country—particularly from elsewhere in Africa.

Post-secondary students from other African countries are also a growing presence in Cape Town—particularly at the University of Cape Town— though these numbers form only a small part of the larger Africanization of the city and are usually temporary and transitory in nature (Ramphele 1999).

Semi-skilled migrants likely form a larger group of foreign-born migrants in Cape Town, such as the fishers referred to above in Hout Bay. Mechanics, tailors, machinists, carpenters and other tradespeople are in considerable demand in the city—particularly in the booming construction sector.

But the largest group of foreign-born Africans in Cape Town are certainly unskilled migrants—people looking for work as labourers (mostly men) and domestic workers (mostly women), or starting up small or microenterprises (men and women) (Rogerson 1999, Peberdy and Dinat 2005). It is here that one can see the highest degree of ghettoization, with migrants of shared ethnic/national identities tending to cluster together, mostly in informal settlements or low-income (African) townships.

Some of this cross-border migration is circular, though the cycles tend to be longer than that of South African–born migrants due to travel times and costs (with the important exception of people who travel to Cape Town and other cities in the country with the expressed intent of buying and selling goods, many of whom go back and forth from their home country on a weekly basis (Peberdy 1998, Dodson 2000)). As a result, many foreign-born Africans—documented or otherwise—consider themselves to be 'transnationals', with one foot in South Africa and one foot (and perhaps a family, a house and a bank account) in their home country, moving back and forth as resources and migration controls permit (Crush and McDonald 2002).

It is this group of un(der)skilled and undocumented foreign migrants that is most vulnerable in South Africa to corruption, abuse, theft, arrest and deportation. It is also this group that may be having the biggest impact on the city of Cape Town, adding cultural diversity, providing cheap labour and putting additional pressures on housing and other basic municipal services.

One final group of foreign-born residents that require mention are refugees and asylum seekers. As of early 2006, South Africa was host to approximately 29,000 recognized refugees and 110,000 asylum seekers—most of whom are from elsewhere in Africa (UNHCR 2006). Cape Town is home to a growing number of these refugees, with 5594 applicants applying for refugee status in 2002 at the UNHCR Refugee Reception Centre in the city (although only 909 of these applicants were approved)—the second highest figure for South Africa that year (SACN 2004, 188). Refugees and asylum seekers are often caught in socioeconomic limbo, however, not always able to work officially and often unable (or unwilling) to make claims on social benefits from the local state.

Regardless of the categories, the movement of people from other African countries to Cape Town seems set to continue for many years to come. As Landau (2005, 3) notes: "Regional inequalities of wealth and threats to human security, combined with South Africa's ever more prominent economic profile, auger for increasing numbers of non-nationals coming to and passing through the country".

Neoliberal austerity in other parts of the continent is to blame for part of this migration, forcing people out of rural areas in search of urban wage employment and creating a stepwise cycle of movement from rural to urban that often ends in South African cities. So too are long-standing civil conflicts in other parts of Africa responsible for the movement, many of them fuelled by ongoing neocolonial projects of resource extraction.

South Africa is heavily implicated in the latter. As the single largest industrial and financial power on the continent, the South African state and South African capital is capable of extending its reach into every corner of the continent, part of the overall "looting" of Africa for its primary products by interests from around the world (Bond 2006b).

Growing trade links—particularly in the services sectors—have given additional impetus to these connections, creating as they do the kinds of transportation and communication corridors that are required for cross-border migration. Roads, railways, air- and seaports facilitate the movement of people, while improved banking and communication facilities make both permanent and temporary migration more feasible for transnational migrants with families back home.

Indeed, it is exactly this kind of cross-border migration that world cities both produce and rely on. As discussed in Chapter 1, world cities from New York to Buenos Aires create infrastructure that both facilitates and depends on international migration, providing as it does some of the cheapest and most submissive labour in the world. From skilled and semi-skilled professionals in the IT sector to unskilled workers servicing the recreational whims of a transnational elite, urban capital requires a pool of un(der)employed labour that it can tap into and discard as required.

This labour equation is complicated somewhat in the South African context by enormously high rates of local unemployment—as high as 90% in some rural areas—begging the question as to why unskilled *foreign* labour would be required at all. The answer, as alluded to above, is that foreign labour—particularly undocumented migrants—tends to be even cheaper and even more compliant than local labour. This is certainly true of underregulated sectors such as construction, farming and domestic work where undocumented migrants would appear to be the preference of many small and large firms as well as independent employers, and the same can be said of some highly formalized sectors such as mining, as the growing percentage of foreign mine workers in South Africa illustrates (Crush et al. 1999).

The fact that undocumented migrants are susceptible to arrest and deportation makes them that much more compliant and more likely to take low-paying, irregular and often dangerous jobs, with some unscrupulous employers going so far as reporting undocumented migrants to police just before pay day.

Access to labour and resources aside, South Africa has also committed itself to a larger agenda of African integration—socially, culturally and politically. The formation of the African Union, the introduction of the New Partnership for Africa's Development (Nepad) and a myriad of other bilateral and multilateral agreements with other countries on the continent have tied South Africa to Africa in ways that it has never before experienced.

Just how deep these social and cultural links might go remains to be seen but there are growing signs of African influence on the streets and in the policymaking rooms of the country—even in Cape Town. Music, food, clothing, newspaper reportage, holiday travel and political discourse all reflect an Africanization of the Capetonian social scene, and, although still marginalized, it is a phenomenon that would have been inconceivable 20 years ago.

These trends are reflected at the level of local government as well. The creation of the United Cities and Local Governments of Africa (UCLGA) organization in May 2005 at a conference in Tshwane, South Africa, is perhaps the best indication of these local-level linkages. Formed out of three previously distinct local government associations originally created along geographic and linguistic lines—the African Union of Local Authorities (predominantly Anglophone), the Union des Villes Africaines (largely Francophone) and the Uniao dos Ciudades y Capitaes Lusofono Africana (solely Lusophone)—the UCLGA is an institutional reflection not only of the urbanization of Africa but of the Africanization of the continent's cities.

Significantly, one of the rationales for forming the UCLGA was that "the African continent will become an essentially urban one during this generation, resulting in significant disruptions in the ways of life, production, social and institutional arrangements" and that these changes are "the main reasons for intense migrations within the continent, from one Local Authority to another, from country to country, and from region to region, but also outside the continent". The intent, therefore, is to "promote African unity in order to overcome these challenges, and to create conditions conducive to the economic integration of Africa into the global economy through the creation of the African Union and its organs, as well as the establishment of the New Partnership for Africa's Development".[1] The rhetoric of Africanization has therefore permeated the institution of local government, if not its ability to manage the experience.

DEAFRICANIZING CAPE TOWN

And yet, Cape Town remains remarkably unchanged from the apartheid era in spatial and cultural terms, remaining for all intents and purposes a very 'white' city. Racial desegregation has been slow to take off throughout South Africa (Christopher 2005), but this is particularly true of Cape Town where geographic segregation along racial lines seems to have intensified rather than diminished, with hard lines drawn in the Cape Flat sands between white, coloured and African residents (with the city's small Asian community largely concentrated in two middle-income townships).

Whites are clustered largely in the northern and southern suburbs, along the Table Mountain chain and coastlines—the most attractive and accessible parts of the city. Coloureds are concentrated largely on the Cape Flats in townships south of the N1 highway and separated from white areas by highways, railway tracks and industrial areas. Africans are concentrated along the N2 highway and in the southeast quadrant of the city in the most remote and sandy parts of the city (see Figure P.1, in the Preface to this book, and Figures 1.2 and 1.3 in Chapter 1).

There is some racial integration in Cape Town, of course. Suburbs that became 'grey areas' during apartheid such as Observatory, Woodstock and Salt River remain somewhat mixed, though even this is limited largely to professional coloureds and middle-income whites and there are increased gentrification pressures that are pushing lower-income people out of these areas.

Upper-income suburbs remain, by and large, lily white. Although many of these suburbs once housed thousands of coloured and African residents prior to the Group Areas Act (e.g. Rondebosch, Constantia, Kalk Bay, Simonstown) forced removals and gentrification pressures in the 1970s created an overwhelmingly white demographic (Western 1996, Pape 2002).

Some upper-income coloured, Asian and African residents have moved back into these wealthier areas since 1994, but it has been estimated that Africans make up only 1% of the upper-income (largely English) southern suburbs of the city and only about 10% of the northern suburbs, concentrated in a few comfortable enclaves such as Parklands that are attracting young African families (*Financial Mail*, October 29, 2004).

The most expensive suburbs along the Atlantic coast, such as Llandudno and Camps Bay, have changed little since the 1980s, as a cheekily entitled article about these suburbs in the *Sunday Times* (October 24, 2004) made clear: "Blacks? We don't have them here!"

Very little integration would appear to be happening in the African townships as well. With the exception of some downwardly mobile coloured families, Cape Town's African townships remain almost entirely African. There is considerably more integration taking place in informal settlements, particularly within and around these African townships, with low-income

African, coloured and even some whites, living in the same areas. But the growth of informal settlements tends to be ghettoized as well, with most made up of one population group, or with racial groups segregated into different geographic clusters within the larger settlement.

New, low-income housing developments also tend to be dominated either by Africans or coloureds, further adding to racial segregation. This is not always the case though. There are examples of low-income housing developments in Cape Town that have proven to be successful at integration, such as Westlake Village in the southern suburbs, which has brought together coloureds and Africans (along with a "handful of white and Indian residents") in a mixed-use development near an upper-income white suburb (Lemanski 2006). Nevertheless, the trend is still toward the development of uniracial low-income housing, and the same would appear to be true of the massive N2 Gateway housing project alongside the African township of Langa.

The most racially integrated parts of Cape Town are coloured townships bordering white or African areas (with the same dynamic occurring throughout the country (Christopher 2005)). Much of this integration is from young whites moving into middle-income coloured communities (largely due to rapidly rising housing costs in white suburbs) as well as the upward mobility of Africans into lower-middle income coloured areas. But this is limited as well.

What are the reasons for this ongoing and intensified racial segregation in the city? There are at least three causes: the impact of neoliberal policies, racism, and xenophobia.

Impact of Neoliberalism

The first, and arguably most important, reason for ongoing racial segregation in Cape Town is the impact of neoliberalism, particularly as it relates to the implementation of housing, basic services and transportation. I have discussed these impacts at length in previous chapters and will only reiterate the point here that neoliberalism has perpetuated and exacerbated the racialized character of the city by creating further class-based inequalities. In a country such as South Africa where class correlates so strongly with race the introduction of neoliberal reforms has served to deepen income-related inequities and entrench spatial segregation along racial lines. As Huchzermeyer (2003, 130) notes with respect to housing policy in Cape Town: "Low-income housing development in South Africa since 1994 has not contributed to the spatial integration of the apartheid urban form. By and large, massive standardised housing projects have perpetuated segregation by income group, allocating the most disadvantaged urban/peri-urban locations to the poorest sectors of society—those qualifying for a fully subsidised housing unit. In the case of the Cape Metropolitan Region, this appears to have taken extreme dimensions". The result: racially segregated housing for coloured and African communities on the periphery of the city.

A more recent addition to this mix has been low-income, black migrants from other African countries, for whom there are even fewer social welfare opportunities. Only citizens and permanent residents are eligible for housing subsidies and most welfare grants (e.g. disability grants, old age pension), leaving non–South Africans "out in the cold" (McDonald 2000a). Access to health care and educational facilities are also largely limited to citizens and permanent residents (though refugees are given limited rights in this regard). Undocumented migrants have virtually no access to state subsidies and are also barred access to banking facilities, making them all the more vulnerable to robbery and making it even more difficult to start their own business to generate income (Landau 2005, 13).

With regard to basic services, foreign migrants are able to access potable water, electricity, refuse collection and other municipal services if they own or rent a home (and pay their bills on time). There are also communal water taps in most informal settlements (though some of these have been set up with prepaid metering devices).

Access to subsidized services is more difficult. In Cape Town, where the free allotment of water and electricity is available to all households, citizenship should not matter, but residents must apply for indigent status to be eligible for additional rates and services rebates, in which case only citizens and permanent residents may apply.

As a result, many low-income migrants from other parts of Africa do not receive even the meagre level of subsidies available to South African citizens, making their lives that much more difficult and ensuring that they live in the most peripheralized and underserviced parts of the city. In Johannesburg, "[m]any buildings housing [foreign] migrants lack electricity or water, and most contravene local government safety and health by-laws" (Kihato 2004, 7). Not as much is known about the living conditions of foreign migrants in Cape Town, but case study evidence suggests the same general pattern, contributing to the racial polarization of the city (McDonald 2000a, Dodson and Oelofse 2002, Sichone 2003).

Economic policy is not the only reason for ongoing segregation in the city, however. The segregational impact of neoliberalism is exacerbated by—and to some extent driven by—racism and xenophobia. Though an ongoing problem throughout the country, Cape Town has its own peculiar set of racial politics, complicated by the emergence of new forms of national chauvinism.

Racism

Although all official legislation discriminating on the basis of race has been abolished in South Africa, not even the most optimistic of observers would argue that racism itself has been excised from the country. The question is: How serious is the problem and how does it manifest itself at the urban level?

My argument here is that racism is remarkably strong in Cape Town—partly because of its history as a 'coloured preference' area and partly because of the nature of its white liberalism—creating a 'double-whammy' of sorts for Africans and exacerbating the racially segregated nature of the city. Blatantly racist attitudes and actions can be blamed for much of this, though there is a materiality to this racism, with both whites and coloureds using race as a way to justify and protect their relative privileges. The end result is a racial discourse and practice that serves to entrench negative racial stereotypes, while at the same time strengthening the city's appeal to a (largely white) transnational elite who do not want to know about (or feel guilty about) their racialized existence.

In developing this argument I adopt Pulido's (2000, 15) definition of (white) racism as that defined by "practices and ideologies, carried out by structures, institutions and individuals, that reproduce racial inequality and systematically undermine the well-being of racially subordinated populations".[2] These practices and ideologies can be carried out at different levels: the personal, the group, the national, etc. "An individual act of racism is just that, an act carried out at the level of the individual. Nonetheless, that individual is informed by regional and/or national racial discourses, and his/her act informs and reproduces racial discourses at higher scales".

Pulido also highlights the question of "intent". Popular notions of racism rest on the concept of purposeful, individual and malicious behaviour. While this is true in some cases, Pulido insists we look beyond overt and institutionalized racism to what she calls "white privilege", the ideologies and practices that reproduce whites' privileged status. In this scenario, "whites do not necessarily *intend* to hurt people of color, but because they are unaware of their white skin privilege, and because they accrue social and economic benefits by maintaining the status quo, they inevitably do.... It is this ability to sever intent from outcome that allows whites to acknowledge that racism exists, yet seldom identify themselves as racists".

This definition of racism helps us to bridge the ideological and material gap between race and class. We can see racism not only as a psychologically and individually constructed phenomenon but as part of a larger societal process shaped and reinforced by—at least in part—the material and class interests of those who have the most to gain from its continuance. This definition does not resolve the underlying tension of whether one factor—race or class—dominates 'in the final instance', but it is at least dialectical in nature, underscoring the multiple ways in which racism evolves and manifests itself.

This dynamic is complicated somewhat by the long-standing myth that white Capetonians were more liberal and less racist than whites in other parts of the country before and during apartheid. While it is true that Cape Town had fewer petty apartheid by-laws and/or enforced these laws less vigorously, the city was no less ruthless than other municipalities in implementing major apartheid regulations such as the Group Areas Act—as the brutal forced removals of tens of thousands of people in the 1960s and 1970s from District Six and other locations in the city attest to.

Nevertheless, the myth continues, with many English-speaking Capetonians in particular having convinced themselves, it would seem, that they were never racist, that apartheid was the fault of irrational Afrikaners, and that they have little, if anything, to atone for. As a result, there has been little in the way of public debate over the nature of white racism in the city and virtually none of the collective soul-searching that was expected to take place as part of the Truth and Reconciliation Commission process, with more palpable impacts in other parts of the country.

This is a broad generalization, of course. Many white Capetonians gave their lives (quite literally) to fighting racism under apartheid, and many continue to do so today. Yet it is true that racist behaviour permeates much of the day-to-day discourse and practice of whites living in the city and dominates the tone of racial interaction.

Another complicating factor is racism amongst coloureds (primarily toward Africans). The roots of this lie in the tactics of 'divide and conquer', with colonial and apartheid governments having been enormously successful at convincing many coloured Capetonians that their real enemy was the African. *Swart gevaar*—the 'Black Peril' in Afrikaans—was the rallying cry of the National Party for decades, forming the basis of its election campaign in the Western Cape as recently as the 1994 national and 1996 local elections in the city, with efforts to paint a picture of Africans flooding into the city to steal the homes and rape the daughters of coloured residents if the ANC were elected (McDonald 1994).

Many coloured Capetonians bought into this racial rhetoric. Western (1996) documented this dynamic in detail in the 1970s and 1980s, and returned to the city in the late 1990s to discover that little had changed, with comments such as "I'll work for the *wit baas* [white boss] but I'll not work for the African", being commonplace (Western 2001, 630). One coloured Capetonian argued strenuously in a letter to the editor of the *Cape Times* that, "Coloureds of the Western Cape do not see themselves as being black.... They have an aversion to the 'black' as an 'African'. In fact, my own people are horrified when you try to explain to them that they are also Africans.... To compare themselves to Africans is a big no-no because they do not see themselves as equal to the African but superior.... The Coloured people are racist as hell—and not only toward Africans but even their own dark-complexioned people" (as quoted in Western 2001, 622).

This coloured racism is perhaps understandable when one considers what has been at stake. The practice of coloured preference labour laws and relatively better investments by the apartheid state in coloured housing, education and health care, meant that coloureds led a slightly more stable and comfortable life than most Africans and they were keen to protect this relative privilege (though the majority of coloureds still lived in poverty under apartheid, and social spending in coloured areas was a mere fraction of that for whites).

Nor can one generalize the phenomenon—with coloured Capetonians having been at the forefront of antiracist and multiracial politics in South Africa in the 1980s, and many still active on these matters today. But the widespread and deeply felt nature of racist attitudes in coloured communities is difficult to deny, as is a pervasive acquiescence to white culture.

Whatever the reasons for this, "racism is running amok in Cape Town" (Dikeni 1996), making many African South Africans "feel like foreigners" in the city (Mniki 2004). Articles in newspapers and magazines with titles such as "Paranoid racist bigots have turned Cape Town into a city without soul" and "Wretched Blacks of Cape Town" (Majavu 2003) capture the mood of many Africans who live here.

Nor are these feelings restricted to low-income Africans. As Namhla Mniki (2004, 27) argues, "To be a black professional of middle-class status living in Cape Town means living in an extremely white world.... I am tired of hidden messages that reinforce that I do not belong here". This discomfort is reflected in the relatively low number of Africans living in upper-income residential areas of the city, with Johannesburg and Tshwane attracting the vast majority of African professionals in the country.

It should also be noted that the vast majority of senior decision makers in Cape Town are white. There is an important new stratum of African bureaucrats and politicians in the municipality, but this layer is thin and overwhelmed by white (and to a lesser extent coloured) bureaucrats, many of whom have been in their posts since the early 1990s and even the 1980s (McDonald 1997, McDonald and Smith 2004). While not all of these old-order bureaucrats should be considered racist—indeed, few if any would make openly racist remarks today—they are part of the larger "practice and ideology" of racism described above and play their part in "reproduc[ing] racial inequality and systematically undermin[ing] the well-being of racially subordinated populations" in an attempt to protect white privilege.

Examples of these ideologies and practices can be found in decisions on where to locate housing developments, sewage treatment plants, refuse dumps, roadways and so on. In the same way that municipal decision makers in the United States have been shown to practice systematic racial discrimination in locating toxic waste dumps and other environmentally damaging facilities in that country (Bullard 1990, 1993), municipal bureaucrats in Cape Town make ongoing and repeated decisions to locate these kinds of noxious facilities in or near African communities and/or to develop housing for African communities near existing facilities, roadways and industrial areas (McDonald 2005).

The decision to locate the massive N2 Gateway low-income housing project beside the busiest highway in the city, and downwind from a large sewage treatment plant and waste transfer station, is perhaps an example. Although the location may have been chosen in part to allow for convenient transportation of residents to work and shopping areas, one can reasonably ask whether the city would have located a white (or even coloured) housing development in this most unpleasant of locations. Does the belief that Africans "like living this way"—as one senior white bureaucrat told me during interviews in the mid-1990s—continue to shape this kind of decision making?

Similarly, one can wonder aloud whether white municipal bureaucrats would cut off the water and electricity supply to low-income white residents in the name of fiscal austerity in the same way they have for low-income black residents, or whether prepaid electricity meters would be rolled out so aggressively in low-income white areas. Under apartheid, so-called 'poor whites' were treated with much more respect.

These are questions that cannot be answered conclusively, of course, because of the complex personal, collective and indirect decision-making processes that take place, but there can be little doubt that systematic and systemic racism continues in the senior echelons of decision making in Cape Town and that African residents suffer the most from this racialized decision-making process.

But it is not just municipal bureaucrats who can be accused of racism in the city. Private companies have been responsible for some of the most racist practices in the country, particularly on the environmental front. As Peek (2002) has documented in the case of air quality in South Durban, petrol refineries and a pulp and paper plant have created some of the most intensely polluted air in the world, affecting close to a quarter of a million low-income black families and leading to the highest recorded levels of asthma in the world. There is also the case of mercury poisoning in Kwa-Zulu-Natal by British multinational Thor Chemicals that killed at least two workers and badly affected many more, what Greenpeace (1994) called one of the worst corporate environmental offences it had ever encountered.

Do corporations behave this way near white communities in South Africa? In short, no. The overwhelming majority of corporate environmental injustices are perpetrated against African communities. The spatial legacies of apartheid are one reason for this continued behaviour, with industrial pollution inevitably affecting those located closest to it, but one cannot avoid the conclusion that racism remains a key factor. How else can one explain the fact that large corporations in South Africa contribute millions of rand annually to the protection of flora and fauna and advertise themselves as environmentally responsible businesses for their wealthy (white) customers, while at the same time contribute to some of the worst environmental health and safety conditions in the world for their African neighbours and employees?

The outcome of these racist attitudes will not be a complete 'deAfricanization' of the city—the underlying economic forces of African urbanization

are too strong for that—but racism will help to justify and conceal the physical separation of racial groups as well as the ongoing racialized division of
labour, and perpetuate the dominance of white cultural practices that have
come to be seen as Cape Town's contribution to global urbanization.

Xenophobia

Complicating matters further is a widespread and stubborn pattern of
xenophobia—defined here as a 'strong dislike of foreigners'. Although no
group of foreign nationals escapes this sentiment entirely, the most venom-
ous and lethal forms of xenophobia have been aimed at black Africans from
elsewhere on the continent, particularly unskilled migrants and those from
outside traditional southern African source countries (McDonald 2000b,
SAMP 2004, Nyamnjoh 2006).

Cape Town is no different from the rest of South Africa in this regard.
Xenophobia has been a national phenomenon since the end of apartheid and
the gradual opening up of borders to—and avoidance of borders by—visitors, traders and job-seekers from elsewhere in Africa. In fact, comparative
international studies show South Africa to be one of the most xenophobic
countries in the world (McDonald et al. 2000, SAMP 2004).

Moreover, it is a widespread problem, with no clear demographic
traits. White and black, rich and poor, educated and uneducated, men and
women—all major demographic and socioeconomic categories of South
African society demonstrate a deep-seated prejudice toward foreigners in
general and African foreigners in particular (SAMP 2004). The one exception to this rule may be upper-income, English-speaking whites, who demonstrate slightly less xenophobic tendencies—though this may be explained
in large part by a growing realization amongst South African (neo)liberals
that xenophobia could undermine access to cheap foreign labour.

What are the impacts of xenophobia in Cape Town? Like racism, there
are many subtle ways in which it manifests itself, but it has also exploded
in quite violent and demeaning patterns. There are many documented
cases—and likely many more that have gone undocumented—of African
foreigners being beaten, raped and/or killed simply because they are foreign, with abuses by police and other officials at government-run detention
and deportation centres proving to be some of the worst instances of all
(Human Rights Watch 1998, Nyamnjoh 2006).

Many foreign migrants of African origin feel like constant targets, easily distinguished in many cases by their dress, complexion and language.
Public spaces such as trains and informal settlements—dangerous enough
for black South Africans—become all the more treacherous for black foreigners, with many migrants living in fear 24 hours a day.

Not all African foreigners live with this level of anxiety—and their
remains a streak of pan-Africanist support amongst South Africans that
provides many foreign migrants with a sense of security (McDonald

2000a)—but study after study in South Africa has shown widespread apprehension among foreign African migrants, even the most skilled and materially secure of these. The situation is no different in Cape Town, as studies have demonstrated here as well (Dodson and Oelesfe 2002, Sichone 2003).

Much attention has been given to the attitudes of national government officials in this regard, with politicians and senior civil servants having been implicated in the fanning of xenophobic flames. Anti-foreigner rhetoric from the state has cooled off since the departure of the volatile head of the Inkatha Freedom Party—Mangosutho Buthelezi—as Minister of Home Affairs from 1996–2004. There would also appear to be a growing recognition on the part of the ANC government that xenophobia is counterproductive in many ways to its neoliberal objectives, though it has not disappeared entirely from within the ANC either.

Less well-recognized is the xenophobia taking place within local government. Local politicians and bureaucrats are as prone to xenophobic tendencies as any other South African, and have demonstrated an increased willingness to express these concerns in public, particularly as they relate to the financial pressures that cross-border migration places on municipalities. Hence the comments by the Chairperson of Salga at its National Conference in 2004: "With the ongoing population growth [in our cities] driven, among other things, by immigration into South Africa, we shall never really have the money we require to deliver on all aspects of local government" (Salga 2004c, 22).

The South African Cities Network has made some efforts to counter these concerns, arguing that sensationalist accounts of "waves" of foreign migrants "flooding" South African cities have been exaggerated, suggesting that the "number of people entering the country legally ... and then staying on illegally have stabilised at a few hundred thousand" (SACN 2004, 42). The organization goes on to directly challenge the negative perception of foreign migrants by municipal officials, noting that "the presence of foreign nationals in South Africa is often placed on the liability side of the balance sheet by city leaders", whereas in reality "cities with diverse, multicultural populations, with significant foreign national minorities well-networked back to home countries, have found that their cosmopolitanism is a major strength in a globalising world" (SACN 2004, 44).

Why is this xenophobia happening at the local and national level in South Africa? Explanations vary, with no agreement as to what is driving the phenomenon (McDonald et al. 2000, Crush 2001, Harris 2002). One possibility is that xenophobia—particularly that aimed at other Africans—is another racialized legacy of apartheid. Other African nations were portrayed by the apartheid state as chaotic and dangerous, helping to justify the rhetoric of racial superiority as well as military forays into the region. No doubt these racialized (and 'pigmentized') images still linger in the minds of many South Africans—white and black—contributing to a continued conceptualization for many that South Africa is somehow *disconnected* from the rest of the continent, as oft-heard comments from South African travellers and business people attest to (e.g. "I just got back from Africa", as though "Africa" were physically separated from South Africa (on this point see Western (2001)).

Another possible explanation is that post-apartheid nation building and internal healing has generated a new kind of nationalism, one that puts South African priorities first and in which citizenship defines who belongs (and benefits) and who does not (Nyamnjoh 2006). A potent contributor to xenophobic rhetoric and action elsewhere in the world (Gellner 1995, Finzsch and Schirmer 1998), nationalism can also mix with racism to rule out particular nationalities based on skin colour/hue, helping to explain the singling out of (darker-skinned) African migrants.

It is also possible that xenophobia could be driven by more basic material needs and wants, and it is here that we must be careful not to 'blame the victim'. Many low-income South Africans complain that (African) foreigners are "stealing jobs" or "taking resources", making what is an already extremely difficult life even harder. Although studies have shown that foreign migrants tend to create jobs rather than "steal" them (Rogerson and Rogerson 1997, Peberdy 1998) the perception of economic competition amongst the poor cannot be denied or wished away.

One thing that is clear about xenophobia in South Africa is that it is not the result of extensive direct contact with foreigners themselves. As numerous surveys in the country have demonstrated, most South Africans have had very little or no contact with migrants from other countries, particularly from elsewhere in Africa, with their opinions based instead on secondhand news from friends, colleagues and the media (Danso and McDonald 2001, McDonald and Jacobs 2005).

This is not to suggest that foreign migrants and refugees are mere victims. Numerous associations have been formed by foreign nationals and South African citizens to address xenophobia and to push for basic rights. Much of this falls on deaf ears at the local government level, but there have been some successes at the national level.[3] For the most part, however, undocumented foreign migrants and refugees remain amongst the most marginalized people in the country.

How might this xenophobia contribute to the deAfricanization of Cape Town? For one, it may deter Africans from elsewhere on the continent from coming to the city, though the growing number of skilled and unskilled foreign African migrants would suggest that this would only be having a dampening affect.

More significant are the sociospatial patterns that xenophobia likely contributes to. African migrants that do come to Cape Town tend to move to African townships and informal settlements, and tend to congregate in a handful of locations. Moreover, they tend to live in certain sections of townships and informal settlements, often clustered into small national/

ethnic groups of Yoruba, Ghanaians or Franco-Africans (Morris 1998, McDonald et al. 2000, Morris and Bouillon 2001, Dodson and Oelofse 2002).

Where foreign African migrants have settled in suburban areas in Cape Town (e.g. parts of Muizenburg in the south end of the city and in Sea Point in the central city), they tend to be clustered in a small number of high-density buildings. In the case of Muizenburg and Sea Point, gentrification pressures are forcing many of these lower-income migrants out, and there have also been explicit efforts on the part of local community organizations to rid the area of what are deemed to be unwanted, criminal elements, with all of the negative stereotypes about foreign migrants being dragged out by the local press.

Even in cases where foreign African migrants might not feel threatened—and may even feel welcomed—they are often reluctant to exercise their rights or take advantage of state subsidies for fear of how this might be perceived by their low-income South African neighbours. In one case that I was personally involved in, a well-liked Ghanaian refugee claimant who had done much to foster good relations between foreigners and South Africans living in Marconi Beam (an informal settlement north of the city centre) was killed by a South African citizen, reputedly because he was given access to an RDP house, via his South African girlfriend, ahead of South African citizens who were also on the waiting list. No arrests were made in this case and the cross-cultural goodwill that had been generated in that particular community quickly dissipated, along with the other foreign nationals in the settlement.

These stories of migrant ghettoization and repression are not unique to South Africa but they are particularly violent and widespread and serve to underscore the insular nature of much of South Africa's urban development. This is the paradox of South Africa's integration with the rest of the continent: the more it Africanizes the less African it becomes, and nowhere is this more true than in Cape Town where there is little recognition, let alone celebration, of the increasingly cosmopolitan nature of its African residents. Although Cape Town needs cheap African labour to build and sustain its world city status it does this by turning its back on the very labour and cultural connections it relies on, focusing instead on a homogenized vision of (white) global urban practices and design.

Whitening Cape Town

By stark contrast, white foreign migrants seem to be welcomed with open arms in Cape Town. Evidence for this can be seen in the fact that the single largest source region for official immigration to Cape Town is Europe—equal, in fact, to the figures for all other source countries in the world combined (though there can be little doubt that the addition of undocumented migrants from SADC and other African countries would overshadow these figures from Europe) (see Table 9.2).

Also of interest is the fact that the 41,803 European immigrants in Cape Town recorded in the 2001 census is much larger, in proportional terms, than the 56,233 recorded for Johannesburg that year, despite the latter being a much larger city and having a much stronger economy, suggesting a preference on the part of European (and North American) nationals for Cape Town.

Economic resources play a large part in the ability of European immigrants to protect themselves from xenophobic behaviour, but by and large this group does not face the same kind of discrimination faced by equally well-off African immigrants and certainly nowhere near the level of xenophobic behaviour faced by low-income and undocumented migrants from elsewhere in Africa.

Can this difference be explained in part by racism? Perhaps, though it is also true that European immigrants can adapt much more readily to the 'white' culture of the city and may signify, in the minds of many Capetonians, the kind of positive world city developments that Cape Town is striving for.

INHERENT TENSIONS

It would appear, then, that Cape Town is being Africanized by domestic and cross-border migration while at the same time shunting these new residents into peripheral, poorly serviced parts of the city where they can take part in the economy (if they can find a job) but will interfere little with the cultural lives of the city's elite.

On the one hand, urban capital (most factions at least) and upper-income residents require pools of cheap labour in producer and consumer services and manufacturing, and African migration is servicing this need. Keeping these migratory flows open requires transportation and telecommunication facilities and some basic level of essential services such as water and electricity. It also requires relatively open migration policies, something that the South African Chamber of Mines and other business interests—along with the neoliberal press—have been pushing for since the late 1990s (McDonald and Jacobs 2005).

On the other hand, there is a desire to control and contain African migration to the city. This balancing act can be managed, in part, with the introduction of neoliberal housing policies, cost recovery and commercialization. This strategy is particularly true for foreign Africans, for whom the state extends very limited fiscal support and subsidies. The state can also control migrants via direct disciplining, of the type discussed in Chapter 8. The Cape Town police spend a considerable amount of time monitoring, harassing and arresting street vendors and hawkers, and there are regular raids in areas deemed to house 'illegal immigrants'. Johannesburg is notorious for these kinds of swoops on African migrants—sometimes with hundreds of police and private security personnel, using helicopters (Landau 2005, 12)—but the Cape Town police have mounted similar sting operations. National government then steps in to detain and deport suspected undocumented migrants.

But it is not just the state that does the policing. As noted earlier, there are community groups that have come together with the expressed intent of expelling foreigners. The largely coloured community of Du Noon in northern Cape Town did just this in early 2001 when about 50 Angolans and Namibians were driven from their homes by South Africans claiming they were "stealing their jobs". At least one person was killed (SAHRC 2001).

Participation in community groups can also prove very difficult for non-nationals. As the discussion of Ward Committees in Chapter 8 made clear, members of official community organizations are hand picked by political leaders, making it easy (and politically beneficial) to exclude foreigners. In other cases it is the fear of reprisal that keeps migrants quiet and compliant: "For the most part, refugees and migrants are a silent group, never engaging with the authorities or drawing attention to themselves for fear of incurring official sanction or social wrath" (Beall et al. 2002, 125).

These tensions can only be contained for so long. Poverty in rural South Africa and in the rest of the continent will continue to drive urban migration, making it increasingly difficult to maintain and police the kinds of racial segregation taking place in Cape Town today, adding to the frustrations and tensions of the city's poor and excluded.

How long this tension can last remains to be seen but there appears to be little interest on the part of the state to address it. As it stands, local government is "partially blind" to the issue, "failing to see and understand what it is that it is trying to control" (Kihato 2004, 8). But it is also true that municipalities have no legislative authority or mandate to deal with immigration and limited financial capacity to deal with the domestic inflow of migrants. Hence Landau's (2005, 17) call for "a heightened need for sub-national actors to assert their influence on the country's immigration and asylum regime. Cities and provinces need to recognize that they can, and indeed must, actively advocate for an immigration regime that helps legalise—rather than marginalise—their residents".

But contrary to Landau's (2005, 16) optimistic view that "South African politics is still an emergent politics providing considerable scope for creative policymaking and statecraft"—or Turok's (2001) equally hopeful claim that urban desegregation can be made to work in South Africa if there is the "political will" to do so—the argument I am making in this chapter is that the structural inequities of (urban) neoliberalism, coupled with the migratory patterns it spawns and the sociospatial demands of a transnational elite, make it impossible to resolve these demographic tensions in a capitalist city. And with the dominant "political will" of Cape Town being that of continued and intensified neoliberalism and world city status, there is little indication of significant policy shifts taking place on this front in the foreseeable future.

In the end, Cape Town will become an increasingly African city, but it will not be one that promotes or celebrates its African-ness—at least not in a way that gives equal opportunity to Africans, coloureds and whites and creates integrated housing and other facilities. Cape Town's (emerging) African heritage will be celebrated instead in sterile, prepackaged ways, lending the city its inevitable claim to exotica while never threatening the social, political or economic control of the city to anyone but its (mostly white) transnational elites.

How this conflict will be managed, and what options exist for a less violent, corrosive future, remains to be seen, but the need for an alternative development path for the city is clear.

Part III

10 Keep Left for Cape Town
Alternative Development Strategies

These trends [of urban inequality] are not ineluctable. They can be reversed and should be reversed.

Manuel Castells, in LeGates and Stout 1996, 496

We either choose to be observers of history, thereby lending our weight to the forces now in control, or we choose to be participants, actively building a new culture.

Lappé and Du Bois 1977, 327

If, as I have argued thus far in this book, neoliberal urban development strategies are destined to generate increased social, spatial and economic inequality, then what are the alternatives? This chapter lays out two broad scenarios: one, a short- to medium-term strategic reformist agenda which calls for Keynesian-style change; the other a more radical political and economic shift that fundamentally alters the social relations of production in Cape Town and South Africa.

The former is relatively straightforward—though by no means easy to implement in this hyper-neoliberal climate. More progressive forms of taxation, larger investments in public transportation, higher density and more mixed urban planning, bigger allocations of 'free' services, a stop to prepaid meters, and so on, are all reasonable and achievable policy objectives that could be implemented in fairly short order and could make significant differences to people's lives without causing wholesale capital flight or severely disrupting the lives of middle- to upper-income Capetonians.

Nor should these initiatives be seen as simply reformist. If done strategically, and if situated within a larger transformative agenda, these seemingly incremental steps can have significant longer-term impacts.

But it is exactly because of the limitations that reformist measures will never work on their own. If one believes that capitalism is *inherently* self-destructive and *necessarily* productive of the kinds of inequalities outlined in this book then there is no alternative but to strive for a non-capitalist world.

As progressive and useful as Keynesian-style reforms may be in the short to medium term, the realities of neoliberal capitalism and the demands of capital accumulation will serve to minimize, eliminate and eventually reverse even the most incremental of these reformist policy options if they are not underwritten by a more radical transformative agenda.

Is this a constraining political and intellectual position to put oneself in? Yes and no. Yes, in the sense that one has to abandon any belief in the ability of market reforms to lead to meaningful, long-term and sustainable policy options for cities, and to call instead for some kind of non-capitalist option. There is no running away from this conclusion, drawing hard lines in the sand between Marxist analysts and those who believe that market reforms can lead to equity and sustainability.

But then again, sand shifts—creating a useful metaphor for the dialectical nature of Marxist thought and the concrete, back-and-forth reality of politico-economic change. In the same way that Marxist theory allows us to see the elastic nature of urban neoliberalism, and capital's ability to adjust to changing political and economic contexts, so too can we use these insights to argue for strategic counter-hegemonic interventions using market-based reforms.

As Saul and Gelb (1981, 4) remind us from an earlier epoch of struggle in South Africa, "while 'reform' is not genuine transformation ... it is not meaningless or irrelevant either, for it can affect the shape of the field of battle". Marais (2001, 40) has made a similar point, referring to the "facile schema" of the anti-apartheid resistance years that saw reform and revolution in "mutually exclusive terms ... where reforms were disparaged as mere attempts to undermine the revolutionary momentum and which, therefore, demanded outright rejection". This exclusivism is equally problematic in the post-apartheid era.

One can push for moderate reforms, therefore, without being a traitor to more radical political goals or theoretical frameworks. Radical history is replete with these kinds of strategic, compromise politics, particularly as the contradictions of capitalism create the conditions and spaces for these reformist interventions.

The trick, of course, is to frame these interventions within broader theoretical and practical objectives. If the goal of a 'free water' policy is simply to contain the demands of the poor to a level of 'basic needs' and intensify the commodification of water—as is the case in South Africa at the moment—then 'reforms' are not what we want.

If, on the other hand, free water policies can be used to change the way in which water is valued more broadly, and how it is used and distributed, then we may have a truly 'radical' policy option on our hands. To decommodify a good or service such as water is a transformative agenda, implying as it does not just the removal of its monetary price—which is, after all, merely a reflection of its commodified labour value—but rather the entire social process behind this pricing mechanism.

Not an easy task, to be sure, but not an impossible one either, and one that is being taken up with varying degrees of success by groups such as the Anti-Privatisation Forum and the Coalition Against Water Privatisation in Johannesburg. Developing strategic reformist policies, while at the same time embedding these within a more radical set of longer-term political objectives, requires a strong counter-hegemonic discourse and theorization, and a broad-based politicization of civil society.

Ultimately, though, there must be a transformative break from the market. What might this non-capitalist world look like? I will talk to some extent in the second half of the chapter about the subjective and objective possibilities in Cape Town—and how socialist policies in one city are constrained by national and international market pressures—but it is not my aim to prescribe radical alternatives. There are ongoing discussions about socialism in the country at the national level, and there are socialist models at various scales being developed elsewhere in the world that can be examined for inspiration and relevance, but any socialist future in the city must be an organic process, not one dictated from above or from outside.

REFORMING CAPE TOWN

Much of what I have to say in this section is implicit in the preceding chapters. For every criticism I have made of pricing, taxation, participation and commercialization as it is being practiced in Cape Town there is a modified version which could have a less deleterious impact on the poor, on social relations and on the environment.

I cannot address all of the possible reformist options for the city in this chapter, and I cannot deal with every policy option in detail. My objective here is simply to indicate the range of possible reforms and how they might be situated within a more radical set of political strategies and objectives.

Of course, the political will on the part of the African National Congress or the Democratic Alliance to implement such incremental reforms in Cape Town is limited, and the economic pressure to remain at the cutting edge of national and global competitiveness makes any progressive, Keynesian-style change in the city extremely difficult. However, self-interest on the part of capital and the petit bourgeoisie to protect their own resources and lifestyles from crime and environmental degradation, and to build a more productive and consumptive workforce, may go some ways toward mitigating hyper-extractive forms of fiscal policy and productive practice.

There is certainly considerable room for a fairer distribution of wealth and resources in Cape Town without making the city uncompetitive in global market terms. And some progress has been made in this regard in the past five years: incremental increases on free allocations of water and electricity, increased investments in basic infrastructure in the townships, and the decision not to introduce prepaid water meters are all indications of the potential gains that can be made within a reformist agenda.

Public Participation

Perhaps the easiest arena for reformist change is that of public engagement. As discussed in Chapter 8, official policy is thick with the rhetoric of public participation, but this promise is so obviously underdeveloped and overmanipulated in Cape Town that the potential for strategic initiatives should be good.

Integrated Development Plans may be the best place to start. Legislation requires public engagement on all IDPs, but to date the only concrete interaction with civil society on Cape Town's IDPs have been the Mayoral Listening Campaigns, drawing, at best, several hundred people to meetings and by no means the poorest of the poor. Worse, Listening Campaign meetings have simply been a review of draft IDPs already drawn up by local government officials rather than a meaningful engagement with citizens about possible IDP scenarios.

A more progressive form of engagement would involve citizens in discussions over a longer period of time and in much larger numbers, giving people an opportunity to learn about the technical and budgetary issues at hand and providing the time and space for more radical ideas to percolate through the consultations.

Participatory budgeting processes in Brazil—though not without their own problems and limitations (Baiocchi 2003)—are perhaps the best known example of the kinds of broad-based participatory mechanisms I have in mind here, but there are examples from other parts of the world where deep public engagement has made a significant difference to the quality of democratic life and to material investments in city planning.

There have even been some attempts in this direction in Cape Town. Chipkin (2005), for example, has demonstrated that a more inclusive form of engagement was attempted in some areas of policy development by an ANC–led administration in the late 1990s, and though I do not agree with his assessment of the degree to which this model could have made a meaningful difference in the city at that time, it is, nonetheless, an indication of the potential for better forms of participatory governance.

Pieterse's (2005) musings on the potential for "dialogical processes" is another indication of possible reform on this front (all the more important given his influential role as a close advisor to the ANC in Cape Town and in the Western Cape province). Pieterse's (2005, 118–20) vision is one of "involving all stakeholders in the city in a comprehensive city visioning exercise", using the "diaological processes of synetics—an approach to solving problems based on creative thinking of a group from different areas of expertise and knowledge [about] whose claims will be addressed, in what sequence and with what resources".

Whilst he is cautious, noting that, "in a context of deep social cleavages in structural inequalities it is not easy to arrive at shared values", Pieterse (2005, 113–23) also insists that a "shared vision of goals, priorities and requirements" can lead to a "transformative, radical political agenda in urban politics in metropolitan Cape Town ... to advance a redistributive agenda".

This "shared vision" is unlikely given the divergent class interests in the city, and the model fails to address the larger structural problems of capital accumulation crises, but the potential to push for greater dialogue and the need for radicalizing its discourse should not be dismissed.

Democratizing Ward Committees, pushing for greater transportation allowances and more convenient meeting times and locations, and tackling controversial issues head on in politicized ways could make a meaningful difference to poverty levels in Cape Town—though it will require considerable time and energy and coordination on the part of progressive citizens, NGOs, social movements and labour groups. "Confronting difference and commonality with 'the other'" will not be as easy or as polite as Pieterse (2005, 121) implies but dialogue is an essential step in any strategic reformist politics.

More Progressive Forms of Budgeting

Reprioritizing national, provincial and local government budgets toward the expansion and improvement of essential services is another area that could see significant gains with reformist intervention. The outrageous amounts of money spent at the national and local level on unnecessary military expenditures, corporate subsidies and physical infrastructure for transnational elites are so out of synch with ANC pledges of 'redistribution', and their targets for service improvements, that much more could be made of these broken promises and skewed investment patterns.

My experience in Cape Town has been that radically-minded individuals and organizations have only fragments of information along these lines. While many suspect the scale and pattern of inequality in the city, it is not until one sees investment patterns stacked up over time and against poverty-reducing objectives that the full scale of these injustices becomes clear. The ANC's (and the DA's) pro-poor rhetoric shrouds these shortcomings.

Nor has there been enough political resistance to the massive private sector investments taking place in the city in locations such as the Waterfront—investments touted as 'public' but which serve in reality as zones of privileged access and as deterrents to state investments in the broader public good. In this respect, activists can and should press for reallocation of existing public funds, as well as a reexamination of the ways in which private monies are spent and the increasingly gated nature of public space. Drawing links between public policy and private wealth is essential to any radicalized debate on community resources and should be drawn further into the critical discourse on the topic.

A stronger focus on more narrowly defined public investments in the city could also have potential benefits. The skewed allocation of existing service resources in suburban areas, the monies spent on roads that benefit the well-to-do, the need for massive investments in housing and basic infrastructure in the townships (and in more mixed, centralized areas of the city), and the need to address information-technology ghettos are part of a very long list of skewed spending and resource allocations. Why is more not being done and said about this in resistance politics in the city?

Mainstream forms of cost-benefit analysis could be politically useful here as well. As has been demonstrated with the cholera outbreak in the country in 2001, underinvestment in basic services ended up costing the state much more in health and productivity costs than adequate investments in water and sanitation infrastructure would have cost (Cottle and Deedat 2002, Hemson et al. 2006). Much more could be done in Cape Town to create a politicized language around basic human rights and the costs of public health hazards due to underinvestment.

Finally, more could be made of the miserly intergovernmental transfers to Cape Town from national government. As discussed in Chapter 5, local government officials in the city complain about their "unfunded mandates"—with the DA going so far as to make this a major platform in their 2000 local government election manifesto—but neither the DA nor the ANC has made this a serious political issue while governing Cape Town.

Questioning "Public"

Although there has been some outright divestiture of state assets and public services in Cape Town, the bulk of municipal facilities remain in public hands. Nonetheless, there has been widespread outsourcing and partnering with the private sector in key services areas and this creeping disinvestment is a long-term threat to state operation and ownership, particularly as local government loses its capacity to run services internally in the future. There are also threats of a renewed interest in outright privatization in the country, particularly in the area of electricity production and distribution, as new generation capacity is being off-loaded to private firms.

The biggest problem, as discussed in Chapter 6, is the corporatization of services in Cape Town. Publicly owned and operated, these entities nonetheless operate at arm's length from city council and under mandates that promote cost recovery over social good and cost savings over public health.

While it is better to keep these services in public hands than to have them outsourced or privatized, progressive NGOs, labour groups and citizen coalitions must continue to challenge city council on the operating principles of these entities and the political distance with which they operate.

Better participatory planning practices—as discussed above—could help in this regard, with citizens involved in budget allocations, pricing decisions and planning for water, sanitation, electricity, refuse collection and other corporatized services in Cape Town. As things stand, these enormously powerful municipal entities operate in a cloud of secrecy with nothing but the most aggregate of figures being released to the public and with virtually no public consultation on major decisions.

Another possible strategy is to push for 'public-public partnerships' (PUPs). Touted as a way to generate synergies from the partnering of different government agencies—within and across different spheres of government—and between state and civil society groups, PUPs have been tried in a variety of different services in different parts of the country with varying degrees of success (Pape 2001, Hall et al. 2005).

Their advantage is that they can utilize economies of scale with respect to skills and resources, and they can build strengths—vertically and horizontally—that might not otherwise be developed. Their disadvantages/limits relate in part to implementation problems (e.g. the Rand Water initiative in Odi) and the difficulties in operationalizing a service across different jurisdictions, organizational cultures and institutional objectives.

More worrying, though, is the fact that PUPs can be a smokescreen for other forms of corporatization. As Hall et al. (2005) warn, public-public partnerships can simply be a step toward further commercialization and even privatization, and a way of deflecting attention from these objectives in the short run in the name of being 'public'.

The challenge, therefore, is to insist not only on keeping services in public hands, but keeping them within a particular type of public ownership: one that involves broad-based dialogue, distributes resources more equitably and operates in the general public interest. This kind of public service delivery will require dramatic ideological changes within the civil service as well as amongst elected officials—a daunting task in Cape Town.

One way of aiming for the latter is to revisit ways in which local government capacity building and training takes place. More money invested in frontline workers—particularly training and capacity to engage in policy debates—could lead to a significant improvement in the depth of public sector skills, as would a reconfiguration of the education programs used to train white-collar officials (most notably, perhaps, by introducing more progressive content and discourse into the Sector Education and Training Authority (Seta) workshops for local government officials).

Fairer Pricing and Less Restrictive Delivery Policies

Aggressive cost recovery policies have perhaps been the biggest flash point for resistance to neoliberalism in Cape Town, with service restrictions, cut-offs and household evictions being concrete expressions of this policy in the city. The Anti-Eviction Campaign made considerable progress in the early 2000s in resisting evictions and, to a lesser extent, challenging service cutoffs and restrictions (Brown 2005, Cassiem 2005).

Little progress was made, however, in making the larger political and economic links between cost recovery at the local level and capital accumulation strategies at the national and international level. For resistance to cost recovery to be more effective in the city, much more will need to be made of this larger politico-economic context.

More will also need to be made of the links between cost recovery, prepaid meters and 'free basic services'. Prepaid meters could be more heavily politicized as an unconstitutional restriction on access to basic services (as per the court challenge put forward by several Johannesburg-based NGOs in 2006). Free services could be challenged for their role in containing consumption at a level that is neither safe nor healthy, and for charging regressive rates beyond that low level.

Neither prepaid meters nor free basic services have received the kind of critical engagement in Cape Town that they have by social movements in Johannesburg and Durban. And although the city did halt its roll out of prepaid water meters in 2005 (likely due to the backlash these meters received elsewhere in the country) it has been able to roll out hundreds of thousands of prepaid electricity meters virtually unchallenged.

So, too, could more be done in Cape Town to challenge the hypocritical ways in which cost recovery is implemented. Not only do low-income households pay more for water and other services as a percentage of their household incomes than upper-income households, they are much more aggressively tracked and penalized for nonpayment. Local government should be forced to conduct its cost recovery more consistently and more progressively, collecting from industrial and commercial defaulters, and by introducing pricing schemes which actually reduce overconsumption by the wealthy (or simply cap their ability to consume, regardless of what they can afford).

More pressure could also be applied on local government to increase the allocation of free water and electricity in the city. At 6kl of water and 50kwh of electricity per household per month, these amounts are insufficient to deal with the needs of the one third of Cape Town's population living below the poverty line. Doubling or quadrupling these amounts has been the call of some organizations in Johannesburg and from some labour groups in Cape Town (notably Samwu) and there may be ground to be gained here in continuing with these demands (despite the fact that the city already sees itself as a national and international leader in this regard).

A complete moratorium on service cutoffs and restrictions could be called for too, with a waiving of payment arrears in low-income areas and a major effort to repair damaged pipes and equipment that lead to faulty billing and wasted water and electricity. A 'water leaks' project by the Environmental Monitoring Group in Cape Town has made some progress in this regard, though it has been difficult and slow (EMG 2005).

Finally, there could be a call for a closure of some or all of the 10 or so golf courses in the metropolitan area, each of which uses between one and three million litres of water a day. Besides being politically symbolic it would help with water conservation strategies and could assist with housing densification and development, with several of the golf courses located close to the city centre. The mayor of Caracas, Venezuela, has threatened to do just this, saying he will expropriate two city-centre golf courses for a mixed housing development (*BBC News*, August 30, 2006).

Capital—big and small—may threaten to leave the city with these kinds of demands for change but the scale of inequality in Cape Town, and the increasingly visible nature of this gap, may allow for tactical interventions in key strategic areas. These are interventions that can make a real difference to people's lives in the short run and can open the door for further interventions and politicization in the long term.

TRANSFORMING CAPE TOWN

But as useful and important as these initiatives may be it is essential not to become trapped in a limited reformist agenda. As Brenner and Theodore (2002, 376) note: "[W]e have every reason to anticipate the crystallization of still leaner and meaner urban geographies in which cities engage in mutually destructive place-marketing policies, in which transnational capital is permitted to opt out from supporting local reproduction, and in which the power of citizens to influence the basic conditions of their everyday lives is increasingly undermined". A rather "grim scenario", as they put it.

Also grim is the political balance of forces on the ground in Cape Town at the moment. Of all the reformist policy interventions I have outlined above none has been sustained over a long period of time in the city. The Anti-Eviction Campaign has effectively collapsed as a coherent social movement and there is no other broad-based political coalition challenging neoliberalism in the city as there has been with the Anti-Privatisation Forum or the Soweto Electricity Crisis Committee in Johannesburg. Both of those organizations continue to attract hundreds of people to their branch meetings, as well as conduct research and even mount candidates for local government elections (though the latter has not been without internal controversy).

Most of the NGOs operating in Cape Town are either neoliberal themselves (in the hopes of winning council contracts) or so meekly opposed to neoliberal policy as to be ineffective. There has been concerted resistance to neoliberalism by some environmental justice organizations in the city (e.g. Environmental Monitoring Group, the Environmental Justice Networking Forum), and some excellent work has been done by the Alternative Information and Development Centre (AIDC) and the International Labour Research and Information Group (Ilrig), but these interventions have been limited by a reliance on (international) donor funding and by limited institutional capacities, and as a result have not been able to sustain widespread political organization or action on the ground.

Organized labour has been the most vocal, with the Cape Town city and Western Cape provincial branches of Samwu being the most active and outspoken opponents to neoliberal policy in the city. Samwu workers have occupied municipal offices to protest the city's neoliberal restructuring plans, and there have been numerous local and national strikes against privatization by Samwu since the late 1990s. With 18,000 members the Cape Town branch of Samwu represents by far the largest, most resourced and most coordinated opposition group in the city.

But Samwu has been largely acting alone. Cosatu leadership in the Western Cape has offered support on strikes and in helping to coordinate some anti-privatization work, but Cosatu's political constraints within the Tripartite Alliance at the national level have limited its ability to contribute to the building of a broader radical labour coalition in Cape Town.

So, too, have efforts to build a coalition of labour and civil society been limited. The Cape Town Anti-Privatisation Forum (formed in 1999 in response to the neoliberalism of the Unicity Commission, and initially known as the Local Government Transformation Forum) has been driven in large part by the local branch of Samwu, but this coalition of some 40 organizations has "not been very stable" and no longer operates as a coherent example of the kind of "social movement unionism" which has managed to bring together labour and social movements to fight neoliberalism in other parts of the world (Lier and Stokke 2006, 812; Xali, forthcoming).

This fracturing of labour and social movement coherence can be attributed in large part to the political tensions inherent in Samwu's membership in Cosatu and the pressures to toe the line in the ANC–alliance (Lier and Stokke 2006). To be critical of the ANC on the ground but supportive of the party in formal political discourse has created an irreconcilable contradiction that may allow for short-term reformism but cannot allow for the more radical transformative break that is ultimately necessary in the city and country.

The fact that there is more than one public sector union in Cape Town complicates matters further, particularly given the conservative political history of the (predominantly white) Independent Municipal and Allied Trade Union (Imatu). Although Imatu has opposed some restructuring in the city, and taken some strike action in collaboration with Samwu over wage negotiations at a national level, Imatu has been silent for the most part on neoliberal initiatives such as City Improvement Districts and outsourcing. At times Imatu has even been supportive of neoliberal reforms, allowing city officials to play a game of divide and conquer with its employees.

Ratepayer groups, not surprisingly, have tended to drive another wedge into the formation of a radical political coalition in the city. Though there are dozens of these neighbourhood-based organizations around Cape Town, many of which are very well-organized, they tend to be driven by middle-class home owners concerned, primarily, with housing values and keeping rates increases to a minimum. Some of the more powerful suburban ratepayer organizations have squashed initiatives for progressive local government taxation (watering down laws on market value assessments on property taxes, for example).

Some township-based ratepayer groups have openly challenged the inequitable distribution of resources in the city, but these groups have failed to take on the larger political and economic questions around neoliberalism and would appear supportive of place-based marketing efforts to attract investors (including the expansion of City Improvement Districts in township areas).

Does this mean there is no hope for a more radical political agenda in the city? Certainly in the short run the situation does not look good. The ANC and DA have both managed to convince a majority of citizens that fiscal austerity is in everyone's interests, that they are doing their best to deliver on basic services, that they are implementing 'pro-poor' policies, that growth for the rich will mean growth for the poor and, most importantly, that there is no alternative but to engage aggressively in a global market economy. The local press perpetuates this philosophy, relentlessly promoting privatization and the 'world-class' vision of city leaders.

Finally, there are relatively few academics in the city pushing for radical change. Some are working diligently toward progressive 'reform' but many have bought into the rhetoric of 'pro-poor' policymaking that serves to reinforce neoliberalism rather than challenge it. Academic funding agencies, NGO donors and journal editors are partly to blame here, lavishing praise and money on mainstream, liberal research and acting as gatekeepers in academic forums.

Cape Town lacks a transformative intellectual hotbed such as the Centre for Civil Society at the University of KwaZulu-Natal in Durban. Although such an institute provides no guarantee of progressive, ethical engagement with labour and civil society—academic vanguardism being a side effect of many progressive movements in South Africa (Desai 2006)—and certainly no guarantee of a socialist agenda, it could at least serve to challenge hegemonic (neo)liberal academic discourse in Cape Town.

Having said this, Cape Town has a long and proud history of radical politics, and there is always a potential for change. Cape Town was a focal point of opposition to apartheid and home to the United Democratic Front (UDF) in the 1980s at the height of apartheid repression. There continue to be active community organizations in the townships and there is a growing politicization of young activists in particular.

Most importantly, the objective conditions for radical change are there. Grinding poverty, growing unemployment, downward pressures on social wages, restricted access to services and public spaces, and rampant crime in the townships are all indicators of enormous and increasing material disparity. Frustrations have erupted from time to time in the form of community protest—often met by violent suppression from the police—and there would appear to be a growing disenchantment amongst Capetonians with the ANC, witnessed in part by falling voter turnout for local elections as well as the election of the opposition DA on two occasions since 2000. These wins by the DA probably represent ideological confusion more than a focused political opposition to neoliberalism, but they do at least suggest that the post-apartheid honeymoon of the ANC has begun to sputter.

Cape Town cannot continue on this path of inequity indefinitely. It may take 10 years, it may take 100 years, but there will be a rupture of social relations along class lines in Cape Town at some point. Capital may be able to diffuse these pressures for some time to come, but the fissures of inequality are too great to contain forever.

What, then, might a radically different Cape Town look like? I am reluctant to comment in too much detail on this topic. This stems in part from a fear of the kind of academic vanguardism alluded to earlier (or, as Harvey (1996, 433) puts it, "the spectre of Lenin"). Direction and coordination from the top is important for any socialist movement but it must, ultimately, be driven from below. Any socialist future in Cape Town or South Africa must be the product of the economic, political, cultural and ideological conditions of the time, not that of an academic blueprint.

However, I am equally leery of what Harvey (1996, 433) calls the "idealized avant-gardism" of postmodernism ("the spectre of Derrida … so entrenched in the academy"). The latter has taken hold of much critical urban theory in South Africa, with countless academics calling for a vague "(re)imaging" of the country's cities. This post-colonial literature is often divorced from material analysis, operating in the realm of normative speculation, detached from the concrete world of prepaid water meters, caps on taxation, or profit-seeking international firms.

It is somewhere between these two spectres that a socialist future will have to be sought in Cape Town—a terrain of political organization and struggle that allows for difference and (re)imagination but does not fall into the trap of unchecked relativism; a practical terrain of change that "desperately cries out for cultivation" (Harvey 1996, 433).

In this sense, I am open to the postcolonial call for "greater articulations between local initiatives and diverse local social groupings across the urban system" and a "more coherent urban form premised on its own organic identities rather than contrived attempts to imitate urban modernities from other contexts" (Swilling et al. 2002, 311). Uncritical and wholesale importation of western and northern conceptions of socialism into the South(ern) African context is bound to fail.

And yet, there are certain universalities that must be grappled with in fighting capitalism's totalizing and homogenizing tendencies. We cannot wish away the reality of dominant, hegemonic rationalities, and these must be fought with equally clear and focused counter-hegemonic discourses. Nor can we ignore the growing call for universal rights (freedom of speech, the right to a healthy environment, etc.) and the need to recognize some form of political, economic and cultural structure that situates socialism within these demands.

To this end, there are a growing number of socialist models elsewhere in the world to which South Africans could look for ideas, inspiration and mistakes. Cuba's experiences over the past 50 years present perhaps the most significant wealth of information, but more recent developments in Brazil, Uruguay, Bolivia, Kerala and, perhaps most importantly, Venezuela, may be more relevant to the highly divided and neoliberalized conditions of contemporary South Africa.

My own preference is for a vibrant, localized form of socialist democracy, which is widely participatory in its political structure and culture, but which is balanced with a centralized decision-making system that ensures equity and (re)distribution in efficient ways. Economically, the nationalization of key sectors such as finance and mining would be essential, as would a halt to any privatization initiatives (as well as an undoing of the commercially oriented corporatization that has taken place in the public and parastatal sectors). Markets—in their limited, organizational sense—could still exist, but a massive decommodification of all essential goods and services would be required.

None of this can take place in a single city such as Cape Town, of course, or even in a single country. As Amin (2006) notes: "Capitalism is a worldwide system; therefore, its victims cannot effectively meet its challenges unless they organise themselves at that same global level".

This does not mean that Cape Town and other cities in the country cannot work toward change on their own. As discussed in Chapter 3, cities are at the epicentre of neoliberal accumulation (and crises) and are therefore the best place to fight for progressive change. The challenge, to borrow one last time from Harvey (1989c, 16), is to devise a geopolitical strategy of city linkages that "mitigates inter-urban competition and shifts political horizons away from the locality and into a more generalisable challenge to capitalist uneven development.... build[ing] alliances and linkages across space in such a way as to mitigate if not challenge the hegemonic dynamic of capitalist accumulation".

Abstract, perhaps, but any socialist vision for Cape Town must be multiscalar in its constitution. Without a larger national, regional and even international shift from market-dominated systems it will be impossible for anything but the mildest of Keynesian reforms to take hold in one place. Inter-urban competition will continue to play in to the interests of transnational capital and undermine efforts to create significant market reforms, particularly in a country such as South Africa where there is no clear urban primacy and where secondary cities play an important role in the national economy.

Cape Town's particular brand of neoliberal capitalism presents its own challenges and opportunities, but ones that must be seen within a larger national, regional and international context of urbanization and market expansion, forcing any serious discussion of socialism in the city to grapple with these larger universal material realities.

In conclusion, Cape Town is ripe for reform and has the potential for larger transformation. Incremental reformist change of the sort described above could make immediate and significant differences to people's lives. The pro-poor, participatory rhetoric of both the ANC and the DA is so underrealized and underfunded in Cape Town that effective lobbying by a well-coordinated coalition of labour, NGOs, civil society and academics could make a notable difference in a relatively short period of time.

The bigger challenge is constructing a language and strategy for more radical change, and building a political coalition that can move with this larger transformative agenda. This will take years of hard work at the grass-roots level, organizing and politicizing. It will also require carefully thought out—though flexible—political vision from above, connected to a larger network of national organizations and drawing on the experiences, insights and resources of international anticapitalist movements.

In this respect, a Socialist Party of some kind, bringing together labour, social movements and other interested organizations would be helpful. Such a new party would likely require a dismantling of the ANC–led Tripartite Alliance, but there may be gains to be made in the shorter term from creating space for more radical elements *within* this coalition and having them link up with other political movements internationally.

Creating these local, national and international configurations will be difficult and painful, but any effective counter-hegemonic movement in Cape Town will have to be as sophisticated and multiscalar as its bourgeois counterparts.

Notes

CHAPTER 1

1. See the website of the Globalization and World Cities (GaWC) project for an extensive data base (www.lboro.ac.uk/gawc/).

CHAPTER 2

1. Sassen (2002, 9) even implies that she has "developed the thesis" about capital fixity, arguing that "[t]his conceptualization allows us to reposition the role of cities in an increasingly globalizing world, in that they contain the resources (including fixed capital) that enable firms and markets to have global operations".

CHAPTER 4

1. Personal interview with the Town Engineer of iKapa, February 10, 1994.
2. The term "metropolitan substructure" refers to the tier of local government below a metropolitan council. Although the term is somewhat cumbersome it is part of the local government restructuring jargon in South Africa and will be retained for purposes of discussion here.
3. As international spokesperson for the South African Civic Organization (Sanco)—the ANC–allied civic which was by far the most dominant nonstatutory actor at the NLGNF—Mayekiso was well-placed to comment on Sanco's rationale for compromise.
4. One of the leading nonstatutory negotiators in Cape Town was also a member of the National Local Government Negotiating Forum, branch chairperson of a local union, part of Cosatu's Economic and Development Task Force and involved in the Western Cape Regional Development Forum, making it very difficult for him to commit the necessary time to local government restructuring debates in the city.
5. The Western Cape United Squatters Association had a long history of involvement with the South African Police, which armed members of the organization in the 1980s in an attempt to stir up violence in the townships and informal areas and to create an armed opposition force to the ANC–allied democratic movement. The Inkatha Freedom Party, although not a signifi-

cant presence in the Western Cape at that time, had an equally antagonistic history with the ANC.

6. The Premier, Hernus Kriel, was a former Minister of Law and Order in the National Party and well-known for his hawkish views. The Minister of Local Government, Peter Marais, rose to prominence in the coloured House of Delegates in the 1980s. A coloured Capetonian who is "absolutely adamant ... that he has no black African blood in him whatsoever" (*Weekly Mail*, June 15, 1995), Marais has been personally blamed for poisoning coloured/African relations in the CMA—most notably with a blatantly racist comic book produced by the National Party for the 1994 provincial elections that claimed that if the ANC won the elections Africans would storm into coloured neighbourhoods, "steal your homes", and "rape your daughters". Fortunately, the publication was quickly banned by the Independent Electoral Commission, but not until thousands of copies had been distributed.

7. The Local Government Demarcation Board was responsible for putting forth proposals on new, nonracial local boundaries, and the Provincial Committee was responsible for making the final decision. The decisions of both of these working groups had enormous repercussions for how boundaries were decided and how municipal resources could be utilized.

8. This opposition included virtually every statutory and nonstatutory body in the inner metropolitan area plus several nonstatutory bodies in the peripheral area. Ironically, most of the statutory groups who opposed the exclusion of these satellite towns during the outer boundary negotiations would use the same arguments themselves when it came to drawing boundaries *within* the metropolitan area by demanding their own, independent status.

9. The Chief Engineer, Mike Marsden, was particularly influential in promoting a balanced substructure arrangement.

10. Information based on replies to questionnaire and interviews with iKapa management in early 1994.

11. Figures based on an estimated population of 425,000 people and a staff of 800 labourers and 100 administrative and managerial personnel at the time.

12. Surveys were sent to each of the 33 waste depots and 13 water depots in the CMA, with the approval and knowledge of the relevant municipal authorities. Depot managers completed the surveys and sent them back within one month. Some follow-up clarifications were conducted telephonically.

13. In some cases depot managers only provided figures for the number of households serviced. In order to obtain per capita figures we multiplied the number of households by three for suburban areas and by five for township areas, as per standard statistical practice in South Africa, in order to give a truer indication of the distributional figures. The figures provided here are also adjusted for the percent of resources that are used for industrial waste management, as per the figures provided by the depot manager. It is worth noting that depots reporting significant proportions of their resources being used for commercial activity were also in suburban-oriented areas, indicating an even higher potential use of resources for domestic waste management activity in these areas.

14. Although occurring in Johannesburg, the removal of ANC ward councillor Trevor Ngwane for his public criticism of the ANC's *iGoli 2002* plan in the late 1990s is a case in point of the ways in which the ANC has dealt with internal dissent at the local level.

CHAPTER 5

1. Manuel's remarks in Parliament on October 26, 2004, were widely reported in the press at the time. The comments attracted a stinging public rebuttal from former Archbishop Desmond Tutu about the Minister's (and the ANC's) callous attitude toward poverty in the country, saying that he will not be "browbeaten by pontificating decrees from on high", adding that "we cannot glibly on full stomachs speak about handouts to those who often go to bed hungry" (as quoted in *IRIN News*, November 23, 2004). Manuel's subsequent comment in a local government magazine that "[h]umility towards the poor is the greatest attribute of a civil servant" rings hollow in this respect (Manuel 2005, 55).
2. Figures obtained from City of Toronto official website at www.toronto.ca, accessed May 18, 2005.
3. Remarkably, SACN (2004, 114) goes on to state that, "in the drive to meet targets for new houses, the fact that most new housing was being developed on the edge of cities went unnoticed". Unnoticed by elite policymakers, perhaps, but certainly not by residents forced to live in these peripheral and generally unappealing locales.
4. In April 2006, 110 low-income residents from Gympie Street in Woodstock were being evicted from their homes in what the IndyMedia (2006) characterized (in a short video documentary) as an aggressive effort on the part of developers to get their hands on some of the last centrally located residential property areas in the city that had not been gentrified. The residents interviewed claim that developers have already taken out advertisements in local newspapers touting the property as a place to invest in tourist accommodation in advance of the soccer World Cup in 2010.
5. Data on number of pools taken from *Cape Argus* (June 1, 2005). Final figures calculated on the basis of 68,250 pools times 50kl/pool/year, divided by 72kl/household/year (the latter being the amount of "free basic water" allocated to each household on an annual basis and a typical rate of consumption).
6. Unless, of course, rail investments also service the elite, as with the announcement in 2005 by national government to spend "at least R20bn" on a high-tech rail link to the Johannesburg International Airport from Johannesburg and Pretoria (*Mail & Guardian*, December 8, 2005).
7. Information on ISPs and the number of Internet users sourced at the UN's Economic Commission for Africa website on May 12, 2005, at www.uneca.org/aisi/nici/country_profiles/South%20Africa/southinter.htm
8. Information sourced at the website dedicated to the cable at www.safe-sat3.co.za, accessed on May 12, 2005.
9. From the website www.capetown.org.za/smartcape, accessed on May 12, 2005.
10. Interview with former City Manager, Dr Wallace Mgoqi, December 6, 2004.
11. Figures vary depending on how procurement deals are factored into the equation. The *Mail & Guardian* estimated a figure of R57bn in its December 10–17, 2004, issue.

CHAPTER 6

1. This section draws on Mcdonald and Ruiters (2005b, 14–19).
2. Similar wording is to be found in the Water Services Act (section 19 (2)) from 1997.
3. This information is drawn from a DPLG memo forwarded to the author by Samwu officials in November 2002. Samwu's requests are articulated formally in Resolutions adopted at its 7th National Congress on 19–22 August 2003, as follows: "*We therefore resolve:* 1. To support and participate in the initiative of establishing a unit such as the Support Unit For Public Provision of Services (SUPPS) and seek to ensure that: (a) It is given a status and access to resources at much more than that of the Municipal Infrastructure Investment Unit (MIIU), given that public sector is acknowledged by both the government and labour to be the preferred option; (b) It promotes the delivery of services by local government in a way that meets the principles set out in the resolution on municipal service standards and tariffs adopted at the 6th SAMWU National Congress, the local government National Framework Agreement, and the 2000 ANC election manifesto; and (c) It does not promote the commercialisation of service delivery".
4. Email communication, John Mawbey.
5. See, for example, chapter 3 of the WRC's 2002 report on its activities, available at www.wrc.org.za/downloads/knowledgereview/2002/Services.pdf. At the time of writing the WRC had provided some funding to the Municipal Services Project to investigate the impact of 'free water' on women, perhaps signalling a small shift in their awareness of the issues.
6. Quote taken from a speech during the election campaign by Ebrahim Rasool, leader of the Western Cape provincial ANC, as quoted in *Cape Argus*, December 13, 2000.
7. It was not possible to discern any attitudinal trends in race and gender terms because the sample was overwhelmingly white (79%) and male (93%), itself a telling feature of the senior echelons of decision making in Cape Town.
8. No page numbers are provided in the document.
9. *Youth Summit on Privatization*, Gugulethu (Cape Town), November 12, 2000, organized by the Alternative Information and Development Centre (AIDC).
10. Interview with Roger Ronnie, General Secretary of Samwu, March 15, 2001.
11. Data collection in mid-2000 found that 11 of the 13 water depots had done some outsourcing (McDonald and Smith 2002), while conversations with Samwu officials in 2005 show that all depots are now outsourcing some functions.
12. It is worth noting here that one of the biggest boosters of the creation of a RED in Cape Town was former ANC Councillor Saleem Mowzer. He is now director of the RED and reputedly earning more than R1.3 a year in salary.
13. The *Cape Times* ran a short, 100-word article on how the "City invites public comment on plans to revamp electricity set-up" on December 15, 2004, at the bottom of page four. When I spoke to the editors at this paper and at the *Cape Argus* they knew virtually nothing about the RED but were interested in learning more and invited me to write a piece which was published in January 2005 in the *Cape Argus*, part of which has been revised for this section of the chapter.

CHAPTER 7

1. These next sections of the chapter draw on McDonald (2002a).
2. Chippy Olver as quoted in *Mail & Guardian*, November 22, 1996.
3. From a half-page advertisement in *Business Day*, March 7, 2002.
4. In a revealing Letter to the Editor of the *Cape Argus* on March 13, 2002, George D van Schalkwyk, the Interim Manager: Revenue and Debt Management for the City of Cape Town, wrote (in response to a previous letter in the paper): "The alleged threat of evictions for water accounts of R100 is incorrect; only accounts exceeding R250 were handed to the attorneys".
5. *Gemini News,* February 22, 2002.
6. Information available at www.eskom.co.za/electrification/faq.htm#installed-base, accessed June 29, 2005.
7. Interestingly, there is nothing in the draft policy about the demeaning and divisive nature of means testing which often creates deep personal and political divisions in already demoralized communities by dividing the poor from the even poorer. Cape Town's concern appears to be merely of an administrative and financial nature.

CHAPTER 8

1. Quote contained in a letter to Samwu. Obtained from Roger Ronnie, General Secretary of Samwu, March 15, 2001.
2. The information in this paragraph and the next comes from an information supplement placed by the city in the *Cape Times*, September 21, 2004.

CHAPTER 9

1. Available at the UCLGA website at www.uclgarica.org/Documents/Founding%20Congress/UCLGA%20FOUNDING%20CONGRESS%20DECLARATION%20ENGL.doc, accessed July 25, 2006.
2. Pulido builds this definition on Omi and Winant's (1994, 55) idea of race as a "concept which signifies and symbolizes social conflicts and interests by referring to different types of human bodies".
3. A September 2006 news release by Lawyers for Human Rights outlines one such victory: "Lawyers for Human Rights represented 16 Somalian refugees and asylum seekers who were expelled by a mob of local residents from the Phahameng Township Modimolle, Limpopo Province, in xenophobic attacks which took place on 20 July 2006. Our clients' shops/ houses were destroyed, their stock stolen and they were threatened with death, apparently for the sole reason that they are foreigners. Subsequent to these attacks, Lawyers for Human Rights requested the Department of Social Development to provide our clients with temporary social relief of distress grants. The Department failed to do so, which led to an application to the Pretoria High Court for appropriate relief. Yesterday, 14 September 2006, the parties reached a settlement which was made an order of Court. The Court order, amongst others, provides that the Minister of Social Development will provide our clients with social relief of distress grants for a period of three months".

References

Abrahamsen, R. 2000. *Disciplining Democracy: Development Discourses and Good Governance in Africa.* London: Zed Books.

Abu-Lughod, J.L. 1989. *Before European Hegemony: The World System A.D. 1250–1350.* New York: Oxford University Press.

ACNielson. 2003. "Customer Perceptions and Needs: Report Prepared for City of Cape Town Water Services", June. Cape Town: ACNielsen.

Ahmad, J. 1995. "Funding the Metropolitan Areas of South Africa", *Finance and Development*, September.

AIDC [Alternative Information and Development Centre]. 2004. "Has Government Abandoned Privatization?", *Alternatives*, October. Cape Town: AIDC.

Allen, K., G. Gotz and C. Joseph. 2001. "Responding to Crisis and Change: *iGoli 2002* and a recent history of local government in Johannesburg", report for the City of Johannesburg, Johannesburg.

Amen, M.M., K. Archer and M.M. Bosman. 2006a. "Thinking Through Global Cities", in M.M. Amen, K. Archer and M.M. Bosman (eds), *Relocating Global Cities: From the Center to the Margins.* Lanham, MD: Rowman & Littlefield Publishers, pp 1–22.

———. (eds) 2006b. *Relocating Global Cities: From the Center to the Margins.* Lanham, MD: Rowman & Littlefield Publishers.

Amin, A. and S. Graham. 1997. "The Ordinary City", *Transactions of the Institute of British Geographers*, Vol 22, No 4, pp 411–29.

Amin, S. 2006. "Towards the Fifth International?", in K. Sehm-Patomaki and M Ulvila (eds), *Democratic Politics Globally: Elements for a Dialogue on Global Political Party Formations*, NIGD Working Paper 1, available at www.nigd.org/globalparties.

ANC [African National Congress]. 1994. The Reconstruction and Development Programme. Johannesburg: Umyanyano Publications.

———. 2000. "ANC Local Government Elections 2000 Manifesto—Together Speeding Up Change, Fighting Poverty and Creating a Better Life for All: The People Shall Govern." Mimeo.

———. 2006. "2006 Manifesto: A Plan to Make Local Government Work Better for You". Available at www.anc.org.za/elections/2006/index.php?id=manifesto. html

Anderson, M. 2004. "Ilitha Lomso and a Community's Struggle for Water", Reclaiming Sustainable Development: Case Study 3. Cape Town: Environmental Monitoring Group.

Anon. 2004. "Further Developments in City of Cape Town", Cape Town and Regional Chamber of Commerce and Industry Business Bulletin, Issue 11, November.

Bahl, R. and P. Smoke (eds). 2003. *Restructuring Local Government Finances in Developing Countries: Lessons from South Africa*. Cheltenham, UK: Edgar Elgar.

Baiocchi, G. (ed). 2003. *Radicals in Power: The Worker's Party (PT) and Experiments in Urban Democracy in Brazil*. London: Zed Books.

Bakker, K.J. 2003. *An Uncooperative Commodity: Privatizing Water in England and Wales*. Oxford: Oxford University Press.

Bakker K.J. and D. Hemson. 2000. "Privatising Water: Hydropolitics in the New South Africa", *South African Journal of Geography*, No 82, pp 3–12.

Barlow, M. and T. Clarke. 2002. *Blue Gold: The Battle Against Corporate Theft of the World's Water*. Toronto: Stoddart.

Barry, A., T. Osborne and N. Rose (eds). 1996. *Foucault and Political Reason: Liberalism, Neo-liberalism and Rationalities of Government*. Chicago: University of Chicago Press.

Beall, J., O. Crankshaw and S. Parnell. 2002. *Uniting a Divided City: Governance and Social Exclusion in Johannesburg*. London: Earthscan.

Beavon, K.S.O. 2006. "Johannesburg 1986–2030: A Quest to Regain World Status", in M.M. Amen, K. Archer and M.M. Bosman (eds), *Relocating Global Cities: From the Center to the Margins*. Lanham, MD: Rowman & Littlefield Publishers.

Begg, I. 1999. "Cities and Competitiveness", *Urban Studies*, Vol 36, Nos 5–6, pp 795–809.

Bell, T. 2004. "The Soccer World Cup and the SA Commuter Rail Crisis", *Business Report*, October 22, 2.

Benton, S. 2005. Interact more, president tells ward committees and councillors, South African Cities Network newsletter, December 20.

Bernstein, A. 1991. "The Challenge of the Cities", in M. Swilling, R. Humphries and K. Shubane (eds), *Apartheid City in Transition*. Cape Town: Oxford University Press.

Berstein, H. 1978. *For their Triumphs and for their Tears: Women in Apartheid South Africa*. London: International Defence and Aid Fund.

Bollier, D. 2003. *Silent Theft: The Private Plunder of Our Common Wealth*. London: Routledge.

Bond, P. 1999a. "Basic Infrastructure for Socio-Economic Development, Ecological Sustainability and Geographical Segregation: South Africa's Unmet Challenge," *Geoforum*, Vol 30, No 1, pp 43–59.

———. 1999b. *Elite Transition: From Apartheid to Neoliberalism in South Africa*. Durban: University of Natal Press.

———. 2000. *Cities of Gold, Townships of Coal*. Trenton, NJ: Africa World Press.

———. 2003. "Johannesburg's Resurgent Civil Society", paper prepared for conference on Aspirant World Cities at Free University (Berlin), August.

———. 2005. "The Geopolitics of Water Commodification in Johannesburg", paper presented at Oxford University, School of Geography, May 25.

———. 2006a. "Neoliberal Urban Policy: Are Those *Planact* Fingerprints?", paper presented at the conference on NGOs as Innovators and Agents of Change: A history interpreted by development practitioners, University of the Witwatersrand, Johannesburg, August 5.

———. 2006b. *Looting Africa: The Economics of Exploitation*. London: Zed Books.

Bonner, P., P. Delius and D. Posel. 1993. "The Shaping of Apartheid: Contradiction, Continuity and Popular Struggle", in P. Bonner, P. Delius, and D. Posel (eds), *Apartheid's Genesis: 1935–1962*. Johannesburg: Ravan Press.

Boshken, H.L. 2003. "Global Cities, Systemic Power, and Upper-Middle-Class Influence", *Urban Affairs Review*, Vol 38, No 6, July, pp 808–30.

Bourdieu, P. 1998. *Acts of Resistance*. Cambridge: Polity Press.

Braudel, F. 1984. *The Perspective of the World—Volume III*. London: Collins.

Bremner, L. 1998. "Participatory Planning: Models of Urban Governance: Porto Alegre and Greater Johannesburg", *Urban Forum*, Vol 9, No 1.

——. 2004. *Johannesburg: One City, Colliding Worlds*. Johannesburg: STE Publishers.

Brenner, N. 1999. "Globalization as Reterritorialization: The Rescaling of Urban Governance in the European Union", *Urban Studies*, Vol 36, No 3, pp 431–51.

——. 2004. *New State Spaces: Urban Governance and the Rescaling of Statehood*. Oxford: Oxford University Press.

Brenner, N. and N. Theodore. 2002. "Cities and the Geographies of 'Actually Existing Neoliberalism'", *Antipode*, Vol 34, No 3, pp 349–79.

Brenner, N. and R. Kiel (eds). 2006. *The Global Cities Reader*. New York: Routledge.

Brook, P.J. and A. Locussol. 2002. "Easing Tariff Increases: Financing the Transition to Cost-Covering Water Tariffs in Guinea", in P.J. Brook and S.M. Smith (eds), *Contracting for Public Services: Output-Based Aid and its Applications*. Washington, DC: World Bank.

Brown, F. 2005. "Housing Crisis in Cape Town, Western Cape, 1994–2004", Research Report No 4, in *RASSP Research Reports 2005, Vol 1*. Durban: Centre for Civil Society, pp 83–106.

Budlender, D. 2002. *The People's Voices: National Speak Out on Poverty Hearings, March to June 1998*. Johannesburg: Commission on Gender Equality, South African Human Rights Commission and South African NGO Coalition.

Buhlungu, S. 2004. The Anti-Privatisation Forum: A Profile of a Post-Apartheid Social Movement, Centre for Civil Society Research Report. Durban: CCS.

Bullard, R. 1990. *Dumping in Dixie: Race, Class and Environmental Quality*. Boulder, CO: Westview Press.

—— (ed). 1993. *Confronting Environmental Racism: Voices from the Grassroots*. Boston: South End Press.

Burchell, G., C. Gordon and P. Miller (eds). 1991. *The Foucault Effect: Studies in Governmentality*. Hemel Hempstead, UK: Harvester Wheatsheaf.

Burrows, R. and B. Loader. 1994. *Towards a Post-Fordist Welfare State?* London: Routledge.

Buur, L. 2005. "Sovereignty and Democratic Exclusion in the New South Africa", *Review of African Political Economy*, Nos 104–105, pp 253–68.

Cameron, R. 1991. "Managing the Coloured and Indian Areas", in M. Swilling, R. Humphries and K. Shubane (eds), *Apartheid City in Transition*. Cape Town: Oxford University Press.

——. 1999. *Democratization of South African Local Government: A Tale of Three Cities*. Cape Town: J.L. van Schaik.

Campagni, R. 2002. "On the Concept of Territorial Competitiveness: Sound or Misleading?", *Urban Studies*, Vol 39, No 3, pp 2395–411.

Carmona Báez, A. 2004. *State Resistance to Globalization in Cuba*. London: Pluto Press.

Cassiem, A. 2005. "The Role of the Law and its Ability to Protect Poor Families Facing Evictions in the Western Cape", Research Report No 6, in *RASSP Research Reports 2005, Vol 1*. Durban: Centre for Civil Society.

Castells, M. 1977. *The Urban Question: A Marxist Approach*. London: Edward Arnold.

——. 1989. *The Informational City: Information Technology, Economic Restructuring, and the Urban-Regional Process.* London: Blackwell.

——. 1996. *The Rise of Network Society.* Oxford: Blackwell.

CAWP [Coalition Against Water Privatisation]. 2004. "The Struggle Against Silent Disconnections: Prepaid Meters and the Struggle for Life in Phiri, Soweto", research report by the Coalition Against Water Privatisation, July, Johannesburg.

CCC [Cape Town City Council]. 1991. Annual Report of the City Planner. Cape Town: CCC.

CCS [Centre for Civil Society]. 2006. Yonk' Indawo Umzabalazo Uyasivumela: New Work From Durban, Centre for Civil Society Research Report, Vol 1. Durban: CCS.

CCT [City of Cape Town]. 2000. Report No R68/2000, July 31, "Closure of the City of Cape Town's Surfacing Undertaking". Mimeo.

——. 2001a. "Assessment of Internal Mechanisms for the Provision of Solid Waste, Water and Sanitation, and Electricity Services in Terms of Section 78(1) of the Local Government Municipal Systems Act: Service Delivery Steering Committee," November 7. Mimeo.

——. 2001b. Water and Sanitation Tariffs—2001/2002 Budget Year, Executive Committee Memo, May 22. Mimeo.

——. 2002a. Taking Stock and Looking Ahead: Digital Divide Assessment of the City of Cape Town, 2002. Cape Town: CCT.

——. 2002b. Introduction to the Economic Development & Tourism Directorate—2002/03. Cape Town: CCT.

——. 2003a. Restructuring Grant Application. Mimeo, July 31.

——. 2003b. Cape Town Energy Strategy: Draft, October. Cape Town: CCT.

——. 2003c. The City of Cape Town's Budget and Municipal Account 2003/04. Cape Town: CCT.

——. 2003d. City of Cape Town City Improvement District By-Law: Final Draft, February 23. Cape Town: CCT.

——. 2004a. City of Cape Town Budget, 2004–2005. Cape Town: CCT.

——. 2004b. Integrated Development Plan: For Review and Comment—2004/2005. Cape Town: CCT.

——. 2004c. Report 2: The Way Forward—High Level Review of the Project to Establish Internal Business Units for Electricity, Water & Sanitation and Solid Waste Management Services, March 12. Cape Town: CCT.

——. 2004d. Minutes of the IDP Public Participation process held at Elsies River Civic Centre, November 22. Cape Town: CCT.

——. 2004e. Report to Executive Mayor on Section 78 Report, January 25. Cape Town: CCT.

——. 2005a. Mayor's Budget Speech, March 31. Cape Town: CCT.

—— 2005b. Draft Integrated Development Plan 2005/06. Cape Town: CCT.

——. 2006a. City of Cape Town Operating Budget, accessed July 15, 2006, at www.capetown.gov.za/budget/2006–2007/Services_Sum_2006_2007.pdf

——. 2006b. City of Cape Town 2006/2007 – 2008/2009 Capital Budget, accessed July 15, 2006, at www.capetown.gov.za/budget/2006–2007/Cap_Budget_Sum_IDP_Theme.pdf

——. 2006c. RED 1 (City of Cape Town Supply Area): Schedule of Electricity Tariffs Effective from 1 July 2006, accessed August 5, 2006, at www.capetown.gov.za/wcmstemplates/Electricity.aspx?clusid=458&IDPathString=5992–6182&catparent=6182#electariff

——. 2006d. Integrated Development Plan 2006–07. Cape Town: CCT.

———. 2006e. State of Cape Town Report 2006: Development Issues in Cape Town. Cape Town: CCT.

CDS [Centre for Development Studies]. 1991. *Local Government and Planning for a Democratic South Africa*. Bellville: University of the Western Cape.

Chavez, D. (ed). 2006. *Beyond the Market: The Future of Public Services*. Amsterdam: TransNational Institute.

Chavez, D. and B. Goldfrank (eds). 2003. *The Left in the City: Participatory Local Governments in Latin America*. London: Latin America Bureau Press.

Chernotsksy, H.I. 2001. "The Growing Impact of Globalization Upon City Policies", *Policy Studies Review*, Vol 18, No 3, Autumn, pp 29–48.

Cherry, J. 2004. "The 'Development State' and Cultures of Participation in Urban Townships", paper presented at a research workshop on "Conflicting forms of citizenship: Mapping the effects of changed urban modes of governance", Port Elizabeth, November 18–19.

Chipkin, I. 2004. "Manenberg Revisited: Producing the Public Domain", unpublished paper, Wits Institute for Social and Economic Research, University of the Witwatersrand, Johannesburg.

———. 2005. "'Functional' and 'Dysfunctional' Communities: The Making of Ethical Citizens", in S.L. Robins (ed), *Limits to Liberation After Apartheid: Citizenship, Governance and Culture*. Athens: Ohio University Press.

Christianson, D. 2004. "The Ramos Plan to be Business-Friendly and Business-like", *Enterprise*, November, pp 37–38.

Christopher, A.J. 2005. "The Slow Pace of Desegregation in South African Cities, 1996–2001", Urban Studies, Vol 42, No 12, November, pp 2305–20.

Clammer, J. 2003. "Globalization, Class, Consumption and Civil Society in South-East Asian Cities", *Urban Studies*, Vol 40, No 2, pp 403–19.

Clark C., J. Green and K. Grenell. 2001. "Does Globalization Challenge the 'Growth Machine'", *Policy Studies Review*, Vol 18, No 3, Autumn, pp 49–61.

Clark, D. 2003. *Urban World, Global City*. London: Routledge.

Clarke, J. and J. Newman. 1997. *The Managerial State*. London: Sage.

Cloete, F. 1995. *Local Government Transition in South Africa*. Pretoria: JL van Schaik.

CMNF [Cape Metropolitan Negotiating Forum]. 1994. CMNF Agreement. Cape Town: Mallinicks.

Coaffe, J. and L. Johnston. 2005. "The Management of Local Government Modernization: Area Decentralization and Pragmatic Localism", *International Journal of Public Sector Management*, Vol 18, No 2, pp 164–77.

Corbett, P. 1992. Post-Apartheid Housing Policy, in D.M. Smith (ed), *The Apartheid City and Beyond: Urbanization and Social Change in South Africa*. London: Routledge.

Cosatu. 2004. *2005–2006 People's Budget Proposal*. Johannesburg: National Labor & Economic Institute.

Cottle, E. and H. Deedat. 2002. *The Cholera Outbreak: A 2000–2002 Case Study of the Source of the Outbreak in the Madlebe Tribal Authority Areas, uThungulu Region, KwaZulu-Natal*. Cape Town: Health Systems Trust and Municipal Services Project.

Crush, J. (ed). 1998. *Beyond Control: Immigration and Human Rights in a Democratic South Africa*. Cape Town: Institute for Democracy in South Africa/ International Development Research Centre.

———. 2001. "The Dark Side of Democracy: Migration, Xenophobia and Human Rights in South Africa", *International Migration*, Vol 38, Issue 6, pp 103–21.

Crush, J., T. Ulicki, T. Tseane and E.J. van Vuuren. 1999. "Undermining Labour: Migrancy and Sub-Contracting in the South African Mining Sector", Migration Policy Series, No 15. Cape Town: Southern African Migration Project.

Crush, J. and D.A. McDonald (eds). 2002. *Transnationalism and New African Immigration to South Africa*. Toronto: Canadian Association of African Studies.

CTRCCI [Cape Town Regional Chamber of Commerce and Industry]. 2004a. Business Guide 2004–2005.

———. 2004b. 200 Years of the Chamber of Commerce and Industry in Cape Town: 1804–2004.

CUPE [Canadian Union of Public Employees]. 2002. Annual Report on Privatization. Ottawa: CUPE.

DA [Democratic Alliance]. 2000. "Local Government Manifesto: For All the People." Mimeo.

———. 2006. "Local Government Election Manifesto 2006", available at www.da.org.za/da/Site/Eng/campaigns/2006/manifestopage.asp?man=1

Danso, R. and D.A. McDonald. 2001. "Writing Xenophobia: Immigration and the Print Media in Post-Apartheid South Africa", *Africa Today*, Vol 48, No 3, pp 114–37.

Davies, B. and J. Day. 1998. *Vanishing Waters*. Cape Town: UCT Press.

Davis, D.E. 2005. "Cities in Global Context: A Brief Intellectual History", *International Journal of Urban and Regional Research*, Vol 29, No 1, March, pp 92–109.

Davis, M. 2004. "Planet of Slums", *New Left Review*, No 26, March/April, pp 5–33.

DBSA [Development Bank of Southern Africa]. 2003. Development Report 2003—Financing Africa's Development: Enhancing the Role of Private Finance. Pretoria: DBSA.

———. 2004. Financial Statements for the Year Ended March 31, 2004. Pretoria: DBSA.

DCCI [Durban Chamber of Commerce and Industry]. 2002. "Water Costs Increases", *Chamber Digest—Official Newsletter of the Durban Chamber of Commerce and Industry*, Issue 3, February 16.

Deacon, H. 1994. "Racism and Leprosy at Robben Island", in E. van Heyningen (ed), *Studies in the History of Cape Town: Volume 7*. Cape Town: UCT Press, pp 45–83.

DEFRA [Department for Environment, Food & Rural Affairs, UK]. 1999. "Water Industry Act 1999: Delivering the Government's Objectives".

Desai, A. 2002. *We Are the Poors: Community Struggles in Post-Apartheid South Africa*. New York: Monthly Review Press.

———. 2006. "Vans, Autos, Kombis and the Drivers of Social Movements", Harold Wolpe Memorial Lecture, Centre for Civil Society, International Convention Centre, Durban, July 28.

Desai, A. and R. Pithouse. 2004. "What Stank in the Past Is the Present's Perfume: Dispossession, Resistance, and Repression in Mandela Park", *The South Atlantic Quarterly*, Vol 102, No 4, Fall, pp 841–75.

De Swardt, C., T. Puane, M. Chopra and A. du Toit. 2005. "Urban Poverty in Cape Town", *Environment and Urbanization*, Vol 17, No 2, October, pp 101–11.

De Wet, P. 2002. *Europe-Africa-Asia Submarine Cable Launched*, ITWeb website, accessed May 27.

Dikeni, S. 1996. "Paranoid Racist Bigots Have Turned Cape Town into a City Without Soul", *Cape Times*, April 9.

Dilla, H. 1999. "Comrades and Investors: The Uncertain Transition in Cuba", in L. Panitch and C. Leys (eds), *Socialist Register 1999: Global Capitalism Versus Democracy*. New York: Monthly Review.

Dinar, A. (ed). 2001. *The Political Economy of Water Pricing Reforms*. Washington, DC: Oxford University Press (for the World Bank).

Dodson, B. 2000. "Women On The Move: Gender and Cross-Border Migration to South Africa from Lesotho, Mozambique and Zimbabwe", in D.A. McDonald (ed), *On Borders: Perspectives on International Migration in Southern Africa*. New York: St Martin's Press.

Dodson, B. and C. Oelofse. 2002. "Shades of Xenophobia: In-Migrants and Immigrants in Mizamoyethu, Cape Town", *Canadian Journal of African Studies*, Vol 34, pp 124–48.

Dolgan, C. 1999. "Soulless Cities: Ann Arbor, the Cutting Edge of Discipline— Postfordism, Postmodernism and the New Bourgeoisie", *Antipode*, Vol 31, No 2, pp 129–62.

Douglass, M. and P. Boonchuen. 2006. "Bangkok—Intentional World City", in M.M. Amen, K. Archer and M.M. Bosman (eds), *Relocating Global Cities: From the Center to the Margins*. Lanham, MD: Rowman & Littlefield Publishers.

DPLG [Department of Provincial and Local Government]. 2002. Quarterly Monitoring of Municipal Finances and Related Activities, Summary of Questionnaires for Quarter Ended 31 December 2001, Pretoria. Mimeo.

———. 2004a. The Municipal Infrastructure Grant 2004–2007. Pretoria: DPLG.

———. 2004b. Strategic Plan: 2004–2007. Pretoria: DPLG.

Drakeford, M. 1998. "Water Regulation and Pre-Payment Meters", *Journal of Law and Society*, Vol 25, No 4, December.

Duménil G., and D. Lévy. 2005. "The Neoliberal (Counter-)Revolution", in A. Saad-Filho and D. Johnston (eds), *Neoliberalism: A Critical Reader*. London: Pluto Press, pp 9–20.

Dunsire, A. 1999. "Then and Now: Public Administration, 1953–1999", *Political Studies*, Vol 47.

DWAF [Department of Water Affairs and Forestry]. 2000. Delivery of Free Water. Mimeo.

———. 2003. Strategic Framework for Water Services. Pretoria: Government Printers.

Dwyer, P. 2004. The Contentious Politics of the Concerned Citizens Forum (CCF), Centre for Civil Society Research Report. Durban: CCS.

Eaton, K. 2004. "Risky Business: Decentralization From Above in Chile and Uruguay", *Comparative Politics*, Vol 37, No 1, pp 1–22.

EDI [Electricity Distribution Industry]. 2004. The Transformer: EDI Holdings Newsletter, October.

Egan, A. and A. Wafer. 2004. The Soweto Electricity Crisis Committee, Centre for Civil Society Research Report. Durban: CCS.

Elliot, J.R. 1999. "Putting 'Global Cities' in their Place: Urban Hierarchy and Low-Income Employment During the Post-War Era", *Urban Geography*, Vol 20, No 2, pp 95–115.

EMG [Environmental Monitoring Group]. 2005. "Water Handbook For South African Activists and Decision-Makers in Urban Areas". Cape Town: EMG.

Ernst, J. 1994. *Whose Utility: The Social Impact of Public Utility Privatization and Regulation in Britain*. Buckingham, UK: Open University Press.

Fee, E., L. Shopes and L. Zeidman (eds). 1991. *The Baltimore Book: New Views of Local History*. Philadelphia: Temple University Press.

Felbinger, C.L. and J.E. Robey. 2001. "Globalization's Impact on State and Local Policy: The Rise of Regional Cluster-Based Economic Development Strategies", *Policy Studies Review*, Vol 18, No 3, Autumn, pp 63–79.

FFC [Financial and Fiscal Commission]. 1997. "Local Government in a System of Intergovernmental Fiscal Relations in South Africa: A Discussion Document" (Midrand). Mimeo.

———. 2004. Submission for the Division of Revenue 2005/06. Pretoria: FFC.

Fiil, M. 2001. "The Electricity Crisis in Soweto", MSP Occasional Papers Series, No 4. Cape Town: Municipal Services Project.

Fiil-Flynn, M. and P. Naidoo. 2004. "Nothing for Mahala: The Forced Installation of Prepaid Water Meters in Stretford, Extension 4, Orange Farm, Johannesburg — South Africa", report by Public Citizen (USA), the Anti-Privatisation Forum (South Africa) and the Coalition Against Water Privatisation (South Africa), Johannesburg.

Fine, B. 2001. *Social Capital versus Social Theory: Political Economy and Social Science at the Turn of the Millennium*. London: Routledge.

———. 2002. "They F**k You Up Those Social Capitalists", *Antipode*, Vol 34, No 4, pp 797–99.

Fine B. and Z. Rustomjee. 1996. *The Political Economy of South Africa: From Minerals-Energy Complex to Industrialization*. Boulder, CO: Westview Press.

Fine, B. and V. Padayachee. 2000. "A Sustainable Growth Path", in J. Coetzee, J. Graaf, F. Hendricks and G. Wood (eds), *Development: Theory and Practice*. Cape Town: Cape Town University Press, pp 269–81.

Fine, R. and D. Davis. 1991. *Beyond Apartheid: Labour and Liberation in South Africa*. London: Pluto Press.

Finzsch, N. and D. Schirmer. 1998. *Identity and Intolerance: Nationalism, Racism and Xenophobia in Germany and the United States*. Washington, DC: German Historical Institute and Cambridge University Press.

Fjeldstad, O.H. 2001. "Intergovernmental Fiscal Relations in the Developing World: A Review of Issues", in N. Levy and C. Tapscott (eds), *Intergovernmental Relations in South Africa: The Challenges of Co-operative Government*. Cape Town: Idasa.

Freund, B. 2002. "City Hall and the Direction of Development: The Changing Role of the Local State as a Factor in Economic Planning and Development in Durban", in B. Freund and V. Padayachee (eds), *(D)urban Vortex: South African City in Transition*. Durban: University of Natal Press.

Freund B. and V. Padayachee (eds). 2002. *(D)urban Vortex: South African City in Transition*. Durban: University of Natal Press.

Friedman, J. 1986. "The World City Hypothesis", *Development and Change*, Vol 17, pp 69–83.

———. 1995. "Where We Stand: A Decade of World City Research", in P.L. Knox and P.J. Taylor (eds), *World Cities in a World System*. Cambridge: Cambridge University Press.

———. 2001. "Intercity Networks in a Globalizing Era", in A.J. Scott (ed), *Global City-Regions*. New York: Oxford University Press.

Friedman, J. and G. Wolff. 1982. "World City Formation: An Agenda for Research and Action", *International Journal of Urban and Regional Research*, Vol 6, No 3, pp 309–44.

García, D.L. 2002. "The Architecture of Global Networking Technologies", in S. Sassen (ed), *Global Networks, Linked Cities*. New York: Routledge, pp 39–70.

Gellner, E. 1995. "Nationalism and Xenophobia", in B. Baumgartl and A. Favell (eds), *New Xenophobia in Europe*. London: Kluwer Law International, pp 6–9.

Gilbert, A. 1998. "World Cities and the Urban Future: The View from Latin America", in F. Lo and Y. Yeung (eds), *Globalization and the World of Large Cities*. Tokyo: United Nations University Press.

GKS [Government of the Kingdom of Swaziland]. 2004. Medium Term Budget Policy Statement, November.

Glazewski, J. 2002. "The Rule of Law: Opportunities for Environmental Justice in the New Democratic Legal Order", in D.A. McDonald (ed), *Environmental Justice in South Africa*. Athens: University of Ohio Press.

Goga, S. 2003. "Property Investors and Decentralization: A Case of False Competition?", in R. Tomlinson, R. Beauregard, L. Bremner and X. Mangcu (eds), *Emerging Johannesburg: Perspectives on the Postapartheid City*. New York: Routledge.

Goldstuck, A.N. 2003. *The Goldstuck Report: Internet Access in South Africa 2004*. Johannesburg: World Worx Inc.

Gordon, I. 1999. "Internationalization and Urban Competition", *Urban Studies*, Vol 36, Nos 5–6, pp 1001–16.

Gotz, G. and A. Simone. 2003. "On Belonging and Becoming in African Cities", in R. Tomlinson, R. Beauregard, L. Bremner and X. Mangcu (eds), *Emerging Johannesburg: Perspectives on the Postapartheid City*. New York: Routledge.

Goubert, J.P. 1986. *The Conquest of Water*. Princeton, NJ: Princeton University Press.

Graham, P. 1995. *Governing at the Local Level: A Resource Guide for Community Leaders*. Pretoria: Idasa.

Graham, S. 1999. "Global Grids of Glass: On Global Cities, Telecommunications and Planetary Urban Networks", *Urban Studies*, Vol 36, Nos 5–6, pp 929–50.

———. 2002. "Communication Grids: Cities and Infrastructure", in S. Sassen (ed), *Global Networks, Linked Cities*. New York: Routledge.

Graham, S. and S. Marvin. 1996. *Telecommunication and the City: Electronic Spaces, Urban Places*. London: Routledge.

———. 2001. *Splintering Urbanism: Networked Infrastructures, Technological Mobilities and the Urban Condition*. London: Routledge.

Greenberg, S. 2005. "The Rise and Fall of Water Privatization in Rural South Africa: A Critical Examination of the ANC's First Term of Office, 1994–1999", in D.A. McDonald and G. Ruiters (eds), *The Age of Commodity: Water Privatization in Southern Africa*. London: Earthscan, pp 206–25.

Greenpeace. 1994. "Wasted Lives: Mercury Waste Recycling at Thor Chemicals", Waste Trade Case Study No 4. London: Greenpeace.

Gu, F.R. and Z. Tang. 2002. "Shanghai: Reconnecting to the Global Economy", in S. Sassen (ed), *Global Networks, Linked Cities*. New York and London: Routledge, pp 273–307.

Gugler, J. (ed). 2004. *World Cities Beyond the West: Globalization, Development, and Inequality*. Cambridge: Cambridge University Press.

Hall, D. 2005. Electricity Privatisation and Restructuring in Latin America and the Impact on Workers, report by PSIRU, University of Greenwich, London.

Hall, D., J. Lethbridge and E. Lobina. 2005. "Public-Public Partnerships in Health and Essential Services", MSP Occasional Paper Series, No 9. Cape Town: Municipal Services Project.

Hall, P. 1966. *The World Cities*. New York: McGraw-Hill.

Hall, P.A. and D. Soskice (eds). 2001. *Varieties of Capitalism*. Oxford: Oxford University Press.

Hanke, S. (ed). 1987. *Prospects for Privatisation*. New York: Academy of Political Science.

Harris, B. 2002. "Xenophobia: A New Pathology for a New South Africa?", in D. Hook and G. Eagle (eds), *Psychopathology and Social Prejudice*. Cape Town: University of Cape Town Press, pp 169–84.

Hart, G. 2002. *Disabling Globalization: Places of Power in Post-Apartheid South Africa*. Durban: University of Natal Press.

Harvey, D. 1982. *The Limits to Capital*. Reissued in 1999. London: Verso.

——. 1989a. *The Condition of Postmodernity*. Oxford: Blackwell.

——. 1989b. *The Urban Experience*. Oxford: Blackwell.

——. 1989c. "From Urban Managerialism to Entrepreneurialism: The Transformation in Urban Governance in Late Capitalism", in *Geografiska Annaler*, Vol 71B, No 1, pp 3–17.

——. 1996. *Justice, Nature and the Geography of Difference*. Oxford: Blackwell.

——. 2000. *Spaces of Hope*. Berkeley: University of California Press.

——. 2003. *The New Imperialism*. Oxford: Oxford University Press.

Hawley, S. 2000. "Exporting Corruption: Privatisation, Multinationals and Bribery," *Cornerhouse Briefing 19*. London: Cornerhouse.

Hay C. and D. Marsh (eds). 2000. *Demystifying Globalization*. London: Macmillan.

Held D. and A. McGrew (eds). 2000. The Global Transformations Reader: An Introduction to the Globalization Debate. Malden, MA: Polity Press.

Heller, P. 2003. "Reclaiming Democratic Spaces: Civics and Politics in Posttransition Johannesburg", in R. Tomlinson, R. Beauregard, L. Bremner and X. Mangcu (eds), *Emerging Johannesburg: Perspectives on the Postapartheid City*. New York: Routledge.

Hemson, D. and H. Batidzirai. 2002. "A Case Study of Dolphin Coast Water Concession", Public Private Partnerships and the Poor Research Series. Loughborough University, UK: Water, Engineering and Development Centre.

Hemson, D., B. Dube, T. Mbele, R. Nnadozie and D. Ngcobo. 2006. "Still Paying the Price: Revisiting the Cholera Epidemic of 2000–2001 in South Africa". MSP Occasional Papers Series, No 10. Cape Town: Municipal Services Project.

Hemson, D. and M. O'Donovan. 2006. "Putting Numbers to the Scorecard: Presidential Targets and the State of Delivery", in S. Buhlungu, J. Daniel, R. Southall and J. Lutchman (eds), *State of the Nation: South Africa 2005–06*. Cape Town: HSRC Press.

Hendler, P. 1991. "The Housing Crisis", in M. Swilling, R. Humphries, and K. Shubane (eds), *Apartheid City in Transition*. Cape Town: Oxford University Press.

Hollingsworth, J.R. and R. Boyer (eds). 1997. *Contemporary Capitalism: The Embeddedness of Institutions*. Cambridge: Cambridge University Press.

Howe, E. 1987. "Responsive Planning of Social Development Programs in the Third World", *Journal of Planning Literature*, Vol 2, Autumn, pp 384–405.

Huchzermeyer, M. 2003. "Low Income Housing and Commodified Urban Segregation in South Africa", in C. Haferburg and J. Oßenbrügge (eds), *Ambiguous Restructurings of Post-Apartheid Cape Town: The Spatial Form of Socio-Political Change*. Hamburg: Lit Verlag.

Human Rights Watch. 1998. *Prohibited Person: Abuse of Undocumented Migrants, Asylum Seekers and Refugees in South Africa*. New York: Human Rights Watch.

Hunter, N. and C. Skinner. 2001. *Foreign Street Traders Working in Inner City Durban: Survey Results and Policy Dilemmas*, Research Report No 49. Durban: School of Development Studies (University of Natal).

Hyden, G. and M. Bratton (eds). 1992. *Governance and Politics in Africa*. Boulder, CO: Lynne Reiner Publishers.

ID [Independent Democrats]. 2006. Election Manifesto for Local Elections 2006, accessed February 25, 2006, at www.id.org.za/IDManifesto_Final_04_01_06.doc

Idasa. 2001. *E-Politics*, Vol 3, No 4, October 19.

IHRG and Samwu [Industrial Health Research Group and the South African Municipal Workers' Union]. 2005. "Who Cares for the Healthcare Workers? The State of Occupational Health and Safety in Municipal Health Clinics in South Africa", MSP Occasional Papers Series, No 8. Cape Town: Municipal Services Project.

ILO [International Labour Organization]. 2000. Labour and Social Dimensions of Privatization and Restructuring on Public Utilities: Water, Gas, Electricity. Geneva: ILO.

IndyMedia. 2006. Gympie Street Residents Face Eviction, video documentary accessed April 5, 2006, at www.southafrica.indymedia.org/news/2006/04/10183.php

Institute, Labour Resource and Research. 2000. Public Sector Restructuring in Namibia—Commercialization, Privatization and Outsourcing—Implications for Organized Labour. Windhoek: Labour Resource and Research Institute.

Jackson, S. 2005. "Coloureds Don't Toyi-Toyi: Gesture, Constraint and Identity in Cape Town", in S.L. Robins (ed), *Limits to Liberation After Apartheid: Citizenship, Governance and Culture*. Athens: Ohio University Press.

Jacobs, J. 1984. *Cities and the Wealth of Nations*. New York: Vintage.

Jauch, H. 2002. "Export Processing Zones and the Quest for Sustainable Development: A Southern African Perspective", *Environment & Urbanization*, Vol 14, No 1, pp 101–13.

Jiji, M. 2005. "Paraffin Deaths: Brutal Evidence of Manufacturers' Low Standards", Paraffin Safety Association of Southern Africa, accessed May 11, 2005, at www.ncf.org.za/docs/publications/consumerfair/paraffin.html

Johnson, J.H. 1967. *Urban Geography*. Oxford: Pergamon.

Kasrils, R. 2003. "Address by the Minister of Water Affairs and Forestry, Budget Vote No. 34", June 6. Cape Town: Parliament of South Africa.

Kawano, R. 1992. *The Global City*. Winfield, BC: Wood Lake Books.

Keeling, D.J. 1995. "Transport and the World City Paradigm", in P.L. Know and P.J. Taylor (eds), *World Cities in a World-System*. Cambridge: Cambridge University Press.

Kerf, M. and W. Smith. 1996. "Privatizing Africa's Infrastructure: Promise and Challenge", Technical Paper No 337. Washington, DC: World Bank.

Khan, F. 1997. *Local Government Transformation in the Durban Metropolitan Area: A Case Study*. Cape Town: Foundation for Contemporary Research.

———. 1998. *Developmental Local Government: The Second-Wave of Post-Apartheid Urban Reconstruction*. Cape Town: Islanda Institute.

Khan F. and P. Cranko. 2002. "Municipal-Community Partnerships", in S. Parnell, E. Pieterse, M. Swilling and D. Wooldridge (eds), *Democratising Local Government: The South African Experience*. Cape Town: University of Cape Town Press.

Khosa, M.M. 1992. "Changing State Policy and the Black Taxi Industry in Soweto", in D.M. Smith (ed), *The Apartheid City and Beyond: Urbanization and Social Change in South Africa*. London: Routledge.

Khunou, G. 2002. "'Massive Cutoffs': Cost Recovery and Electricity Services in Diepkloof, Soweto", in D.A. McDonald and J. Pape (eds), *Cost Recovery and the Crisis of Service Delivery in South Africa*. London: Zed Books.

Kihato, C. 2004. "Nepad, the City and the Migrant: Implications for Urban Governance", Migration Policy Series, No 12. Cape Town: Southern African Migration Project.

King, A. 1990. *Urbanism, Colonialism and the World-Economy*. London: Routledge.

Knox, P.L. and P.J. Taylor (eds). 1995. *World Cities in a World System*. Cambridge: Cambridge University Press.

Kraak, G. 1993. *Breaking the Chains: Labour in South Africa in the 1970s and 1980s*. London: Pluto Press.

Kriesler, P. and C. Sardoni. 1998. *Keynes, Post-Keynesianism and Political Economy*. New York: Routledge.

Landau, L. 2005. "Migration, Urbanisation and Sustainable Livelihoods in South Africa", Migration Policy Series, No 15. Cape Town: Southern African Migration Project.

Lapavitsas, C. 2005. "Mainstream Economics in the Neoliberal Era", in A. Saad-Filho and D. Johnston (eds), *Neoliberalism: A Critical Reader*. London: Pluto Press, pp 30–41.

Lappé, F. and P. Du Bois. 1977. *Food First: The Myth of Scarcity*. London: Souvenir Press.

Larner, W. 2000. "Neo-Liberalism: Policy, Ideology and Governmentality", *Studies in Political Economy*, No 63, Autumn, pp 5–25.

LeGates, R.T. and F. Stout (eds). 1996. *The City Reader*. New York: Routledge.

Lehohla, P. 2006. "Studies Reveal the Circular Nature of Urban Migration", *Business Report*, May 4.

Lemanski, C. 2006. "Spaces of Exclusivity or Connection? Linkages Between a Gated Community and its Poorer Neighbour in a Cape Town Master Plan Development", *Urban Studies*, Vol 43, No 2, pp 397–420.

Lemon, A. (ed). 1991. *Homes Apart: South Africa's Segregated Cities*. Cape Town: David Philip.

———. 2002. "The Role of Local Government", in S. Parnell, E. Pieterse, M. Swilling, and D. Wooldridge (eds), *Democratising Local Government: The South African Experience*. Cape Town: University of Cape Town Press.

Lever, W.F. and I. Turok. 1999. "Competitive Cities: Introduction to the Review", *Urban Studies*, Vol 36, Nos 5–6, pp. 791–93.

Levy, N. and C. Tapscott (eds). 2001. Intergovernmental Relations in South Africa: The Challenges of Co-operative Government. Cape Town: Idasa.

Leys, C. 2001. *Market-Driven Politics: Neoliberal Democracy and the Public Interest*. London: Verso.

LGDB [Local Government Demarcation Board for the Western Cape]. 1994. Report No 1: Outer Boundary for the Proposed Cape Transitional Metropolitan Council. Cape Town: LGDB.

———. 1995. Report No. 13: Proposed Substructure Boundaries for the Cape Metropolitan Area. Cape Town: LGDB.

LGWSETA [Local Government Water and Related Services Sector Education Training Authority]. 2004. Annual Report: April 2003–March 2004. Johannesburg: LGWSETA.

Lier, D.C. and K. Stokke. 2006. "Maximum Working Class Unity? Challenges to Local Social Movement Unionism in Cape Town", *Antipode*, Vol 38, No 4, pp 802–24.

Lodge, T. 2002. *Politics in South Africa: From Mandela to Mbeki*. Cape Town: David Philip.

Loftus, A. and D.A. McDonald. 2001a. "Of Liquid Dreams: A Political Ecology of Water Privatization in Buenos Aires," *Environment and Urbanization*, Vol 12, No 2.

———. 2001b. "Lessons From Argentina: The Privatization of Water in Buenos Aires", MSP Occasional Papers Series, No 2. Cape Town: Municipal Services Project.

Lorrain, D. 1991. "Public Goods and Private Operators in France", in R. Batley and G. Stoker (eds), *Local Government in Europe: Trends and Developments*. London: Macmillan.

Mabin, A. 1995. "Negotiating Local Identities: Local Government and Space in South African Cities", paper presented to Canadian Research Consortium on Southern Africa, Queen's University, Kingston, October 27.

———. 1999. "From Hard Top to Soft Serve: Demarcation of Metropolitan Government in Johannesburg", in R. Cameron (primary author), *Democratization of South African Local Government: A Tale of Three Cities*. Cape Town: JL van Schaik.

Majavu, M. 2003. "Wretched Blacks of Cape Town", *ZNet Magazine*, accessed October 12, 2005, at www.zmag.org/sustainers/content/2003-10/12majavu.cfm

Makino, K. 2004. "Social Security Policy Reform in Post-Apartheid South Africa: A Focus on the Basic Income Grant", Centre for Civil Society Research Report No 11. Durban: CCS.

Malangu, N. 2005. "Paraffin Poisoning in Children: What Can We Do Differently?", *South African Family Practice*, March.

Mammon, N. and K. Ewing. 2006. "Urban Nodes and Corridors—The Role of Public Transport in Urban Cape Town: The Case of Klipfontein Corridor", paper presented at Planning Africa 2006 Conference, Cape Town, March 22.

Manuel, T. 2005. "Budgeting Challenges in the Developmental State", *Delivery: The Magazine for Local Government*, No 2, Summer, pp 54–55.

Marais, H. 2001. *Limits to Change: The Political Economy of Transition*. Cape Town: Cape Town University Press.

Marcotullio, P.J. 2003. "Globalization, Urban Form and Environmental Conditions in Asia-Pacific Cities", *Urban Studies*, Vol 40, No 2, pp 219–47.

Marcuse, P. and R. van Kempen. 2000. *Globalizing Cities: A New Spatial Order?* Oxford: Blackwell.

Marks, R. and M. Bezzoli. 2000. "The Urbanism of District Six, Cape Town", in D.A. Anderson and R. Rathbone (eds), *Africa's Urban Past*. Oxford: James Currey.

Mattes, R., J. Crush and W. Richmond. 2000. "The Brain Gain: Skilled Migrants and Immigration Policy in South Africa", *Migration Policy Series*, No 20. Cape Town: Southern African Migration Project.

Mayekiso, M. 1994. "From the Trench to the Table", *Work in Progress*, No 95.

———. 1996. *Township Politics*. New York: Monthly Review Press.

Mayher, A. and D.A. McDonald. Forthcoming. "The Print Media and Privatization in South Africa".

McCann, E. 2004. "Urban Political Economy Beyond the 'Global City'", *Urban Studies*, Vol 41, No 12, pp 2315–33.

McCarney, P. (ed). 1996. *Cities and Governance: New Directions in Latin America, Asia and Africa*. Toronto: Centre for Urban and Community Studies.

McCarney, P., M. Halfani and A. Rodriguez. 1995. "The Emergence of an Idea and its Implications for Urban Research in Developing Countries", in R. Stren and J. White (eds), *Urban Research in the Developing World, Volume Four: Perspectives on the City*. Toronto: Centre for Urban and Community Studies.

McCarthy, J. 1991. "Class, Race, and Urban Locational Relationships", in R. Humphries, K. Shubane and M. Swilling (eds), *Apartheid City in Transition*. Cape Town: Oxford University Press.

McDonald, D.A. 1994. "How the West was Won: The Coloured Vote in the Western Cape", *Southern Africa Report*, Vol 9, No 5, pp 10–14.

———. 1997. "Neither From Above, Nor From Below: Municipal Bureaucrats and Environmental Policy in Cape Town, South Africa", *Canadian Journal of African Studies*, Vol 30, No 2, pp 315–40.

———. 1998. "Three Steps Forward, Two Steps Back: Ideology and Urban Ecology in the New South Africa", *Review of African Political Economy*, No 75.

———. 2000a. "We Have Contact: Foreign Migration and Civic Participation in Marconi Beam, Cape Town", *Canadian Journal of African Studies*, Vol 34, No 1, pp 101–24.

——— (ed). 2000b. *On Borders: Perspectives on International Migration in Southern Africa*. New York: St Martin's Press.

———. 2002a. "The Theory and Practice of Cost Recovery in South Africa", in D.A. McDonald and J. Pape (eds), *Cost Recovery and the Crisis of Service Delivery in South Africa*. London: Zed Books.

———. 2002b. "Up Against the (Crumbling) Wall: Privatization and Environmental Justice in South African Cities", in D.A. McDonald (ed), *Environmental Justice in South Africa*. Athens and Cape Town: Ohio University Press and University of Cape Town Press, pp 292–325.

———. 2002c. "The Bell Tolls for Thee: Cost Recovery, Cutoffs and the Affordability of Municipal Services in South Africa", in D.A. McDonald and J. Pape (eds), *Cost Recovery and the Crisis of Service Delivery in South Africa*. London: Zed Books.

———. 2005. "Environmental Racism and Neoliberal Disorder in South Africa", in R.D. Bullard (ed), *The Quest for Environmental Justice: Human Rights and the Politics of Pollution*. San Francisco: Sierra Club Books.

McDonald, D.A. and J. Crush (eds). 2002. *Destinations Unknown: Perspectives on the Brain Drain in Southern Africa*. Johannesburg: Africa Institute.

McDonald, D.A. and S. Jacobs. 2005. "(Re)writing Xenophobia: Understanding Press Coverage of Cross-Border Migration in Southern Africa", *Journal of Contemporary African Studies*, Vol 23, No 3, pp 295–325.

McDonald, D.A., L. Mashike and C. Golden. 2000. "The Lives and Times of International Migrants in Post-Apartheid South Africa", in D.A. McDonald (ed), *On Borders: Perspectives on International Migration in Southern Africa*. New York: St Martin's Press, pp 168–96.

McDonald, D.A. and J. Pape (eds). 2002. *Cost Recovery and the Crisis of Service Delivery in South Africa*. London: Zed Books.

McDonald, D.A. and G. Ruiters (eds). 2005a. *The Age of Commodity: Water Privatization in Southern Africa*. London: Earthscan.

———. 2005b. "Theorizing Water Privatization in Southern Africa", in D.A. McDonald and G. Ruiters (eds), *The Age of Commodity: Water Privatization in Southern Africa*. London: Earthscan.

McDonald, D.A. and L. Smith. 2002. "Privatizing Cape Town: Service Delivery and Policy Reforms Since 1996", MSP Occasional Papers Series, No 7. Cape Town: Municipal Services Project.

———. 2004. "Privatizing Cape Town: From Apartheid to Neoliberalism in the Mother City", *Urban Studies*, Vol 41, No 8, pp 1461–84.

McDonald, D.A., L. Zinyama, J. Gay, R. Mattes, and F. de Vletter. 2000. "Guess Who's Coming to Dinner: Perspectives on Cross-Border Migration from Lesotho, Mozambique and Zimbabwe to South Africa", *International Migration Review*, Vol 34, No 3, pp 812–40.

McInnes, P. 2005. "Entrenching Inequalities: The Impact of Water Inequalities on Water Injustices in Pretoria", in D.A. McDonald and G. Ruiters (eds), *The Age of Commodity: Water Privatization in Southern Africa*. London: Earthscan.

McKenzie, K. 2004. "Two Paths to Recovery: Johannesburg Versus Cape Town", *Delivery: The Magazine for Local Government*, No 1, Spring, pp 28–30.

McKinley, D. and A. Veriava. 2005. *Arresting Dissent: State Repression and Post-Apartheid Social Movements*. Johannesburg: Centre for the Study of Violence and Reconciliation.

Meer, S. 1999. "The Demobilization of Civil Society: Struggling with New Questions", *Development Update*, Vol 3, No 1, pp 109–18.

Merrifield, A. 2002. *Dialectical Urbanism: Social Struggles in the Capitalist City*. New York: Monthly Review Press.

Meyer, D.R. 2002. "Hong Kong: Global Capital Exchange", in S. Sassen (ed), *Global Networks, Linked Cities*. New York: Routledge.

MIIU [Municipal Infrastructure Investment Unit]. 2000. Homepage on the World Wide Web, www.miiu.org.za/mission.html

Minaar, A., S. Pretorius, and M. Wentzel. 1995. *Who Goes There? 'Illegals' in South Africa*. Pretoria: HRSC Press.

Miraftab, F. 2003. "The Perils of Participatory Discourse: Housing Policy in Post-apartheid South Africa", *Journal of Planning Education and Research*, Vol 22, pp 226–39.

———. 2004. "Making Neo-Liberal Governance: The Disempowering Work of Empowerment", *International Planning Studies*, Vol 9, No 4, November, pp 239–59.

———. 2006. "Spatiality of Post-Apartheid City: City Improvement Districts and Urban (Dis)integration in a Neoliberalizing Cape Town", paper presented at the Association of American Geographers Annual Conference, Chicago, March 10.

Mkokeli, S. 2005. "Inside an Effective Ward Committee", *Delivery: The Magazine for Local Government*, No 2, Summer, pp 64–66.

Mniki, M. 2004. "Black in a White World", *Mail & Guardian*, November 12–18, p 27.

Moodley, S. 2004. "2010: A Soccer Odyssey", *Delivery: The Magazine for Local Government*, No 1, Spring, pp 44–46.

———. 2005. "Municipalities Bridge the Digital Divide", *Delivery: The Magazine for Local Government*, No 2, Summer, pp 60–61.

Moosa, V.A. 1997. Appropriation Bill: Debates of National Council of Provinces, *Hansard*. Cape Town: Government Printers, pp 909–48.

Moran, S. 2000. "Fluid Categories: Water Systems Management in Post-Communist Poland". Graduate Geography Department PhD Dissertation. Worcester: Clark University.

Morris, A. 1998. "'Our Fellow Africans Make Our Lives Hell': The Lives of Congolese and Nigerians Living in Johannesburg", *Ethnic and Racial Studies*, Vol 21, pp 1116–36.

Morris, A. and A. Bouillon (eds). 2001. *African Immigration to South Africa: Francophone Migration of the 1990s*. Pretoria: Protea/IFAS.

Mramba, B.P. 2004. Speech by the Minister for Finance to the National Assembly for the Estimates of Government Revenue and Expenditure for the Financial Year 2004–05, June 10, accessed May 18, 2005, at www.tanzania.go.tz/budgetspeech/2004/financeE.htm

MSP [Municipal Services Project]. 2000. "Survey of Municipal Workers in the CMA," report for the Unicity Commission, Cape Town, May 30. Mimeo. Available at www.queensu.ca/msp/pages/Project_Publications/Reports/survey.htm

Mulgan, R. 1997a. "Contracting Out and Accountability", *Australian Journal of Public Administration*, Vol 56, No 4, pp 106–16.

———. 1997b. "The Processes of Public Accountability", *Australian Journal of Public Administration*, Vol 56, No 1, pp 25–36.

———. 2000. "Comparing Accountability in the Public and Private Sectors", *Australian Journal of Public Administration*, Vol 59, No 1, pp 87–97.

Murray, M.J. 1994. *The Revolution Deferred: The Painful Birth of Post-Apartheid South Africa*. London: Verso.

Nahnsen, A. 2003. "Discourses and Procedures of Desire and Fear in the Re-making of Cape Town's Central City: The Need for a Spatial Politics of Reconciliation", in C. Haferburg and J. Oßenbrügge (eds), *Ambiguous Restructurings of Post-Apartheid Cape Town: The Spatial Form of Socio-Political Change*. Hamburg: Lit Verlag.

Naidoo, P. and A. Veriava. 2005. "Re-membering Movements: Trade Unions and New Social Movements in Neoliberal South Africa", Centre for Civil Society Research Reports, Vol 1. Durban: CCS.

Nefale, M. 2004. "A Survey on Attitudes to Prepaid Electricity Meters in Soweto", research report. Johannesburg: Centre for Applied Legal Studies.

Nyamnjoh, F.B. 2006. *Insiders and Outsiders: Citizenship and Xenophobia in Contemporary Southern Africa*. London: Zed Books.

Olcay-Unver, I.H., R.K. Gupta and A. Kibaroglu (eds). 2003. *Water Development and Poverty Reduction*. London: Kluwer Academic.

Oldfield, S. and K. Stokke. 2004. Building Unity in Diversity: Social Movement Activism in the Western Cape Anti-Eviction Campaign", Centre for Civil Society Research Report. Durban: CCS.

O'Meara, D. 1983. *Volkskapitalisme: Class, Capital, and Ideology in the Development of Afrikaner Nationalism, 1934–1948*. Cambridge: Cambridge University Press.

———. 1996. *Forty Lost Years: The Apartheid State and the Politics of the National Party 1948–1994*. Johannesburg: Ravan Press.

Omi, M. and H. Winant. 1994. *Racial Formation in the United States from the 1960s to the 1990s*. New York: Routledge.

Padayachee, V. 2002. "Financing Durban's Development: 1970–99", in B. Freund and V. Padayachee (eds), *(D)urban Vortex: South African City in Transition*. Durban: University of Natal Press.

Palley, T.I. 1998. *Plenty of Nothing: The Downsizing of the American Dream and the Case for Structural Keynesianism*. Princeton, NJ: Princeton University Press.

———. 2005. "From Keynesianism to Neoliberalism: Shifting Paradigms in Economics", in A. Saad-Filho and D. Johnston (eds), *Neoliberalism: A Critical Reader*. London: Pluto Press, pp 20–30.

Pape, J. 2001. "Poised to Succeed or Set Up to Fail? A Case Study of the First Public-Public Partnership in Water Delivery", MSP Occasional Papers Series, No 1. Cape Town: Municipal Services Project.

——. 2002. "The Struggle Against Encroachment: Constantia and the Defence of White Privilege in the 'New' South Africa", in D.A. McDonald and J. Pape (eds), *Cost Recovery and the Crisis of Service Delivery in South Africa*. London: Zed Books.

Pape, J. and D.A. McDonald. 2002. Introduction, in D.A. McDonald and J. Pape (eds), *Cost Recovery and the Crisis of Service Delivery in South Africa*. London: Zed Books.

Parker, M. 2000. *Proposed Policy Framework to Inform the Process of Convergence to a Common Metropolitan-Wide Tax and Tariff Structure*, draft, commissioned by the Unicity Commission, pp 1–19.

——. 2001. *City of Cape Town Administration—Unbilled Areas*, draft memorandum, February.

Parnell, S. and A. Mabin. 1995. "Rethinking Urban South Africa", *Journal of Southern African Studies*, Vol 21, No 1.

Parnell, S., E. Pieterse, M. Swilling and D. Wooldridge (eds). 2002. *Democratising Local Government: The South African Experience*. Cape Town: University of Cape Town Press.

Patel, R. 2005. "Power Lines, and the Struggle for Democracy in Bayview". Centre for Civil Society discussion paper, accessed July 25, 2005, at www.nu.ac.za/ccs/default.asp?10,24,10,1984. Durban: CCS.

PDG [Palmer Development Group] and School of Governance, University of Western Cape. 2001. *Corporatization of Municipal Water Service Providers Research Report*. Cape Town: Water Research Commission.

Peberdy, S. 1998. "Trading Places: Cross-Border Traders and the South African Informal Sector", Migration Policy Series, No 6. Cape Town: Southern African Migration Project.

Peberdy, S. and N. Dinat. 2005. "Migration and Domestic Workers: Worlds of Work, Health and Mobility in Johannesburg", Migration Policy Series, No 40. Cape Town: Southern African Migration Project.

Peck, J. and A. Tickell. 2002. "Neoliberalizing Space", *Antipode*, Vol 34, No 3, pp 380–404.

Peek, S.B. 2002. "Doublespeak in Durban: Mondi, Waste Management and the Struggles of the South Durban Community Environmental Alliance", in D.A. McDonald (ed), *Environmental Justice in South Africa*. Athens and Cape Town: Ohio University Press and University of Cape Town Press, pp 202–20.

Peet, R. 2002. "Ideology, Discourse, and the Geography of Hegemony: From Socialist to Neoliberal Development in Postapartheid South Africa", *Antipode*, Vol 34, No 1, January, pp 54–84.

Pendleton, A. and J. Winterton (eds). 1993. *Public Enterprise in Transition: Industrial Relations in State and Privatized Corporations*. New York: Routledge.

Petras, J.F. and H. Veltmeyer. 2001. *Globalization Unmasked: Imperialism in the 21st Century*. London: Zed Books.

Petrella, R. 1995. "A Global Agora vs. Gated Communities", *New Perspectives*, Winter, pp 21–22.

PGWC [Provincial Government of the Western Cape]. 2004. Allocations to Gazette 6119 of 1 April.

——. 2005. Western Cape Medium Term Budget Policy Statement 2005–2008, Eastern Cape Provincial Treasury. Cape Town: Government Printers.

Pieterse, E. 2002. "Participatory Local Governance in the Making: Opportunities, Constraints and Prospects", in S. Parnell, E. Pieterse, M. Swilling and D. Wooldridge (eds), *Democratising Local Government: The South African Experience*. Cape Town: University of Cape Town Press.

———. 2005. "Political Inventions and Interventions: A Critical Review of the Proposed City Development Strategy Partnership in Cape Town", in S.L. Robins (ed), *Limits to Liberation After Apartheid: Citizenship, Governance and Culture*. Athens: Ohio University Press.

Pilger, J. 1998. *Hidden Agendas*. London: Vintage.

Pirie, G. 2005. "Researching Cape Town, 1990–2004", *Urban Forum*, Vol 16, No 4, October–December, pp 336–51.

Polanyi, K. 1944 [1957]. *The Great Transformation*. New York: Basic Books.

Pollock, A. and D. Price. 2000. "Globalization? Privatization! WTO and Public Services," *Health Matters*, Vol 41, Summer.

Poon, J.P.H., B. Eldredge and D. Yeung. 2004. "Rank Size Distribution of International Financial Centres", *International Regional Science Review*, Vol 27, No 4, October, pp 411–30.

PSIRU [Public Services International Research Unit]. 2005. *Evaluating the Impact of Liberalisation on Public Services*. University of Greenwich: PSIRU.

Pulido, L. 2000. "Rethinking Environmental Racism: White Privilege and Urban Development in Southern California", *Annals of the Association of American Geographers*, Vol 90, No 1, pp 12–40.

PWC [PriceWaterhouseCoopers]. 1999. *Corporatization Models for Water and Waste Water Directorates*, July. Cape Town: PWC.

———. 2000. *Feasibility Study: Water and Wastewater Utility Company*. Cape Town: PWC.

———. 2001. "Assessment of Internal Mechanisms for the Provision of Solid Waste, Water and Sanitation, and Electricity Services for the City of Cape Town: Executive Summary," October 29. Mimeo.

Qotole, M., M. Xali and F. Barchiesi. 2001. "The Commercialisation of Waste Management in South Africa", MSP Occasional Papers Series, No 3. Cape Town: Municipal Services Project.

Ramphele, M. 1993. *A Bed Called Home: Life in the Migrant Labour Hostels of Cape Town*. Cape Town: David Philip.

———. 1999. "Immigration and Education: International Students at South African Universities and Technikons", Migration Policy Series, No 12, Cape Town: Southern African Migration Project.

RED [Regional Electricity Distributor One]. 2006. Business Plan and Budget 2006–2009, January. Cape Town: RED.

Reddy, P.S. 1999a. "Local Government Democratization and Decentralization: Theoretical Considerations, and Recent Trends and Developments", in P.S. Reddy (ed), *Local Government Democratisation and Decentralisation: A Review of the Southern African Region*. Cape Town: Juta Press.

———. 1999b. "South Africa: Local Government Democratisation and Decentralisation Revisited", in P.S. Reddy (ed), *Local Government Democratisation and Decentralisation: A Review of the Southern African Region*. Cape Town: Juta Press.

———. 1999c. *Local Government Democratisation and Decentralisation: A Review of the Southern African Region*. Cape Town: Juta Press.

Reitzes, M. and S. Bam. 2000. "Citizenship, Immigration, and Identity in Winterveld, South Africa", *Canadian Journal of African Studies*, Vol 34, pp 80–100.

Renzetti, S. 2001. "An Empirical Perspective on Water Pricing Reforms", in A. Dinar (ed), *The Political Economy of Water Pricing Reforms*. Washington, DC: Oxford University Press (for the World Bank).

Rimmer, P.J. 1998. "Transport and Telecommunications Amongst World Cities", in F. Lo and Y. Yeung (eds), *Globalization and the World of Large Cities*. Tokyo: United Nations University Press.

Roberts, A.S. 2000. "Less Government, More Secrecy: Reinvention and the Weakening of Freedom of Information Law", *Public Administration Review*, Vol 60, No 4, pp 308–20.

Robins, S.L. 2005. Introduction, in S.L. Robins (ed), *Limits to Liberation After Apartheid: Citizenship, Governance and Culture*. Athens: Ohio University Press.

Robinson, J. 2002. "Global and World Cities: A View From Off the Map", *International Journal of Urban and Regional Research*, Vol 26, No 3, pp. 531–54.

———. 2003. "Johannesburg's Futures: Beyond Developmentalism and Success", in R. Tomlinson, R.A. Beauregard, L. Bremner and X. Mangcu (eds), *Emerging Johannesburg: Perspectives on the Postapartheid City*. New York: Routledge.

———. 2006. *Ordinary Cities: Between Modernity and Development*. New York: Routledge.

Rogerson, C.M. 1999. "Building Skills: Cross-Border Migrants and the South African Construction Industry", Migration Policy Series, No 11. Cape Town: Southern African Migration Project.

———. 2004. "Towards the World-Class African City: Planning Local Economic Development in Johannesburg", *Africa Insight*, Vol 34, No 4, pp 12–21.

———. 2005. "Globalization, Economic Restructuring and Local Response in Johannesburg: The Most Isolated 'World City'", in K. Segbers, S. Raiser and K. Volkman (eds), *Public Problems—Private Solutions? Globalizing Cities in the South*. Aldershot, UK: Ashgate, pp 17–35.

Rogerson, C.M., and J. Rogerson. 1997. "The Changing Post-Apartheid City: Emergent Black-Owned Small Enterprises in Johannesburg", *Urban Studies*, Vol 34, pp 84–103.

RSA [Republic of South Africa]. 1994a. Local Government Transition Act of 1993. Cape Town: Government Printers.

———. 1994b. RDP White Paper: Discussion Document. Cape Town: Government Printers.

———. 1994c. White Paper on Water and Sanitation. Pretoria: Government Printers.

———. 1995a. "Municipal Infrastructure Investment Framework," Ministry in the Office of the President and the Department of National Housing, June 12. Mimeo.

———. 1995b. The RDP: The First Year Reviewed. Cape Town: Office of the President.

———. 1996a. *Constitution of the Republic of South Africa*. Pretoria: Government Printers.

———. 1996b. *Local Government Transition Second Amendment Act (Act 97 of 1996)*. Pretoria: Government Printers.

———. 1996c. *National Sanitation Policy White Paper*. Pretoria: Government Printers.

———. 1997a. *White Paper on Water Policy*. Pretoria: Government Printers.

———. 1997b. *Towards a White Paper on Local Government in South Africa: A Discussion Document*. Pretoria: Government Printers.

———. 1998a. The Municipal Structures Act, No 117. Pretoria: Government Printers.

———. 1998b. The White Paper on Local Government. Pretoria: Government Printers.

———. 1998c. Draft White Paper on Energy Policy. Pretoria: Government Printers.

———. 1998d. National Water Act. Pretoria: Government Printers.

———. 2000a. Local Government: Municipal Systems Act, 2000. Pretoria: Government Printers.

———. 2000b. Draft: Local Government: Property Rates Bill. Pretoria: Government Printers.

———. 2000c. The White Paper on Municipal Service Partnerships. Pretoria: Government Printers.

———. 2000d. Municipal Infrastructure Investment Framework (MIIF): Draft, Department of Provincial and Local Government, February. Mimeo.

———. 2003a. Local Government: Municipal Finance Management Act (Act 56 of 2003). Pretoria: Government Printers.

———. 2004a. National Treasury, Medium Term Expenditure Framework. Pretoria: Government Printers.

———. 2004b. Breaking New Ground: A Comprehensive Plan for the Development of Sustainable Human Settlements. Pretoria: Government Printers.

———. 2004c. Local Government: Municipal Property Rates Act (Act 6 of 2004). Pretoria: Government Printers.

———. 2004d. Public Private Partnership Manual, National Treasury. Pretoria: Government Printers.

Ruiters, G. 2002. "Debt, Disconnection and Privatisation: The Case of Fort Beaufort, Queenstown and Stutterheim", in D.A. McDonald and J. Pape (eds), *Cost Recovery and the Crisis of Service Delivery in South Africa*. London: Zed Books.

———. 2005. "Knowing Your Place: Urban Services and New Modes of Governability in South African Cities", paper presented at Centre for Civil Society, University of KwaZulu-Natal, Durban, October 6.

Saad-Filho, A. and D. Johnston. 2005. Introduction, in A. Saad-Filho and D. Johnston (eds), *Neoliberalism: A Critical Reader*. London: Pluto Press, pp 1–9.

SACN [South African Cities Network]. 2003. *A South African Urban Renewal Overview*. Johannesburg: SACN.

———. 2004. State of the Cities Report. Johannesburg: SACN.

———. 2005. Patterns of Migration, Settlement and Dynamics of HIV and AIDS in South Africa. Johannesburg: SACN.

———. 2006. State of the Cities Report. Johannesburg: SACN.

SAHRC [South African Human Rights Commission]. 2001. "Du Noon Expulsion of Foreign Nationals", *Protecting Human Rights*, Vol 1, No 3, p 3.

Salga [South African Local Government Association]. 2004a. National Conference Commission Guide. Pretoria: Salga.

———. 2004b. Conference Resolutions, 2004 National Salga Conference, September 30. Pretoria: Salga.

———. 2004c. Chairperson's Report, 2004 National Salga Conference, September 30. Pretoria: Salga.

Salo, E. 2005. "Negotiating Gender and Personhood in the New South Africa: Adolescent Women and Gangsters in Manenberg Township on the Cape Flats", in S.L. Robins (ed), *Limits to Liberation After Apartheid: Citizenship, Governance and Culture*. Athens: Ohio University Press.

SAMP [Southern African Migration Project]. 2004. "Regionalizing Xenophobia? Citizen Attitudes to Immigration and Refugee Policy in Southern Africa", Migration Policy Series, No 30. Cape Town: Southern African Migration Project.

Sampson, A. 1999. *Nelson Mandela: The Authorised Biography*. Johannesburg: Jonathan Ball.

Samson, M. 2003. Dumping on Women: Gender and Privatisation of Waste Management. Cape Town: Municipal Services Project and Samwu.

Sassen, S. 1988. The Mobility of Labour and Capital: A Study in International Investment and Labor Flow. Cambridge: Cambridge University Press.

———. 1991. The Global City: New York, London, Tokyo. Princeton, NJ: Princeton University Press.

———. 1994. *Cities in a World Economy*. Thousand Oaks, CA: Pine Forge.

———. 1995. "Immigration and Local Labour Markets", in A. Portes (ed), *The Economic Sociology of Immigration: Essays on Networks, Ethnicity and Entrepreneurship*. New York: Russell Sage Foundation.

———. 1996. *Losing Control? Sovereignty in an Age of Globalization*. New York: Columbia University Press.

———. 1998. *Globalization and its Discontents: Essays on the Mobility of People and Money*. New York: New Press.

———. 1999. *Guests and Aliens*. New York: New Press.

———. 2000. *Cities and Their Cross-Border Networks*. New York: Routledge.

———. 2001. *The Global City: New York, London, Tokyo*, second edition. Princeton, NJ: Princeton University Press.

——— (ed). 2002a. *Global Networks, Linked Cities*. New York: Routledge.

———. 2002b. "Locating Cities on Global Circuits", in S. Sassen (ed), *Global Networks, Linked Cities*. New York: Routledge.

———. 2003. *De-Nationalization*. Princeton, NJ: Princeton University Press.

———. 2004. Epilogue, in J. Gugler (ed), *World Cities Beyond the West: Globalization, Development, and Inequality*. Cambridge: Cambridge University Press.

———. 2006. Foreword, in M.M. Amen, K. Archer and M.M. Bosman (eds), *Relocating Global Cities: From the Center to the Margins*. Lanham, MD: Rowman & Littlefield Publishers, pp ix–xii.

Saul, J.S. 1993. *Recolonization and Resistance: Southern Africa in the 1990's*. Toronto: Between the Lines.

Saul, J.S. and S. Gelb. 1981. *The Crisis in South Africa: Class Defence, Class Revolution*. New York: Monthly Review Press.

———. 1986. *The Crisis in South Africa*. London: Zed Books.

Schofield, R. and J. Shaol. 1997. "Regulating the Water Industry, Swimming Against the Tide or Going Through the Motions", *The Ecologist*, Vol 27, No 1, January/February.

Sclar, E.D. 2000. *You Don't Always Get What You Pay For: The Economics of Privatization*. Ithaca, NY: Cornell University Press.

Seekings, J. 2000. *The UDF: A History of the United Democratic Front in South Africa, 1983–1991*. Athens: Ohio University Press.

———. 2002. "The Broader Importance of Welfare Reform in South Africa", *Social Dynamics*, Vol 28, No 2, Winter, pp 1–38.

Sexton, S. 2001. "Trading Health Care Away? GATS, Public Services and Privatisation," *Cornerhouse Briefing 23*. London: Cornerhouse.

Shirley, M.M. 1999. "Bureaucrats in Business: The Roles of Privatization versus Corporatization in State-Owned Enterprise Reform," *World Development*, Vol 27, No 1, pp 115–136.

Short, J.R. 2004a. "Black Holes and Loose Connections in a Global Urban Network", *The Professional Geographer*, Vol 56, No 2, pp 295–302.

———. 2004b. *Global Metropolitan: Globalizing Cities in a Capitalist World*. Routledge: New York.

Short, J.R., C. Breitbach, S. Buckman, and J. Essex. 2000. "From World Cities to Gateway Cities", *City*, Vol 4, pp 317–40.

Shubane, K. 1991. "Black Local Authorities: A Contraption of Control", in M. Swilling, R. Humphries and K. Shubane (eds), *Apartheid City in Transition*. Cape Town: Oxford University Press.

Sichone, O. 2003. "Together and Apart: African Refugees and Immigrants in Cape Town", in D. Chidester (ed), *What Holds Us Together: Social Cohesion in South Africa*. Cape Town: HSRC Press, pp 120–40.

Sihlongonyane, M.F. 2004. "The Rhetoric of Africanism as a World African City", *Urban Forum*, Vol 34, No 4, pp 22–30.

Simon, D. 1995. "The World City Hypothesis: Reflections from the Periphery", in P.L. Knox and P.J. Taylor (eds), *World Cities in a World System*. Cambridge: Cambridge University Press, pp 132–55.

Simone, A. 2004. *For the City Yet to Come: Changing African Life in Four Cities*. Durham, NC: Duke University Press.

Smith, D.M. (ed). 1992. The Apartheid City and Beyond: Urbanization and Social Change in South Africa. London: Routledge.

Smith, L. 2005. "South Africa: Testing the Waters of Public-Public Partnerships", in B. Belanyá, B. Brennan, O. Hoederman, S. Kishinoto and P. Terhorst (eds), Reclaiming Public Water: Achievements, Struggles and Visions from Around the World. Amsterdam: TNI.

Smith, L. and E. Fakir. 2003. The Struggle to Deliver Water Services to the Indigent: A Case Study on the Public-Public Partnership in Harrismith with Rand Water. Johannesburg: Centre for Policy Studies.

Smith, L., A. Gillet, S. Mottiar and F. White. 2005. "Public Money, Private Failure: Testing the Limits of Market Based Solutions for Water Delivery in Nelspruit", in D.A. McDonald and G. Ruiters (eds), *The Age of Commodity: Water Privatization in Southern Africa*. London: Earthscan, pp 130–48.

Smith, M. 1998. "The Global City—Whose Social Construct is it Anyway? A Comment on White", *Urban Affairs Review*, Vol 33, No 4, pp 482–88.

Smith, N. 1984. *Uneven Development: Nature, Capital, and the Production of Space*. New York: Blackwell.

———. 1996. *The New Urban Frontier: Gentrification and the Revanchist City*, New York: Routledge.

Smith, N., P. Caris and E. Wyly. 2001. "The 'Camden Syndrome' and the Menace of Suburban Decline: Residential Disinvestment and its Discontents in Camden County, New Jersey", *Urban Affairs Review*, Vol 36, No 4, March, pp 497–531.

Social Dynamics. 2002. Special issue on "Welfare Reform in South Africa", J. Seekings and D. Skinner (eds), Vol 28, No 2.

Soni, D.V. 1992. "The Apartheid State and Black Housing Struggles", in D.M. Smith (ed), *The Apartheid City and Beyond: Urbanization and Social Change in South Africa*. London: Routledge.

Sparks, A.H. 1995. *Tomorrow is Another Country: The Inside Story of South Africa's Road to Change*. Sandton: Struik Book Distributors.

SSA [Statistics South Africa]. 2005. Mid-year population estimates, South Africa 2005. Statistical release P0302.

Starr, P. 1988. "The Meaning of Privatization", *Yale Law and Policy Review*, No 6.

Stoker, G. 1989. "Local Government for a Post Fordist Society", in J. Stewart and G. Stoker (eds), *The Future of Local Government*. Basingstoke, UK: Macmillan.

Strange, S. 1995. "The Limits of Politics", *Government and Opposition*, Vol 30, pp. 291–311.

Sussman, G. 1997. *Communication, Technology, and Politics in the Information Age*. London: Sage.

Swilling, M. 1996. "Building Democratic Local Urban Governance in Southern Africa: A Review of Key Trends", in P. McCarney (ed), *Cities and Governance: New Directions in Latin America, Asia and Africa*. Toronto: Center for Urban and Community Studies.

Swilling, M., W. Cobbett and R. Hunter. 1991. "Finance, Electricity Costs, and the Rent Boycott," in M. Swilling, R. Humphries and K. Shubane (eds), *Apartheid City in Transition*. Cape Town: Oxford University Press.

Swilling, M., R. Humphries and K. Shubane (eds). 1991. *Apartheid City in Transition*. Cape Town: Oxford University Press.

Swilling, M., A. Simone, and F. Khan. 2002. "'My Soul I Can See': The Limits of Governing African Cities in a Context of Globalization and Complexity", in S. Parnell, E. Pieterse, M. Swilling, and D. Wooldridge (eds), *Democratising Local Government: The South African Experience*. Cape Town: University of Cape Town Press.

Swyngedouw, E. 1992. "The Mamon Quest, 'Glocalization', Interspatial Competition and the Monetary Order: The Construction of New Scales", in M. Dumford and G. Kafkalas (eds), *Cities and Regions in the New Europe*. London: Belhaven Press, pp 39–67.

———. 1997. "Neither Local Nor Global: 'Glocalization' and the Politics of Scale", in R Cox (ed), *Spaces of Globalization*. New York: Guilford, pp 137–66.

Taylor. P.J. 2000. "World Cities and Territorial States Under Conditions of Contemporary Globalization", *Political Geography*, Vol 19, No 1, pp 5–32.

———. 2004. *World City Network: A Global Urban Analysis*. New York: Routledge.

Taylor-Gooby, P. 2000. *Risk, Trust and Welfare*. Houndsmill, UK: Macmillan.

Thahane, T.T. 2005. Budget Speech to Parliament for the 2005–2006 Fiscal Year, Ministry of Finance and Development Planning, Government of Lesotho, February 16.

Thale, R. 2004. "Smoothing the Road to Economic Growth", *Enterprise*, November, pp 121–24.

Thomas, W. 2003. "Western Cape Business Prospects—2004", paper presented at the BER Conference: The South African Economy—Challenges and Prospects, Stellenbosch, November 13.

Thrift, N. 1999. "Cities and Economic Change: Global Governance?", in J. Allen, D. Massey and M. Pryke (eds), *Unsettling Cities*. London: Routledge.

Tomlinson, R. 1990. *Urbanization in Post-Apartheid South Africa*. London: Unwin Hyman.

———. 1994. *Urban Development Planning*. London: Oxford University Press.

Tomlinson, R., R. Beauregard, L. Bremner and X. Mangcu. 2003a. Introduction, in R. Tomlinson, R. Beauregard, L. Bremner and X. Mangcu (eds), *Emerging Johannesburg: Perspectives on the Postapartheid City*. New York: Routledge.

———. 2003b. "The Postapartheid Struggle for an Integrated Johannesburg", in R. Tomlinson, R. Beauregard, L. Bremner and X. Mangcu (eds), *Emerging Johannesburg: Perspectives on the Postapartheid City*. New York: Routledge.

———. 2003c. *Emerging Johannesburg: Perspectives on the Postapartheid City*. New York: Routledge.

Turok, I. 2001. "Persistent Polarization Post-Apartheid? Progress Towards Urban Integration in Cape Town", Urban Change and Policy Research Group, Discussion Paper.

Tyner, J.A. 2006. "Laboring in the Periphery: The Place of Manila in the Global Economy", in M.M. Amen, K. Archer and M.M. Bosman (eds), *Relocating Global Cities: From the Center to the Margins*. Lanham, MD: Rowman & Littlefield Publishers.

UN-Habitat. 2001. *Cities in a Globalizing World: Global Report on Human Settlements 2001*. London: Earthscan.

UNHCR [United Nations High Commission for Refugees]. 2006. "Squatter Camp in South Africa Underscores Need for Urban Refugee Policy Review", *News Review*, February 23, accessed July 23, 2006, at www.unhcr.org/cgi-bin/texis/vtx/news/opendoc.htm?tbl=NEWS&id=43fdc3f82

Unicom [Unicity Commission]. 2000a. "Discussion Document: Developing the Future City of Cape Town, Building a Unified City for the 21st Century: A Summary of the Proposed Service Delivery and Institutional Change Proposals for the Term of Office of the New City of Cape Town". Cape Town: Unicity Commission.

———. 2000b. "Strategic Recommendations". Cape Town: Unicity Commission.

Urban Studies. 2003. Special Issue on "The Nested City", edited by RC Hill and K Fujita, Vol 40, No 2.

USN [Urban Sector Network]. 1998. *Developmental Local Government in South Africa: A Handbook for Urban Councillors and Community Members*. Johannesburg: USN.

van der Merwe, I.J. 2004. "The Global Cities of Sub-Sahara Africa: Fact or Fiction?", *Urban Forum*, Vol 15, No 1, pp 36–47.

van Heyningen, E. (ed). 1994. *Studies in the History of Cape Town*. Cape Town: UCT Press.

van Ryneveld, P., S. Parnell and D. Muller. 2003. *Indigent Policy: Including the Poor in the City of Cape Town's Income Strategy*. Cape Town: CCT.

van Zyl, P.S. 2005. "V&A Waterfront, The Story of its Development: An African Success Story in the Integration of Water, Working Harbour, Heritage, Urban Revitalisation and Tourism Development", accessed February 1, 2006, at www.capeinfo.com/WCregions/CapeTown/CityBowl/VAWdev.asp

Wacquant, L. 1999. "How Penal Common Sense Comes to Europeans: Notes on the Transatlantic Diffusion of the Neoliberal *Doxa*", *European Societies*, Vol 1, pp 319–52.

Wallace, D.A. 2004. *Urban Planning/My Way: From Baltimore's Inner Harbor to Lower Manhattan and Beyond*. Chicago: Planners Press, American Planning Association.

Watson, V. 1994. "Housing Policy, Sub-Letting and the Urban Poor: Evidence from Cape Town", *Urban Forum*, Vol 5 No 2, pp 27–43.

———. 2002. *Change and Continuity in Spatial Planning: Metropolitan Planning in Cape Town Under Political Transition*. London: Routledge.

Watts, M. 1999. "Commodities", in P. Cloke, P. Crang and M. Goodwin (eds), *Introducing Human Geographies*. London: Arnold.

WCEDF [Western Cape Economic Development Forum]. 1993. *The Way Forward: Cape Metropolitan Area Interim Metropolitan Development Framework*. Cape Town: WCEDF.

———. 1995. *Metropolitan Spatial Development Framework: A Guide for Spacial Development in the Cape Metropolitan Region*. Cape Town: WCEDF.

Wesgro. 2001a. The Call Centre Industry in the Western Cape Province, South Africa, Wesgro Background Report, July. Cape Town: Wesgro.

———. 2001b. The Film and Television Industry in Western Cape Province, South Africa, Wesgro Background Report, January. Cape Town: Wesgro.

Western, J. 1996. *Outcast Cape Town*. Berkeley: University of California Press.

———. 2001. "Africa is Coming to the Cape", *The Geographical Review*, Vol 71, No 4, October, pp 617–40.

Whelan, P. 2002. "Local Government Finance Reform", in S. Parnell, E. Pieterse, M. Swilling and D. Wooldridge (eds), *Democratising Local Government: The South African Experience*. Cape Town: University of Cape Town Press.

Whincop, M.J. (ed). 2003. *From Bureaucracy to Business Enterprise: Legal and Policy Issues in the Transformation of Government Services*. Aldershot, UK: Ashgate.

Williams, C.C. 2002. "A Critical Evaluation of the Commodification Thesis", *The Sociological Review*, Vol 50, No 4, November.

Williams, C.C. and J. Windebank. 2003. "The Slow Advance and Uneven Penetration of Commodification", *International Journal of Urban and Regional Research*, Vol 27, No 2.

Williamson, O.E. 1990. "The Firm as a Nexus of Treaties: An Introduction", in U. Maki, B. Gustafsson and O.E. Williamson (eds), *The Firm as a Nexus of Treaties*. London: Sage, pp 1–25.

Wolch, J. and M. Dear (eds). 1989. *The Power of Geography*. Boston: Unwin Hyman.

Wolpe, H. 1988. *Race, Class and the Apartheid State*. Paris: UNESCO.

Wooldridge, D. 2002. "Introducing Metropolitan Government in South Africa", in S. Parnell, E. Pieterse, M. Swilling and D. Wooldridge (eds), *Democratising Local Government: The South African Experience*. Cape Town: University of Cape Town Press.

World Bank. 1989. *Sub-Saharan Africa: From Crisis to Sustainable Growth*. Washington, DC: World Bank.

———. 1991a. Aide Memoire I [Cape Town]. Mimeo.

———. 1991b. Aide Memoire II [Cape Town]. Mimeo.

———. 1992. *Governance and Development*. Washington, DC: World Bank.

———. 1994. *World Development Report 1994: Infrastructure for Development*. New York: Oxford University Press.

———. 1999. Urban Property Rights Project Appraisal Document, Report No 18245 PE, July 15, Poverty Reduction and Economic Management Unit, Latin America and the Caribbean Region, accessed May 8, 2002, at www.worldbank.org/sprojects/Project.asp?pid=P039086

———. 2000. *Cities in Transition: World Bank Urban and Local Government Strategy*. Washington, DC: World Bank.

———. 2001. "Information and Communication Technology, Poverty, and Development in Sub-Saharan Africa and South Asia", Africa Region Working Paper Series, No 20, August. Washington, DC: World Bank.

Xali, M. 2002. "They Are Killing Us Alive: A Case Study of the Impact of Cost Recovery on Service Provision in Makhaza Section, Khayelitsha", in D.A. McDonald and J. Pape (eds), *Cost Recovery and the Crisis of Service Delivery in South Africa*. London: Zed Books.

Xali, M. Forthcoming. *Seeking Trade Union and Community Organisation Linkages in the Cape Town Metropolitan Area: Possibilities for New Trade Unionism and New Social Movements*. Cape Town: Ilrig Research Report.

Zuern, E. 2004. Continuity in Contradiction? The Prospects for a National Civic Movement in a Democratic State: SANCO and the ANC in Post-Apartheid South Africa, Centre for Civil Society Research Report No 26. Durban: CCS.

INTERVIEWS

Roger Ronnie, General Secretary of Samwu, March 15, 2001.

John Mawbey, National Education Director, South African Municipal Workers' Union, email communication, November 15, 2004.

Albert Schuitmaker, Executive Director, Cape Town Regional Chamber of Commerce and Industry, personal interview, November 18, 2004.

Roland Langley, Chairperson of the Cape Town Civil Society City Wide Forum (CTCSCWF), November 27, 2004.

Wallace Mgoqi, former City Manager of Cape Town, email communication, December 6, 2004.

David Schmidt, special advisor to the Mayor, personal interview, December 6, 2004.

Japie Hugo, Director: Planning and Environment, City of Cape Town, telephonic interview, December 7, 2004.

Index

For Product Safety Concerns and Information please contact our EU
representative GPSR@taylorandfrancis.com
Taylor & Francis Verlag GmbH, Kaufingerstraße 24, 80331 München, Germany

www.ingramcontent.com/pod-product-compliance
Ingram Content Group UK Ltd.
Pitfield, Milton Keynes, MK11 3LW, UK
UKHW021606240425
457818UK00018B/404